Chile

& Easter Island
a travel survival kit

Alan Samagalski

Chile & Easter Island - a travel survival kit
First Edition

Published by
Lonely Planet Publications
Head Office: PO Box 88, South Yarra, Victoria 3141, Australia
Also: PO Box 2001A, Berkeley, CA 94702, USA

Printed by
Colorcraft, Hong Kong

Photographs by
Alan Samagalski

Illustrations by
Dennis Sheehan
Chris Lee-Ack

Cover
Front: 17th century church, Poconchile, Atacama
Back, top: Torres del Paine, Magallanes
Back, bottom: Ahu Tahai, Easter Island

First published
July 1987

Although the author and publisher have tried to make the information as accurate as possible, they accept no responsibility for any loss, injury or inconvenience sustained by any traveller using this book.

National Library of Australia Cataloguing in Publication Data

Samagalski, Alan.
  Chile & Easter Island, a travel survival kit.

  Includes index.
  ISBN 0 908086 99 7

  1. Chile – Description and travel – 1981– – Guide-books.
  1. Title.

918.3'04647

The Author

Alan Samagalski came to Lonely Planet several years ago, after spending some time on the Indian sub-continent and going astray from the Melbourne University Genetics Department and a stumbling career at Melbourne's legendary Last Laugh Theatre Restaurant and Comedy Café. Excursions to exotic parts of Australia soon led to long forays in Hong Kong and China from which emerged an updated *Hong Kong, Macau & Canton* and the voluminous *China – a travel survival kit*. Alan has also contributed to Lonely Planet's *Indonesia – a travel survival kit, South-East Asia on a Shoestring* and *Bali & Lombok – a travel survival kit*. *Chile & Easter Island – a travel survival kit* is his first book on a South American country.

Acknowledgements

First and foremost, thanks to Geoff Crowther whose *South America on a Shoestring* provided a strong base to work from when this book was being researched. Also, thanks to all those travellers whose information has found its way into this guide from Geoff's; you'll find yourselves credited in the current edition of *South America on a Shoestring*.

Thanks to the Chileans and others along the way who translated, explained, filled me in on background, resolved various mysteries, or pointed me in worthwhile directions. Thanks also to Michael Buckley (co-author of Lonely Planet's *China – a travel survival kit* and *Tibet – a travel survival kit*) for his piece on Alexander Selkirk and the Juan Fernández Islands.

This book is also the product of the efforts of other workers at Lonely Planet, including Richard Everist who edited, Fiona Boyes who drew the maps, Todd Pierce who designed the cover, Alison Porter who typeset, and Chris Lee-Ack and Valerie Tellini who did the paste-up.

A Warning & a Request

The first thing to remember is that this book only covers Chile, Easter Island and a small part of Argentina; be warned against extrapolating information about health, crime and transport to other South American countries. The scope of this book is also limited. It's not intended, for instance, to cover trekking or climbing. Hopefully, however, it will point you in the right directions, save you lots of money, and provide you with a starting point for learning about Chile.

The second thing to remember is that things change. Prices go up, good places go bad, bad places go bankrupt and nothing stays the same. So, if you find things better or worse, recently opened or closed, or simply different, please write and tell us about them and help make the next edition even better! In return for worthwhile information we'll send you a free copy of any Lonely Planet book you request. To make this information available as soon as possible it is also included in the quarterly Lonely Planet Newsletter (see page 278 for more information).

Contents

Introduction

Most people with any interest in Latin America know something of the politics of Chile and the events of 1973 when the communist president, Salvador Allende, was overthrown by a military coup, some of the instigators of which still hold power in Chile today. Politically and economically Chile was – until the coup – an oddity in Latin America, if not the envy of many other Latin Americans. By comparison with other Latin American countries Chile was a relatively industrialised, prosperous nation. It had also managed to maintain some semblance of a democratic tradition, despite several interventions by the military since it won independence from Spain in the early 19th century.

Few people know much else about Chile, however, or have much idea of what the country actually *looks* like. The traditional images which most westerners associate with Latin America have no place in Chile; there are no Aztec

sundials, no Mayan pyramids, no mysterious Inca ruins. The powerful images generated by the American Indian cultures which once ruled in Mexico, Central America and Peru do not relate to this country, where the majority of people have far more in common with Europeans and North Americans than they do with the early Indian inhabitants.

Encompassing only the narrow strip of land between the Pacific Ocean and the high peaks of the Andes – never more than 180 km wide, but with a coastline stretching over 4300 km – Chile has one of the most varied landscapes in the world. It includes the almost waterless Atacama Desert in the north, the snow-covered volcanoes, forests and tranquil lakes of the centre, and the wild and windswept glaciers and fjords of the far south. It has magnificent trekking country with several national parks where guanacos, rheas, seals, pink flamingos and penguins can be seen. It boasts some of the world's finest salmon and trout fishing. Just a few hours drive from Santiago you can ski for no less than five months of the year on the slopes of the Andes, or swim year-round at the Pacific beaches.

Chile also has two Pacific outposts: Easter Island, with its giant stone statues, has long been a drawcard for explorers, adventurers, anthropologists, archaeologists and tourists; and the Juan Fernández Islands, famed as the home, for four years, of the Scotsman Alexander Selkirk, on whose experiences Daniel Defoe based the novel *Robinson Crusoe*.

The country is a goldmine of undiscovered nooks and surprises – and its people, even by Latin American standards, are remarkably friendly and hospitable to foreigners. In the past it's mostly been seen as a detour from Peru or Bolivia, but there's no reason why Chile couldn't be a destination in its own right!

Chile

Facts about the Country

HISTORY

The history of modern Chile begins with the invasion of the Spanish under Pedro de Valdivia, a *conquistador* who led a small force into Chile from Peru, founded Santiago and several other Chilean cities, and became the first governor of the new Spanish colony. The subjugation of Chile was a bloody affair. Valdivia divided up the land amongst his soldiers as if 'among thieves as though it were a dead jackass' (as one writer eloquently put it) and returned his prisoners with their noses and ears cut off. He met his own end at the hands of the Araucanian Indians in the south. One version of the story has his head cut off and passed around on a pike. Another has him tied to a tree while molten gold, the metal which the Spanish expended so much energy and blood to acquire, was poured down his throat by his Indian captors.

The Indian Settlers

The ancestors of the Indians who Valdivia subdued entered the American continent over 20,000 years ago when the Bering Straits between Siberia and America were dry land. By 1500 BC, after spending thousands of years as semi-nomadic hunters and gatherers, many Indian groups had adopted maize farming as the basis of their existence and developed permanent settlements.

In Mexico, Central America and the northern regions of South America, sophisticated Indian civilisations arose. By 300 AD the Maya – a collection of culturally related but politically independent city-states and tribes in Central America – had developed a system of hieroglyphic writing and accurate calendars, and had constructed massive temples and public buildings. Many other Indian groups developed their own distinctive civilisations, con-tributing to the heritage of the Aztecs who made their appearance in Mexico around 1200 AD. The civilisations of the central Andes reached their zenith in the Inca empire, a tribe who made its first appearance around the 11th Century AD in Peru. By the time the Spanish arrived on the scene the Inca empire spanned most of Peru, Bolivia, Ecuador and the northern parts of Chile and Argentina.

Further to the south lived the Araucanian Indians – today known by their own name, *Mapuche* – and other Indian groups who lived as hunters and gatherers. Prior to the arrival of the Spanish the Incas exacted tribute as far south as the Bío Bío River, but beyond that point the Mapuche successfully resisted both Inca and Spanish domination. Dispersed over a large area, with no central political leadership or authority, it was impossible for the Spanish to achieve a quick and final victory over the Mapuche as they did over the Aztecs and Incas.

The Spanish Conquest

Interloping French and British managed to slice off small pieces of land for themselves, but it was primarily the Spanish and Portuguese who were respons-ible for bringing Central and South America under European control. A treaty in 1494 divided the world between Portugal and Spain, at that time the two principal contenders for the discovery, conquest and exploitation of overseas possessions. A line was drawn dividing the world in two, and all the land east of the line was granted to Portugal and all the land west of the line was granted to Spain. By chance, this placed the coast of Brazil – as yet unknown to Europeans – within the Portuguese sphere and the rest of America within the Spanish sphere.

It is difficult to grasp the speed with

17th century Spanish conquistadors

which the Spanish 'discovered' and subsequently conquered the New World. Christopher Columbus first landed in the Caribbean Islands in 1492. By 1550 the Spanish presided over an area which extended from the southern part of what is now the USA to central Chile, and had founded most of what are now Latin America's largest cities, including Lima, Santiago, Asunción and La Paz.

This whole affair was carried out by a rabble of adventurers, opportunists, desperadoes, misfits and men-of-fortune. Small in numbers, what they had on their side was determination, an exceptional ruthlessness, horses and firearms which terrified the Indians, the willingness of Indian tribes to ally with the Spanish against their Inca and Aztec masters, and the good fortune to enter Central and South America when the Indian empires were vulnerable to attack.

The conquest of the Aztecs was achieved in two years by a force of just 550 men, 16 horses and a few cannon, under the command of Hernán Cortés. The conquest of the Inca empire was not so swift although the timing of the Spanish was impeccable. In 1531, Francisco Pizarro landed on the coast of Ecuador with a force of 180 men and 27 horses and marched southwards. The Inca empire had been split by civil war and the Spanish managed, through a combination of deceit and treachery, to capture and murder the emperor. Even so, it was not until 1572 that the last Inca stronghold was finally overrun. As for Pizarro, he had been assassinated in 1541 by supporters of a rival conquistador, Diego de Almagro, in revenge for Pizzaro executing Almagro.

The Conquest of Chile

Just before his death, Pizarro set the wheels in motion for the conquest of Chile. The first attempt had been made around 1537 by a force under the leadership of Diego de Almagro, but this turned back after a fruitless venture into the region. Pizarro then handed the task of conquering Chile to Pedro de Valdivia. Valdivia's expedition set out from Peru in 1540, crossed the desert, reached the fertile central plains of Chile in 1541, subdued the local Indians and founded the city of Santiago.

South of the Bío Bío River, Valdivia met the Mapuche Indians, who learnt to manage horses and devise combat tactics which were successful against the Spanish cavalry. Valdivia was captured and killed by the Mapuche in 1554. Between 1599 and 1604 all major Spanish settlements south of the Bío Bío were destroyed by the Indians and had to be abandoned. The Spanish soldier and poet Alonso de Ercilla, who fought against the Indians and was impressed by their military qualities, sang their praises in the epic poem *La Araucana*:

They are confident, emboldened,
Dauntless, gallant, and audacious.
Firm inured to toil and suffering
Mortal cold and heat and hunger.

The last resistance of the Mapuche to foreign rule was not suppressed until the 19th century. Today their descendants live in the south of Chile, like the Aboriginals of Australia and the Maoris of New Zealand, a dispossessed minority in what was once their own land.

The Foundation of Modern Chile

Valdivia laid the foundations for the modern Chilean state. The first Spanish colonisers in Chile were soldiers, and since they knew little about building, agriculture or mining it was the Indians who had to do the work. A soldier would receive an *encomienda* which meant that the Indians of a certain area were 'commended' or allotted to him and he made them work. No Indian – regardless of sex or age – was exempt. By distributing the Indians and land into encomiendas Valdivia laid the foundations for a Chilean oligarchy which would dominate Chilean history until the 20th century.

The racial makeup of Chile also changed. Valdivia's expedition included only one Spanish woman, so his men married the local Indian women. Children of mixed Spanish and Indian blood – *mestizos* – resulted from these relationships, and after 50 years there were more mestizos in Chile than there were full-blooded Spanish. Military campaigns against the Indians, the killing of troublesome Indians by the *encomenderos*, epidemics of smallpox, measles and typhus, forced labour, and the further intermingling of the Spanish and mestizos all helped reduce the size of the Indian population.

By the end of the 18th century, the Indians outside the territory directly controlled by the Mapuche had almost completely disappeared as a race. Today, most Chileans are mestizos; the Chilean upper classes and recent European migrants and their offspring are the chief exceptions.

The Division of the Land

Valdivia not only rewarded his soldiers with allotments of Indians but also with land. Some received whole valleys stretching from the Andes to the Pacific. Others received more moderate grants but immediately began to enlarge them by taking over bordering land. The process went on until the large farm estate became the dominant unit of Chilean agriculture.

Contemporary banknote showing the founder of Chile, Pedro de Valdivia

So long as the landowners faced problems in holding onto their forced labourers the encomienda system was maintained, with the Indians remaining wards of their masters. But as the estates gradually consumed all the best land, and as the labourers found no alternative but to work on the estates, the system gradually changed. From the old encomiendas and land grants arose the *hacienda*, and the Indian labourer became the *inquilino* or tenant. The labourers and their families now worked for their master in exchange for certain rights. They were allowed to live in a hut on the estate, to pasture some animals, and to use part of the land to grow crops. In effect the *hacendado* reigned like a feudal lord presiding over Indian and mestizo serfs.

By the end of the Spanish colonial period the hacienda (or *fundo* as it's more commonly called in Chile) formed the basic unit of Chilean society and was much more important than the small towns. Even by the middle of the 20th century the division of the land had not essentially changed, with a very large quantity of arable land still concentrated in the hands of a few owners.

The Independence Movements

Within a few decades of Columbus' landing in the Caribbean, Spain found itself with an empire twice the size of Europe. The exploitation of its resources was monopolised by the Spanish. Only Spanish-born immigrants were allowed to settle in the New World. Heretical Protestants from other parts of Europe were excluded, thus preserving the wealth of the conquered territories for Spain. Yet the empire which lasted for some 300 years was suddenly swept away in the early years of the 19th century. In 1808, Spain controlled an area stretching from California to Cape Horn and from the mouth of the Orinoco River to the shores of the Pacific; 17 years later she retained only Puerto Rico and Cuba.

There were many factors involved in the development of the independence movements in Latin America. One was the rise of a class of *criollos* (*creoles*), people of Spanish descent born in the Americas who considered themselves American rather than Spanish.

More importantly, trade was primarily regulated in the interests of Spain and was under the rigid control of the Spanish Government. To facilitate the collection of taxes all trade had to pass through Porto Bello (on the Caribbean shore of the Panamanian isthmus) or the port of Veracruz in Mexico. This was an extraordinarily cumbersome system (goods exported from Argentina first had to be sent to Peru!) and it hampered the economic development of Latin America. Ironically, the influx of gold and silver from the New World into Spain encouraged extravagance, stimulated inflation and discouraged industry. Eventually Spain could no longer provide the manufactured goods which the American colonies demanded. As a result, by the latter part of the 18th century the colonies were becoming increasingly self-sufficient, maintaining their own administrations, defence forces and economies.

Spain also had to contend with interloping European nations. The British, Dutch and French all acquired minor bases in Latin America. By the 18th century the British were lending a sympathetic ear – in the interests of advancing British trade in the region – to suggestions that the Spanish colonies should be helped to acquire independence.

The successful North American war of independence against Britain, the overthrow of the French monarchy at the end of the 18th century, Napoleon's seizure of Spain which weakened links between Spain and its American possessions (allowing a period of temporary self-government for the colonies), and the influence of an enlightened intellectual trend in Europe, have all been cited as reasons for the sudden upsurge of Latin

American independence movements in 1808-10. The fact that the colonial armies were composed mainly of criollos and mestizos, and not Spanish troops, made it possible for the Latin Americans to fight Spain.

The Revolutionary Wars

Revolutionary movements rose and ferocious wars of independence were fought. Each of the uprisings was spontaneous and localised, and although they seem to have risen out of similar circumstances they were unconnected with each other. From Venezuela, a revolutionary army fought its way to the Pacific side of the mountains and then marched south towards Peru. Another army, under the command of José de San Martín, set forth in 1817 from Argentina, marched over the mountains into Chile, occupied Santiago and then sailed northwards up the coast and entered Lima. There was no real master plan behind this giant pincer movement, but by 1825 Spain had been completely ejected from all its Latin American colonies except Cuba and Puerto Rico.

The liberating army which marched from Argentina to Chile included Chilean refugees who had fled Chile when Spain reimposed her rule after the Napoleonic Wars. Spain had been unable to reimpose her rule in Argentina due to the presence of a strong criollo army which had consolidated itself during the Napoleonic Wars. At the head of these Chilean contingents San Martín placed a Chilean with the rather unlikely name of Bernardo O'Higgins, the son of an Irish immigrant who had become Viceroy of Peru under Spanish rule.

O'Higgins became head of the new Chilean republic, while San Martín pushed on to drive the Spanish from Peru, transporting his army in ships either seized from the Spanish, or bought from British or North American owners, often with the aid of British and North American finance. British and North American merchants also financed the purchase of arms and ammunition, knowing that the removal of the Spanish would allow them to set up their own businesses on the continent. The command of the Chilean navy was given to the Scotsman Thomas Cochrane, a former officer in the British navy.

The Early Years of Independence

The Spanish administrative divisions provided the political framework for the new countries which emerged from the wars and Latin America broke up into some 17 independent republics. When Chile became an independent state it was but a fraction of its present size, with undecided boundaries with Bolivia in the north, Argentina to the east and the independent Mapuche Indians to the south of the Bío Bío River.

Although other Latin American coun-

Old banknote showing the first President of Chile, Bernardo O'Higgins

tries came out of the wars in a state of economic distress, Chile quickly achieved a degree of political stability which permitted rapid development of agriculture, mining, industry and commerce, all of which sought new areas in which to expand. The population was more homogeneous and less racked by the racial problems of other Latin American countries.

O'Higgins dominated the Chilean Government for the first five years after independence. A pragmatic 'enlightened despot' he was concerned about cultural and economic progress, tax reform, initiating immigration, improving transport and extending education to even the poorest Chileans. He concentrated power in his own hands in order to enforce reform in the face of vested interests. Possibly because his reforms threatened the wealth and power of the land-owner class he was overthrown in 1823 by a revolt supported by the army.

Latin America had won political independence but it had yet to undergo a social revolution. The essential structure of society remained the same, with the criollos and other members of the Latin American upper-classes stepping into the shoes of the departed Spanish. Chile was dominated by the interests of the large land-owners who exercised great political power and sought to run the country like a big hacienda for their own benefit. Following the overthrow of O'Higgins a period of conflict followed, including a civil war in 1830 which delivered Chile firmly into the hands of the landed gentry. In 1833 they secured a new constitution which excluded the landless and illiterate – the majority of the population – from the franchise. Great power was granted to the president who, of course, was the nominee of the landowners.

British Economic Penetration

Not only was the country dominated by the interests of the landowners but a new force also appeared on the scene – the British capitalists. Both Britain and the USA favoured the independence of Latin America from Spain so that they could gain access to its raw materials and markets. As early as 1811, Chile had opened its ports to free trade with friendly and neutral countries. The British had been quick to exploit the rift in the Spanish monopoly, and increased their activity after independence.

In the 1820s, British consulates were established in several Chilean towns and British merchants settled in large

Expansion of Chile

From Peru
Arica
Iquique
From Bolivia
Antofagasta

0   100   200km

Copiapó

ARGENTINA

Valparaíso — Santiago

PACIFIC
OCEAN

Río Bío Bío

Temuco — From the Mapuche

Puerto Montt

Effectively occupied 1800

Territorial consolidation 1800-1880

Expansion 1882-1883

numbers. Chile exported wheat, beef, hides, tallow, copper, gold and silver, and imported most of her manufactured goods from Britain and British India. With money to invest, raw materials to be gained, and manufactured goods to be marketed, Britain became the dominant foreign force in the Chilean economy.

The economic development of Chile in the 19th century was based on the use of foreign money to finance the exploitation of her hitherto neglected natural resources; nitrate and copper became the basis of her new prosperity. Not until the end of the 19th century would Britain face a serious challenge from other foreign powers (the USA and Germany) for economic dominance in Chile.

The Expansion of Chile

Having won independence from Spain and built a fairly strong, stable nation, the Chileans entered into their own period of imperialism. The last campaigns against the Indians in the south were fought and won in 1883. To the north the War of the Pacific (1879-83) ended in the victory of Chile over Peru and Bolivia and the annexation of the nitrate-rich Atacama Desert.

The victory sparked off an economic boom, inspired confidence in the future (at least amongst the upper classes) and led to the belief that Chile was on the way to becoming one of the world's great powers. There was only one sour note; preoccupation with the war in the north had compelled Chile to sign a treaty which gave eastern Patagonia to Argentina.

Since potential territory in the east was lost, Chile looked seawards. The country had a strong, British-trained navy, to which it largely owed its victory in the War of the Pacific. Naval heroes and battles became the highlights of national history – and still are today. Chile therefore had the potential to establish and protect large scale maritime commerce. Situated on the trade and emigration route around Cape Horn, Chile was conveniently placed to establish close links with Europe and the USA.

Before the opening of the Panama Canal, Valparaíso and the ports of the nitrate mining centres in the north were major ports of call for international shipping. Chilean vessels visited Australia, Asia and Polynesia, and Chilean extremists even advocated the annexation of the Philippines (then in Spanish hands). Chile's first overseas possession, however, was a more humble one: the annexation of Easter Island in 1888 made Chile the first Latin American country to control territory in Polynesia.

Reforms Under Balmaceda

Chile had emerged from the War of the Pacific considerably enriched with the annexation of the nitrate and copper-rich Atacama Desert. Nitrate was exported to fertilise the farms of Europe and the USA, with much of the money to finance the mining operations being provided by British investors. Nitrates alone provided Chile with the major share of her income for some 40 years.

Expansion of the mining industries led to the development of a new working class and to the rise of a class of *nouveau riche*, both of whom demanded a say in the running of the country. Political power still lay in the hands of the landowners, but as the urban working and middle classes grew, so did their demands for representative government and welfare legislation.

The first president to tackle Chile's uneven sharing of wealth and power was José Manuel Balmaceda, who was inducted in 1886. He proposed state ownership of the railroads, spoke of breaking the monopoly of the British capitalists, of setting up Chilean-owned nitrate companies, and introducing tariff protection to aid the development of Chilean industry. Balmaceda began to carry out numerous public works, expanding the rail network, building new roads, telegraph lines, bridges, docks, water supply systems, hospitals and schools.

Such policies naturally met with a violent reaction from the British who saw their economic interests being threatened, and from the Chilean upper classes who objected to paying taxes to finance social services. In 1890 the Congress rejected Balmaceda's budget, voted to depose him, and appointed a naval officer, Jorge Montt, to head a provisional government. Montt's troops occupied the northern mining towns while Balmaceda held out in the central valley. The inevitable civil war resulted in the death of perhaps 10,000 Chileans and the defeat of Balmaceda – who is said to have shot himself after months of asylum in the Argentine legation.

Alessandri to Ibáñez

The Chilean working class would have to wait until 1920 for their next hope of social reform – the election of President Arturo Alessandri Palma. As a cure for the parliamentary deadlock which had plagued Chile since the civil war he proposed increased powers for the president. To break the power of the central valley aristocracy he demanded greater self-rule for the outlying provinces. For the relief of the government treasury he advocated an income tax on corporations and individuals, and a high tax on land. To aid the working class he advocated laws which would increase wages, shorten hours, and provide insurance against illness, accident, old age and death.

His reforms were not easily carried out. Blocked by the conservatives in Congress for four years, he succeeded in winning only one major reform – the enactment of a labour code which recognised the right of labour unions to organise freely with leaders of their own choice, restricted child labour and introduced a worker's health insurance plan.

Army opposition forced Alessandri to resign in 1924. The following year a coup

restored him for six months until he was once again deposed. For several years the presidency was held by a dictatorial army officer, Carlos Ibáñez del Campo, who had led the coups which restored and once again deposed Alessandri. Despite many initial successes, misguided or miscarried economic policies coupled with the world depression, led to widespread opposition which forced Ibáñez into exile. A period of political turmoil followed until Alessandri returned as president from 1932 to 1936.

The confusion following Ibáñez's ousting resulted in the re-alignment of political groupings in Chile. Small socialist groups merged to form the Socialist Party in 1933 – the future president, Salvador Allende, was a member. Splits between Stalinists and Trotskyists divided the Communist Party and splinter groups from existing radical and reformist parties created many new parties. The industrial trade unions increased their membership and became increasingly powerful.

Despite the turmoil in the early 1930s, for the next 40 years Chile managed to escape the coups, rebellions and revolutions which beset most Latin American countries after the Great Depression. The military did not overtly interfere in Chilean politics between 1932 and 1973. Fair elections took place on schedule, there were no illegal changes of government, and the power of the presidents remained checked.

The Trade Unions

The early history of the Chilean labour movement is a fragmentary one. Prior to the 1880s there were sporadic, spontaneous protests, rebellions and strikes. After that the labour movement developed as an organised, militant, political force. Periodic depressions in the nitrate industry resulted in unemployment amongst the miners and forced many of them to migrate to the northern ports and central valley. As industrial unrest increased, and border disputes with Bolivia and Argentina continued, the conservative government of President Montt began to expand the army. The labour movement became the military's principal target and the military leadership began to see itself as an agent of law and order and to think in terms of a permanent role for the armed forces in the government of the country.

In the first decades of the 20th century, large trade unions were formed, such as the Chilean Workers Federation (FOCH) which originally began as a conservative-led railway workers union but developed into a militant organisation linking socialists, anarchists and syndicalists. Although internal power struggles reduced the union's membership, by the 1920s it was a major force amongst miners, maritime and tram workers, and some rural labourers. The anarchists and syndicalists became significant forces on the docks, construction works, and amongst craftsmen. In Chilean Patagonia aggressive labour movements grew up amongst the workers on the cattle and sheep ranches and in the meat and hide processing plants.

Rural Problems

Although the unions had some influence in the countryside, by the 1920s some 60% to 75% of Chile's rural workers were still largely isolated on large haciendas which controlled 80% of agricultural land in the central valley. The inquilinos remained at the mercy of the landowners for access to land, housing and daily needs. As a result, their votes belonged to the landowners who used them to keep their seats in Congress and maintain the existing system of land ownership.

The Alessandri Government helped maintain this system, partly in response to the demands of the urban leftist parties. These pressed for lower food prices and restrictions on the export of agricultural produce in order to counter rising food prices and shortages. Price controls and restrictions on food exports were introduced, and the price of agricultural produce was kept artificially low, passing the burden of price and export controls on to the producer. This kept the urban consumer happy, and the goodwill of the landowners was maintained because they were allowed to keep control over their land and workers. The leftists, although not all of them, had sold out the rural workers in the interests of political expediency.

As industry expanded and the government introduced new public works, employment opportunities increased and the lot of the urban worker improved. But the lot of the rural worker declined rapidly; real wages dropped forcing many to migrate to the towns in search of work. The inquilinos suffered a decrease in the quality and quantity of their land allotments, supplies of firewood, seed, fertiliser and other help, as well as their rights to graze animals. Most haciendas failed to introduce modern agricultural techniques, resulting in a decline in production and the increasing backwardness of Chilean agriculture. Police enforced evictions of rural workers, broke up newly formed rural unions, and allowed the landowners to retain control of the countryside.

Foreign Investment & Influence

Despite increased industrialisation during the first decades of the 20th century, Chile did not achieve economic independence. US investments boomed in the first two decades of the century (mainly in nitrate, copper and iron mining). German investments grew rapidly in the 1890s and soon dominated the electric power industry and urban trolley car system. British interests dominated the mining industry in the north and the sheep grazing ranches in Tierra del Fuego.

WW I settled the rivalry between the three countries. Germany was eliminated and Britain was reduced to a debtor nation. This left the US corporations, which now controlled the Chilean copper mines, as the new cornerstone of the Chilean economy (nitrate mining had lost its significance due to the invention of synthetic nitrate during the war).

In 1947, Chile signed the Rio Treaty for the 'security' of the western hemisphere and the following year joined the Organisation of American States (OAS), both tailored to the anti-communist policies of the USA. Under the Mutual Security Act of 1951 and the Mutual Defense Agreement of 1952, the US began to send military advisors and instructors to Chile and to train Chilean officers in the US – thus helping to cement political and professional relationships and secure the political sympathy of the Chilean military towards the US.

In the late 1950s and early '60s, Chile was hit by a wave of foreign investment. A whole zoo of foreign multinationals and companies moved in: General Motors, Ford, Chrysler, Fiat, Leyland, Citroen, General Telephone & Electronics, Remington Rand, the First National City Bank and the Bank of America. In a country where the majority of the population still needed more food, clothing, housing and transport systems, foreign investment produced goods which were geared for rich, developed nations.

Elections: 1952 to 1961

In 1952 the former dictator General Carlos Ibáñez won the presidential election as an authoritarian but 'above politics' candidate. Under Ibáñez, reforms were introduced to curtail the power of the landowners in Chilean politics by eliminating their control over the votes of their labourers. The Law for the Permanent Defense of Democracy (which had been instituted in 1948 in order to ban the Communist Party) was also revoked. Despite the political reforms, Ibáñez's economic policies lost him the support of both the working and upper classes, and brought high inflation and a significant decline in living standards.

The elimination of a law which banned the Communist Party allowed a new coalition of socialists and communists – the Popular Action Front (FRAP) – to contest the 1958 presidential elections with Salvador Allende as their candidate. Jorge Alessandri, the son of Arturo Alessandri, represented the Conservative Party and the (inaptly named) Liberal Party coalition. Eduardo Frei represented the newly-formed Christian Democrat Party, a moderate, reformist party whose short-term goals were very similar to FRAP's but whose philosophical basis was Christian humanism.

Alessandri won the election with just under 32% of the vote, to Frei's 21% and to Allende's 29% (Allende had managed only 5% of the vote in the 1952 election). However, with the rural vote now firmly wrenched away from the conservatives by electoral reform and the new political parties, the 1961 congressional election saw FRAP and the Christian Democrats out-poll and out-seat the Conservative and Liberal parties.

Congress was now controlled by powerful opposition groups which were committed to real land reform. In 1962, Alessandri was virtually forced to adopt land reform programmes which began a 10-year assault on the haciendas. Though not a great deal was actually done while he remained as president, the new laws did provide a legal basis for expropriating land from the large estates and transferring them to small holders.

The Christian Democrat Period

The 1964 presidential election saw a two-way battle. FRAP again supported Allende and the Christian Democrats and the conservative groups (who viewed the Christian Democrats as the lesser of two evils) supported Frei. In the campaign that followed, both the Christian Democrats and FRAP promised agrarian reform, supported rural unionisation, and promised an end to the hacienda system.

President Salvador Allende

The right and centre of Chilean politics were united against Allende. The USA backed Frei and provided the Christian Democrats with large sums of money to help him win the election; perhaps more than half his campaign was financed by the US. A tremendous barrage of anti-communist propaganda was dispersed. Frei won the election with about 56% of the votes to Allende's 39%.

The Christian Democrats were genuinely committed to social reform, and having won the election, efforts were made to control inflation, improve the country's balance of payments, carry out large-scale rural reform, and improve public health, education and social services. Whatever the Christian Democrats did, however, threatened the privileges of the traditional elite, or the influence of the radical left. Fearful of losing their supporters to the Christian Democrats the FRAP parties urged faster and more extensive action, no matter how successful the Christian Democrats were.

Rather than reducing dependence on foreign capital the Frei Government sought to attract more. By 1970 over a hundred US corporations had investments in Chile, but capital-intensive production failed to reduce unemployment. Too few jobs were created to cope with migration to the cities, and rings of shanty-towns grew at an alarming rate.

The Christian Democrats were also faced with the often-violent MIR (the Left Wing Revolutionary Movement) which had joined with the Mapuche Indians in the south in organising land seizures and had spread its influence into the urban slums. The movement was led by André Pascal Allende, a nephew of Salvador Allende. Other leftist parties also gave support to strikes and land occupations by rural labourers.

Frei was unable to implement reforms fast enough to satisfy the leftists, and was obstructed in Congress by the National Party (formed by the merger of the Conservative Party and Liberal Party in 1965). He was also confronted by dissension within his own party over the pace and objectives of rural reform.

Although the Christian Democrats did improve living conditions for thousands of rural workers and made impressive gains in education and public health, inflation, dependence on foreign markets and capital, and unequal distribution of wealth continued to be major problems. To a large extent however, the Christian Democrats had instituted policies which the Allende Government would implement more extensively.

Allende Comes to Power

As the 1970 presidential election approached, the coalition of leftist groups – now calling itself Popular Unity (*Unidad Popular*) – once more chose Allende as their candidate. Popular Unity advocated radical changes. Nationalisation of banks, insurance companies and other key elements in the economy was proposed. All agricultural estates more than the equivalent of 80 hectares of irrigated land were to be expropriated. Changes to the presidential and parliamentary systems were to be made.

The 1970 election pitted Allende against the Christian Democrat candidate Radomiro Tomic (who gave the impression of being as radical as Allende) and the aged Jorge Alessandri who stood as an independent. Alessandri appealed to the old elite and middle classes with the prospect of restoration of law and order which they believed had eroded under the Christian Democrats. Since the Christian Democrats' reforms had alienated their right-wing supporters, a victory for Alessandri was generally predicted. As it turned out, Allende won 36.3% of the vote to Tomic's 27.8% and Alessandri's 34.9%.

Under the Chilean constitution, if the winner was short of an absolute majority of votes, Congress had to confirm the result and could in theory name the runner-up as president. By rights, Allende should have been confirmed as president, but since the Christian Democrats controlled the deciding votes in Congress they used their power to push through a number of constitutional amendments designed to limit the course of Allende's Government. With no choice other than to lose the presidency for the fourth time, Allende backed down to the demands of the Christian Democrats and was subsequently confirmed as president in October 1970.

The First Years of Allende

If Frei had faced a storm of opposition then Allende faced a hurricane. Allende had no revolutionary army to enforce his will. He headed a multi-party coalition which was still divided on the objectives of the new government. He faced a hostile Congress and an entrenched bureaucracy. He had polled only a third of the vote and therefore lacked a truly popular mandate to rule. As a leftist he evoked the instant hostility of the US Government under Nixon and Kissinger and right-wing extremist groups called for his overthrow by violent means.

The short-term economic policies of the Allende Government aimed to make a massive redistribution of income to benefit the poor. Wage increments to the urban and rural poor were made significantly higher than inflation. By coupling this with increased government spending, the government hoped to stimulate the demand for goods and encourage private enterprise to increase production. An increase in income and demand for goods, plus a reduction in unemployment, was expected to bring the country out of the economic recession inherited from Frei.

However, demands by farmers and workers for the expropriation of farms and factories, and the apprehension of private investors over the extent of the government's nationalisation policies, worked against any substantial private investment programmes. Instead of investing for the future, private business sold off stock or disposed of farm machinery and livestock. Wages and demand for goods increased, but production declined, causing shortages of goods, rising prices and black markets. Inflation soared to over 300% by mid-1973, reducing the real income of workers to less than it was when Allende came to power. Agricultural production declined and the government had to use scarce foreign exchange to import food.

In an attempt to deal with shortages in the cities and towns the government organised public companies to compete with private wholesalers and distributors. However, this directly threatened the viability of Chile's numerous shopkeepers and vendors and helped turn them against the government. The activities of the MIR (which Allende could not, or would not, control) continued, and stories circulated about the development of armed pro-government workers' organisations in Santiago's factory belt.

The establishment of friendly relations

between Chile and Cuba, and the expropriation of US copper companies and other foreign companies, further provoked the hostility of the US Government. Later hearings in the US Congress clearly indicated that President Nixon and Henry Kissinger played an active role in attempts to bring down the Allende Government. The US attempted to disrupt the Chilean economy by cutting off credit from international finance organisations, while providing both financial and moral support to Allende's opponents. It maintained friendly relations with the Chilean military, *increased* military aid while other aid was being cut off, and later, helped plan the military coup which eventually brought down the government.

Faced with these awesome problems the government attempted to reduce the conflict by negotiating clearly defined limits on the extent of socialisation with the opposition groups. But neither the left-wing extremists who believed that socialism could only be brought about by force, nor rightists who believed it could only be halted by force, allowed the government any room to find a peaceful solution to the crisis.

The Right-Wing Backlash

In October 1972, the government was faced with a massive strike by shopkeepers, professionals, bank clerks, right-wing students, and even some urban and rural working-class groups. The strike was brought about by the independent truckers association which demanded that the government drop its plans to create a state-owned trucking enterprise. Supported by the Christian Democrats and the National Party, the strike quickly became a direct challenge to the Allende Government.

With the possibility of a government collapse looming, the government declared a state of emergency. Ironically, this meant that the military was now responsible for maintaining law and order and for enforcing censorship on the opposition media. The Army Commander-in-Chief, General Carlos Prats, was invited to serve as Minister of the Interior and an air force general and an admiral were also included in the presidential cabinet. The truckers' strike was settled in November with the government promising not to nationalise transport or wholesale trading, and to return private enterprises occupied by workers during the strike to their owners.

Despite the economic crisis Popular Unity managed to poll 44% of the votes in the March 1973 congressional election – enough to prevent the Christian Democrats and National Party from gaining sufficient seats to carry out their plan to impeach Allende. It was obvious from the vote that popular support for Allende had actually *increased* significantly since the 1970 election.

Hard on the heels of the congressional election, in June 1973, came an attempted military coup. This was unsuccessful but the pressure continued to mount. Absurd stories spread, claiming Popular Unity had a plan for killing all 100,000 members of the military. The extreme right was calling for the military to revolt and overthrow the government. Military units, under a gun control law passed in 1972, started going into the factories, shanty towns and government offices, ostensibly to search for guns, disarm workers and prevent a leftist insurrection.

In July 1973 the truckers and other right-wing groups once more went on strike, supported by the entire political opposition. Prats resigned soon after, apparently having lost the support of the military. He was replaced by General Augusto Pinochet who both Prats and Allende thought was loyal to the principal of constitutional government. The following month the opposition parties called on the military to re-establish the 'rule of the constitution and the law' and three weeks later came the coup.

The Coup

On 11 September 1973, Pinochet led a military coup which overthrew the Popular Unity Government and resulted in the death of Allende and thousands of his supporters. The presidential palace in Santiago was bombed by air force jets. What happened to Allende, who was in the palace, is unclear. Some reports suggest he was killed by soldiers in the palace, while others suggest he committed suicide. Other parts of Santiago, including factories and working class neighbourhoods, were bombed and attacked by soldiers.

Thousands of leftists and suspected leftists were arrested. Many were herded into Santiago's National Stadium and Chile Stadium where brutal beatings and numerous summary executions were carried out. Like Nazis during the 1930s, bonfires were made out of left-wing literature and government publications. Possession of left-wing literature meant arrest. A curfew was imposed and people were shot for being on the streets during it. How many people were killed or simply 'disappeared' at the time of the coup and in the years after it is unknown; estimates range from as few as 2500 to as many as 80,000. Over 850,000 workers were sacked from their jobs for political reasons. Hundreds of thousands of Chileans left the country.

The Chilean military claims it was necessary to use force to remove Allende because his government had brought about economic chaos and was planning, using clandestinely amassed weapons, to overthrow the democratic institutions of the country. The origins of the 'economic chaos' were to some extent the vague Popular Unity policies on the nationalisation of industry and farms, but it is too easy to say that Allende brought the coup on himself. The real causes of the 'economic chaos' were the strikes of right-wing businessmen and professionals, artificially induced scarcities of commodities and food, foreign manipulation of the Chilean economy, and the creation of a black market.

Had Allende been intent on murdering the military and civilian opposition leaders and imposing communism on Chile, he would have embarked on armed rebellion rather than trying to gain power legally by standing for election four times over a period of 18 years. When the coup came it was plain to see that all the guns were in the hands of the military.

Towards the end, Allende had decided to resolve the political crisis *peacefully* and *legally* with another election, but was prevented from doing so by the military coup. At the time of the coup Allende remained in the presidential palace, refusing to surrender and flee the country while his supporters were left to be massacred by the military. In doing so he ensured his own death, but also his own integrity and the integrity of the Popular Unity Government. The last words belong to him; they are part of a radio address given just before the presidential palace was bombed:

... My words are not spoken in bitterness, but in disappointment. They will be a moral judgement on those who have betrayed the oath they took as soldiers of Chile .... They have the might and they can enslave us, but they cannot halt the world's social processes, not with crimes, nor with guns .... May you go forward in the knowledge that, sooner rather than later, the great avenues will open once again, along which free citizens will march in order to build a better society. Long live Chile! Long live the People! Long live the workers! These are my last words, and I am sure that this sacrifice will constitute a moral lesson which will punish cowardice, perfidy and treason.

GOVERNMENT

Since the military coup of 1973, Chile has been headed by a junta made up of the commanders of the armed forces. After the coup the junta dissolved the National Congress, banned the country's leftist parties, placed all other parties in an

ADVERTENCIA:
LA POLITICA
ES DAÑINA PARA
LA SALUD

MINISTERIO DEL INTERIOR

Warning: Politics is bad for your health
– 'Hoy' 6 January 1982

which the army numbers 57,000 (including 30,000 conscripts). Very rigid, highly disciplined and obedient to its commanders, the Chilean army owes its structure to foreign influence. In the late 19th century a Prussian army officer, Emil Koerner, was contracted to reform the Chilean officer training academy. As head of general staff from 1891 to 1910 he introduced German instructors, uniforms, discipline and modern military equipment. Much of this has stuck and even today Chilean soldiers in their parade uniforms look like they've marched down from a Nuremburg rally.

It is commonly believed that the Pinochet regime is an aberration in Chilean history, and that the Chilean army has normally been apolitical. In fact, since independence from Spain, Chile has had four civil wars, some 10 successful coups, and a number of unsuccessful coups, uprisings and mutinies.

'indefinite recess' and prohibited all other political activities. All the remaining political parties were banned in 1977.

The President

The head of the junta is General Augusto Pinochet Ugarte, who assumed the office of president in 1974 and has held it ever since. Unlike some other Latin American dictatorships which rest on the collective rule of the junta, Pinochet is very much the real ruler in Chile. Although a plebiscite is planned for 1989 to confirm either Pinochet or his nominee as president until 1997, it seems unlikely that Pinochet will voluntarily relinquish the presidency. Barring his incapacitation or death, or an uprising by the armed forces, Pinochet (born 1915) is likely to continue as Chile's dictator for some years to come.

The Army

Pinochet's power is based on his command of the Chilean army. The total strength of the armed forces is about 101,000, of

The Security Forces

Underpinning the junta is a system of repression, murder and torture. Torture of political prisoners by members of the Chilean security forces has been reported regularly since the junta seized power in 1973. Those detained and tortured because of their political activities come from a broad range of Chilean society, from doctors and lawyers to shanty-town dwellers.

Although torture and ill-treatment has been used by both the *Carabineros* (uniformed police) and *Investigaciones* (plain-clothes police) it is the National Information Centre (*Central Nacional de Informaciones – CNI*) which has been most frequently cited as responsible for torturing political prisoners.

The most common physical tortures described in testimonies to Amnesty International include beatings, electric shocks and burns to sensitive parts of the body, rape and sexual abuse of women, drugging, sleep deprivation, submerging the victim's head under water, and the 'parrots perch' where the victims are trussed into a crouching position with their arms hugging their legs and are hung upside down from a pole which is slipped through the gap between their knees and elbows, and are then given electric shocks and have water squirted at high pressure into their mouths and noses.

The 'parrot's perch' torture

International assassination has also been a forte of the Chilean security forces since the coup. General Prats was murdered in Buenos Aires a year after the coup. Bernardo Layton, a Christian Democrat leader, narrowly escaped being killed in a bomb attack in Rome in 1975. Orlando Letelier, Chile's foreign minister under Allende, was killed by a car bomb in Washington in 1976. All these acts have been attributed to Chilean agents or people associated with them.

Opposition Groups

All opposition parties operate although they're officially banned. Street demonstrations against the government and opposition political meetings continue. Opposition newspapers and magazines are widely available and carry many articles critical of the government. There have even been attempts made to prosecute Pinochet in the courts. This, however, should not be taken as an indication that there is some great blooming of freedom in Chile. The regime is so secure that it needn't worry about the opposition, and any that does get out of hand can be dealt with by the police and army.

In lieu of free elections it's difficult to say how many Chileans support the regime. Certainly there are many who believe that Pinochet is the saviour of the country, and you'll meet Chileans who will *implore* you to return home and tell everyone how good life is under the present government. Their reasons include bad memories of, and experiences during, the Allende years, a tremendous fear of communism, and a belief in the need for strong government and a stable society.

The opposition groups cover a wide range including the political left-wing, the centre and even some right-wing people. The Roman Catholic Church and the trade union movement are two major focuses for dissent. The problem is that the opposition groups fail to agree on an acceptable alternative to Pinochet and have no means of toppling him even if they did. Pinochet is exceptionally adept at exploiting divisions between the opposition groups, keeping them weak and distrustful of each other.

Ironically, some of the political parties supported the coup against Allende in the expectation that the military would hand back power to civilians. Just one month before the coup, in a statement which prophesied exactly the situation the opposition parties are now in, Allende advised an opponent:

You are looking for a military dictatorship. And from somewhere, not that I believe there's anything after death, but still, if there is, I shall look down on you all and find you all together, casting about for ways to get out of power the military man you replace me with. I shall see you all there, plotting and planning it, but with a great deal more difficulty than you are having now, how to get rid of the soldier you put in my place. Because it won't cost you much to get him in. But by heaven, it will cost you something to get him out!

The left-wing of the Christian Democrat party opposed the coup; the right-wing supported the coup, but turned against Pinochet when it became clear he would not hand back power to civilians. The National Party supported the coup; a number of National Party leaders have since come out against Pinochet, but overall the party backs the regime. The MIR still operates and a number of acts of violence over recent years have been attributed to it. The Communist Party, once a moderate group which favoured an alliance with the Christian Democrats during the Allende years, has joined with the MIR in advocating armed opposition to the Pinochet regime.

The union movement is fraught with problems. Many of the older more experienced leaders were killed at the time of the coup, or disappeared, were imprisoned, or forced into exile after it. Many of the unions appear to be bankrupt, have neither paid full-time organisers nor buildings from which to operate. With 30 to 35% unemployment and low wages it's difficult to rebuild the union movement. Under the government's labour plan, strikes are declared illegal by the government after 60 days duration. Picketing by strikers or soliciting money to help striker's families is illegal, and employers are allowed to use non-union labour to break strikes.

Despite the problems, many of the militant trade unions, including leftist and Christian Democrat-led unions, are actively involved in the struggle against the dictatorship and have allied themselves under a common leadership.

Pinochet supporters brandish his photo

The Future

The immediate problem for the opposition groups is the removal of Pinochet. The long-term problems are even more complex. The history of Chile has been one of conflict between those who have attempted to better the lot of ordinary Chileans, and an economic and political order which has rested on the subjugation and coercion of the working class. A comment attributed to Diego Portales, who ruled Chile as a virtual dictator in the 1830s, captures the tone of Chilean politics in the 19th and 20th centuries:

> The stick and the cake, justly and opportunely administered, are the remedies with which any nation can be cured, however inveterate its bad habits may be.

Ever ready to use the stick, Portales' autocratic rule spared Chile the anarchy that many other Latin American countries experienced after independence. But Portales failed to solve the country's internal problems, and passed them on to future generations to deal with: How can you make Chile a free country while maintaining political order? How do you achieve economic progress without exploiting the working classes? How do you maintain social order without the use of political repression? How do you keep the army out of politics?

ECONOMY

When the junta seized power its support for private enterprise and 'law and order' appealed to right-wing businessmen and professionals who had opposed Allende. The junta promised to combat inflation, restore private property, and purge the country of leftists.

Since the junta had little knowledge of economics or public affairs when it came to power, civilian advisers played the dominant role in determining policy. The junta opened the way for economists espousing a theory variously described as 'libertarianism' or the 'new economic orthodoxy'. This is an extreme form of *laissez-faire* economics, which attempts to leave economic control entirely to individuals and international market forces.

A group of right-wing, economic advisers (the so-called 'Chicago Boys' who were either graduates of, or had links with, the University of Chicago) gained the ear of Pinochet. Their plan for restructuring the economy appears to have been worked out prior to the coup, and given to high-ranking military officers and opposition politicians. If nothing else it must have created the impression that *someone* knew how to cope with the economic chaos which would face Allende's successor.

When Pinochet took power the Chicago Boys were able to place themselves in key

'Workers are asking for a wage rise.'
'Well sack them.'
'But what about the social costs?'
'We're not paying them.' – 'Hoy', 8 July 1981

positions in the banks and government, and the military ensured the implementation of their policies. Prices were freed while wages remained frozen. Tariffs were reduced. Interest rates for savings were frozen by state-owned banks but raised by private companies, causing a flood of personal savings into private hands. Government spending was cut and indirect taxes were introduced. Many nationalised industries were broken up and sold off to private business. A new investment code was set up to attract foreign capital and the US copper companies were compensated for their nationalised copper mines.

In the short term, the rate of inflation fell, domestic demand shrank and imports decreased. The growth of 'non-traditional' exports helped to compensate for the decline in the price of copper on the world market. But the cost of this 'success' was enormous. Industrial production dropped and some industries disappeared never to be seen again. Wages continued to fall and unemployment increased to almost 20% of the workforce by the beginning of 1976. Chile's already ramshackle social security system broke down as firms going into bankruptcy defaulted on their social security insurance payments, and the government refused to pay unemployment benefits to those made redundant. In some urban shanty towns unemployment rose to as high as 80% or more, and only the church-organised soup kitchens kept people from starving.

Faced with the collapse of their internal markets employers were forced to find markets abroad for their produce. 'Non-traditional' exports such as fruit, vegetables, wine and even basic consumer products like shoes flowed abroad. In keeping with the Chicago Boys' policies, tariffs were further lowered, even though Chilean industry was hardly surviving in its own markets.

As the banks were sold to private owners, the rate of interest they were allowed to charge was freed from government controls, and subsequently soared. Firms trying to borrow money to stave off bankruptcy found themselves in huge debt to private banks and finance companies. Not surprisingly the financiers – sometimes the Chicago Boys using foreign loan money – were able to buy up Chilean industry at very cheap prices and develop personal business empires.

As inflation continued to fall, real wages and salaries began to rise again, increasing the demand for goods and services. Since the battered local industry was often incapable of responding, the demand was met by importing manufactured goods.

Foreign investment in Chile also failed to eventuate in the quantity and form that was expected. Although wages were low the size of the local market was too small to interest foreign companies who, in any case, could export goods to Chile's unprotected markets from better situated countries with equally cheap wages. Chile was therefore forced to depend on the export of primary products such as minerals, timber, fruit and seafood in order to earn foreign exchange.

Private enterprise borrowed large sums of money from overseas to finance expansion, but this was only sustainable so long as exports increased (as they did in the second half of the 1970s) and the money was invested productively. Problems began to develop after 1979 when the peso was tied to the US dollar. When the US dollar was revalued upwards the peso went with it. Consequently imports were very cheap and prices of Chilean exports abroad were expensive, and this created a growing deficit in Chile's balance of trade.

The crunch finally came in the early 1980s when the world recession hit the price of copper and other minerals which were still Chile's chief exports. The trade deficit grew as the fixed exchange rate forced up the price of exports on the contracting international market. Foreign lending continued however, and Chile's indebtedness (almost all of it created by foreign loans to private banks and firms) grew. By the end of 1981 loan repayments were eating up three-quarters of Chile's export earnings. Interest rates climbed, bankruptcies increased and unemployment soared.

In 1982 the government sought to counter the trend by devaluing the peso and by further reducing wages, but inflation soon wiped out any benefits which Chilean exporters may have gained. With interest rates rising both locally and internationally the banks' debt problems worsened. The peso was then allowed to float and immediately plummeted by 40% against the US dollar. With the Chicago Boys' policies in shambles the government was forced to backtrack and at the beginning of 1983 it took over direct management of key private banks and finance houses, revealing the massive foreign debts these businesses had accumulated.

The cost of the Chicago Boys' policies has been high – especially for Chile's poor. The social security system, once the most extensive in Latin America and benefiting 70% of the population, has been gutted. Although the inflation rate is low in comparison to some other Latin American countries, this has been at the cost of producing massive unemployment. Perhaps 25 to 30% of the national workforce is unemployed and in some poor districts and amongst the young the figure may be much higher. Wages are extraordinarily low with the minimum wage set at just US$60 *per month*. A lot of Chileans live very close to the bone and how they continue to make ends meet is a mystery.

POPULATION & PEOPLE

Chile is a country of some 12 million people, the majority of whom are *mestizos* of mixed Spanish and Indian ancestry. Over the centuries many distinctions have been made between the different mestizo groups. The 'pure blood' Spanish are set apart from the 'mainly white' mestizos, the 'Indian' mestizos, Indians, blacks, mulattos (with mixed black and European ancestry) and *zambos* (with mixed black and Indian ancestry).

Since there are few blacks in Chile, the most important non-European element in the population are the American Indians. Around 95% of Chile's population is caucasian or *mestizo*, and about 3% are American Indian. About 90% of the population is Roman Catholic but there are also other religions, including Lutherans, Jews, Presbyterians, Mormons and Pentacostals.

Unlike Argentina or Brazil, the growth of Chile's population in the 19th and 20th centuries did not rely on successive waves of immigration from Europe. At the end of the 19th century only a few per cent of Chile's population were foreign born. After 1848, several thousand Germans settled in the south where, to this day, many people speak German as well as Spanish. Other immigrants included French, Italians, Yugoslavs (there is a large concentration of Yugoslavs in Tierra del Fuego), European Jews, and Palestinians.

Immigration from Europe did not change the structure of Chilean society, but it did add a non-Spanish element to the middle and upper classes. The old Chilean aristocracy (the original landed gentry) is mainly of Spanish Basque origin, but some of Chile's 'best' families have British or French names like Edwards, Lyon or Subercaseaux. Despite their small numbers the European immigrants became very powerful in Chile's economy, owning a large share of rural estates and commercial and industrial establishments.

About three-quarters of Chile's population lives in the central valley, which covers a fifth of the country's total area. About a third of the total population is crammed into Santiago and its surrounding regions, making it the fifth or sixth largest city in Latin America. Only a fifth of Chile's population can be classed as rural and this figure is gradually decreasing, a trend found throughout Latin America.

Although they say nothing about particular sub-groups of the population, statistics suggest that in some ways Chileans are relatively well off in comparison to other Latin Americans. Infant mortality rates are relatively low: in Chile about 4% of children die before reaching the age of one year, compared to 13% in Bolivia, 8% in Brazil and 9% in Peru. Average life expectancy in Chile is 68 years, compared to 51 years in Bolivia, 64 in Brazil and 58 in Peru.

GEOGRAPHY

Few countries as small as Chile – it covers an area about the size of France – can boast such a formidable variety of landscapes: Andean summits, snow-capped volcanoes, valleys, deserts, fjords, glaciers, and countless lakes and beaches. For 4300 km this narrow country runs along the south-west coast of South America between the Andes mountains and the Pacific Ocean, yet it is never more than 180 km wide.

The territory now occupied by Chile is the result of a number of military adventures: first by the Spanish conquistadores then by the Chileans themselves. Only at the end of the 19th century did Chile reach its present boundaries, extending from the city of Arica in the north to the islands of Tierra del Fuego and Navarino in the south. Chile also holds the Pacific islands of Rapanui (Easter Island) and Juan Fernández, and claims a large slice of Antarctica.

The country has a number of fairly distinct regions. In the north the great Atacama desert stretches for some 1000 km from the Peruvian border towards central Chile. The area around Copiapó is often regarded as the desert's southern end. The only water is provided by river valleys and underground sources which sustain the scattered farming oases and river-valley farming communities. Other than that there is no surface water, and some weather stations have *never* recorded any rainfall. In a sense, it is one of the most 'perfect' of deserts.

South of this desert, parts of the regions of Atacama and Coquimbo form a transition zone from desert to steppe land and then to the fertile central valley of Chile. The desert gives way to scrub and bush which becomes richer as you approach the centre and rainfall increases. Like the northern desert this is a region rich in minerals, and since there are a number of rivers cutting through the region it has been possible to establish large-scale agriculture and sizeable towns.

At the southern boundary of San Felipe de Aconcagua Province the fertile region known as the Chilean Heartland or the Central Valley begins. The heartland contains something like 70% of the country's total population and provides the lion's share of its industrial jobs. There are also copper mines in the provinces of Santiago, Valparaíso and O'Higgins. Here you find the capital of Chile – Santiago – containing almost a third of the country's population, as well as Valparaíso which is Chile's major port. The heartland is Chile's chief farming region, ideal for orchards, vineyards, cereal crops and livestock.

Unfortunately central Chile and the band of adjacent provinces are amongst the world's most geologically unstable regions and many of Chile's major cities (including Copiapó, La Serena, Valparaíso, Santiago, Talca, Chillán, Concepción and Valdivia) are constantly under threat of damage or destruction by volcanic eruptions and earthquakes.

At the Bío Bío River the heartland gives way to what was once Chile's great frontier, the home of the Mapuche (Araucanian) Indians and now a region of cereal and pasture lands. Although this is known mainly as a rural area the majority

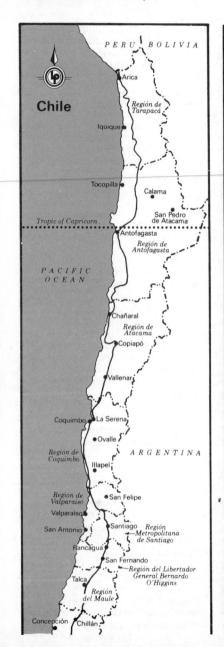

of the population live in the towns and cities, of which Temuco and Concepción are the most important.

South of the Toltén River lies the magnificent Lake District, a sprawl of snow-capped, active volcanoes and lakes, covering the provinces of Valdivia, Osorno and Llanquihue. Apart from being a destination for overseas and domestic tourists, agriculture and timber are also important industries.

The land south of the city of Puerto Montt comprises a third of Chilean territory, but holds just a few per cent of the country's population. This is a land of heavy rainfall, storms and bitterly cold winds, lashed by rough seas. Offshore, Chiloé, Chile's largest island, comprises dense forest and numerous small farms. The mainland province of Aisen is made up of canals, lakes, islands and mountains, interspersed by grasslands which support a large sheep-grazing industry. This is Chile's last frontier and its isolated settlements are only now being joined by road.

The coastline further south is a maze of bleak fjords, where great glaciers slide down mountain slopes to meet the sea. In the far south of South America lies Magallanes Province, or Chilean Patagonia. The country's most southerly city, Punta Arenas, lies on the Straits of Magellan. Before the opening of the Panama Canal in 1914 this southern passage made Punta Arenas and Valparaíso major ports of call for inter-national shipping, but the prosperity of the south is now dependent on oil and gas.

Across the straits lies Tierra del Fuego, split between Chile and Argentina, where oil extraction and sheep-grazing are the main industries. Chile effectively comes to an end with the island of Navarino, separated from Tierra del Fuego by the Beagle Channel, the site of Puerto Williams, the most southerly settlement in the world with a permanent population. Between Puerto Williams and Chilean Antarctica there is a scattering of small islands and on the southern flank of one of these islands lies the famous *Cabo de Hornos* or Cape Horn.

As diverse as the country may be there is one unifying feature – the Andes. In the far north at Lago Chungará near the Bolivian border the range is a string of awesome volcanoes; from Santiago's Santa Lucía the mountains look like an invincible phalanx advancing on the city; from Aisen the mountains are barren peaks decorated with glaciers.

In fact, the Andes make up much of Chile. Between Copiapó and the Bío Bío River the range occupies one-third to one-half of the country's width. It contains some of the highest peaks in South America, including Mt Salado which rises some 6900 metres (22,500 feet).

Though passable, this great mountain range made transport and communications difficult and generally isolated Chile from the rest of South America.

Facts for the Visitor

VISAS

Visas are required by very few people. Most West European nationalities and citizens of Britain, Canada, the USA, and Australia do not require visas. New Zealand passport holders *do* require a visa; the fee varies but is usually about US$8. Check on the current situation before you depart for Chile.

Most people are given an entry stamp on arrival which allows them to stay for up to 90 days, and this can be renewed for an additional 90 days. If you want to stay longer than six months it's probably simplest to make a short trip to Argentina or another adjoining South American country, then return and start your six months all over again. The tourist visa can be extended at the Ministry of National Affairs, Moneda 759 (2nd floor), Santiago (tel 82413, ext 271); it's open Monday to Friday from 9.30 am to 2.30 pm.

Don't turn up at a border without a visa – unless you're absolutely certain one will be issued on the spot. You could easily find yourself tramping back to the nearest Chilean consulate.

Visas for Adjoining Countries

The adjoining South American countries of Argentina, Bolivia and Peru all have embassies in Santiago and consulates in several other Chilean towns. Argentina has an embassy in Santiago and consulates in Punta Arenas, Puerto Montt, Arica and Antofagasta. Peru has an embassy in Santiago and a consulate in Arica. Bolivia has an embassy in Santiago and consulates in Arica, Calama and Antofagasta.

For the full story on Argentine visas see the chapter on Patagonia. New Zealanders can now get visas, but at the time of writing British nationals were still having problems. If you want to get to Chilean Patagonia and Tierra del Fuego and you can't get an Argentine visa the only alternative is to take one of the infrequent ships, or fly to Punta Arenas. Flying won't actually increase the cost of your trip by much since travelling through Argentinian Patagonia is quite expensive, but it does mean you miss out on an interesting side-trip. And without an Argentine visa your travelling in Tierra del Fuego (which is split between Chile and Argentina) will be very restricted.

PAPERWORK

The only essential document is your passport. You do not need an International Health Certificate. If you're planning to drive (there are many car rental firms) then you should take along an International Driving Permit. These are available from national motoring organisations.

If you're a shoestring traveller another useful document is a Youth Hostels Association membership card, although for many Chilean hostels you also need a Chilean YHA card. See the Places to Stay section in this chapter for more details.

If you are south of Puerto Montt and planning to leave for Argentina it may be necessary to get your passport stamped by an official in a department of the Chilean police known as *Investigaciones*. This rule seems to be fading out: it wasn't necessary to report to Investigaciones in Punta Arenas before leaving for Argentinian Tierra del Fuego, nor to report to the Argentine police before exiting to Chile.

CUSTOMS

Your duty free allowance includes 400 cigarettes, or 100 cigars, or 500 grams of tobacco; 2½ litres of alcoholic beverage; and a reasonable quantity of perfume. Negotiating customs is usually straightforward and officials usually only check

Contemporary 1000 peso banknote

your bags for fruit, which is strictly prohibited to prevent the spread of diseases and pests. It's also illegal to transport fruit from northern Chile and there are numerous checkpoints along highways in the Atacama Desert where all baggage is searched.

MONEY

The unit of currency is the Chilean peso (Ch$). Notes come in denominations of 100, 500, 1000 and 5000 pesos, though the 100 peso note is gradually being phased out. Coins come in denominations of 1, 5, 10, 50 and 100 pesos.

There are two sets of coins in circulation: the silver-coloured 1, 5, 10 and 50 peso coins are gradually being phased out and replaced with smaller copper-coloured 1, 5, 10, 50 and 100 peso coins.

The peso has been floating against the US dollar and is falling in value. The exchange rate, at the time of writing, is around US$1 = Ch$180, but take that as a rough guide only! The rate of the Chilean peso's devaluation is mild by South American standards, but it is hefty enough to make it worth quoting prices in this book in US dollars.

There is no limit on the export or import of local currency but you will probably find your Chilean pesos utterly useless outside Chile – except in a few border towns.

Changing Money

US dollars are the best currency to take with you to Chile – US cash can be changed almost anywhere. You can change pounds sterling, Australian dollars, yen, deutschmarks and other strange currencies at banks (banco) and change houses (casa de cambio) in Santiago, but elsewhere you may as well roll them up and use them as cigarette papers. Leave your coins in the pinball machines back home – no one will change them.

Take the bulk of your money in travellers' cheques, but make sure you bring cheques from a major company like American Express, Thomas Cook or Citibank. Cheques from small banks will be impossible to change!

Apart from cheques, you should take some US cash with you – it's not possible to change travellers' cheques in small places or when the banks (and casas de cambio) are closed. It's also more convenient to change a few dollar bills just before you leave a country rather than a hefty travellers' cheque.

Keep a record of your cheque numbers

and the original bill of sale in a safe place, in case of theft. Replacement is a lot quicker if you can produce these records – and if you don't look like a desert rat that just crawled out of a hole in the Atacama. Even so, replacement is not always as fast as companies make out; this is particularly the case with American Express. Their suspicion is justified to an extent, as in some parts of South America there's a substantial black market for travellers' cheques and many travellers sell their cheques, then claim they've lost them and demand replacements.

Take sufficient US$20 and US$50 cheques to avoid having large amounts of excess currency when you want to leave a country. It appears to be impossible to reconvert Chilean pesos to a hard currency, so avoid flying home with a bunch of useless pesos. Probably the best you will manage while you're travelling will be to exchange them for another South American currency. If you're crossing a border to Argentina, Peru or Bolivia you should get some of the appropriate new currency, or US cash, before you cross – at some of the more obscure border towns you cannot change travellers' cheques.

If you run out of money and have more at home, ask your bank to send a draft to you; make sure you specify the city and the bank branch. Transferred by cable, money should reach you in a few days, but you can run into complications even with supposedly reliable banks. If you send money by mail it will take at least two weeks and often longer. Chilean banks will give you your money in US dollars if you ask.

Black Market
There is a black market of sorts for US cash. It's very open, especially in Santiago where you'll be approached by dealers, particularly along Huérfanos, Agustinas and Ahumada in the centre of the city. The black market rate is about 12.5% above the official rate. The street changers will probably take you to what seem like obscure offices to make the deal – don't worry about this as it's quite normal and safer for both of you. In fact because Chile is so desperate for foreign capital the black market seems to be officially sanctioned.

If you have US-dollar travellers' cheques then it's better to convert to cash dollars first and then change the cash for pesos. If you have American Express cheques this is easy. Go to the American Express Banking Corporation, Agustinas 1360, and cash your cheques for US dollars (there's about 1% commission which can be paid in Chilean pesos), then change your cash on the street. You can often get the street rate at hotels, or in shops which sell imported goods (shops selling electrical and electronic goods and pharmacies, for example).

Credit Cards
Credit cards, particularly those which allow you to withdraw cash or to buy cheques (American Express and Visa), can be very useful. You'd be surprised how many apparently impecunious travellers have a credit card up their sleeve. They're also useful if you are required to show 'sufficient funds' before you enter another South American country.

Bargaining
Probably the only things you'll have to haggle over are long-term accommodation and purchases from markets, particularly handicrafts. Otherwise, prices for hotel rooms are almost always fixed, and displayed in the foyer – the only exceptions are some of the very cheap hotels.

THEFT
Yes, things can get stolen in Chile. Yes, people can get mugged in Santiago. But of all the South American countries, Chile rates as one of the safest. It's *unlikely* you'll come up against bag-slashers or pick-pockets like you do in Peru or Colombia. A strong sense of

paranoia, however, still made me refrain from carrying valuables in a shoulder bag. Carrying things close to your skin is not only comforting but also makes them harder to lose or forget!

You can fall asleep on buses and trains and your bags will still be where you left them when you wake up. I wouldn't leave gear lying around bus terminals, but you don't have to watch your bags like a hawk when you pull into a wayside stop. Still, it's a good idea to get some baggage insurance before you leave home!

Tried and proven methods (none are foolproof) for carrying money and valuables include money belts, hidden pockets, pouches hung round the neck and worn next to the skin, and vests with inside pockets.

Definitely do *not* leave any valuables in a hotel room. A lot of Chilean hotel rooms have token locks, and in the south many don't have any locks at all! Even if your hotel staff are honest you can't guard against other people rifling through the rooms. No-one's going to steal your faded old jeans but travellers' cheques and money will certainly wander off. Likewise, don't leave valuables on a beach while you go for a swim.

Use the hotel safe if there is one and you think the keepers can be trusted – if not carry important things with you. The risk of theft is not as great as in some parts of South America, but a certain amount of discretion is strongly advised!

CLIMATE

Chile has formidable extremes of heat and cold. You bake in the Atacama Desert and freeze in Patagonia. You can cook to a crisp on Easter Island, and die of exposure on Tierra del Fuego. Be prepared for these extremes, plus rapid changes from one to another, wherever you are.

Chile has several distinct climatic regions. In the north, the Atacama Desert is one of the driest, hottest places on earth. It can be seeringly hot during the day but piercingly cold during the early hours of the morning. The coast tends to have higher humidity, more cloud and lower average temperatures. If you leave the desert and head towards Bolivia you must cross mountain passes which are several thousand metres high, so while others are sunbathing on the beaches at Arica you can be up to your knees in snow.

The Chilean heartland, centred on Santiago and Valparaíso, has a Mediterranean climate with temperatures averaging 28°C (82°F) in January, dropping to an average of 10°C (50°F) in July. Evenings and nights can be cold and you will need some warm clothes even during summer. The rainy season in the Santiago area is from May to August. Though it will still be warm and dry in the north of the country during this time, it will be stormy and cold in the far south. It's worth remembering how narrow Chile is: in one or two hours you can drive from Santiago to ski resorts where there is skiing for no less than five months of the year.

Heading due south of Santiago brings you to the Lake District, the region roughly between Temuco and Puerto Montt. This area also has a pleasant Mediterranean climate during the summer months, although biting winds can suddenly sweep off the lakes and mountains. Wind-surfing, swimming and sun-bathing are popular on the many black volcanic beaches of this area. Winter brings snow to the higher ground, around places like Petrohué, Puella, Lago Todos los Santos, and some of the hill resorts and chalets. During winter some of the passes between Chile and Argentina may be blocked by snow, so ask before you set out. Generally speaking you can expect sudden changes in the weather and you must be prepared for fog and stormy weather, even in summer.

Southern Chile is characterised by almost continuously cold weather. The one peculiar exception to the general rule is the region around the village of Chile

Chico in the Región Aisén which has a warm micro-climate similar to the Chilean heartland.

South of the 40th latitude Chile has some of the stormiest country in the world. Chiloé Island, the large island to the south of Puerto Montt, has fewer than 60 days of sunshine per year and up to 150 days of stormy weather. In summer both the island and the adjacent mainland can have warm days, but the nights are cold and if you travel by ship you are whipped by icy winds.

Further south, in Magallanes Province (southern Chilean Patagonia) and Tierra del Fuego, temperatures drop to a summer average of just 11°C (52°F), and to a winter average of about 4°C (39°F). Temperatures on Tierra del Fuego can drop so low that even sheep are killed. There are cold, gusty winds even on sunny summer days. Rainfall is heavy – more so in the interior than on the coasts – and can be expected at any time of the year.

Puerto Williams, almost as far south as you can go in Chile without bumping into Antarctica, can have pleasant days of warm sunshine in summer, followed by days of rain and terrible cold. Rug up for crossing stretches of water in this region; they can be stormy and terrifying year-round, even on the large vehicle ferries.

The best time to visit Patagonia and Tierra del Fuego is in the southern summer (December to February). Heavy snows set in from July. In the middle of the year in southern Patagonia and Tierra del Fuego there are just seven hours or so of daylight per day. The cold can be kept out but the wind pounds you day in and day out. You really need windproof clothing – particularly if you intend to trek, camp or hitch.

HEALTH

No vaccinations are required to enter Chile, and the country is free of malaria and yellow fever. Generally speaking, as far as health is concerned, Chile harbours only three real problems: altitude, extremes of climate, and a change of diet.

Altitude – Mountain Sickness

Although you are more likely to be affected by altitude on the altiplano of Ecuador, Peru and Bolivia (average height 3000 to 4000 metres) you can experience *soroche* (mountain sickness) crossing some of the high mountain passes from Chile into Bolivia and Argentina, if you stop at places like Lago Chungará on the Chile/Bolivian border, or do some trekking.

Mountain Sickness, Soroche, Altitude Sickness, Acute Mountain Sickness (AMS) – whatever you call it – can, in extreme cases, be fatal. In all probability however, you will only be lightly affected. AMS is totally unpredictable – athletes have suffered from it, and those who've had no problems at high altitude before have suddenly come down with it.

AMS starts to become noticeable at around 3000 metres, becomes pronounced at 3700 metres, and then requires adjustments at each 500 metres of additional elevation after that. If you make a sudden ascent (by bus or plane) and intend to stay at a high altitude you need to take it easy for three to four days, possibly longer. Lie low for the first few days, move around in slow motion, drink plenty of fluids, reduce or eliminate smoking, and do not drink alcohol.

Your body has to undergo a physiological change to absorb more oxygen from the rarefied air. This means it has to build up more red blood-cells, and this takes time. Until this happens (a month or more is required for *full* adjustment), the heart and lungs must work harder – 50% or more – to compensate.

The brain absorbs 40% of the blood's oxygen intake so it's not surprising that you get headaches if not enough oxygen is coming through. Mild symptoms to be expected over 3000 metres are headaches and weakness; loss of appetite; shortness

Volcán Osorno

of breath; insomnia, often accompanied by irregular breathing; mild nausea; a dry cough; slight loss of co-ordination; and a puffy face or hands in the morning. If you experience a few of these symptoms you probably have a mild case of altitude sickness which should pass. You should rest until the symptoms subside but if the symptoms become more severe or do not improve you may have to descend to a lower altitude. Monitor your condition carefully and realistically.

Severe altitude sickness brought on by a rapid ascent to high altitudes can result in pulmonary oedema (the lungs fill with fluids), or a cerebral oedema (fluid collects on the brain) which is fatal within two days. Symptoms of severe altitude sickness include marked loss of co-ordination, dizziness, and walking as if intoxicated; severe headaches; serious shortness of breath with mild activity; severe nausea and vomiting; extreme lassitude, loss of interest in food, conversation, and self-preservation; abnormal speech and behavior, progressing to delirium and coma; reduced urine output; bubbly breath, or persistent coughing spasms that produce watery or coloured sputum.

The only cure for AMS is immediate descent to lower altitudes. When any combination of these severe symptoms occur, the afflicted person should descend 300 to 1000 metres *immediately*, the distance increasing with the severity of the symptoms. When trekking, such a descent may even have to take place at night (responding quickly is vital), and the disabled person should be accompanied by someone in good condition.

AMS often seems to be a function of reduced fluid intake. Make sure you drink as much as you can, even if you have to force it down. Loss of appetite can wear down your resistance – so try and keep up food intake. Carbohydrates are supposed to be good for countering AMS. There's no cure for AMS except for descent to lower altitudes, but oxygen can provide temporary relief, and a pain-killer for headaches and an anti-emetic for vomiting will help relieve the symptoms.

In South America the traditional relief for soroche is provided by *mate de coca* – tea made from coca leaves. You can get this in most cafés in Peru and Bolivia (not in Ecuador). You can also buy the leaves legally in general stores or from market stalls, throughout Peru and Bolivia. The leaves also find their way down into Chile. If you chew the leaves you have to add ash or some bicarbonate of soda (mild alkalis) so the cocaine will leach out of the leaves.

On a brighter note, once you have acclimatised and built up your red blood-cells, the altered blood-chemistry will stay with you for a few weeks. This means that if you descend to lower altitudes from the Altiplano you will feel like Superman or Wonder Woman.

Heat – Heat Exhaustion & Sunburn

In hot climates – like the Atacama and Easter Island – you sweat a great deal and lose both water and salt. Make sure you drink sufficient liquid and have enough salt in your food to make good the losses (a teaspoon of salt a day is sufficient). If you don't you run the risk of suffering from heat exhaustion and cramps.

Heat can also make you impatient and irritable, especially if you're a speedy person; try to take things at a slower pace. Getting around Easter Island and the Atacama is *hot* work; make sure you carry a water-bottle with you!

Good sunglasses are an absolute necessity on Easter Island and in the desert. Sunburn is a *real* problem in these places and regardless of how good a tan you have you need a powerful sun-block, some headgear which shades your whole face and neck, and a light long-sleeved shirt to cover your arms. Make no mistake about how formidable the Easter Island and Atacama sun can be!

Cold – Hypothermia

At the other end of the temperature scale hypothermia is a simple but effective killer – usually referred to as 'exposure'. Basically the body loses heat faster than it can produce it and the core temperature of the body falls. It's deceptively easy to fall victim to it through a combination of wind, wet clothing, fatigue and hunger, even if the air temperature is well above freezing. Hypothermia's symptoms include a loss of rationality – so people can fail to recognise their own condition and the seriousness of their predicament.

Symptoms of hypothermia are exhaustion, numb skin (particularly toes and fingers), shivering, slurred speech, irrational or violent behaviour, lethargy, stumbling, dizzy spells, muscle cramps and violent bursts of energy. This can progress to collapse, unconsciousness and death. Anticipate the problem if you're cold and tired, and recognise the symptoms early. Immediate care is important since hypothermia can kill its victims in as little as two hours.

The first response should be to find shelter from wind and rain, remove wet clothing and replace with warm dry clothing, drink hot liquids (not alcohol) and eat some high calorie, easily digestible food. These measures will usually correct the problem if symptoms have been recognised early. In more severe cases it may be necessary to place the patient in a sleeping bag insulated from the ground, with another person if possible, while they are fed warm food and drinks. Do *not* rub the patient, place him/her near a fire, give food or drink to an unconscious patient, remove wet clothes in the wind, or give him/her alcohol.

You could face this problem if you're trekking, day-walking or hitching anywhere in southern Chile. Be prepared for cold, wet and windy conditions. Get undercover before you get soaked, keep your sleeping bag dry, and if you're day-walking and don't have the proper gear (*not* a good idea) turn back if the weather looks threatening. Warm, waterproof clothes are essential; they should should retain insulating qualities when wet (wool and various synthetics *not* cotton) and protect all parts of the body, including hands, feet, neck and head. Solid shoes are also essential. Thermal underwear – at least a thermal underwear top – is a good investment.

Diarrhoea & Dysentery

Montezuma's Revenge, the Inca Two-Step and other endearing terms describe an experience you'll have sooner or later, so accept it as inevitable and know how to deal with it. Although Chile and Argentina are much more hygienic than some of their northern neighbours the problem can arise simply from a change in food – it doesn't necessarily mean you've caught something. Amongst other things, oily food, seafood saturated in vinegar, and strange creatures you're not used to eating can bring on diarrhoea.

Avoid rushing off to the pharmacy and filling yourself with antibiotics at the first signs. The best thing to do is eat nothing and rest, avoid travelling and drink plenty of liquid (tea or *mate* without sugar or milk). Many cafés in Latin America serve camomile tea (*te de manzanilla*) which is excellent for this. Otherwise drink mineral water (*agua mineral*). About 24 to 48 hours should do the trick. If you really can't cope with starving, keep to a diet of yoghurt, lemons, and boiled vegetables. After a severe bout of diarrhoea or dysentery you will be dehydrated and this often causes painful cramps. Relieve these by drinking fruit juices or tea into which a small spoonful of salt has been dissolved; maintaining a correct balance of salt in your blood stream is important.

If starving doesn't work or if you really have to move on and can't rest, there is a range of drugs available. *Lomotil* is probably one of the best though it's come under fire recently in medical literature. The dosage is two tabs three times daily for two days. If you can't find that then try *Pesulin* or *Pesulin-O* (the latter includes tincture of opium). The dosage is two teaspoons four times daily for five days.

Ordinary 'Traveller's Diarrhoea' rarely lasts more than about three days. If it lasts for more than a week you must get treatment, move on to antibiotics or see a doctor. There are many different varieties of antibiotics and you almost need to be a biochemist to know what the differences between them are. They include *Tetracyclin*, *Chlorostrep*, *Typhstrep*, *Sulphatriad*, *Streptomagma* and *Thiazole* to name just a few. Avoid *Enterovioform* which used to be sold widely in Europe but which is next to useless for treating gut ailments and is suspected of causing optic nerve damage. Keep to the correct dosage; overuse will do you more harm than good.

If you're unfortunate enough to contract dysentery there are two types: bacillary, the most common, acute and rarely persistent; and amoebic, persistent and more difficult to treat. Both are characterised by very liquid shit containing blood and/or excessive amounts of mucus.

Bacillary dysentery attacks suddenly and is accompanied by fever, nausea and painful muscular spasms. Often it responds well to antibiotics or other specific drugs. Amoebic dysentery builds up more slowly, but is more dangerous, so get it treated as soon as possible. See a doctor. If that's not possible *Flagyl* is the most commonly prescribed drug. The dosage is six tabs per day for five to seven days. *Flagyl* is both an antibiotic and an anti-parasitic drug. It is also used for the treatment of giardia and trichomoniasis but should not be taken by pregnant women.

Drinking Water

Chilean cities have a decent, chlorinated water supply and you can drink from the tap. On Easter Island the water is rather strong-tasting bore water and takes some time to get used to. If you're trekking in the Chilean mountains draw your water from springs or small streams; if you have any doubts about the purity of the water boil it or use water purifying tablets such as *Halazone*, *Sterotabs* or *Potable Aqua*. These tablets are effective against most micro-organisms but not against amoebic dysentery. To kill this you need an iodine-based steriliser. The only trouble with iodine is that it makes the water taste foul – but this is a small price to pay.

Medical Supplies

Medical supplies and drugs are available from pharmacies so there's not much point bringing things you *might* need – though if there's something you'll *probably* or *definitely* need then you can save time by bringing it with you. Prices for drugs vary quite a bit across South America; in Peru, Bolivia and Brazil they tend to be quite cheap but in Argentina, for instance, four tabs of an antibiotic can cost US$20 and you need a seven to 10 day course.

Health Insurance

Get some! You may never need it but if you do it's worth a million. There are lots of travel insurance policies available and any travel agent will be able to recommend one. Get one which will pay for your flight home if you are really sick. Make sure it will cover the money you lose for forfeiting a booked flight, and that it will cover the cost of flying your travelling companion home with you. Pay a visit to your dentist and get your teeth checked and treated before you set out.

Books

A useful book to browse through is *The Traveller's Health Guide* (Roger Lascelles, London, 1979) by Dr A C Turner. For a run-down on problems faced by trekkers and campers in Chile see Hilary Bradt's and John Pilkington's *Backpacking in Chile & Argentina* (Bradt Enterprises, 1980)

LANGUAGE

Chileans, along with the vast majority of people in Latin America, speak Spanish (the exception is Portuguese-speaking Brazil). There are variations, however, between the Spanish spoken in different regions and countries, caused by variations in the original imported Spanish dialects and the influence of indigenous languages. The most important distinction is between 'highland' and 'lowland' Spanish.

Highland Spanish is found in the Mexican mountains and the plateaus of the Andes and tends to sound 'clipped'. Some of its consonants are more forcefully articulated than in lowland Spanish. Vowels – particularly unstressed ones – have a habit of disappearing, and confusions between 'e' and 'i' and between 'o' and 'u' can arise, especially where bilingualism is common. There are many other peculiarities.

Lowland Spanish is characterised by a relaxation of consonants to the extent that they can almost disappear. In Chilean Spanish 's' often becomes 'h' (for example *los hombres* is pronounced 'loh hombreh' and *las mamas* is pronounced 'la mama') leaving the openess of the final vowel and the context of the sentence to distinguish plural from singular.

Chileans, tend to speak rapidly and somewhat lazily so that many phrases are hard to understand. There are also significant differences between the Spanish spoken in Spain and that spoken in South America. In Spain 's' and 'c' before 'e' are pronounced 'th', but are 's' or 'c' in Latin America. Throughout Latin America personal pronouns (I, you, he, she, we, they) are rarely used, being implied in the verb.

Another common feature of American Spanish is the 'll' sound which is usually pronounced as a 'y' rather than the more correct 'ly'. The main exception to this rule is Argentina where the 'll' sound is pronounced as a soft 'j' or like the 's' in 'pleasure' so that Rio Gallegos is pronounced something like 'Rio Ga-shay-go' with the final 's' dropped. In Chile it is pronounced 'Rio Ga-yay-go'.

Even the vocabulary differs. In Central America the word for 'matches' is *cerillos*, but in South America it's the mediaeval Spanish word *fosforos*. The word for 'toilet' is generally *servicio* or *bano* but can also be *urinario*, *sanitario*, *retrete* or *excusado*. In Chile it is usually one of the first two, though toilets are often simply marked *hombres* or *señoras*. The definite article can also vary between Latin America and Spain: *el radio* becomes *la radio* for example.

'Ch' is considered to be a separate letter in the Spanish alphabet and words beginning with it are listed in the dictionary after the words beginning with 'c'. 'll' and 'ñ' are also separate letters and words beginning with them are listed after 'l' and 'n' respectively. Vowels written with an accent are accented for stress and are not considered to be separate letters, although accents are sometimes important for distinguishing meaning.

Learning Spanish

To set off for Chile without some knowledge of Spanish is very short-sighted. At the most basic level you *have* to know enough Spanish to cope with everyday problems. You could resort to a phrasebook, but life becomes a lot easier if you don't have to! You will also find that all through the country people will want to talk to you; if you don't speak Spanish your exchanges aren't going to get past a few limited clichés and you'll start to feel trapped in a linguistic bubble.

English is quite commonly spoken in Chile, but not enough to allow you to get around easily. Fortunately, Spanish is a relatively straight-forward language and it's easy to learn the necessary rudiments quickly. Go to an evening course; buy a phrasebook and a grammar and learn from them; borrow or buy a record/cassette course (they can be quite cheap

and well worth the investment); or, if you can, find someone from Latin America.

When you get to Latin America don't worry about making mistakes. Spanish-speaking Latin Americans are not snobbish about their language and don't look down on people who speak Spanish poorly. Communication is what they look for, not perfect pronunciation and grammar. Another advantage is that many words are similar to English or French – you can often figure out what they mean.

Pronounciation

The letters f, k, l, m, n, p, t, y and ch are pronounced as they are in English. The exceptions are listed below, but remember there will be variations from country to country.

a is like 'a' in 'cart' but fairly short

e is like 'a' in 'late' or like the 'e' in 'get'

i is like 'ee' in 'feet'

o is like 'o' in 'rope' or in 'hot'

u is like 'oo' in 'loot'

y is regarded as a vowel when alone or at the end of the word. At these times it is pronounced like 'ee' in 'feet'

b is generally pronounced as in English, but between vowels it makes a sound midway between 'b' and 'v'.

c is pronounced like 's' in 'sit' before e and i, otherwise it is like 'k' in 'kit'.

d is generally pronounced like 'd' in 'dog' though less distinctly. Between vowels and at the end of a word it is more like 'th' in 'this'

g is pronounced like 'ch' before e and i, otherwise like 'g' in 'go'

h is always silent

j is like 'ch' in the Scottish 'loch'. Thus the word *bajo* would be pronounced something like 'ba-ko'.

ll is pronounced as 'y' as in 'yet' in Chile, and as a soft 'j' or 's' sound as in 'pleasure' in Argentina.

ñ is like 'ni' in 'onion' or like the 'ny' sound in 'canyon'.

qu is like 'k' in 'kit'.

r is usually rolled, particularly at the start of a word.

rr is very strongly rolled.

s is generally like 's' in 'sit' but in Chile it is usually dropped if it appears at the end of a word. Thus *las ciudades* becomes 'la ciudade'.

v tends to be like 'b' in 'bad' but not as distinct. Between vowels it makes a sound mid-way between 'b' and 'v'.

x is usually like 'x' in 'taxi', and like 's' in 'sit' if before a consonant.

z is like 's' in 'sit'

Some Basic Grammar

In the space available here it is impossible to give a full run-down on Spanish grammar but this brief section will point out some things worth following up. You should should buy a *small* Spanish/English dictionary and a comprehensive phrasebook which includes some grammar and pronunciation. The Berlitz *Latin-American Spanish for Travellers* tends to emphasise Mexico but it's clear, concise, easy-to-use and very useful in Chile.

Nouns in Spanish are masculine or feminine. The definitive article (the) agrees with the gender and number of the noun. For example, the Spanish word for 'train' is *tren*, a masculine noun, 'the train' is *el tren* and the plural is *los trenes*. The Spanish word for 'house' is *casa*, a feminine noun, 'the house' is *la casa* and the plural is *las casas*. The indefinite articles (a/an) work in the same way: *un lapiz* (a pencil) is masculine singular, and *una carta* (a letter) is feminine singular. Most nouns that end in 'o' are masculine and those that end in 'a' are generally feminine. Normally, nouns that end in a vowel add 's' to form the plural, and those that end in a consonant add 'es'.

Adjectives also agree with the noun in gender and number, and usually follow it. Possessive adjectives (my/*mi*, your/*tu*, and so on) agree with the thing possesed, not with the possessor. For example 'his suitcase' is *su maleta* while 'his suitcases' is *sus maletas*. A simple way to show possession is to use the preposition 'de' which means 'of'. For example 'Robert's room' would be *la habitacion de Roberto* or literally 'the room of Robert'.

Comparatives are formed by adding *mas* (more) or *menos* (less before the adjective. For example, *alto* is 'high' and *mas alto* is 'higher' and *lo mas alto* is 'the highest'.

Demonstrative pronouns are also affected by gender: *este* is the masculine form of 'this' while *esta* is the feminine form and *esto* is the neutral; forms for 'these', 'that' and 'those' also change according to gender.

Personal pronouns (I, you, he, she and so on) vary and there are polite and familiar forms of 'you' as there are in French. There are three main categories of regular verbs; those which end in 'ar' such as *hablar* (to speak), those which end in 'er' such as *comer* (to eat) and those which end in 'ir' such as *reir* (to laugh), but there are also a number of irregular verbs which must be learnt.

At the Hotel

hotel
    hotel, pensión, residencial
room
    habitación

I'd like a ...
Quisiera una ...
Is there ...?
Hay ...?
May I have ...?
Puede darme ...?
single room
habitación sencilla
double room
habitación doble
What is the price ...?
Cual es el precio ...?
per night
por noche
for full board
por pensión completa

That's too expensive
Es demasiado caro.
Have you have anything cheaper?
Tiene algo más barato?
May I see the room?
Puedo ver la habitación?
No, I don't like it.
No, no me gusta.
the bill
la cuenta

Toilets
In Chile the toilet is usually called *baño* or *servicio*, and is sometimes marked simply *hombres* or *señoras*.

General

May I have ... ?	*Puede darme ... ?*
I'll have some ...	*Tomaré ...*
Where?	*Dónde?*
Where is?	*Dónde está*
Where are?	*Dónde están?*
When?	*Cuándo?*
What?	*Qué?*
How?	*Cómo?*
How much?	*Cuánto?*
How many?	*Cuántos?*

Useful Words

and	*y*
to	*a*
for	*para*
at	*a*

in	*en/dentro*
with	*con*
without	*sin*
before	*antes*
after	*después*
soon	*pronto*
already	*ya*
now	*ahora*
immediately	*immediatamente*

Civilities

Yes	*Sí*
No	*No*
Please	*Por favor*
Thankyou	*Gracias*
Hello	*Alló*
Good morning	*Buenos días*
Good afternoon	*Buenas tardes*
Good evening	*Buenas tardes*
Good night	*Buenas noches*
Goodbye	*Adiós*

I don't speak much Spanish
No hablo mucho español
I understand
Comprendo
I don't understand
No comprendo

Transport

bus	*bus*
ship	*barco, buque*
train	*tren*
plane	*avión*
car	*carro* or *car*
taxi	*taxi*
bicycle	*bicicleta*
motorcycle	*motocicleta*

I'd like a ticket to ...
Quiero un billete para ...
What's the fare to..?
Cuál es el precio a..?
When is the next plane for..?
Cuándo sale el próximo avión para ... ?
When is the train for..?
Cuándo sale el tren para..?
When is the first train for..?
Cuándo sale el primero tren para ...?

first/last/next
   primer/último/próximo
first/second class
   primera/segunda clase
single/return (round-trip)
   ida, ida y vuelta
sleeper coach (train)
   coche cama

Around Town
Post Office
   la oficina de correos
Tourist Information Centre
   Centro de Información Turística
Airport
   el aeropuerto

Post & Communications
letter	*carta*
parcel	*paquete*
postcard	*un tarjeta*

I want to send this by ...
   Quiero mandar esto ...
air mail
   por correo aéreo
registered mail
   certificado
stamps
   estampillas or *franco*
I want to place a personal (person to person) call.
   Quiero hacer una llamada personal.
reverse charges
   cobro revertido

Countries
Australia	*Australia*
Argentina	*Argentina*
Bolivia	*Bolivia*
Canada	*Canada*
France	*Francia*
Great Britain	*Gran Bretaña*
Japan	*Japón*
New Zealand	*Nueva Zelandia*
Perú	*Peru*
United States	*Estados Unidos*
West Germany	*Alemania Occidental*

Numbers
1	*uno*
2	*dos*
3	*tres*
4	*cuatro*
5	*cinco*
6	*seis*
7	*siete*
8	*ocho*
9	*nueve*
10	*diez*
11	*once*
12	*doce*
13	*trece*
14	*catorce*
15	*quince*
16	*dieciséis*
17	*diecisiete*
18	*dieciocho*
19	*diecinueve*
20	*veinte*
21	*veintiuno*
22	*veintidós*
23	*veintitrés*
24	*veinticuatro*
30	*treinta*
31	*treinta y uno*
32	*treinta y dos*
33	*treinta y tres*
40	*cuarenta*
41	*cuarenta y uno*
42	*cuarenta y dos*
50	*cincuenta*
60	*sesenta*
70	*setenta*
80	*ochenta*
90	*noventa*
100	*cien*
101	*ciento uno*
102	*ciento dos*
110	*ciento diez*
120	*ciento veinte*
130	*ciento treinta*
140	*ciento cuarenta*
150	*ciento cincuenta*
160	*ciento sesenta*
170	*ciento setenta*
180	*ciento ochenta*
190	*ciento noventa*
200	*doscientos*

300	*trescientos*
400	*cuatrocientos*
500	*quinientos*
600	*seiscientos*
700	*setecientos*
800	*ochocientos*
900	*novecientos*
1000	*mil*
1100	*mil cien*
1200	*mil doscientos*
2000	*dos mil*
5000	*cinco mil*
10000	*diez mil*
50000	*cincuenta mil*
100000	*cien mil*
1000000	*un millón*

Days of the Week

Monday	*lunes*
Tuesday	*martes*
Wednesday	*miércoles*
Thursday	*jueves*
Friday	*viernes*
Saturday	*sábado*
Sunday	*domingo*

Time

Telling time follows a logical pattern. For example, 10 o'clock is *las diez*. 11 o'clock is *las once*. 11.05 is *las once y cinco*. 11.15 is *las once y cuarto*. 11.30 is *las once y media*. Then after the half hour has passed 11.35 would be *veinticinco para las doce*, 11.45 would be *cuarto para las doce* and 11.55 would be *cinco para las doce*. 12.10 would *las doce y diez* and so on. Some useful terms to know are:

in the morning	*por la mañana*
during the day	*durante el día*
in the afternoon	*por la tarde*
in the evening	*por la tarde*
at night	*por la noche*
yesterday	*ayer*
today	*hoy*
tomorrow	*mañana*
the day after tomorrow	*pasado mañana*
next week	*la semana próxima*

BOOKS

Before you start to read about Chile it's worth reading about South America, since it's impossible to understand how modern Chile has developed without some understanding of early Indian settlement and the Spanish and Portuguese conquest.

Books on Latin America

A good starting point is the *History Of Latin America* by George Pendle (Penguin, 1973) a pocket-sized account of the period from the Spanish conquest to the mid-1970s; it's very readable though it contains hardly anything about South America prior to the Spanish invasion.

The story of the South American independence wars is told in John Lynch's *The Spanish-American Revolutions 1808-1826* which gives a detailed country-by-country account of the wars against Spain.

The most bitter account of the consequences of economic imperialism in South America, and the social and political struggles of the continent following independence from Spain is Eduardo Galeano's *Open Veins of Latin America: Five Centuries of the Pillage of a Continent* (Monthly Review Press, NY and London, 1973). It's one of the best books ever written about Latin America.

Books on Chile

Probably the best overview of Chilean history and politics from the time of the Spanish conquest to the late 1970s is *Chile – The Legacy of Hispanic Capitalism* (Oxford University Press, New York, 1979) by Brian Loveman. The book gives an intelligent, no-holds-barred account of the struggle of the Araucanian Indians and the Chilean working classes against the Spanish and Chilean elite.

The Allende years and the subsequent coup, with so many political parties and conflicting interests, has produced an awesome number of books which describe the events from every conceivable angle.

A very readable account of the Allende years is given in *Allende's Chile* (International Publishers, New York, 1977) by Edward Boorstein, a US economist who worked for the UP government.

For a first-hand account of what happened in the countryside during the Allende years read *Agrarian Reform Under Allende – Peasant Revolt in the South* (University of New Mexico Press, Albuquerque, 1977) by Kyle Steenland who lived in Chile's Cautin Province during 1972-73.

For background on the USA's involvement in the campaign against Allende read *The United States & Chile – Imperialism & the Overthrow of the Allende Government* (Monthly Review Press, New York, 1975) by James Petras and Morris Morley.

Amongst the people murdered by the military at the time of the 1973 coup was the Chilean folk-singer Victor Jara, something of a South American Woodie Guthrie if comparisons need to be drawn. His story is told by his English wife Joan Jara in *Victor – An Unfinished Song* (Jonathan Cape, London, 1983). It's a personal account of life in Chile during the 1960s and 1970s.

US citizens Frank Teruggi and Charles Horman were killed at the time of the 1973 coup, and the US embassy in Santiago was later accused of being implicated in the death of Horman. The story was recounted in a book by Thomas Hauser which became the basis for the 1982 film *Missing*. The US ambassador to Chile at the time, Nathaniel Davis, includes his side of the story in his book *The Last Two Years of Salvador Allende* (Cornell University Press, 1985).

The Chilean military regime's official account and explanation of the coup is the *White Book* (*Secretaría General de Gobierno*) which is available in both Spanish and English. Another is *Hoy y Ayer* (*Today & Yesterday*) which is available in Chile in Spanish.

Chile: The Pinochet Decade by Phil

O'Brien and Jackie Roddick (Latin America Bureau, London, 1983) covers the first years of Pinochet's rule, concentrating on the economic policies devised by the so-called 'Chicago Boys'. From the same organisation and written by a number of contributors is *The Poverty Brokers – the IMF & Latin America* which includes a discussion on Chile.

If you have any doubts about the brutality of the Chilean military government then try and see the documentary *Chile: Hasta Cuándo?* by Australian film-maker David Bradbury (who also made *Nicaragua: No Pasarán*).

'Chile: How Long?'

Other Books

There is a voluminous literature available on Easter Island spanning the 250 years since the first Europeans landed on the island. A number of books are listed in the in the Easter Island chapter.

The most comprehensive and readily

available account of the far south of Chile and Argentina is *Tierra del Fuego* by Rae Natalie Prosser Goodall, first published in Argentina in 1970. It will tell you everything from how many Indians were wiped out by measles epidemics to when the first lifts (elevators) were installed (no kidding). It's printed in both Spanish and English and can be bought from bookshops in Chile and Argentina.

Two popular traveller's accounts of southern Chile and Argentina are Paul Theroux's *The Old Patagonian Express* (Penguin, 1980) and Bruce Chatwin's *In Patagonia* (Pan Books, London, 1979).

Though it was written by the Columbian author Gabriel Garcia Marquez, *One Hundred Years of Solitude* (Picador, 1978) is as applicable to Chile as it is to the rest of South America – and humanity in general. Before you read too far into it though, consider what Marquez says about the book in *The Fragrance of Guava* (Verso Editions, London, 1983) – a conversation between Marquez and another Columbian author.

Other Guides

In a guidebook of this size and scope it's not possible to cover every conceivable aspect of travel in Chile. Hopefully it will give you some starting points and make the routine aspects of travelling easier and cheaper. The following books can help you with a few other alternatives.

Lonely Planet's *South America on a Shoestring* by Geoff Crowther is a lengthy book but rather more concise than *The South American Handbook*. It's an overview of the entire continent designed for shoestring (budget) travellers. If you intend going to another Latin American country check Lonely Planet's growing list of guides to the continent. In 1986 *Ecuador & the Galapagos Islands – a travel survival kit*, by Rob Rachowiecki was available, and guides to Peru, Brazil, Bolivia, Argentina and Columbia were in the making – check your bookshop.

The South American Handbook edited

by John Brooks (Trade and Travel Publications, Bath, UK) is generally regarded as the standard guide to the continent and it lists everything from saunas in Potosi to manzanilla trees in Willemstad (Bolivia and Netherlands Antilles respectively, didn't you know?). It's an impressive collection of information, but since it caters for every type of traveller from rich kids and yuppies down there's lots of information which is no use to the budget traveller.

Trekking Guides

For trekkers, there's a series of guidebooks on South America written by George and Hillary Bradt and published by Bradt Enterprises, including the very amusing and informative *Backpacking in Chile & Argentina plus the Falkland Islands*. Their *South America: River Trips* includes a description of rafting down Chile's Bío Bío River.

Health Guides

A good health guide – particularly if you intend doing some far-ranging travel in South America is *The Traveller's Health Guide* (Roger Lascelles, London, 1979) by Dr Anthony C Turner.

Phrasebooks

The Berlitz phrasebook, *Latin-American Spanish for Travellers* is a good one to bring with you; it's oriented to Mexico but is clear, concise, easy to use and it works well in Chile. A dictionary is also worth bringing. One that has been recommended is the paperback *University of Chicago Spanish-English, English-Spanish Dictionary* which has many more entries than most pocket-sized dictionaries; it also contains words used in Latin America but not in Spain.

Periodicals

The *South American Explorer* published by the South American Explorers Club, Avenida Portugal 146, Lima, Peru, is a quarterly with an annual subscription of

US$10 plus US$5 for overseas mail. The magazine is free to members of the club who pay an annual subscription of US$25. The club provides services, support and information to travellers, scientific researchers, mountaineers and explorers as well as selling a wide range of books, guides and maps dealing with South America. The magazine is well worth subscribing to. The Club's mailing addresses are: 2239 East Colfax Avenue 205, Denver, CO 80206, USA; and Casilla 3714, Lima, Peru.

Adventurer's Club News is published monthly by the Adventurers Club of Los Angeles, 706 West Pico Boulevard, Los Angeles, CA 90017, and is sent free to members. It contains articles of interest to travellers and is a good source of information for many parts of the world.

MAPS
Maps Available in Chile
The best and most practical map of Chile you're likely to come across is the *Gran Mapa Caminero de Chile*, published by the Informaciones Unidas Para América Latina. You often see it sold by the magazine and newspaper vendors on the streets in Santiago – it costs about US$1.60. It's very detailed, and clearly and accurately labelled. If you can't find it on the streets or in the shops then INUPAL is at Portal Fernández Concha 960, Plaza de Armas, Santiago (tel 71 5791). It is also sold in some specialist bookshops in the United States.

The *Atlas Caminero de Chile* published by Silva & Silva Ltda, Casilla 16374, Santiago (tel 229 2298) is as detailed as the *Gran Mapa* and even clearer. The main problem with it is that the country is broken up into small pieces. However, if you intend doing some wide-ranging travel it would make life very easy if used in conjunction with the *Gran Mapa*.

For detailed maps go to the retail office of the *Instituto Geográfico Militar de Chile* at Alameda Bernardo O'Higgins 240, near the Holiday Inn Crowne Plaza in Santiago. This sells the most detailed maps of the country available to the general public – useful if you're intending to do some trekking.

Street maps of Chilean cities and towns are available throughout the country; look in kiosks, newspaper stands and tourist offices.

Maps Available Outside Chile
It's useful to get a couple of maps before you land in South America – one of Chile and one of the whole continent – to orient yourself.

The best maps of South America you are likely to lay hands on are those by an independent cartographer, Kevin Healey, of Melbourne, Australia, called *A Contemporary Reference Map of South America*. Two maps cover the South American continent – one the north, the other the south. Their scale is 1:5,000,000 – twice as big as Bartholomew's map which is 1:10,000,000. Unfortunately even at this scale Chile doesn't fare too well. It is useful, however, if you're travelling through Argentina to southern Chile – the scale works well for Argentina.

If you can't get hold of Healey's maps then Bartholomew's *America, South* is the next best though you should be wary of some of the roads marked on it, especially in Amazonia.

Maps of Easter Island
There are a number of maps for Easter Island, most of them very poor. For details see the chapter on Easter Island.

POST & COMMUNICATIONS
Chile has good international and domestic post and communication systems though you will find that charges for overseas parcel post and international telex, telephone and telegram charges are quite hefty. Telex, telephone, telegraph and postal rates from Santiago are:

Telexes

Telexes to Australia are US$4.50 per minute; and to West Germany, the USA and Britain US$3.40 per minute.

Telegrams

Telegrams to Australia are US$1.20 per word; and to West Germany, the USA and Britain US$0.70 per word.

Telephone

Telephone calls for three minutes to the USA and Canada are US$9.40 station to station, and US$12.50 person to person. Charges for a three-minute call to anywhere else in the world other than Latin America are US$11.20 station to station, and US$15 person to person. Charges for a six minute call are slightly less than double. International telephone charges tend to go up quite rapidly – usually every month. Lines are usually good, wherever you call from in the country, and it generally takes only a short time to put your call through.

Post

An ordinary letter costs about US$0.06 to send anywhere in Chile. An airmail letter costs US$0.40 to the USA and US$0.55 to anywhere else in the world. Allow quite a bit of time for letters and postcards to get through, particularly to Australia where it can take three weeks or more!

Unlike some Latin American countries sending parcels is a straightforward process in Chile, although you may have to have the contents inspected and passed by a customs officer before they can be accepted by a postal clerk. So don't wander in and try to post a neatly sealed parcel. Everything you are likely to need for wrapping parcels can generally be bought from the vendors who hang around on the pavements outside the larger post offices.

Poste Restante

Have letters sent to you c/o *Lista de Correos* followed by the name of the city you want the letter to go to. Mail addressed in this way will always be sent to the main post office.

Instead of using the post offices you can also use American Express if you have their cheques; they operate a mail service for customers and have an office in Santiago. Some embassies will also hold mail for their citizens; among them are Australia, Canada, West Germany, Israel, Switzerland and the USA. British embassies will no longer hold mail. Any letters addressed for collection to a British embassy will be sent to the main post office.

To collect mail from a post office (or from Amex or an embassy) you need to produce your passport as proof of your identity. Most post offices hold mail for one to two months after which, if they're not collected, they get sent back to the country of origin. Chilean post offices charge a few cents per letter as a fee for the lista de correo service.

If you're not getting expected letters ask them to check under every conceivable combination of your initials not forgetting they might also be under 'M' (for Mr, Ms, etc) or 'S' (for Señor, Señora). The confusion arises because of the naming system in Latin countries. If you were called Juan García Moreno, for example, 'Juan' would be your first or given name, Garcia your father's name, and Moreno your mother's name. A post office employee would file such a letter under 'G'. In a non-Latin country, of course, it would be filed under 'M'. To avoid this confusion address a letter in block capitals, leave out all titles (Mr, Mrs, Señor, etc) and underline the person's surname.

HOLIDAYS

Chile has a number of public holidays: 1 January (New Year's Day); Easter (dates vary); 1 May; 21 May (Navy Day); 15 August; 18 & 19 September (Independence Days); 12 October (Columbus Day); 1 November (All Saints Day); 8 December (Immaculate Conception); 25 December (Christmas Day).

PLACES TO STAY

In Chile you can usually get a roof over your head for around US$2 to US$5 per night. Obviously a great deal depends on what you're satisfied with in terms of comfort and cleanliness, how much running around you're prepared to do after a long journey, and whether you're in a city or a small town. In general, however, most low budget accommodation in Chile is good value.

Hospedajes

The cheapest places go under the title of *hospedaje* or *residencial*. Distinctions are somewhat academic, but a hospedaje is usually a family house with a room or two for rent. These are often excellent value; they have hot water and you share the lounge with the family. Hospedajes are sometimes permanent affairs but are often only temporary. Some of these places are mentioned in this book; others

can be found by asking at the tourist offices, or in small towns, especially in the south, by walking around the streets.

Residencials

A residencial is a small permanent hotel with a number of rooms to rent, often run by a family who also lives in the same building. They're usually fairly basic, providing only a bed, table and chair in an otherwise bare room. Usually clean sheets and blankets are provided. Some of them have heating units in the rooms, some don't; some have rooms with attached bathrooms, but usually there are shared toilets and showers. Most have hot water, particularly those in the south, though you often have to pay extra for it. Places in the north, and sometimes in Santiago, often only have cold water.

Although they're always quite basic and often spartan, the quality of the hospedajes and residencials varies quite a bit. Some of these places – especially in Santiago – have windowless rooms (resembling solitary confinement cells) and beds with sagging mattresses (designed for prisoners with curvature of the spine). Some are just large rooms divided up with paper-thin masonite into separate compartments. Others have friendly managers and decent little rooms, but bathrooms and toilets that look like they haven't been cleaned since the colonial era. Others are bright, clean and comfortable, with hot water included in the price or at an extra charge of US$0.50 to US$1.

On the whole the managers and owners of most of the cheaper places are friendly to foreigners, even if you don't speak much Spanish. Some have a safe in which you can leave your valuables. Many cheap hotels, residencials and hospedajes either have no locks for the rooms, or token locks as a statement of intent. Although theft is not as common in Chile as it is in some other South American countries *don't* leave valuables lying around your room. Give them to the manager if you think he/she can be trusted, if not carry them with you.

The price of rooms in residencials and hospedajes will often include breakfast. The quality and quantity of this will obviously vary. In the very cheapest hotels and residencials it's often just a cup of coffee and maybe a piece of bread with butter or jam. If you pay more your breakfast may well be a whole buffet consisting of fruit juice, bread, butter, jam, biscuits, eggs, and a pot of coffee. It's worth thinking about paying extra for a place which offers a good breakfast because you'll rarely be able to buy one for the same price in a restaurant.

Hotels & Pensiones

Hotels and *pensiones* are generally somewhat more expensive than residencials and hospedajes though the distinction is often obscure. Most pensiones tend to have slightly better facilities, and services of a higher standard. For anything from one to a few dollars more than you pay in an hospedaje you will probably have a private shower and toilet. Quite a few have their own restaurant, but so do some residencials.

The term hotel is usually applied to mid-range and up-market places. At the bottom end of this price bracket are hotels which provide you with a small room, attached bathroom and toilet, hot water, private telephone (who are you going to ring anyway?), television set, and occasionally even a small refrigerator. These usually have a restaurant which is fairly inexpensive but not shoestring cheap.

Beyond this there's not much difference until you get to places like the Holiday Inn Crowne Plaza in Santiago which is an international-standard, five-star hotel with luxury rooms, swimming pool, room service, shopping arcades and so on. You can always find excellent mid-range hotels in the larger towns right through Chile, though international and luxury standard hotels are largely restricted to Santiago and Valparaíso/Viña del Mar.

Chalets

Look out for some of the fine mid-range hotels found in the Lake District, usually located on the shores of the lakes or by thermal springs in the mountains. These are often run by people of German descent, are built like central-European chalets, and have mineral water swimming pools, hot therapeutic baths, and their own restaurants. They're expensive by shoestring standards but they're usually good value and well worth trying.

Youth Hostels

Youth Hostels in Chile are something of a mystery to me. They seem to be found in, or have some connection with, places like sports stadiums, refugios, camping grounds, schools and educational institutions. In some instances there is conflicting evidence as to where the hostel is actually located, and most only seem to be open in the first two or three months of the year, during the holiday season.

They're usually only a dollar or two per night for a dormitory, which makes them just about the cheapest accommodation in Chile, bar camping grounds. It seems you can use some of them if you have an International YHA card, but to use others (they can be found in just about every major town between Arica and Punta Arenas) you must have a Chilean YHA card.

Youth Hostel members are supposed to be entitled to a 20% discount on 1st and 2nd class rail travel between Santiago and Puerto Montt and intermediate stations; and a 50% discount on Transmarchilay ferries from Chiloé Island to Puerto Chacabuco.

For more information on youth hostels try the national office Asociación Chilena de Albergues Turísticos Juveniles (tel 39 2705) at Villavicencio 352, 3rd floor, Edificio Diego Portales, Santiago. Or get the international Youth Hostel handbook which lists hostels in each country before you go.

Camping & Refugios

The tourist office in Santiago gives away a useful pamphlet simply called 'Camping' which lists campsites throughout Chile and gives details of their facilities. Once upon a time you used to be able to pitch a tent in the national parks for free, but now you have to pay a dollar or two per day per tent and sometimes more. *Refugios* are huts set up in the national parks to provide shelter for walkers and trekkers.

FOOD

From battling *soroche* (altitude sickness) with coca leaf tea on the border with Bolivia to holding down sea urchins in the stormy climes of Punta Arenas, such are the delights of eating in Chile. The point is that eating does not have to be an endless succession of *empanadas*, the simple baked pastries stuffed with meat, vegetables or cheese which usually form the staple food for penniless travellers.

If empanadas are as far as you get with Latin American food then you really are missing out on an extraordinary variety of cuisines which have been influenced by the original Indian settlers, the Spanish invaders and colonisers, and later European and African immigrants. The influence has also worked the other way – the tomato was unknown in Europe before the Spanish conquest of America.

Each Latin American country has developed a distinctive cuisine. Corn-based food like *tortillas*, and soups and beans are the backbone of the Mexican diet. In Peru it's potato with corn. In Argentina the going thing is meat, from a grilled cow dished up with a pile of chips to elaborate meat stews and *matambre arrollado* – rolled beef stuffed with spinach, onion, carrots and eggs. Chile has something of everything to offer, with some fine seafood as its own contribution.

Places to Eat

If you're on a tight budget you can eat cheaply from many small restaurants in the towns and cities. A sign of a good restaurant is locals eating there – restaurants aren't empty if their food is good and cheap. Another good hunting ground for cheap eats are city markets. There is usually at least one large, covered market in the central district of Chilean cities, which provides a roof for many small, cheap restaurants. If you stick to places like these you can be sure of eating cheaply.

Eating places fall into a number of categories: *bars* serve snacks and both alcoholic and non-alcoholic drinks; *cafeterías* and *hosterías* are straightforward restaurants; *confiterías* are primarily cake shops but also serve coffee, tea and other drinks; *snack bars* sell fast-food and the English words are used to describe them; and finally, the fully-fledged *restaurantes* are distinguished by their quality and service. The distinctions are never exact and *restaurante* can be applied to everything from the simplest to the most illustrious.

Almost all eating houses serve alcoholic and non-alcoholic drinks. Except in places run and worked by families it is customary – and expected – that you tip waiters 10% of the bill. The menu is *la carta*; the bill is *la cuenta*.

Many cafés put on a cheap set-meal (*comida corrida*) both for lunch (*almuerzo*) and dinner (*comida* or *cena*). Breakfast (*desayuno*) is rarely a set-meal and you generally order whatever you like. Following the European custom you will often find that you get exactly what you ask for. If you ask for chicken and rice that's what you get – if you want trimmings you must ask for them. If you want salad ask for *ensalada*; vegetables are *verduras*.

Some of the most common dishes are listed below but it's impossible to mention all the possibilities. You need a dictionary and a phrasebook with a good food section; try the Berlitz Latin American phrasebook.

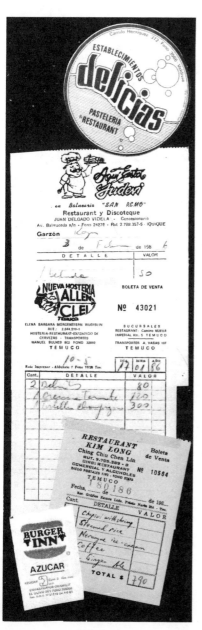

Snacks

Empanadas are similar to Cornish pasties; they're stuffed with vegetables, or combinations of vegetables, meats and cheese. Two or three of these with a coffee should set you up for the morning. Empanadas can be fried (*fritas*) or baked (*al horno*). In some other countries empanadas are known as *saltenas*.

Humitas is better known in western cookbooks as 'seasoned puréed corn' – corn kernels and milk mashed into a thick pulp. This is found in one form or another in every Latin American country. It is frequently wrapped in corn husks and steamed; when served this way it is known as *humitas en chala*.

There are various types of bread worth trying. *Chapalele* is a bread made with potatoes and flour and boiled in hot water. *Milcao* is another type of bread made with potatoes. *Sopaipa* is a bread made from wheat flour and fruit, but is not baked; it's recognisable by its dark brown exterior.

For breakfast the usual eggs and bread rolls are the main alternatives to empanadas. *Huevos fritos* are fried eggs, *revueltos* are scrambled, and *pasados* or *a la copa* are boiled or poached. As far as the last two are concerned, *bien cocidos* means well-cooked and *duros* means hard. *Tostadas* is toast, and *pan* is bread; eat these with *mantequilla* which is butter, *mermelada* which is jam, or *jamón* which is ham, or *queso* which is cheese.

Main Course

Lunch is the biggest meal of the day. The only trouble with comidas corridas (set menus) is that they tend to be almost exactly the same wherever you are, and by the time you get to Chile you may be bored with them. They usually consist of a thick soup, usually of potato or maize with some meat, a main course of rice with chicken or a slice of grilled meat, and a dessert.

For the biggest standard meal in Chile

ask for *lomo a la probe*. An enormous slab of red meat decorated with two fried eggs, hemmed in by french-fries and buried in a tip-truck load of rice descends on your table – or at least it should if the restaurant is worth its weight in cholesterol.

Popular places for meat dishes are the *Parilladas* or steak houses and grills, which cook everything from steak to sausages over charcoal fires. Wonderful if you like to eat meat and a complete loss if you don't. They're not particularly cheap but are nevertheless good value. Ordinary restaurants usually serve up chicken; common dishes include *pollo con papas fritas* – chicken with fried potatoes, and *pollo con arroz* – chicken with rice.

Desert (*postre*) is commonly ice cream (*helado*). *Helado de fresa* is strawberry flavoured and *helado de chocolate* and *helado de vainilla* require no further explanation. Also try rice pudding (*arroz con leche*) and cakes (*tortas*).

Seafood

Good seafood is always available in the coastal towns. The richest dish you'll probably ever come across is *curanto*, a combination of seafood, chicken, pork, lamb, beef and potato. Curanto is eaten with *chapalele* and *milcao* bread and is a speciality of Chiloé Island and the southern regions of Chile.

Soup is *caldo* or *sopa*. Popular soups are *sopa de mariscos* which are delicious fish soups found in both Chile and Argentina, or *cazuela de mariscos* which are fish stews. Fish soup is *sopa de pescado*. Try the soups using the conger eel (*congrio*) and abalone (*locos*).

A few terms worth knowing are: fish – *pescado*; shrimp – *camarones*; prawns – *camarones grandes*; crab meat – *carne de cangrejo*; mussels – *mejillones*; oysters – *ostiones (ostras)*; shellfish – *concha*; clams – *almejas*; sea urchin – *pilluelo, erizo*; squid – *calamares*; octopus – *pulpo*.

Try the eating places at the fish markets in the large coastal towns like Puerto Montt. Be warned that some of these dishes require a cast-iron stomach. There is some good seafood to be found in Chile – particularly the seafood soups and stews – but a lot of it requires some getting used to.

Ethnic Food

Santiago has a large selection of 'ethnic' restaurants. There are eight pages of restaurants and bars listed in the Santiago yellow pages. Seek out Brazilian restaurants for boiled black beans (the famous *feijao*), grilled or barbecued meats and manioc flour. There are also Indian (Hindustani, not Mapuche) curry houses, Italian pasta specialists, Chinese noodle shops, and Mexican tortilla dispensaries, amongst many others.

Many Chinese restaurants can be found in the towns of the Atacama Desert like Iquique and Arica; these are known as *chifas* and are generally cheap, good value, and a pleasant change from South American food.

Vegetarianism

Vegetarianism is a growing movement in South America and it isn't confined to Hari Krishna devotees. There are some vegetarian restaurants in Santiago, and you might find some in the larger towns. If you tell the waiter at an ordinary restaurant that you don't want meat they'll put something together for you. This is more difficult in Argentina where the idea is to devour a sheep or steer at an evening sitting; fears of heart disease are thrown to the *pampas* winds.

Every town has a market with a wide variety of fruit and vegetables for sale – the Chilean heartland is a fine fruit producing region and its produce is exported to the southern regions of the country. Remember that it is absolutely forbidden to carry fruit from northern Chile to the centre, or to import it from foreign countries.

Fast Food

Santiago also has the largest number of fast-food restaurants – mostly poor imitations of Kentucky Fried Chicken or McDonalds. There are other fast-food chains around which serve a variety of food including rather bland pizzas. I only came across one restaurant – in Punta Arenas – which made decent pizzas. The Dino's group is common in the towns south of Santiago and on the whole they're not bad places to eat.

As you nibble on a french fry and and suck on a greasy chicken bone, you may well reflect that there must be a better way .... Unless you learn to understand enough Spanish to decipher the menu boards outside restaurants, or overcome your shyness and get waiters to point out what's available in the kitchen, you may find yourself eating fast-food more often than your body will forgive you for.

Drinks

Top of the list and easy to consume in great quantities (before it strikes you down like a whack over the head with a dead guanaco) is a powerful yellowish-coloured spirit called *pisco*. It's a grape brandy, served with lemon juice or syrup. *Pisco sour* is served with ginger ale (*chilcano*) or with vermouth (*capitán*).

Gol is a translucent yellow alcoholic drink made with butter, sugar and milk and then then left for two weeks to ferment. It's drunk in the south of the country but you probably won't find it in the restaurants.

Yerba mate is herbal tea. *Yerba* is the name of the herb, *mate* is the cup from which it is drunk and *bambia* is the pipe with which the tea is sucked from the cup. The herb is a greenish colour, ground to about the size of ordinary tea leaves. It is mixed with hot water and drunk through the *bambia* which has a filter at the end to prevent the leaves being sucked up, and looks rather like something you'd use to snort cocaine. A proper *mate* is roughly spherical with a small hole in the top.

When the liquid is finished more hot water is poured in. This drink is consumed in both the north and south of Chile, but is much more common in Argentina. If you can't find it in the restaurants then buy it in small packets from the shops and supermarkets.

Guinda is a cherry-like fruit used to make a drink called *guindado*. The fruit is bottled with water and allowed to ferment for two to three months into a dark-red alcoholic liquid. New guindado is an orange colour. Again, you probably won't find it in restaurants.

Bars and restaurants commonly sell draught beer (known as *chop* and pronounced 'shop') which is cheaper than the bottled beer *cerveza* and often just as good.

Fine wines are produced in Chile; some are world-class and they're certainly the cheapest in South America. *Vino tinto* is red wine, *vino blanco* is white wine; *seco* is dry, *dulce* is sweet.

Other drinks available include *jugos* or fruit juices: *naranja* is orange; *toronja* is grapefruit; *piña* is pineapple; *mora* is blackberry; *maracuya* is passion fruit; *sandía* is watermelon and *limón* is lemon.

All your favourite multinational soft-drinks like *Sprite*, *Coca-Cola* and *Fanta* are sold in Chile. *Sprite* is pronounced 'essprite' for some unfathomable reason. Water is safe to drink almost everywhere in Chile, although in Santiago it tastes heavily chlorinated.

Café con leche means coffee with milk but is literally milk with coffee; a teaspoon of coffee is scooped into your cup which is then filled with hot milk. Likewise, *té con leche* is milk with tea that tastes like muddy water. *Café con agua* or *café negro* is coffee with hot water only. If you don't want milk with your tea it will be served black, probably with sugar and a slice of lemon.

THINGS TO TAKE

The old traveller's rule still applies: travel light. An overweight pack or carry bag will quickly become a nightmare, particularly if it's hot. Don't join that diminishing minority of travellers who stagger around in a pool of sweat, dwarfed by an enormous pack. The main thing to remember is that if you need something – from windsurfers, skis and trekking gear to everyday necessities – you can buy it in Chile.

Personal preference largely determines the best way to carry your stuff. A large zip-up bag with a wide shoulder strap is easy to get on buses and easy to put down and pick up, but it's hard to carry for long distances and throws you off balance if its heavy. A backpack is most convenient if you have a lot of walking to do. There is no prejudice about backpacks and their owners – Chileans and Argentinians all travel with backpacks, so you just blend into the crowd. A very useful type is one with an internal frame and a cover which zips over and protects the straps so they don't get snagged when the bag is stowed in the bowels of buses or planes.

After that, what you take largely depends on what you want to do and where you want to go. If you intend to camp or trek keep the difficulties of Chile's climate in mind. In the far south of Chile the wind blows almost unceasingly and a stove will be useless unless it has a wind-shield. Likewise you have to have a tent whose flaps can be well secured so that they don't keep you awake flapping in the wind.

I generally found that even the cheapest places in Chile provided sufficient blankets and gave me more if I asked for them, so sleeping bags are not essential. Camping gear will, however, give you extra freedom of movement and may cut down on accommodation costs; if you don't bring it with you, you could buy it in Chile.

Clothing which copes with extremes of climate is essential if you intend travelling extensively – see the sections on Climate and Health to give you some idea of what you'll need. If you're travelling right through Central and South America you can keep the weight of your pack down by initially taking clothes for hot and temperate climates and buying things like sweaters and ponchos when you need them, in places like Ecuador, Peru, Bolivia and Chile. You'll find these to be relatively cheap compared with the prices at home and the quality is usually very good. Warm jackets, socks, solid footwear, and gloves, scarves and headgear will all be essential! Thermal underwear, at least a thermal underwear top, is a good investment. In the far south your clothing must be wind and waterproof.

Don't forget small essentials like a combination pocket knife or Swiss Army knife; needle and cotton and small pair of scissors; contraceptives; sunglasses; swimming gear and so on. All the usual stuff like toothbrushes, paste, shaving cream, shampoo, and tampons can be bought in Chile. The only places you may have difficulty getting things are remote towns, small villages or isolated places like Easter Island.

Getting There

Chile is expensive to get to. If you're doing an extended overland journey through Latin America then Chile means just one more border to cross, but if you want to go directly from the USA, Australia or Europe it's a long way to fly.

Discount Air Tickets

There are a number of factors which influence a search for a cheap ticket: whether you can buy your ticket in advance, how flexible you can be about your travelling arrangements, how old you are (flights can be cheaper if you are less than 27 years old), whether you have a student card, and how extensive your South American itinerary is.

One of the best sources of information about cheap air fares is the monthly magazine, *Business Traveller*, which is distributed internationally and is available direct from 60/61 Fleet St, London EC4, UK, and from 13th floor, 200 Lockhart Rd, Hong Kong.

The main types of cheap air tickets are:

APEX & Super-APEX (Advance Purchase Excursion) – these tickets must be bought 14 days to two months in advance. They are usually only available on a return basis. There are minimum and maximum stay requirements, no stop-overs are allowed, and there are cancellation charges.

Excursion Fares are priced mid-way between an APEX and a full economy fare. There are no advance booking requirements but a minimum stay abroad is often obligatory. Their advantage over APEX tickets is that you can change your bookings and/or stop-overs without surcharge.

Point-to-Point is a discount ticket which can be bought on some routes in return for the passenger waiving his or her rights to a stop-over.

ITX (Independent Inclusive Tour Excursion) –

these tickets are often available for popular holiday destinations. Officially they are only available as holiday package deals which include hotel accommodation, but many agents will sell you one of these and issue you with phony hotel vouchers in case you're challenged at the airport (very rare).

Economy Class is indicated by 'Y' on the airline ticket and is the full economy fare. Tickets are valid for 12 months.

Budget Fares can be booked at least three weeks in advance but the actual travel date is not confirmed until seven days prior to travel. There are cancellation charges.

MCO (Miscellaneous Charges Order) – this is a voucher which can be exchanged with any IATA airline for a flight of your choice. It's principal use is as a flexible alternative to a specific onward ticket (Panama, Colombia, Venezuela, Guyana, and Trinidad require travellers to have an onward ticket or an MCO of appropriate value).

Standby can be one of the cheapest ways of flying though APEX may be even cheaper. You simply turn up at the airport or at an airline's city terminal, without a ticket, and if there are spare seats available you can get them at a considerable discount. It's become so common since the early 1970s that most airline counters now have a separate standby section. To give yourself the best chance of getting on a flight on the day of your choice, get your name placed on the waiting lists as early as possible. It's first come, first served.

RTW or 'Round the World' tickets can be a cheap way of travelling. There are some excellent deals available and you may well pick up one of these for less than the cost of a return excursion fare. You must travel round the world in one direction and you cannot back-track; you are usually allowed five to seven stop-overs – the number allowed often depends on the price paid; tickets are valid for a year although in some cases you can extend their validity by paying the difference between the price you paid and the current price. These tickets are often offered by a combination of airlines, with each airline carrying you part of the way.

Bucket Shops

In addition to the official ticket structure there are unofficially discounted tickets available through certain travel agents – known in Britain as 'bucket shops'. The tickets which these bucket shops sell are sold to them by the airlines at a considerable discount. The airlines believe that it's better to fill as many seats as possible, even if some of the passengers are travelling on tickets which are sold cheaper than the official prices.

Generally bucket shop tickets are lower in price than APEX tickets, and without the advance purchase or cancellation penalty requirements (though some agents do have their own penalties for cancellation). Most bucket shops are well-established and scrupulous, but it's not unknown for fly-by-night operators to set up office, take money (on deposit or in full), and then disappear before they've given you a ticket. Most bucket shops insist on a deposit for a ticket but don't hand over the full amount until you have the ticket in your hands. Tickets bought from a bucket shop are indistinguishable from those bought from an airline.

If you're travelling on a student-discount ticket make sure you have a student card or you may be required to repay the discount at the airport. Tickets, regardless of where they are bought, are non-transferable; airlines usually check that the name on the ticket and the name on the passport match when you check in.

In Europe, two of the best places for buying cheap tickets are London and Amsterdam. In both places there are numerous bucket shops and their services and prices are well advertised. In Asia the cheapest places are Hong Kong, Penang, Singapore and Bangkok. Australians and New Zealanders have been unlucky in the past because of protectionist government policies, but there are now many places offering cheap deals. In the USA, deregulation has made it much easier for travellers to find cheap air tickets, and there are a number of discount outlets in Canada.

Considerations

A return ticket is nearly always cheaper than two single tickets – unless the only flying you plan to do is between Europe and America on standby. And with few exceptions, it's cheaper to add places to a long-haul ticket rather than buy a series of short hops.

Buying airline tickets in some American countries is a decidedly uneconomic proposition because of sales taxes which range from three to 21%! Costa Rica is one possible exception: cheap tickets are available from OTEJ, a student organisation. There appears to be no discounting at all in Chile.

If you are coming from Australia and want to work your way overland through Central America to South America the cheapest options generally entail flying to a southern USA city like San Francisco, Los Angeles or Houston. If you only want to go to South America you'll generally find it cheaper to fly direct to Santiago or Buenos Aires (the first via Tahiti, and the second via New Zealand).

If you are coming from Europe it is cheaper to fly to the USA first, but look into the cost of flights direct to Mexico as they may not be much more expensive than flights to the US. If you don't want to go through Central America then the cheapest places to fly to are in Colombia and Venezuela. If you do decide to fly direct to Colombia or Venezuela remember that both countries demand onward tickets before they will allow you in. Travel agents won't sell you a one-way ticket unless you have an onward ticket or MCO.

When looking at the examples of air fares given in this chapter bear three things in mind: the cost of a ticket depends on whether you fly peak, shoulder or low season; air fares are always increasing; and no matter how cheaply you buy a ticket someone else will always get one cheaper!

TO/FROM THE USA & CANADA

To find cheap tickets scan the travel sections of the Sunday papers for likely looking agents – the *New York Times*, *San Francisco Chronicle-Examiner* and the *Los Angeles Times* are particularly good. American Student Council Travel (SCT) and Student Travel Network are both clued-up about cheap tickets and interesting routes, and you don't have to be a student to use their services. Make sure you include them on your rounds of agents.

Student Travel Network

Los Angeles – Suite 507, 2500 Wilshire Boulevard (tel (213) 380 2184)

San Diego – 6447 El Cajon Boulevard (tel (619) 286 1322)

San Francisco – Suite 702, 166 Geary St (tel (415) 391 8407)

Honolulu – Suite 202, 1831 South King St (tel (808) 942 7455)

Dallas – 6609 Hillcrest Avenue (tel (214) 360 0097)

Student Council Travel

New York – 205 East 42nd St (tel (212) 661 1450); 356 West 34th St (tel (212) 23 4257); and 356 West 34th St (tel (212) 239 4257)

Los Angeles – 1093 Broxton Avenue (tel (213) 208 3551)

San Diego – 5500 Atherton, Long Beach (tel (213) 598 3338); UCSD Student Center, B-023, La Jolla (tel (619) 452 0630); and 4429 Cass St (tel (619) 270 6401)

San Francisco – 312 Sutter St, San Francisco (tel (415) 421 3473); 2511 Channing Way, Berkeley (tel (415) 848 8604);

Boston – 729 Boylston St, Suite 201 (tel (617) 266 1926)

Seattle – 1314 Northeast 43rd St (tel (206) 632 2448)

Discount Tickets in Canada

Travel Cuts is Canada's national student travel agency and has offices in Vancouver, Victoria, Edmonton, Saskatoon, Toronto, Ottawa, Montreal and Halifax – you don't necessarily have to be a student to use their services.

Flights from the USA

It is worth considering flying to Lima, Peru, and then working your way overland to Chile. By some strange quirk one of the best deals from the USA to South America is to Lima – but via Canada! Tickets are available on Canadian Pacific from Vancouver and Toronto to Lima for US$600 return – including a connecting CP flight from San Francisco or Los Angeles to Vancouver. Otherwise a direct return flight from New York to Santiago will cost US$1050 and from the West Coast about US$1150.

Flights from Chile

LAN-Chile has four flights a week from Santiago to Miami and New York, either via Lima or Caracas. The one-way economy fare to Miami is US$699, and to New York US$797. Connections can also be made to other US cities. Ladeco also flies Santiago to Miami and connects to other US cities.

TO/FROM AUSTRALIA & NEW ZEALAND

There are two ways of getting to Latin America from Australia and New Zealand: via the USA, or direct to Santiago or Buenos Aires. There are a number of travel agents offering cheap air tickets out of Australia, although there's not much they can do for Latin America. However, they may be able to provide you with cheap tickets to the USA or cheap Round-the-World tickets, so they're definitely worth contacting.

Student Travel Australia (STA) is very good and they have a number of offices; you don't have to be a student to use their services. In Brisbane you should check out the Brisbane Flight Centre (tel (07) 229 9211). In Melbourne, Sydney and

Brisbane try the Flight Shops: Melbourne (tel (03) 67 6921), Sydney (tel (02) 233 2296) and Brisbane (tel (07) 229 9958).

Look for *Student Traveller* a free newspaper published by Student Travel Australia and distributed on campuses, and check the advertisements in Saturday's *The Age* or *The Sydney Morning Herald*.

Student Travel Australia

Melbourne – 220 Faraday St, Carlton (tel (03) 347 6911)

Hobart – Union Building, University of Tasmania, (tel (002) 34 1850)

Sydney – 1A Lee St, Railway Square, (tel (02) 212 1255)

Adelaide – Level 4, The Arcade, Union House, Adelaide University (tel (08) 223 6620)

Perth – Hackett Hall, University of WA, (tel (09) 380 2302)

Canberra – Concessions Building, Australian National University, (tel (062) 470 8005)

Brisbane – Shop 2, Societe General House, 40 Creek St (tel (07) 221 9629)

To the USA

From Australia the cheapest way to get to the USA is to fly to Los Angeles or San Francisco from Sydney or Melbourne. The one-way fare from Australia to Los Angeles or San Francisco is A$1013; the return fare varies from A$1446 in the low season to A$1966 in the high. You won't find any special deals for the LAN-Chile flight but by shopping around you should be able to knock fares to the USA down by several hundred dollars.

To Chile

If you want to fly direct to South America from Australia then your first option is to fly to Santiago via Tahiti and Easter Island with a combination of Qantas or UTA and LAN-Chile. Qantas flies once weekly Melbourne-Sydney-Tahiti. UTA fly once weekly Sydney-Tahiti.

Both these flights connect with the once-weekly LAN-Chile flight to Santiago which calls in at Easter Island. You can stop off at the island if you like but you will be there for a week before you can get the next flight on to Santiago; you would, by the way, be mad to miss the opportunity!

From New Zealand there are twice-weekly flights from Auckland to Tahiti with Air New Zealand and once-weekly flights with UTA. Depending on which Air New Zealand flight you take you either connect with the LAN-Chile flight or stopover for one or two nights before flying out.

For more information contact the LAN-Chile offices at: 10th floor, American Express Tower, 388 George St, Sydney 2000 (tel (02) 231 1355). Peak season for flying out of Australia is the few months around Christmas and the New Year; the rest of the year is off-peak.

Sydney to Santiago The cheapest one-way fare is APEX for A$1180. The economy-class return is A$1915 (off peak) and A$2170 (peak).

Melbourne & Brisbane to Santiago The cheapest one-way fares from these cities are A$1236. The economy-class return is A$1981 (off-peak) and A$2238 (peak).

Auckland to Santiago The cheapest return fares are NZ$2768 (off-peak) and NZ$2999 (peak).

To Argentina

The other alternative – though no cheaper than the Qantas/UTA and LAN-Chile combination to Santiago – is the Air New Zealand and Aerolineas Argentina combination from Australia to Buenos Aires via New Zealand and the southern Argentinian city of Río Gallegos. This is an interesting way of entering the continent, and once you're in Río Gallegos or Buenos Aires you can cross into Chile very easily. A return excursion fare from the east coast of Australia to Buenos Aires will cost around A$2200.

TO/FROM BRITAIN & EUROPE

In Britain there are a number of magazines (in addition to *Business Traveller*) which have good information about flights and agents. These include: *Trailfinder*, free from the Trailfinders Travel Centre, 48 Earls Court Rd, London W8 6EJ: *Time Out*, the London weekly entertainment guide which is widely available in London or from Tower House, Southampton St, London WC2E 7HD; *LAM*, a free weekly magazine for entertainment, travel and jobs; and *The News & Travel Magazine (TNT)* which is another free weekly magazine.

If you simply want to fly from Europe to the USA one-way there's no point in going to a bucket shop since a one-way standby ticket is the cheapest ticket you can get. It is possible, however, to save money on a return ticket by going to a bucket shop. Almost all the airlines operating between major European cities and the USA offer stand-by fares. It's a good idea to ring around the airlines the night before you want to leave to check seat availability and then get to the appropriate terminal as soon as it opens in the morning.

To the USA

There's an excellent choice of flights from London to the US. The cheapest is London-New York by Virgin Atlantic (an off-shoot of Virgin Records) which costs US$129 one-way. For bookings and seat availability ring 01-200 0200. You should also check out People's Express which flies London-Newark (across the river from New York). Many bucket shops offer return tickets on this route for less than the price of two Virgin Atlantic one-way tickets. A return flight to New York can be as low as US$239. Fares to San Francisco from London range upwards from US$168 one-way and US$336 return.

To Latin America

If you want to go direct from Europe to Latin America the bucket shops come into their own with numerous possibilities.

From London, the cheapest places to fly to are generally Bogota, Colombia (from £190 one-way and £380 return) and Caracas, Venezuela (from £180 one-way and £360 return). Other fares from London include flights to Lima for £205 one-way and £410 return, and to Buenos Aires and Santiago both of which can cost as little as £247 one-way and £494 return.

Another route which has become quite popular is from East Berlin to Lima via Cuba using cheap Aeroflot or Interflug flights.

Discount Air Tickets

Two reliable London bucket shops are Trailfinders at 46 Earls Court Rd, London W8; and the Student Travel Association at 74 Old Brompton Rd, London SW7 or 117 Euston Rd, London NW1 (and other addresses). One company which specialises in cheap fares and tours to Latin America is Journey Latin America, 16 Devonshire Rd, Chiswick, London, W2 2HD.

Similar fares to those from London are available from other European cities but there are one or two outstanding bargains. One company which is very popular is Point Air-Mulhouse, 4 Rue des Orphelins, 68200 Mulhouse, France (tel (89) 42 4461), and 54 Rue des Ecoles, 75006 Paris, France. This company is a travel club though anyone is entitled to join for a small fee. It offers no-frills flights to various Latin American destinations including Lima and La Paz. For further details of their schedules and fares write (in French) for their brochure. You need to book seats as far in advance as possible as there's often heavy demand for tickets. Other agencies in Paris which deal in cheap fares are Le Point, 2 Place Wagram, and Uniclam-Voyages, 63 Rue Monsieur le Prince.

The Netherlands, Brussels and Antwerp are among other good places for buying discount air tickets. WATS, de Keyserlei 44, Antwerp, Belgium, has been recommended. In Zurich try SOF

Travel (tel (01) 301 3333) and Sindbad, 3 Schoffelgasse, and in Geneva try Stohl Travel (tel (022) 31 6560).

TO/FROM PERU

There are two means of entering Chile from Peru; one is by road from Tacna in the far south of Peru, and the other is on the Lima-Santiago flight.

Tacna-Arica

The only overland crossing point is from Tacna in Peru to Arica in the extreme north of Chile. There is a choice of *taxi colectivo*, bus, or daily train. The colectivos are the most convenient and they leave from Calle Mendoza in Tacna, and from Chacabuco between Baquedano and Colón in Arica. For details see the section on Arica.

Flights

The Peruvian airline AeroPerú has flights between Santiago and Lima four days a week; the fare is US$262. They have daily flights from Lima to Tacna for US$79; from Tacna you can cross by land to Arica in Chile. In Peru you must re-confirm flights 48 hours before departure regardless of what you are told to the contrary. Neglect to do this and you probably won't have a seat even though you have been told it is confirmed.

TO/FROM BOLIVIA

There are three ways of entering Chile from Bolivia; either by road or rail from La Paz to Arica; by rail from La Paz to Calama; or by air from La Paz to Santiago via Arica and Iquique.

La Paz-Arica

There is a choice of train or bus along this route. The *ferrobuses* have been discontinued and there is now only an ordinary train in either direction twice a month. The actual dates vary each month so you need to make enquiries either at the station or at the tourist office in Arica or La Paz. It's easiest to take the bus

between the two places. There are two bus companies which cover the route: Pullman Martínez at the Terminal de Buses in La Paz and at Pedro Montt 620 in Arica; and Litoral at the Terminal de Buses in La Paz and Chacabuco 454 in Arica. For details see the section on Arica.

La Paz-Calama

You can only do this journey by train. The passenger trains only start from Calama – not from Antofagasta – so you must first go to Calama from Antofagasta by bus. There are once-weekly trains in either direction. For full details see the section on Calama.

Flights

The Bolivian airline Aero Boliviano has flights two days a week between Santiago and La Paz; a one-way fare is US$152. LAN-Chile also flies Santiago-La Paz and the fare is US$206.

TO/FROM ARGENTINA

All train services to Argentina have been suspended so the only way to get between the two countries is by road or air. There are a number of crossing points, the main ones being Santiago-Mendoza, several connections through the Lake District, and between Chilean and Argentinian Patagonia and Tierra del Fuego.

In the past, on the southern routes (south of Puerto Montt), you had to report to Chilean *Investigaciones* (the plain clothes police force) at Coyhaique, Puerto Natales, Punta Arenas or Porvenir before turning up at the Argentinian border. The same sort of system applied if you were crossing from Argentina to Chile – you had to report to the Argentine police. This rule seems to have been abandoned on both sides of the border, but it may be wise to check just in case; it may still apply to some crossings.

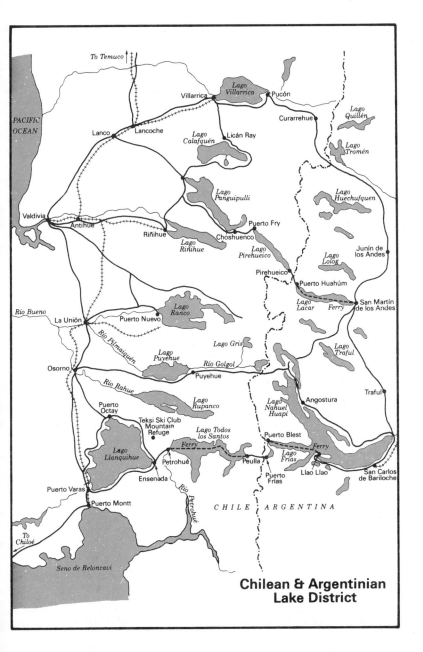

Chilean & Argentinian Lake District

Flights

There are a number of flights between Chile and Argentina. LAN-Chile flies Santiago to Buenos Aires (US$187, daily); and Ladeco flies Santiago to Mendoza (US$60, two days a week). Aerolíneas Argentina have a number of flights including Punta Arenas to Río Grande (US$30, two days a week) and Río Gallegos (US$36, two days a week).

Antofagasta to Salta

There are buses at least once a week between Antofagasta and Salta run by Buses Gemini which has offices in Antofagasta and Calama; see those sections for details. There is no longer any international train along this route, though Argentine railways still runs a service to Socompa near the border. Take warm clothing with you as it gets *very* cold going over the mountain passes at any time of year!

Santiago to Buenos Aires & Mendoza

There are several companies which cover this route and you can book at either the Terminal de Buses Norte, Calle General MacKenna; or at the Terminal de Buses Sur, Alameda Bernardo O'Higgins 3800, both in Santiago. There are also colectivos which cover the route and you can find them at the Terminal de Buses Sur. The route is open all year – there is now a tunnel under the pass. Many of the same companies also operate daily buses to Buenos Aires. For more details see the Santiago chapter.

Through the Lake District

There are basically four different routes across the Lake District to or from the Argentinian side, three of them terminating at San Carlos de Bariloche and the other at Zapala or Neuquén where there are trains and buses to Buenos Aires. The most popular is the route from Puerto Montt via Lago Todos los Santos, since it has the most spectacular scenery and involves a variety of trips on buses and boats. Details of each route can be found in the relevant sections in this book, but the gist of the story on the main routes is:

Puerto Montt to San Carlos de Bariloche, via Todos los Santos There are two ways of doing this trip. One is with a through ticket with one of the bus companies operating out of Puerto Montt or Puerto Varas. However the best (and cheapest) way of doing this trip is in stages, with overnight stops at Ensenada, Petrohué or Peulla. In winter make enquiries before you set off as the road can sometimes be blocked with snow.

The first stage takes you from either Puerto Montt or Puerto Varas on the daily bus (except Sundays) to Petrohué. At Petrohué you catch a ferry to Peulla at the other end of the lake. From Peulla a bus takes you over the border to Puerto Frías in Argentina.

The next step is Puerto Frías-Puerto Allegre-Puerto Blest-Puerto Pañuelo-San Carlos de Bariloche. The first part of this involves crossing Lago Frías on a small launch, followed by a short bus ride to Puerto Blest. From there you board another lake steamer and go to Puerto Pañuelo. There is another short bus hop from there to San Carlos de Bariloche.

Osorno to San Carlos de Bariloche via Lago Puyehue & the Puyehue Pass This is an all-road journey which passes beside four lakes – snow may occasionally cause delays. There are daily buses from Osorno to Bariloche, and several times a week to Zapala, Mendoza, Rosario and Buenos Aires. There are also direct buses from Puerto Montt to Bariloche, all of them going via Osorno and Puyehue.

Valdivia to San Carlos de Bariloche via Lago Panguipulli, Lago Pirehueico, Lago Lacar & San Martín de los Andes It is no longer possible to go from Valdivia to Riñihue on Lago Riñihue and then by boat from there to Choshuenco. There are no regular boats crossing Lago Riñihue (though you can still charter your own) and the road which skirts the southern end of the lake to Enco is now closed. The new route goes via Panguipulli. In winter, make enquiries as it's sometimes blocked by snow.

The first step of the journey is by bus from Valdivia to Panguipulli. From Panguipulli you go by road to Choshuenco. There is no longer a launch service on Lago Panguipulli so you must go by road to Puerto Fry (sometimes spelt Puerto Fuy or Puerto Fui). The third step is the ferry across Lago Pirehueico to Pirehueico. From Pirehueico to Puerto Huahun you can either walk or take a local bus. Argentinian customs is cleared at Puerto Huahun. The next step is Puerto Huahun-San Martín de los Andes via Lago Lacar; there is a ferry across the lake between the two towns which connects with the buses from Pirehueico and Puerto Huahun. From San Martín de los Andes there are daily buses in either direction to Bariloche.

From Panguipulli there is an alternative route into Argentina via Lago Calafquén and the Carrirrine Pass. And there are also bus companies in Valdivia which allow you to do the Valdivia-Bariloche trip in one hop.

Northern Route, via Villarrica & Puesco, to Junín de los Andes
This road route between Chile and Argentina goes across the Tromen Pass, which can be blocked by snow for four months. The first step is to go by bus from Valdivia or Temuco to either Villarrica or Pucón. From Villarrica you take a bus to Curarrehue. Between Curarrehue and Junín de los Andes there is no public transport so you'll have to hitch.

The Southern Routes
South of Puerto Montt there are a number of crossings into Argentina which allow you to detour through Argentinian Patagonia in order to get to Tierra del Fuego and the far south of Chile. The main routes are listed below, but there are too many forms of transport and connections to list them all.

Coyhaique to Comodoro Rivadavia This is something of a mystery route. There appears to be a continuous road between the two towns and there may be direct buses. Alternatively you may have to take a bus to Balmaceda first and cross from there.

Chile Chico to Los Antigos The first step is to take a bus or taxi colectivo to Puerto Ibáñez on the shores of Lago Carrera. Next you take a ferry across the lake to Chile Chico. From Chile Chico you hire a jeep or ford an unbridged river to the Argentinian township of Los Antigos. You then bus or hitch to Caleta Olivia via Perito Moreno, and turn south down the coast to Río Gallegos.

Puerto Natales to Río Gallegos This is a relatively quick and convenient means of crossing from Argentina to Chile. Daily buses from Río Gallegos take you to Río Turbio, from where you catch one of the regular buses (departures about every half hour all through the day) over the mountains to Puerto Natales.

Punta Arenas to Navarino & Tierra del Fuego There is a daily ferry from Punta Arenas to Porvenir. If the weather is too rough for the ferry you have to take one of the daily flights from Punta Arenas to Porvenir. From Porvenir there are buses twice a week to Río Grande via San Sebastián and there are daily buses from Río Grande to Ushuaia.

From Ushuaia there is a ferry once a week (more often in the tourist season) to Puerto Williams on the island of Navarino. From Puerto Williams you can fly to Punta Arenas (three flights a week) or take the once-monthly ship *M/N Argonauta*.

If you've come down through Chile via Punta Arenas and Porvenir and continued on to Ushuaia by road and then want to head back up to Río Gallegos, it's cheaper to try and get on a flight between either Ushuaia or Río Grande and Río Gallegos.

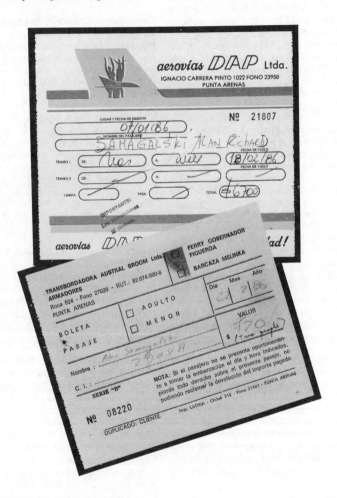

Getting Around

Except for the occasional winter journey in a 2nd-class railway carriage (if the heating fails to work) travel in Chile is a dream come true, with generally good roads, fast and punctual bus services, reasonably cheap flights and a number of useful passenger shipping services.

It is easy to work out an itinerary for this long and narrow country as you can start at one end and work your way through to the other with hardly any backtracking or detours.

AIR

Because of the enormous distances in Chile, you may want to take the occasional flight if your time is limited. A flight can also save tedious backtracking; for instance, you can overland through Chilean and Argentinian Patagonia to Tierra del Fuego and fly from Punta Arenas back to Santiago or Puerto Montt. Flying will probably be no more expensive than a combination of bus fares and accommodation (unless you take a direct bus).

There are two national airlines: LAN-Chile and Ladeco. Both have domestic and international services. There are also some smaller airlines, such as DAP – which connects Punta Arenas with Tierra del Fuego. It's generally thought Ladeco is cheaper than LAN-Chile but this isn't true. The only difference is that Ladeco services more cities than LAN-Chile.

LAN-Chile offers 21-day air passes known as the 'Visit Chile Pass'. The cities you can fly to include Arica, Iquique, Antofagasta, Santiago, Puerto Montt, Coyhaique, Punta Arenas and Easter Island. Depending on the route you choose the passes cost US$249, US$288, US$449 or US$488 (the latter two include Easter Island). The passes must be bought outside Chile; they can only be used by foreigners and non-residents of Chile; they are valid for a maximum of 21 days, but there is no minimum restriction; and fares can be changed without prior notice and intermediate stops can be omitted.

International and domestic flights can be paid for in Chilean pesos without having to produce bank receipts. This means that if you change US dollars on the black market you can reduce the cost of your air tickets by more than a tenth. The airport departure tax for international flights is US$5 and for domestic flights it's about US$0.55. Confirm reservations for return or onward flights at least 48 hours prior to departure for domestic flights, and 72 hours before international flights. Your reservation may be cancelled if you arrive at the airport less than 30 minutes prior to departure. Both Ladeco and LAN-Chile have a computerised booking service, so you can book domestic and international flights from their offices anywhere in the country.

Airport Transport
Often LAN-Chile and Ladeco will provide a bus between the town centre and the airport (either their own bus or one run by a local company); the cost is included in your air ticket. In a few places however, you still have to use public transport or a taxi to get to the airport. Enquire about arrangements when you buy your ticket.

BUS

All the main roads are surfaced and only in the rural areas do you come across dirt and gravel roads. All the buses on the main roads are comfortable (some of them are luxurious), well-maintained, fast and punctual. They generally have a toilet and provide coffee and tea on board.

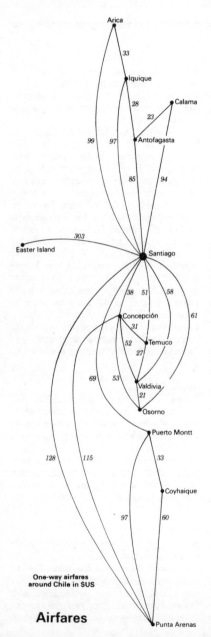

Airfares

One-way airfares
around Chile in $US

When you consider the distances from one city to another they're a bargain. The trains are even cheaper.

In Chile, theft is not a great worry; you can fall asleep, or get off a bus for a snack, and your bags will stay where you left them. You can't afford to be this nonchalant at the bus terminals themselves – although they're not nearly as bad as the terminals in the Andean countries to the north.

Most Chilean cities have a central bus terminal where all the bus companies are gathered, although in some cities the bus companies have their own separate terminals. At the central bus terminals the individual bus companies all have their own offices. The bus terminals are well organised and even if your Spanish isn't up to much it's a breeze finding the right ticket office since schedules and fares are always prominently displayed – unlike in many Brazilian bus terminals.

You rarely need to book a ticket more than a few hours in advance. On really long trips like Arica to Santiago (if you're crazy enough to go straight through) and on minor rural routes which are serviced by a single company (in the Frontier or Lake District, for instance) it's wise to book seats as soon as possible. Seats on buses are numbered.

Fares vary from one company to the next and there are often promotion deals (*ofertas*) which can cut the normal fare in half, so it's worth comparing prices. Student reductions (usually about 25%) are also sometimes available; enquire when you buy your ticket. You may not have much success getting discounts in northern Chile but they're quite common in the Lake District. You won't get a student discount in addition to an oferta.

There are ordinary buses and sleeper buses. Sleeper buses (*bus cama*) have reclining seats and foot rests similar to those in 1st class on planes, and cost about twice the price of ordinary buses. The sleeper buses go on long hauls (like

Arica to Santiago, or Santiago to Puerto Montt) and usually depart at night. Although the ordinary buses on these long routes are very comfortable the sleeper buses are worth considering.

Things are a bit different on the back roads. Although the main roads and many of the minor roads are surfaced, that still leaves about 70,000 km which are gravel or dirt. Transport on these back roads is slower, the buses are less frequent, older and stripped down to basics. You might get one or two buses a day between some small rural towns and they'll be packed like sardine tins with Mapuche Indians and their baskets of fruit and vegetables.

On weekends, public holidays and during the Chilean holiday season (around January and February) buses can be packed out – on main routes and back roads. Sometimes the bus company will let you stand in the aisle if there are no seats available, but this seems to only apply to short trips.

RAIL
With the exception of the Arica-La Paz and Calama-La Paz lines which take you from Chile to Bolivia, there are no passenger services on the railways north of Santiago; the lines you see marked on maps of the country are either goods lines or disused lines which once linked the nitrate mining towns and ports. The trains of greatest interest to travellers are those from Santiago to Valparaíso, and Santiago to Puerto Montt via Concepción and Osorno. Trains are worth considering if you're doing a long haul, but for short trips you'll generally find the buses much more frequent and convenient.

Santiago-Valparaíso
These trains leave from Estación Mapocho in Santiago. The trip takes three hours and costs US$1.60. Check the timetable as it may change. Currently trains depart Santiago for Valparaíso at 8.35 am (daily), 12.40 pm (Monday to

Saturday), 4.40 pm (daily), and 7.25 pm (daily). They depart Valparaíso at 7.25 am (daily), 11.30 am (daily), 2.30 pm (daily), and 6.40 pm (daily).

Santiago-Puerto Montt
The trains from Santiago to Puerto Montt run via Talca, Chillán, Temuco, Valdivia, Osorno and Puerto Varas. All trains going south from Santiago start from Estación Central.

Tickets for trains going south can be bought either at Estación Central or in the centre of Santiago at the railways booking office (the Venta de Pasajes Informaciones – look for the yellow sign) in the Galeria Libertador, Alameda O'Higgins 851. This office is open Monday to Friday from 9 am to 6 pm and on Saturday from 9 am to 1 pm.

Classes South-bound trains basically have two classes: *salón* and *economía*. *Rápido* trains usually only have salon class available. Train fares from Santiago for salon and economy class are:

Destination	Salón	Economia
Concepción	US$7.80	US$5.00
Temuco	US$10.60	US$6.10
Valdivia	US$12.20	US$7.20
Osorno	US$12.80	US$8.30
Puerto Montt	US$13.30	US$9.70

In addition to the salón and economia classes there are more expensive private compartments on some trains (such as those to Concepción, Valdivia and Puerto Montt). A shared compartment to Valdivia would cost US$22.35 (lower bunk) and US$16.65 (upper bunk). To Puerto Montt the costs are US$24 (lower bunk) and US$18.35 (upper bunk). Youth Hostel Card holders are entitled to a 20% discount on tickets for both classes.

It's worth considering getting a bunk on long overnight journeys; Santiago to Valdivia, for instance, takes 20 hours. If you do travel in the ordinary cars think seriously about spending some extra money and using salón rather than economia. In winter the heating in economia doesn't always work so it can get very cold.

Timetable Departure times from Santiago may change so check an official timetable. There are a number of trains which go only as far as Chillán or Linares, and not all trains stop at every station. For a full timetable get the leaflet called *Itinerario – Trenes al sur* from the railway stations, the tourist office or the Venta de Pasajes Informaciones in Santiago.

Train	Destination	Departure
Rápido	Concepción/ Temuco	8.15 am daily
Expreso	Concepción	8.30 am daily
Rápido	Concepción	1.30 pm daily
Rápido	Concepción	5.30 pm daily
Rápido	Vald/Osorno/ Pto Montt	6.30 pm daily
Rápido	Temuco/ Valdivia	8.30 pm daily
Expreso	Tem/Vald/ Osorno/Pto Montt	9.15 pm daily
Rápido	Concepción	10.30 pm daily
Expreso	Concepción	11.00 pm daily

Approximate journey times from Santiago are: Concepción – 9 hours; Temuco – 13 hours; Valdivia – 17 hours; Osorno – 18½ hours; Puerto Montt – 20 to 22 hours.

CAR

Some of the pros and cons of driving a car in Latin America are covered in Lonely Planet's *South America on a Shoestring*, though you'll probably find driving in Chile will be straight-forward.

The advantages of a car include freedom from timetables, the ability to stay wherever you like (particularly if you bring camping equipment), the opportunity to get off the beaten track, and the chance to stop when you see something interesting. The number of times I've been on buses which have stormed past immense geoglyphs in the Atacama Desert, Indian *ruca* houses in the frontier area, 18th century churches on Chiloé, or herds of guanacos in Magallanes, is too frequent and frustrating to bear thinking about! In some places – like Easter Island – a car is definitely the best way to get around.

The chief disadvantages include expense, the difficulty of arranging safe garaging (particularly if you go trekking), and isolation, because you don't have the opportunity to meet people on public transport and in cheap hotels.

If you can gather up a few people to share the costs you'll find hiring a car is quite cheap. You can either rent a car from one of the rental firms or hire a taxi and driver for the day. Rates to hire a taxi are, of course, entirely negotiable.

A number of international and local car rental firms operate in Chile, including Hertz, Avis, National, Dollar, and Budget. The Automobile Club of Chile (*Automóvil Club de Chile*) also rents cars. Rates start from around US$11 per day plus US$0.12 per km and US$4 per day insurance for a small car like a Daihatsu Charade. Large cars can be rented for around US$27 a day plus US$0.27 per km and US$4.50 per day insurance. Weekly rates and rates with unlimited km are also available from some companies.

The larger companies like Hertz and the Automobile Club of Chile have offices in the major cities (Hertz, for example, can be found in all the major cities of the north, several cities in the Chilean heartland including Valparaíso and Santiago, and in Concepción, Temuco, Valdivia, Osorno, Puerto Montt and Punta Arenas in the south) but it's also worth checking out local car rental companies and comparing their rates. Petrol is around US$0.47 per litre.

HITCHING

Both Chile and Argentina are pretty good

Distances by Road from Santiago

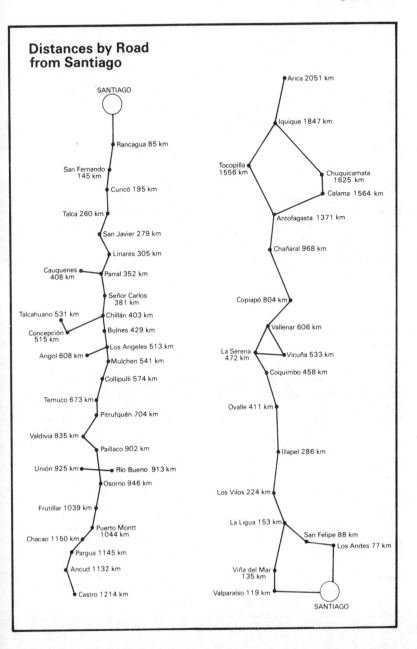

SANTIAGO

Rancagua 85 km

San Fernando 145 km

Curicó 195 km

Talca 260 km

San Javier 279 km

Linares 305 km

Cauquenes 408 km

Parral 352 km

Señor Carlos 381 km

Talcahuano 531 km

Chillán 403 km

Concepción 515 km

Bulnes 429 km

Los Angeles 513 km

Angol 608 km

Mulchen 541 km

Collipulli 574 km

Temuco 673 km

Pitrufquén 704 km

Valdivia 835 km

Paillaco 902 km

Unión 925 km

Río Bueno 913 km

Osorno 946 km

Frutillar 1039 km

Puerto Montt 1044 km

Chacao 1150 km

Pargua 1145 km

Ancud 1132 km

Castro 1214 km

Arica 2051 km

Iquique 1847 km

Tocopilla 1556 km

Chuquicamata 1625 km

Calama 1564 km

Antofagasta 1371 km

Chañaral 968 km

Copiapó 804 km

Vallenar 606 km

La Serena 472 km

Vicuña 533 km

Coquimbo 458 km

Ovalle 411 km

Illapel 286 km

Los Vilos 224 km

La Ligua 153 km

San Felipe 88 km

Los Andes 77 km

Viña del Mar 135 km

Valparaíso 119 km

SANTIAGO

for hitching – except south of Puerto Montt and in Patagonia where the distances are huge and the traffic is sparse. The time of the year is also an important consideration; you probably have more chance of getting a lift in the Lake District during the tourist season when there are more vehicles, but there is also more competition as young backpacking Chileans are really into hitching too! Bring some warm clothes with you; it can get *very* cold.

BOAT

A road is being constructed south of Puerto Montt which will eventually extend as far as Villa O'Higgins. There are buses operating along parts, but some stretches of it are either unfinished or not yet begun. Until it is completed the only way of getting south of Puerto Montt is by air, ship, or a ship/bus combination. There are several useful sea routes along the Chilean coast.

Puerto Montt to Puerto Chacabuco

Empresa Marítima del Estado (*Empremar*), Avenida Suiza 248 in Santiago (tel 57 2650), and at Portales 1450 in Puerto Montt (tel 2547) operate ships from Puerto Montt to Puerto Chacabuco (close to Puerto Aisén and Coyhaique) calling at several places in route including Chaitén, Puerto Cisnes and Puerto Aguirre. The boats sail from Puerto Montt twice a week on Tuesdays and Thursdays.

You can travel either economy or tourist class which is, on average, twice as much as economy class. Economy class fares from Puerto Montt are: Chaitén US$5.60 (16 hours), Puerto Cisnes US$10 (two days), Puerto Aguirre US$11.70, and Chacabuco US$30 (three days). The ship continues another half day to the Laguna San Rafael glacier in the summer months (December to March).

There is also a tourist ship which takes sightseers to the Laguna San Rafael glacier several times each year. This is the *Skorpios* and the cheapest passage is during the spring-fall season when you can get a double cabin for US$650 *per person*, or a cabin of your own for US$975. Summer prices are even higher. Enquire at Angelmo 1660 (tel 2952) in Puerto Montt, or at MacIver 484, 2nd floor, (tel 33 6187) in Santiago.

Puerto Montt to Puerto Natales

Naviera Magallanes (*Navimag*), Angelmo, Puerto Montt (tel 3318), operate the long haul boats south to Puerto Natales. In Puerto Natales they have their office at the port; in Punta Arenas they're at Independencia 830 (tel 22593).

These ships depart Puerto Montt about three times a month and take three days to get to Puerto Natales. The exact departure days at either end vary depending on what sort of cargo is being loaded so you need to make enquiries.

The fares per person are US$487 to US$926 (single cabin), US$256 to US$487 (double cabin) and US$86 (2nd class). The fares include all meals. It's sometimes possible to travel in the restaurant on the ship for half the 2nd class fare.

Chiloé Island to the Mainland

There are three connections between Chiloé Island and the mainland. The first is with the Cruz del Sur ferries which operate between Chacao at the northern tip of the island, and Pargua across the straits on the mainland.

The second and third connections are made by the Transmarchilay Ltda ferries which operate between Chiloé and Chacabuco and Chaitén. Transmarchilay Ltda has offices at Libertad 669, Ancud (tel 317); 21 de Mayo 417, 2nd floor, Coyhaique (tel 21971); Pedro Montt 265, Quellón (tel 290); O'Higgins, Puerto Chacabuco (tel 144); O'Higgins 243, Chaitén (tel 272); Costanera, Chonchi (tel 66); and Angelmo 1668, Puerto Montt (tel 4654).

Patagonia & Tierra del Fuego

There is a daily ferry link between Punta Arenas and Porvenir; see those sections for details. Punta Arenas is also linked to Puerto Williams by a monthly voyage of the *M/N Argonauta* which carries tourists; in Punta Arenas enquire at the Agencia de Viajes Turismo Aventour Ltda (tel 23572) at Navarro 1255.

There is a weekly ferry (on Sundays) between Puerto Williams, on the Chilean island of Navarino, to Ushuaia in Argentinian Tierra del Fuego. There are more ferries during the tourist season when extra trips are put on for tour groups. See the Puerto Williams and Ushuaia sections for more details.

Weird & Wonderful

If you've ever wanted to sail 'round the Horn' then this could be your big chance. Alain Caradec (c/o Brouazin, 20 Rue Dauphine, 35400, St Malo, France) runs the charter yacht *Basile* out of Punta Arenas to Cape Horn and the surrounding area. These trips last about 20 days each (more if the weather is bad and the yacht has to take shelter) and cost around US$1000 per person, plus your share of the diesel fuel. He only takes about six people per trip so if you want to go, write to him well beforehand. He probably only does these trips in the early months of the year.

Atacama Desert

The Atacama is the most 'perfect' of deserts with regions where it has *never* been known to rain and not a single variety of plant or animal life can be found – or has ever been known to exist.

At higher altitudes there are cacti which survive by drawing moisture from the thick fogs which occasionally descend. In some parts the fog provides enough moisture for tiny oases called *lomas*, which attract birds and insects not commonly found in deserts. There is even one type of plant which grows underground, drawing enough light for photosynthesis through translucent sand. In other areas there is underground water, but for the most part, water is provided by rivers which cut their way through the desert from the Andes, forming deep valleys along which agricultural settlements have developed.

For thousands of years the original Indian inhabitants fished along the coast or farmed along river valleys. Their most impressive creations were enormous murals (*geoglyphs* – made by grouping dark stones together on a light sand background) which decorate the barren mountain ridges. They include images of people, animals, geometric shapes and possibly even deities, at places like the Lluta Valley near Arica, and Sierra Unida and Pintados near Iquique. Modern day artists, with 90% of the inspiration and 10% of the technical skill of these early inhabitants, have littered the hill slopes along roadways with giant grafitti and rudimentary pictures.

Northern Chile is part of South America's western coastal desert which extends northwards through Peru and into Ecuador. The southern boundary of the Atacama is taken as the farming belt around Copiapó, and until the War of the Pacific in the 19th century, Copiapó marked the northern boundary of Chilean territory. Prior to the war the desert to the north was Peruvian and Bolivian territory, but disputes over treaties, and the presence of thousands of Chilean workers in the guano fields (accumulated bird droppings valued as fertiliser) and mines in the Bolivian region caused tensions between Chile and Bolivia.

In Antofagasta, for example, about 75% of the population was Chilean, and a Chilean company produced all the nitrate. A Bolivian attempt to increase the tax on this company's exports and the company's refusal to pay provided an excuse for Chile to go to war. The War of the Pacific (1879-83), as it was called, set Chile against Bolivia and Peru. In early 1880, after bloody fighting, the Chileans moved into Arica and Tacna. They went on to occupy Lima, which they held until 1883.

Chile gained the copper and nitrate-rich lands that are now the Chilean regions of Tarapacá (formerly Peruvian territory) and Antofagasta (formerly Bolivian territory), enlarging Chilean territory by a third. Eventually Tacna was handed back to Peru; Arica remained a Chilean port although Bolivia was permitted to export through it and still does today. The war led to the rapid expansion of the Chilean army and further territorial gains when the Mapuche Indians were defeated in the south.

Most of the large towns in the Atacama – Iquique, Calama, Antofagasta, Tocopilla – owe their existence to the silver, gold, nitrates, copper and iron of this region. Iquique owes its existence to the discovery of silver at Huantajaya and later, in the 19th century, to nitrate mining. At Caracoles, 200 km north of Antofagasta, a silver strike attracted some 10,000 fortune-seekers, transforming Antofagasta into a

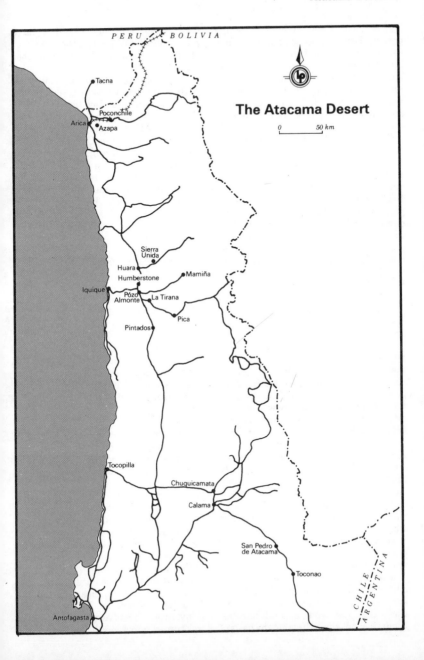

PERU BOLIVIA

The Atacama Desert

0   50 km

Tacna

Poconchile
Arica
Azapa

Sierra
Unida

Huara
Humberstone
Mamiña

Iquique
Pozo
Almonte   La Tirana

Pica

Pintados

Tocopilla

Chuquicamata

Calama

San Pedro
de Atacama

Toconao

CHILE
ARGENTINA

Antofagasta

major town. Later it and Tocopilla prospered from copper and nitrate mining. Mining towns like Humberstone, near Iquique, flourished during the nitrates boom, died when it ended, and are now rusting ghost towns. Some of them are now being repopulated as new extraction techniques make processing of low-grade ore profitable.

One of the chief beneficiaries of the War of the Pacific was the British speculator John Thomas North. Prior to the war, in 1875, Peru expropriated nitrate holdings and issued bonds to their former owners. During the war, the value of these bonds plummeted, and North, using capital obtained from the banks in Chile, bought as many as he could. After the war, Chile decided to return ownership to the holders of the bonds - and John North found himself in a very healthy position. He then moved to gain control of all the other industries on which the nitrate industry depended and before long he and his allies had turned Chile's new northern provinces into their private fiefdom.

The Chilean economy's dependence on nitrates and copper has meant that since the 19th century the Atacama has played an extraordinary role in determining the political fortunes of Chile. The wealth of the desert meant a steady flow of revenue into government coffers and this allowed Chilean politicians to avoid major social and political issues until well into the 20th century. They could depend on tax revenues from the mining industry to finance government services and did not have to address the idea of a wide-based and equitable taxation system. The north was also home to strong trade unions and when workers returned to the south they took with them experience of class organisation, strikes, and sometimes massacres by the police and military.

After WW I the nitrate industry declined as the fields were exhausted and synthetic nitrates (invented during the war) took over from natural nitrates. From then on copper became the basis of

the Chilean economy - and a large proportion of it came from the Atacama, although there were other mines further south.

The largest open-pit copper mine in the world is at Chuquicamata, near Calama. Until it was nationalised by the Allende Government this mine was under the control of a US company, giving the US significant influence in Chilean affairs. In the 1960s and 1970s copper accounted for something like 70% to 80% of the total value of Chilean exports - as Allende put it, the Atacama copper mines provided the 'salary of Chile'. This dependency on a single export, however, made the Chilean economy vulnerable to even small changes in the prices received for it.

South of the Atacama Desert, there is a transition zone from desert to steppes and then to the fertile central valley. This transition zone was once called the 'region of ten thousand mines' and is also known as the 'little north' (*norte chico*). It was once a great silver mining region and it's still an important copper and iron mining area. A number of rivers cross the region making some extensive agriculture possible although it contains only a small percentage of Chile's total arable land.

ARICA

Where bloody battles were once fought for the acquisition of honour, desert and minerals, wealthy Bolivians now come to lie on the beaches, and Peruvian Indians come to sell handicrafts and vegetables. Arica is a year-round resort town, with beach weather every day of the year - there is *never* any rain. Despite its arid surroundings Arica is an attractive place, nestled below a spectacular headland from the top of which are sweeping views of the ocean and desert.

Until the War of the Pacific, Arica was part of Peru. The Chileans seized the Peruvian province of Tacna and the Bolivian province of Antofagasta. Bolivia was turned into a land-locked country -

and the Bolivians have never quite forgotten it! Today, aside from being a resort and peddler's town, Arica is also a free port. Almost half the exports of Bolivia flow out through Arica, via the railway line which links the town with the Bolivian capital of La Paz.

In 1883 a treaty between Peru and Chile recognised Chilean ownership of Tacna and Arica for 10 years, on the condition that a plebiscite was held at the end of that time. The plebiscite, of course, never took place and the three countries squabbled until 1929 when Peru and Chile finally signed another treaty allowing Peru to recover Tacna while Chile retained Arica – Bolivia was simply left out of the negotiations.

Despite its distance from the Chilean heartland and its somewhat shaky position with regards to Bolivia, the Chileans built a large hydro-electric power station on the Lauca River and used the electricity to power automobile and electronics industries that were set up in Arica in the 1960s. By the 1970s Arica had become a city of 120,000 people (rising from 20,000 in just two decades) and a major manufacturing centre.

In 1975, in order to resolve the lingering dispute with Bolivia, Pinochet made a surprising offer to give a piece of Chilean territory (to the north of the Arica-La Paz railway) to Bolivia to provide it with a corridor to the sea, in return for some Bolivian territory to the south. Unfortunately the 1929 treaty between Peru and Chile stated that neither country could

Fortune teller's advertising leaflet

cede any part of the Tacna region to Bolivia without the agreement of the other. Peru stopped the new scheme by proposing that a special zone (including Arica) be established and administered by all three countries. Chile backed off.

The Bolivians attempted to start negotiations again in 1977. In 1978, after talks had failed to eventuate, they moved troops up to the Chilean border. That same year Chile almost found itself at war with Argentina as well. One of the dilemmas facing Latin American countries is that without a powerful army they are at the mercy of adjoining countries – but with a powerful army they are at the mercy of their own generals. There is no better place to contemplate this balance of weakness than the front-line beach resort of Arica.

The town, by the way, has much more to offer than sunbathing, swimming and politics. This is also the terminus for the Arica-Bolivia road which winds its way up the mountain slopes and through the incredible Lauca National Park set around Lago Chungará. Pre-Inca Indian forts, herds of vicuña and alpaca, and massive snow-covered volcanos on the border are just some of the things thrown in with the deal. The town is a pleasant resting point for any odysseys south through Chile, east to Bolivia, or north to Peru.

Information

Tourist Office The tourist office is at Prat 375 (2nd floor), and is staffed by fairly helpful people. Make sure you get hold of the useful booklet *Arica – Guía de Turismo y Compras*, which is free at the tourist office, many hotels and travel agencies. The tourist office also has a useful map of the city.

Bank Most of the change-money guys are to be found at the junction of 21 de Mayo and Colón. They offer better rates than the banks. There are several permanent casas de cambio around the centre of town which will change US cash and travellers' cheques, and Peruvian, Bolivian and Argentinian currency.

Post & Communications The post office and Telex Chile are in the same building at Prat 375. Telex Chile is open Monday to Friday 8.30 am to 8 pm, Saturday 9 am to 2 pm, and Sunday and holidays 9 am to 1 pm. Long-distance phone calls can be made from the telephone office at the corner of Colón and 21 de Mayo.

Consulates The Argentine Consulate (tel 31322) is at Manuel Rodríguez 95. The Bolivian Consulate (tel 31030) is at Bolognesi 344, open Monday to Friday 9 am to 2 pm, although these hours may vary at different times of the year. The Peruvian Consulate (tel 31020) is at Yungay 304, at the corner with Colón, open Monday to Friday 9 am to 1 pm.

Things to See

Arica is one of the few places where you can catch some warm sea south of Ecuador. The best beaches are along the Avenida Costanera where there are a number of sheltered coves.

There are a few reminders of earlier

1 Tourist Office & Post Office	10 Residencial Núñez
2 San Marcos Church	11 Hotel Lynch
3 LAN-Chile	12 Residencial El Cobre
4 Ladeco	13 Residencial La Blanquita
5 Collectivos to Tacna	14 Hotel Diego de Almagro
6 Bus Terminal	15 Residencial Sotomayor
7 Bolivian Consulate	16 Residencial Madrid
8 Peruvian Consulate	17 King Hotel
9 Residencial Patricia	18 Argentine Consulate
	19 Hotel El Paso

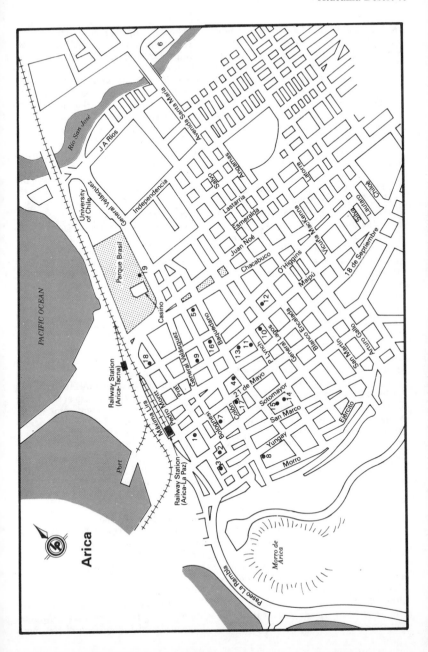

Arica

years around town, like the old German-built locomotive, vintage 1924, which used to pull trains on the Arica-La Paz line. It now stands in the Plazoleta Estación (also called the Parque Gral Baquedano) at the corner of 21 de Mayo and Pedro Montt.

The Iglesia San Marcos de Arica was designed by Alejandro Gustavo Eiffel in 1875. This is the light-blue church which faces the Plaza Cristóbal Colón. Apart from his famous tower, Eiffel's achievements include the Estación Central (Central Train Station) in Santiago.

The Museo Argueológico San Miguel de Azapa is in the Azapa Valley 12 km from the town. The museum has an excellent collection of exhibits which chronicle the various civilisations which have come and gone in the area, since the 7th century BC until the arrival of the Spanish. The museum is open Monday to Friday from 9 am to 5 pm and on Saturdays from 1 to 6 pm. To get there you'll have to hire a colectivo. Alternatively, some of the companies which run tours around the surrounding area and to Lago Chungará (see details following) include the museum on their itineraries.

Places to Stay - bottom end

The cheapest place is the *Residencial Núñez* at Maipú 516 near the corner with Patricia Lynch. It costs just US$1.20 per person; it's basic but it has clean sheets and hot water. The *Residencial El Cobre* at Lagos 672 is slightly more expensive, but clean and good value.

The *Residencial Patricia* at Maipú 269 has double rooms for US$3.40, which is good value in this town. Although the rooms themselves are clean (there's not much to get dirty) the toilets and bathrooms are consistently grotty. If you're on your own you pay for a double room – there are no singles. The people who run the place aren't too friendly, and although it seems to be popular with other South Americans it can't really be recommended.

Moving up-market slightly, the *Residencial La Blanquita* (tel 32064), Maipú 472, is clean, has hot water when the pressure allows and is good value at US$2.70 a single and US$4 a double. Similar, and highly recommended by many travellers, is the *Residencial Madrid* (tel 31479) at Baquedano 685, which is clean, has hot water and costs US$2.40 a single and US$4 a double. Another which you can try in this range is the *Residencial Sotomayor*, Sotomayor 442, which costs US$2.35 per person but has no hot water.

Places to Stay - middle

One of the best places is the *Hotel Lynch* (tel 31581) at Lynch 589, which costs from US$4 to about US$5 single and US$7 a double without a bathroom; and around US$13 a double with a bathroom. There's a discount of 5% (yes, a whole 5%) for those staying more than two days but you'll probably have to ask to get it. It's a large place built around a central courtyard, so you probably won't get much traffic noise. Rooms are very simple, but both the rooms and bathrooms are very clean. Highly recommended.

Try the *Hotel Diego de Almagro* (tel 32927) on Sotomayor, just near the corner with Lynch. Bright, clean rooms with a private bathroom, TV, telephone and double beds are US$10 a single, and US$13.30 a double.

Similar to the Diego de Almagro, the *King Hotel* (tel 32094) is on Colón, just near the corner with 21 de Mayo. Singles are US$7.80 and doubles are US$11.70.

Places to Stay - top end

Top of the list is the *Hotel El Paso* (tel 31965) on Velásquez which is set in a pleasant garden and has singles from US$22.80 and doubles from US$26.

Places to Eat

There are plenty of cafés along 21 de Mayo, 18 de Septiembre, Maipú, Bolognesi and Colón. One of the most popular is the *21* on 21 de Mayo 201 at the junction with Colón; it has hamburgers, coffee and beer but is relatively expensive. Some of the cheapest places are along the latter two streets – you can get soup, a starter, a hamburger and a fruit juice for a dollar or two. The *Rotisería Colón* at Colón 325 is worth trying.

Arica, like other towns in northern Chile, has its fair share of Chinese restaurants. Try the *Chifa Chin Huang Tao* at Patricia Lynch 317; as Chinese restaurants go this place is fairly expensive but the food is good and the manager is friendly. Another Chinese place is the *Restaurant Shanghai* at Maipú 534, near the corner with Patricia Lynch.

Getting There

From Arica you can head north to Tacna in Peru, south to Iquique and Santiago, or east to Bolivia.

Air Ladeco (tel 32596) is at 18 de Septiembre 370. LAN-Chile (tel 31261) is at 7 de Julio 148 opposite the Plaza de Cristóbal Colón. Lloyd Aéreo Boliviano (tel 31124) is at Patricio Lynch 298 at the corner with Sotomayor. Aero Perú has an agent in the basement of the same building housing the LAN-Chile office.

Both LAN-Chile and Ladeco fly from Arica to Antofagasta (three times a week), Iquique (daily), and Santiago (daily).

If you can afford it, the Santiago to Arica flight is one of the most spectacular in Chile, with awesome views of the enormous cliffs along the northern coast.

Bus & Colectivo The new bus terminal is on Diego Portales at the junction with Santa María. It's quite a long way from the centre so allow 45 minutes if you're walking.

There are daily buses (some during the day, others at night) to Iquique (about US$5, four hours), Antofagasta (about US$12 to US$14, 10 hours) and Santiago (about US$32, 27 to 28 hours). Book a day

in advance if possible, especially for the daytime buses.

Taxi colectivos also depart from the bus terminal for Iquique; there are several companies and they each charge about US$8.30 per person.

On the road from Arica to Iquique you pass the Geoglyphs de Chiza on a hillside on the right-hand side. About 47 km out from Iquique you drive past Humberstone, an old nitrate mining ghost-town, now completely deserted apart from a few scrap metal salvagers and tourists.

There are international buses to La Paz in Bolivia, and to Tacna and Arequipa in Peru. Some of these may have offices at the bus terminal. If not, for buses to La Paz go to Pullman Martínez at Pedro Montt 620, and Litoral at Chacabuco 454. Litoral has buses direct from Arica to La Paz twice a week; they take about 24 hours and cost about US$28.

It may also be possible to get buses direct to Lima for around US$25; try at the bus terminal, but if there are no buses just take a colectivo to Tacna and catch a bus from there.

Taxi colectivos to Tacna (several companies) go from Chacabuco between Baquedano and Colón. They leave whenever they're full, throughout the day. One-way to Tacna is US$2.20 and a return fare is US$3.30. The buses cost about the same as the trains but they're neither as convenient nor as fast as the colectivos.

Rail The railway station for trains to Tacna is at Máxima Lira 891. If you're taking the train to Tacna in Peru you need to turn up about half an hour before departure to give the police time to get through exit formalities. There are departures twice daily for Tacna (one in the late morning and one in the early afternoon) and the journey takes about 1½ hours and costs US$1. You will generally find the colectivos much easier and more straightforward.

The railway station for trains to La Paz

is in front of the Plazoleta Estación, at the corner of Pedro Montt and 21 de Mayo. The ferrobuses along this route have been discontinued and there is now an ordinary train in either direction twice a month. The actual dates vary so you need to make enquiries at the station or the tourist office. You must change trains at the border and this can take hours because there's a lot of smuggling going on and there are interminable bag searches. The change-over station is at about 4000 metres, so it can be snowing even if it's baking in Arica. Don't use this route unless you have warm clothes!

The fare from Arica to La Paz is around US$13 for 1st class and about US$10.50, 2nd class. If you need somewhere to stay at the border ask at the houses; you can sleep in a barn for a few soles and they'll give you blankets. You can generally change money on the train at Ollagüe but make sure you know what the current rates are before changing money as the rates are not always very good. Generally, it's much better taking the buses on this route.

Getting Around

Taxis from the town centre to the bus terminal will cost you US$1.10. A taxi colectivo is cheaper and will cost about US$0.20 per person. There are also local buses on this route.

Ladeco has a bus connecting with all their flights and LAN-Chile probably does the same. It's 14 km from the town to the airport.

Cars can be rented from Allen Rent-a-Car (tel 51121) at Velásquez 750. Cheapest cars start from about US$14.50 a day plus around US$0.13 per km (the first 50 km is free) and US$3 insurance per day. This is worth considering, particularly if you want to go up to the Lauca National Park but don't want to take a tour. Beware of ruts, potholes, landslides, gaping holes and ravines!

Tours available from various agents include the national park, the city of

Arica, local archeological sites and the museum, Tacna (across the border in Peru), day-trips to Iquique, and even to Machu Picchu. There is a Peruvian consulate in Arica where you can get a visa if you need one. Several tour companies are listed in the section on the Lauca National Park.

LAUCA NATIONAL PARK

The Lauca National Park lies north-east of Arica beside the Bolivian border, at altitudes between 3000 and 6300 metres. It's a magnificent area, especially around Lago Chungará which sits between two snow-capped volcanoes and is supposedly the highest lake in the world. There's a lot of wildlife in the park and you'll see vicuña, alpaca, vizcacha, condor and waterfowl even on a short visit.

Getting There

The park is about 120 km from Arica and straddles the Arica-La Paz highway. The drive from Arica takes about four hours. The cheapest way of getting to the park is to take the Arica-La Paz bus and get off near Lago Chungará where there is an information centre with a few beds and a kitchen. Take food and warm clothing with you.

If your time is limited or you prefer something more organised, check the tourist agencies in Arica which organise tours. These include Huasqui-Tour, Turismo Payachatas, Parina Tour and Jurasi.

Payachatas, at Bolognesi 330 (near the corner with Sotomayor) offer a one-day tour by VW Kombi which leaves Arica at 7.30 am and returns at 8.30 pm. It costs US$13.90 and includes a light breakfast en-route. Travellers who have taken this tour have recommended it highly.

Jurasi Tour at Bolognesi 370 also have trips to Lago Chungará, either in a VW Kombi at US$13.90 per person or by car at US$16.60 per person. The people are friendly and the company is highly recommended.

Remember that you'll be going higher than 4000 metres (13,000 ft) and you may feel some effects of altitude sickness – particularly headaches and shortness of breath. If you intend staying above 3000 metres read the Health section in the Facts for the Visitor chapter. Some of the tour companies may take oxygen bottles on the trip. Whatever you do, take warm clothing! It can be blisteringly hot in Arica and still be snowing in the park.

The Lluta Valley

The first place of interest en route to the park is the Lluta Valley just outside Arica and on the road to Poconchile. On a mountain ridge on your right (as you head away from Arica) you can see a large mural of Indian geoglyphs – pictures made by grouping dark stones together against light-coloured sand. Images of alpaca, people and what appear to be birds (possibly condors) can be seen. Many similar geoglyphs can be seen throughout the northern desert, notably at Pintados near Iquique where a huge mountain ridge is covered in pictures.

Poconchile

At the side of the road there is an adobe church, originally built in the 17th century, reconstructed in the 19th, and restored during this century. This is one of the oldest churches still standing in Chile. As the road climbs higher up the side of the desolate mountains you look down into the deep, narrow river valley of Poconchile and its corridor of agricultural land. As you turn away from the river valley and start climbing into the mountains you can look down and see a strip of cleared land resembling an aircraft runway; it is not known who built it, or when, or why it was constructed.

The Old Road

For quite a distance the road follows a dry river bed that looks as if it hasn't seen water for centuries. About 50 years ago a road was built in the river bed on the assumption that water would never again run in it – a freak flood washed the road away, although some pieces of it can still be seen.

Candle Holder Cactus

Between 1300 and 1800 metres in altitude you'll see the appropriately named 'candle-holder' cactus (*cactus candelabros*). They look like they've just marched off a set for *Dr Who*. These cacti grow just five to seven *millimetres* a year and flower for 24 hours just once a year. The cacti, and other plants, take their moisture from the fog which descends on the mountains and from humidity in the air; there is no ground water and no rain, although you will often see clouds.

Copaquilla

At Copaquilla there is a restored Indian fortress, which pre-dates the Incas by 200 years, and was built to protect Indian farmlands in the valley below. Copaquilla is the name of the valley, and the fortress is set on a clifftop above it.

The Park

After Copaquilla the road winds its way around the mountains until you gradually leave the desert. The candle-holder cacti disappear and at 2000 metres you enter the national park. Although it's bone dry at low altitudes, at high altitudes it can snow during summer. Keep your eyes open for llama, vicuña, alpaca, pink flamingos, and huemuelle herds.

Alpaca are kept by the local Indians and their fleece is shorn and made into gloves, ponchos and hats, some of which are sold to tourists. The Indians at the settlement at Parincota sell beautiful ponchos and clothing made from alpaca wool – very cheap and very warm.

The Cameloids

The llama is a 'cameloid' – a member of the camel family, as is the vicuña, the alpaca and the guanaco. In Chile you can see alpaca and vicuña around Lago Chungará and guanaco in

Llama

the Torres del Paine National Park and on grazing land near Punta Arenas in the far south. Argentina is home to 90% of Latin America's guanacos.

Cameloids are adapted to mountainous terrain, with pads on their toes which assist them on rock and gravel slopes. The split upper lip, the long, curved neck, and long legs are characteristic of camels and cameloids. These creatures – or some variation of them – have been around for about 40 to 45 million years, originating in North America and spreading into South America and Asia only two to three million years ago.

Domestication of the llama and alpaca began about 4000 to 5000 years ago, possibly around Lake Titicaca. Today there are no alpacas or llamas which live independently of people. The animals are kept for their milk, meat, fleece and manure (which is used as fuel); and are used as transport by the Indians of Peru and Bolivia. They have been indispensable to human survival in parts of South America.

The llama was the Inca empire's primary means of transportation, but when the Spanish destroyed the empire and introduced sheep the llama population plummeted. Today there are about 3.7 million llamas and about 3.3 million alpacas. Most llamas can be found in the mountains, particularly in Bolivia, and most alpacas can be found in Peru. Their coats can be a single colour or a mixture of white, brown, grey and black. The alpaca's coat is longer than the llama's.

The vicuña is the smallest of the cameloids, a sleek animal which grazes in alpine grasslands between 3700 to 4800 metres (12,000 to 15,700 ft), and is non-migratory. Prized for their wool these animals were almost hunted into extinction; by the 1950s there were 400,000 left and by the late 1960s just 15,000. Today it's protected and its numbers have increased to over 80,000. Most can be found in Peru. They have a cinnamon-coloured coat, sometimes with a white 'bib' on the chest, and white undersides.

The guanaco is twice as large as a vicuña and

is much more flexible in its grazing habits. It can survive in desert grasslands, savannahs, and forest and at altitudes from sea-level to about 4250 metres (13,900 ft). It is either migratory or sedentary, and unlike the vicuña it can draw its water from foliage and does not need to drink. There were huge numbers of guanaco in South America when the Spanish arrived, some estimates ranging as high as 30 to 35 million on the Argentine pampas alone. Today there are between 500,000 and 600,000 and over 90% of these are in Argentina. They have a cinnamon-brown coat with white undersides.

IQUIQUE

During the 19th century the products of the mining towns were shipped out through port towns like Antofagasta and Iquique, now large towns of well over 100,000 people each. It's hard to imagine that last century many of the port towns were not much more than a collection of tin shanties huddled at the base of barren cliffs, fed with minerals by railway lines stretching like umbilical cords into the interior.

At Iquique and Antofagasta the wealthy built luxurious mansions (many can still be seen), water was piped in over long distances from the valleys, and topsoil was imported for the obligatory central plaza and private gardens. Eventually these towns were as comfortable for the rich to live in as those further south. Iquique is a good example with its Plaza de Armas complete with a clock tower and a 19th century theatre with corinthian columns, and many stately homes. Nearby ghost towns like Humberstone, and rusting nitrate-ore crushing plants are the last reminders of where the wealth came from.

Iquique is still one of the largest ports and towns of the north, but it has a very different feel to the other towns at this end of the country. It's ringed by packing-crate houses and its beaches are buffeted by powerful waves and awesome rips. During the day it's blisteringly hot and every night the town centre is as loud as

New Year's Eve. Convoys of honking cars advertise marriages, but strip joints, pick-up bars and other places of solace continue to ply their trade. Amidst the party the cheap hash-houses are filled with loners eating and drinking and whiling away the time watching TV.

On the roads heading northwards out of Iquique you see innumerable crosses and roadside shrines plastered with the number plates of fallen highway heroes. It's all a bit inappropriate for a town whose name is said to be derived from an Indian word meaning 'rest and tranquillity'.

Information

Tourist Office The tourist office is at Pinto 436, next to the Ladeco office and opposite the Hotel Phoenix. They have a free leaflet which tells you what's on in Iquique including concerts, films, sports and other events.

Bank The Banco de Chile is on Prat, facing the Plaza Prat, and will change foreign currency and travellers' cheques. It's open from about 9 am to 2 pm Monday to Friday.

Post & Communications The post office is on Bolívar, between Labbe and Patricio Lynch. It's open Monday to Friday 8.30 am to 12.30 pm and 3 to around 7 pm; Saturdays from 9 am to 1 pm. The telephone office is at the corner of Tarapaca and Ramirez.

Navy Museum

It's worth checking out the Navy Museum at the junction of Esmeralda and Pinto. It's open Tuesday to Saturday 9.30 am to 12.30 pm and 2.30 to 6 pm, and on Sundays and holidays from 10 am to 1 pm; entrance costs about US$0.10.

Museum Regional

The Museum Regional is at Sotomayor 706 and is interesting and well laid out. There's even a mock Indian village out

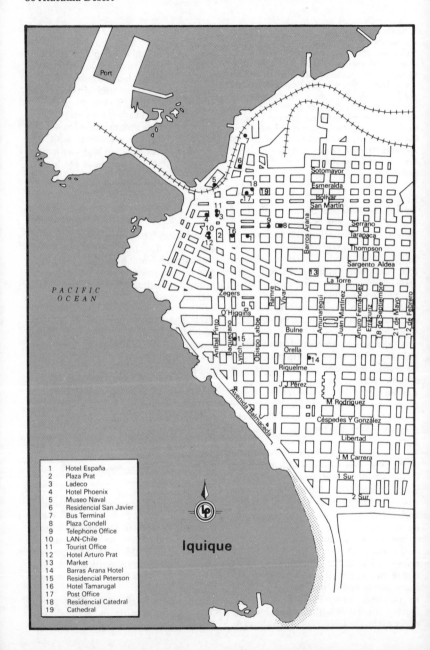

1	Hotel España
2	Plaza Prat
3	Ladeco
4	Hotel Phoenix
5	Museo Naval
6	Residencial San Javier
7	Bus Terminal
8	Plaza Condell
9	Telephone Office
10	LAN-Chile
11	Tourist Office
12	Hotel Arturo Prat
13	Market
14	Barras Arana Hotel
15	Residencial Peterson
16	Hotel Tamarugal
17	Post Office
18	Residencial Catedral
19	Cathedral

Iquique

the back with mud-brick houses and mannequins dressed in Indian costumes. There's a large collection of Indian relics including raft and canoe paddles, fishing hooks and sinkers, rope, fishing harpoons, arrows and arrow holders made of animal hide. There are also several disintegrating Indian mummies on display rather less intact than the ones you can see in the museum at San Pedro de Atacama. One of the bodies in the Iquique museum has a deliberately malformed, elongated skull. There's also an exhibition of Indian ceramics and weaving, and photos of the early days of Iquique. The museum is open Monday to Friday 9 am to 1 pm and 3 to 7 pm, and on Saturday from 10 am to 1 pm. Admission is about US$0.15

Beaches

The Playa Bravo is a large beach, but it's far too rough for swimming, with big, dumping waves – bring your air-tanks and personal life-saving squad because this place really lives up to its name. It's a long stretch of greyish-white sand, not bad for sun-bathing. The easiest way to get there is by taxi colectivo from the centre of town – US$0.30 per person. Further up and around a rocky headland is the Playa Cavancha, which is good for swimming, but rather crowded and not terribly attractive.

Places to Stay - bottom end

There's a cluster of residencials on Amunategui between Sargento Aldea and Thomson: the *Residencial Victoria* at 770 is US$1.40 per person; the *Residencial Viena* at 729 is US$1.10 and is not bad – spartan but clean, and the people are friendly; and the *Residencial Lucerna* at 723 is US$1.10 per person. There are one or two others but they're almost all permanently full with workers. If you're really on a low low budget then give them a try – the *Viena* is definitely worth a look.

My pick of the residencials in Iquique is the *Residencial José Luis* at San Martín

601, at the corner with Ramírez. Singles are US$4.30 and doubles are US$7.20, with attached bathrooms; it has cool, clean rooms, all with large double beds.

My next choice would be the *Residencial Catedral* on Labbe, opposite the large cathedral. Singles are US$4.70, doubles are US$7, and doubles with a private bathroom are US$10. There are two levels of rooms set around a pleasant courtyard and garden, and both the rooms and bathrooms are very clean.

Try the *Residencial Peterson* at Patricio Lynch 1257 which is US$3.30 a double, including bathrooms. The hotel is OK and the people are friendly; it may do for the night.

The *Hotel España* at Tarapacá 465, near the Plaza Prat, can't really be recommended although you may be able to tolerate it for a night or two. You should think about taking a room with a bathroom, because the common bathrooms are fairly scungy. The hotel itself resembles a large warehouse divided into small boxes and you should bring a pair of earplugs to guard against the hordes of kiddies as well as the permanent residents' TVs punching through the thinly partitioned walls. Rooms without private bathrooms are US$2.20 a single and US$4.20 a double; rooms with private bathrooms are US$4.90 a single and US$8.40 a double.

Two cheap places near the bus station which may be worth trying are the *Residencial Esmeralda* at the corner of Esmeralda and Lynch, and the *Residencial Aluimar* at San Martín 486, between Lynch and Obispo Labbe.

Places to Stay - middle

One of the best places in Iquique is the *Hotel Phoenix* (tel 21315) at Aníbal Pinto 451. The simple rooms are clean and bright and the people are friendly. Singles are US$7, doubles are US$12, including a private bathroom and breakfast. There's a restaurant and pool hall on the ground floor.

Although it's a bit of a walk out of the centre, the *Hotel Barros Arana* (tel 24420) at Barros Arana 1330, near the corner with Orello, is well worth the effort. Singles with a bathroom are US$8.80, and doubles are US$13.30. They're clean, fresh-looking rooms all with TVs and private bathrooms. Highly recommended.

Places to Stay – top end

One of Iquique's top hotels is the *Hotel Arturo Prat* (tel 21414) on Pinto facing the Plaza Prat. Singles are US$25.70 and doubles are US$29.20.

The *Hotel Tamarugal* is at Tarapacá 639, just near the corner with Prat. Singles with private bathrooms and TVs are US$17.20 and doubles are US$22.80 – it's on a par with the *Barros Arana* which is half the price so the main advantage of staying at the *Tamarugal* is that you're in the centre of town.

At the Playa Cavancha is the *Hotel Cavancha* (tel 21158) on Los Rieles 250 which has rooms from US$30 a single and US$40 a double – or US$60 a single and US$75 a double for rooms facing the beach. The price includes breakfast. The beach is hardly scenic and I wouldn't troop down to Iquique just for a swim.

Places to Eat

Try the Chinese restaurants around town – there are lots of them. The *Chifa Chai-Wha* at Thomson 917 is very cheap and you can get a simple Chinese meal for around US$2 per person. Also very cheap and with generous helpings is the *Restaurant Chifa Can Loon* at Tarapacá 780. Others are the *Chifa Tung Fong* on Tarapacá between Barros Arana and Amunategui, and the *Chifa Ming Wang* at Barros Arana 668, near the corner with Thomson.

The city's trendiest snack bar is probably the *Restaurant Garbo* (an unfortunate coincidence, but *garbo* is actually a Spanish word meaning elegant) on Tarapacá between Barros Arana and Vivar. *La Merienda*, on Tarapacá between Barros Arana and Amunategui, has very filling humitas.

On the Plaza Prat at the corner of Prat and Tarapacá, the *Jugoslavenski Dom Club Social* is worth trying; its menu includes seafood. The place you should not miss is the illustrious *Club Español* two doors down on Prat; its incredibly ornate interior is painted in Moorish style and eating in the dining room is like eating inside an Arabian painting. A meal at the *Club Español* will set you back about US$8 to US$11 per person. If you can't afford the meal prices you should at least visit for a drink and gaze at the decor through an alcoholic haze.

The *Restaurant Circolo Italiano* at Tarapacá 477 serves pasta. Try the *Sociedad Protectora de Empleados de Tarapacá* at Thomson 207, at the corner of Thomson and Pinto facing the Plaza Prat – it's open to foreign tourists.

Getting There

Air Ladeco (tel 24794) is at the corner of Pinto and Serrano, facing Plaza Prat. LAN-Chile (tel 21479) is at the corner of Pinto and Tarapacá, facing Plaza Prat. Ladeco has flights from Iquique to Antofagasta (three days a week); Arica (daily); and Santiago (daily). LAN-Chile has flights from Iquique to Arica (daily); and Santiago (daily).

Bus There are numerous bus companies with offices at the bus terminal on Patricia Lynch. There are several bus companies which run day and night buses to Santiago and Arica. Most of these bus companies also have an office in town, so there's no need to walk all the way out to the bus station for tickets.

Typical fares from Iquique are: Antofagasta, US$10; La Serena, US$20; Valparaíso, Viña del Mar and Santiago, US$26; Arica, US$5; Calama, US$5.60.

For taxi colectivos to Arica try Agencia Turistaxi at Barros Arana 897A, at the corner with Latorre; there are several vehicles per day in that direction. Bus companies, the addresses of their offices, and the destinations they service are:

Fénix Pullman Norte, Pinto 531 next to the Hotel Phoenix, and Barros Arana 881; to Santiago and Arica.

Buses Carmelita, Barros Arana 831; several departures daily to Arica and to Santiago.

Bus Julita St Rosa, Barros Arana 831; daily to Pica and, except on Sundays, to Mamiña.

Buses Ramos Cholele, Barros Arana 851; daily to Santiago.

Kenny Bus, Amunategui, near the corner with Sargento Aldea; to Calama, departing about 9 pm daily and arriving in Calama about 5 or 6 am.

Buses Cuevas & González, Sargento Aldea, between Amunategui and Barros Arana; several departures daily to Arica, daily to Calama and Chuqui.

Getting Around

For tours of the surrounding region try Iquitour at Tarapacá 465, next to the Hotel España. They have tours, every day except Sunday, departing about 9.30 am, which go to Pica, Humberstone, Santa Laura, Museo Pozo Almonte, La Tirana, Hayca, Canchane and Matilla. They cost US$14 and include lunch. They also have tours to the Termas de Mamiña, Santa Laura and Humberstone. Unfortunately – and inexplicably – there seem to be no tours which take in Sierra Unida.

It should be possible to arrange a one-day tour with a taxi driver for around US$40 to US$45 (perhaps rather less if you're a better bargainer) covering Sierra Unida, Pintados, Humberstone, La Tirana and Pica.

AROUND IQUIQUE

There are a number of geoglyphs near Iquique, including the mural sprawled across the side of the mountain ridge at Pintados, and the enormous image of a man, on the side of a hill known as Sierra Unida.

The Atacama is not the only place where giant images can be found. Huge men delineated by stones can be found near Blyth in California. They are almost impossible to detect from ground level and are clearly meant to be seen *from above*.

The desert between the Nazca and Ica Valleys of Peru is criss-crossed by a vast picture book of lines, geometric figures and images, made by clearing away a layer of dark-brown stones to expose lighter-coloured soil beneath. Of all the known images designed on the ground these are the most extravagant. Some of the lines run for several km, unswervingly straight over plateaux and mountains, while others form giant enclosures (some say like runways). Like the Blyth figures, they seem to have been laid out to be viewed from above.

Nor are such images found only in the Americas. At least 50 giant figures are known in England. They were made by exposing the chalk which lies just beneath the turf, particularly in the West Country. In England, however, the designs were laid out on hillsides and can be clearly seen from ground level.

One theory explains the Nazca lines by proposing that the Indian builders could fly using hot air balloons made with rope and cloth. Others theories suggest that the designs represent an enormous observatory, with the lines aligned with the rising and setting of celestial bodies and the animal figures representing the constellations. But it seems only a small number of lines were aligned with stars and planets, allowing for the date the designs were built. The simplest theory is that the designs are meant to be seen by heavenly gods, not by people.

The Chilean geoglyphs, like the designs in England, are made on the sides of mountains rather than on flat desert plains, and can be viewed from the ground. It is not known how long ago the figures and designs were made or who or what they represent. One theory is that the Chilean geoglyphs were once signposts for Inca or pre-Inca traders. The giant figures may represent celestial beings or mythological figures, but it's always possible that they were produced without any religious or mystical motivation at all. They may simply be an artistic creation by a desert-dwelling people who used the materials which were available to them – dark stones on a canvas of light-coloured desert sand.

The Giant of the Atacama

The Giant of the Atacama, laid out on the slope of Sierra Unida, is the largest representation of a human figure in the world – a massive 120 metres long!

Twelve rays emanate from the human figure's head (which is square and supported by a thin neck), four from the top and four from each side, the eyes and mouth are square, the torso is long and narrow, the arms are bent (one hand appears to be an arrowhead), the size of the feet suggest the figure is wearing boots, and there are odd protrusions from the knees and thighs.

At its side is another odd creature sporting what appears to be a tail – perhaps a monkey, although others interpret it as a reptile of some sort. The two figures are set amidst a complex of lines and circles, and on one side of the hill (facing the Huara-Chuzmisa road, visible as you approach the hill) there are a number of enormous clearings resembling runways.

The Huara-Chuzmisa road is surfaced, as is the Arica-Iquique highway. Only the very short stretch (about a km) of road leading from the Huara-Chuzmisa road to the hill itself is across the desert. The only way to visit the site is to hire a car or taxi in Iquique (forget about hitching).

Strangely, very few Chileans seem to have an accurate idea of the location of the Giant of the Atacama. When I was trying to find it I was given vague estimates of its location which ranged between Arica and Antofagasta, until the tourist office in Iquique finally came good. For some reason the ordinarily reliable *Gran Mapa Caminero de Chile*, which shows innumerable geoglyph sites, makes no mention of either the Sierra Unida or Pintados sites.

The best views of the giant would be from the air but the whole figure – including the head – can be clearly made out if you stand several hundred metres back from the base of the hill. Avoid climbing on the hill since doing so damages the pictures. The hill itself is completely alone on an immense desert plain.

The Giant of the Atacama

Pintados

This is one of the biggest outdoor murals in the world – the whole side of a mountain ridge is adorned with some 390 individual geoglyphs grouped in 60 panels. From close up it is almost impossible to discern what most of the figures represent, but from a distance you can make out images of people, llamas, circles, squares, chequerboard patterns and even a gigantic arrow. Try to refrain from climbing up the mountain ridge and over the geoglyphs as this will inevitably damage them.

Pintados lies some distance off the Iquique-Antofagasta highway. It's actually a derelict railway yard with a number of ruined buildings and rusting rolling stock still on the dilapidated rails. The mountain ridge forms a huge barrier behind this old settlement, running roughly parallel with the highway. The only way to visit this site is by car, taxi or tour from Iquique.

Humberstone

A former nitrate-mining town and now an eerie ghost town, Humberstone is on the Iquique-Arica highway about 47 km due east of Iquique. It's now totally deserted apart from curious tourists and some scrap metal merchants. Walk around and you'll find the main plaza flanked by a large theatre, a church and a market. Almost all the original buildings are still standing, although they're crumbling into dust.

At one end of the town the electrical generating plant still stands and you can see the remains of the train line running across the desert to the Oficina Salitera Santa Laura (the ore crushing plant) in the distance just to the side of the road to Iquique. A rusting steam locomotive, railway cranes, shovels, wheelbarrows – many things have been left as if everyone deserted the town simultaneously. With a bit of imagination you can almost see the ghosts.

Humberstone is not the only ghost town in the Atacama Desert. Some are now being repopulated as modern processing techniques make excavation of low grade ores profitable.

CALAMA

Calama sits on the high plain in the middle of the Atacama Desert and is the commercial centre for the nearby open-cast copper mines of Chuquicamata

which are the largest in the world. Coming up from Antofagasta, you can see the smoke pouring out of the stacks at Chuquicamata for miles before you arrive.

For travellers the town is a jumping-off point for visits to the oasis villages of San Pedro de Atacama (on the edge of the Salar de Atacama), Toconao, Chiu Chiu and, of course, the copper mine at Chuquicamata. It's also the terminus of the Calama-La Paz railway which is used by many travellers on their way to and from Bolivia.

Information

Tourist Office The tourist office is on the corner of Vicuña MacKenna and Latorre. The staff are enthusiastic and friendly and have free maps of Calama and the surrounding region. Only some halting English is spoken.

Bank You *cannot* change travellers' cheques in Calama or Chuqui in the banks, hotels or restaurants. You can change US cash and that's all. To do this go to the Banco de Chile on Vivar, just near the corner with Vargas, or to the Banco de Credito. Another possibility is the Tramaca Bus Terminal.

Post & Communications Telex Chile is at Abaroa, between Ramírez and Vargas. The post office is on the Plaza Heroes de la Concepción; it's open Monday to Friday 8.30 am to 1 pm and 3.30 to 6 pm; and Saturday 9 am to 12 noon.

Consulates The Bolivian Consulate is at Vicuña MacKenna 1976, and is open Monday to Friday from 9 am to 12.30 pm and 3.30 to 6.30 pm (hours may vary). If you are taking the train to Bolivia make sure you get your passport stamped here first, before buying the train ticket. In the past there were reports that the consul demanded money for what should have been a free stamp but this doesn't appear to be the case anymore.

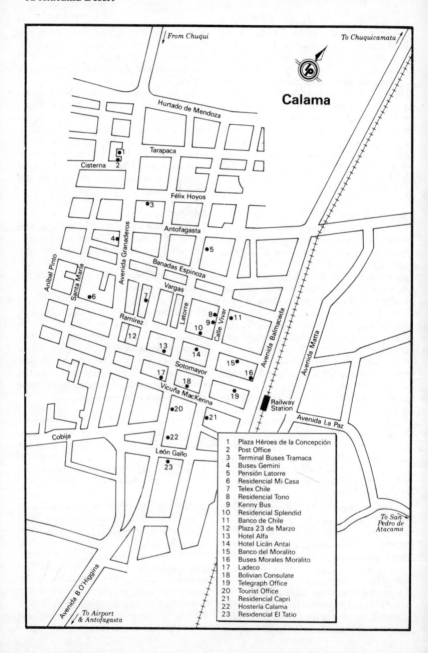

Calama

1   Plaza Héroes de la Concepción
2   Post Office
3   Terminal Buses Tramaca
4   Buses Gemini
5   Pensión Latorre
6   Residencial Mi Casa
7   Telex Chile
8   Residencial Tono
9   Kenny Bus
10 Residencial Splendid
11 Banco de Chile
12 Plaza 23 de Marzo
13 Hotel Alfa
14 Hotel Licán Antai
15 Banco del Moralito
16 Buses Morales Moralito
17 Ladeco
18 Bolivian Consulate
19 Telegraph Office
20 Tourist Office
21 Residencial Capri
22 Hostería Calama
23 Residencial El Tatio

Places to Stay - bottom end

The *Residencial Tono* at Vivar 1968, has been popular with travellers for years. It has clean sheets and adequate blankets, and costs US$2.20 per person in double rooms. Hot showers cost around US$0.35 extra. It's clean and fairly quiet.

The *Residencial Capri* (tel 21 2870) at Vivar 1639, is friendly, very clean and costs US$2.20 a single and US$4.40 a double. You may find the rooms rather dingy since they only have windows facing into the passageway, otherwise it's good value. There's hot water in the showers in the mornings and it's surprisingly quiet. Recommended.

Somewhat more expensive, the *Residencial Splendid*, Ramírez 1960 is a clean, homely, secure hotel popular with local salesmen and the like. It costs around US$2.70 a single and US$5.30 a double - a bit more for rooms with their own bathroom. There's plenty of hot water in the mornings and evenings. Breakfast (two fried eggs, bread, coffee) is available for an additional US$0.80 and is good value.

Another place I'd recommend is the *Residencial El Tatio* at Gallo 1987, which has rooms at US$4 per person. This doesn't include your own bathroom or breakfast so it's relatively expensive. However, it's very clean, has hot water and the people are friendly.

Other cheapies worth trying are the *Pensión Latorre*, Latorre 2091, and the *Residencial Mi Casa*, Ramírez 2262.

Places to Stay - middle

The *Hotel Lican Antai* (tel 21 2817) at Ramírez 1937 has singles for around US$14.50 and doubles for US$17.80 including a private bathroom. You don't really get that much for your money but it's bright, clean and airy, and by Calama standards it's a great place.

Places to Stay - top end

At the top of the range is the *Hostería Calama* (tel 21 1115) at Latorre 1521, with singles for US$18.90 and doubles for US$23.30, which includes a private bathroom and breakfast. The *Hotel Alfa* (tel 21 2496) at Sotomayor 2016 is the same price. Check out the middle-range *Hotel Lican Antai* first – you may not find the more expensive alternatives worth the extra money.

Places to Eat

There are dozens of bars, restaurants and holes in the wall serving snacks around the main plaza and streets in the centre of town; Sotomayor and Ramírez are two good hunting grounds. Look for small, non-descript places for the cheapest eats – if a place is popular with ordinary workers it means it's cheap.

The *Hotel Restaurant Victoria* at Vargas 2102 on the corner of Abaroa is an average-price cheapie with meals from around US$3 and cheap bottles of house wine; the *escalopa kaul* makes a tasty meal, but remember to ask for side-dishes or you won't get any. The *Restaurant Osorno* on the corner of Granaderos and Espinoza offers four-course meals for a few dollars.

Try the *Restaurant Tong Fong* on Ramírez between Granaderos and Santa María, and the *Restaurant Chi Kang* on Espinoza between Latorre and Vivar. The *Club Yugoslavia* on Abaroa facing the Plaza de 23 Marzo is slightly more up-market.

The mainstays of nightlife in Calama are the discotheques/strip/pick-up joints. Men are expected to buy cigarettes and drinks for the girls, and since these places only serve spirits you're up for at least US$2.50 per drink. If you're interested, try the *Topless Lucifer Discotheque* at Ramírez 1812 just near the corner with Balmaceda, and the *Topless Marbella* at Sotomayor 1886 near the corner with Vivar.

Getting There

From Calama you can head north to Iquique and Arica, south to Antofagasta,

Nightclub hoarding

east by train to Bolivia, or by bus to Salta in Argentina.

Air Ladeco (tel 21 1355) is at Vicuña MacKenna 2016. LAN-Chile is at Sotomayor 2076 between Latorre and Abaroa. Ladeco has flights from Calama to Antofagasta six days a week, and to Santiago six days a week. LAN-Chile has flights from Calama to Santiago six days a week.

Bus Typical fares from Calama are: Arica, US$9; Iquique, US$6.40; Santiago, US$22.80; Antofagasta, US$3.30; San Pedro de Atacama, US$2.40. Bus companies operating out of Calama include:

Tramaca, Felix Hoyes near the corner with Granaderos; 11 or 12 departures daily for Antofagasta; at least once daily to Arica (around 9 pm); once daily to Iquique (around 10 pm); twice daily to Santiago with connections to Viña del Mar and Valparaíso; and daily to San Pedro de Atacama (see that section for details).
Kenny Bus, Calle Vivar between Vargas and Ramírezhas; daily to Antofagasta; daily to Iquique (around 10 pm).
Fleche Norte, Ramírez 1930; several departures daily to Santiago via Antofagasta.
Buses Gemini, Granaderos near the corner with Espinoza; daily to Antofagasta, Arica and Iquique; on Sundays to San Pedro de Atacama (see that section for details); and every Wednesday to Salta in Argentina.
Buses Libac, corner of Espinoza and Abaroa; daily to Santiago and Antofagasta.

Rail Trains to La Paz in Bolivia depart once a week, on Wednesday afternoon, and the journey takes about 36 hours. The train station in Calama is on Balmaceda, at the top end of Sotomayor. Tickets are sold on Tuesdays between about 3 and 4.30 pm and on Wednesdays between 8.30 am and 12.45 pm. Fares to La Paz are around US$16.45 (one class only).

Take your passport when buying tickets and make sure you have a Bolivian visa if you need one. You have to change trains at Ollagüe and that often involves a four-hour wait. It's very cold at the frontier – temperatures can drop to –15°C so don't go on this train unless you have warm clothing! The Bolivian trains are in reasonable condition, but the Chilean trains are like cattle trucks.

AROUND CALAMA

Places of interest near Calama, apart from the copper mine, include San Pedro de Atacama, and the village of Chiu Chiu (where you can find fine examples of cactus-wood carving). There is no public bus to Chiu Chiu so you'll have to hire private transport – this will be expensive unless you can get a group together.

If you can foot the bill the best man to contact in Calama is Luis Gutiérrez, Angamos 2687, Pob Santa Rosa. He organises tours to remote spots in the border region as well as to San Pedro de Atacama, Toconao and the geysers. His vehicles will take up to eight people and cost a total of about US$100 including food. Alternatively you can hire your own car; Hertz (tel 21 1380) is at Latorre 1510.

THE CHUQUICAMATA COPPER MINE

Chile is the biggest copper producer in the world, and production has been steadily increasing all through this century. Copper mining in Chile during the 20th century has relied on the bulk mining of relatively low-grade ore using foreign capital, and techniques originally developed in the copper mines of western

USA. El Teniente, south-east of Santiago, was the first big mine in Chile to be developed in this way (by Kennecott Copper, a US company) and is the largest underground copper mine in the world.

In 1911 the huge Chuquicamata deposit was discovered. The original owners sold it to the US Anaconda Company and in 1916 excavations began – today it is the largest opencast copper mine, and the largest single supplier of copper in the world. The pit is 350 to 400 metres deep and is responsible for half of Chile's total copper output – which makes its responsible for at least a quarter of Chile's total annual income from exports.

The scale of the Chilean copper industry has given it remarkable importance in the politics of the country. By the 1960s the three largest mines accounted for over 80% of Chile's copper production, over 60% of the total value of exports and 80% of government revenue from taxes.

With the Chilean economy so tightly wrapped up with the production of copper, the idea of nationalising the copper industries inevitably developed. Leftists in the National Congress – including Allende – introduced nationalisation bills in the early 1950s, but support for nationalisation also grew amongst the Christian Democrats and other non-leftist parties. In the late 1960s during the Christian Democrat Government of President Frei, Chile gained a majority share-holding in the Chilean assets of the Anaconda and Kennecott companies.

In 1971, the Congress – including the National Party members – voted unanimously in favour of nationalising the copper industries. After the overthrow of Allende in 1973, agreement was reached between the US companies and the new military government about compensation for the loss of their mines. The US companies have since returned, though the large mines are still run by the state *Corporacion del Cobre de Chile*

(CODELCO), and refining is also under the control of a state organisation.

Tours

Chuquicamata – Chuqui for short – is about 20 km from Calama. The mine and smelter plant can visited on guided tours on Mondays, Wednesdays and Fridays at 1 pm; they leave from the Public Relations Office (*Relaciones Públicas*) in Chuquicamata.

The tour lasts about three hours and costs about US$0.80. Bring your passport for identification. Children under the age of 12 are not permitted on the tour, and photography inside the processing works is, at least officially, prohibited. After a video you're taken in a bus past the first mine and up to a hill where you can look down on the entire processing works, then you visit the smelters.

You have to wear proper shoes, long pants and a long-sleeved garment if you want to go inside the smelter building. They do provide jackets but it would be better to bring your own. Helmets and protective glasses are provided.

Copper Processing

Chuquicamata mines low-grade copper ore and it is only because such large quantities of material are processed that production is economical.

The ore is quarried by blasting and power-shovel work. At the mining stage, material is classified as ore or waste depending on the copper content. The material with sufficiently high metal content is dumped into a crusher, beginning a treatment process which reduces it to fine particles. The metal is then separated from the rock by a flotation process.

The flotation process separates and concentrates the copper by using chemically induced differences in surface tension to carry it to the surface of pools of water. The large pools of blue solution at the processing works are the concentrators where this process is taking place.

The copper concentrate is turned into a thick slurry from which the copper is finally extracted by heating it in the smelters.

Places to Eat

The mine's canteen is near the public relations office so if you go there around 12 noon you can enjoy a cheap meal. The food is OK and the service is good, though you may only get a set menu. To get there go to the public relations building and then walk past the caterpillar earth mover; the canteen is the building with a sign 'SOCIAL' on the front. There are also several cheap restaurants in the town centre near the bus and taxi colectivo station.

Getting There

The public relations office is at Puerto Uno. To get there from Calama take a taxi colectivo – it should cost about US$0.50 per person, and they leave from the corner of Abaroa and Ramírez at the Plaza de 23 Marzo. These will take you to the central bus terminal in Chuqui where you have to get a local taxi colectivo (about US$0.30) to take you the last two km to the public relations office (it's a long and *very* hot walk). It may be possible to get the taxi colectivo from Calama to take you the whole way, but you will have to pay extra for this. When the tour finishes there will often be local taxi colectivos waiting to take you back to the Chuqui bus station.

There are public buses from Calama to Chuqui which can be caught from the corner of Granaderos and Ramírez. These cost about US$0.25, but they only go as far as the Chuqui bus terminal where you'll have to catch a taxi colectivo or walk the two km to the mine. The buses go quite frequently, but the colectivos are more frequent.

If you're going to Calama from Antofagasta on a Monday, Wednesday or Friday, you could save some time by taking a bus which takes you straight through to Chuqui and tour the mine

before heading back to Calama. All the long-distance bus companies have offices and terminals in Chuqui. You could also tour the mine and get a bus straight back to Antofagasta if you don't want to hang around Calama; check departure times and allow for the tour to run longer than expected.

SAN PEDRO DE ATACAMA

This is an oasis village at the edge of the Salar de Atacama, a completely flat and mostly-dry salt lake. On the eastern side of the Salar rise enormous volcanoes – as far as the eye can see. Some of them are snowcapped, and some of them are still active – and smoking. You can see one of the highest extinct volcanoes in the Andes, Licancábur, which rises some 5900 metres, and the surrounding area has some of the weirdest, most awesome landscapes imaginable. The oasis itself is very relaxing and if you're in the area it deserves at least several days devoted to it.

San Pedro is just one of the oasis villages in the region, but it is the most important; about 120 km south-east of Calama, and 2436 metres above sea-level, it's home to about 1600 people. Almost all the dwellings are stone and mud brick. Many of them are enclosed in separate compounds by mud-brick walls and others are built in long rows.

The villagers' incomes seem to come from a number of sources: some work in the local sulphur mine; others farm; a few run shops; there are three or four hotels which cater to the tourist trade; and handicrafts, including wood carvings and woollen ponchos, are sold to tourists. It is still, to some extent, a subsistence economy, and village bartering is important.

The Museum

The area around the village has been inhabited since pre-historic times. In 1955 the former village priest, Father Le Paige, with the help of villagers and the

Top: Landscape, near San Pedro de Atacama
Bottom: Road between Lago Chungara and Arica, 4000 metres above the Atacama Desert

Top: Valley of the Moon, near San Pedro de Atacama
Left: Candle-holder cactus, Atacama Desert
Right: Clock tower, Iquique

UNIVERSIDAD   DEL   NORTE

"Museo Arqueológico San Pedro de
Atacama   R.P. Gustavo   Le Paige"

COLABORACION   PARA   CONSERVAR   Y   DIFUNDIR

EL PATRIMONIO NATURAL Y CULTURAL DE CHILE

Auspicio MINISTERIO DE EDUCACION Exenta N°0316,
18-VIII-1982. D.L. N°825-1980 Y D.L. N°3.454 1980

Adultos s 60   25 737

University of the North (in Antofagasta), began to put together one of the most remarkable and interesting museums in South America.

The museum gives an overview of the history and archaeology of the whole area, and an extraordinary range of Indian artefacts and remains are on display. Some of the most interesting are the mummies of Indian children and adults, including a child buried in a pottery urn, and skulls which show deliberate malformation. All the bodies are in a good state of preservation because they were buried in arid, salty soil. There are also fragments of ancient woven fabrics, pottery, tools, jewellery, and even a collection of paraphernalia for preparing, ingesting and smoking psychedelic plants and mushrooms. It's exceptionally well organised and cared for, but all the captions are in Spanish.

The museum is just near the main plaza. Its full name is the *Museo Arqueológico Gustavo Le Paige de Walque* and it's open Monday to Friday from 8 am to 12 noon and 2 to 6 pm and on weekends from 10 am to 12.30 pm and 3 to 7 pm. Admission is US$0.30.

Around the Plaza

Almost 450 years ago Chile's first unwanted European tourist, Pedro de Valdivia, came this way with his band of warriors, and Indians who were used as pack-animals, on an expedition which must have looked more like a migrating troop of nomads than a conquering army.

They brought everything they needed for the colonisation of a new country: European grains (mainly wheat), domestic animals (mainly pigs and chickens), and agricultural tools. Valdivia set out from Cuzco in Peru with only 14 or 15 men, but others joined him along the way, to make up a total of 150 Spanish soldiers. Peruvian Indians carried the supplies. Women and children also went with the expedition, although there was only one Spanish woman among them, Inés Suárez, Valdivia's mistress.

On one side of San Pedro de Atacama's main plaza stands a restored adobe house, typical of the early colonial period, which was originally constructed in 1540, apparently for Valdivia. On the other side stands the local church; originally built in the 16th century, it is one of the oldest churches in Chile. The present building makes use of local cactus wood, thatching, clay, and large straps of leather instead of nails.

Places to Stay & Eat

In San Pedro stay at the *Residencial La Florida* just down from the plaza. Although spartan it's generally clean, sheets and blankets are provided, and it's run by a friendly family assisted by a bombastic parrot. The rooms are arranged around a pleasant courtyard and cost US$1.40 per person in double or triple rooms – if you're travelling alone you'll get a room to yourself. Good meals are available for around US$2 (three courses) and beer, soft drinks, tea and coffee are available. My one criticism is that the common bathrooms (cold showers only) and toilets could do with a good clean!

If the Florida is full try the similar *Residencial El Pukara* next door; it's also run by a friendly family.

The *Residencial y Restaurant Chiloé* at the edge of town is also similar to the Florida (although the toilets and bathrooms are clean) and costs US$1.70 per person. There's a restaurant attached.

The *Hostería San Pedro* has the best accommodation in the oasis and charges a relatively modest US$13 a single and US$17.80 a double. The co-proprietor is an Australian woman and she has put together a brief pamphlet which describes some of the attractions in and around the oasis. The hotel is very comfortable and also has a restaurant attached. It's also the only hotel with hot water – solar heated.

Electricity in San Pedro de Atacama is only available from dusk to around 9.30 pm.

Other than the residencials and the hostería, there is the *Restaurant Juanita* on the plaza. There are also a number of small tiendas in the village where you can buy bread, cheese, fruit, vegetables, wine, beer and canned food, so there's no need to bring these from Calama. Local *vino* at the bottle shop/bar just down the street from *La Florida* costs under a dollar and is very palatable. You meet a lot of local people there in the evenings.

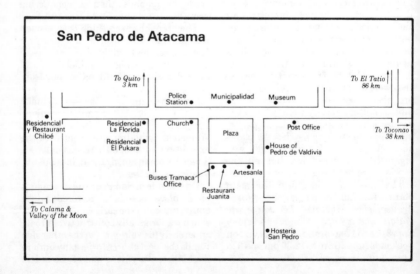

San Pedro de Atacama

To Quito
3 km

Police Station

Municipalidad

Museum

To El Tatio
86 km

Residencial y Restaurant Chiloé

Residencial La Florida

Residencial El Pukara

Church

Plaza

Post Office

To Toconao
38 km

House of Pedro de Valdivia

Buses Tramaca Office

Restaurant Juanita

Artesanía

To Calama & Valley of the Moon

Hostería San Pedro

Shopping

There is a good craft shop on the plaza where you can find excellent carved cactus wood. They also sell ponchos made from llama and alpaca wool. Crafts are also sold at the *Hostería San Pedro*.

Getting There

From Calama, Tramaca has buses to San Pedro every day at 9 am, except Sunday when they leave at 11 am. The journey takes about 1½ hours along a surfaced road and offers spectacular vistas of snow-covered mountains and volcanoes; the bus drivers will often stop to let you take photographs. The buses depart from San Pedro for Calama daily, around 6 pm to 7 pm from the main plaza – check with the driver. The fare is around US$2.20 one-way and US$4.40 return. It's sometimes possible to hitch but there's very little traffic.

Buses Gemini, on Granaderos just near the corner with Espinoza, runs buses to San Pedro and back on Sundays only, departing Calama around 9 am.

Morales Moralito, at the corner of Balmaceda and Sotomayor, has departures for San Pedro and Toconao at 4 pm on Tuesdays, Thursdays and Saturdays. Buses depart Toconao for Calama on Wednesdays and Fridays at 8 am and on Sundays at 6 pm. The fare is about US$3.

AROUND SAN PEDRO DE ATACAMA
Valley of the Moon

On the other side of the Salar is the famous Valley of the Moon, so-called because of its strange, wind-sculptured rock formations (yes, I know there's no wind on the moon!), all in glorious technicolour. It's about eight km from the oasis and you touch its southern end when you drive in from Calama. The best time to see the valley is supposed to be at sunset or when there's a full moon and the light reflects off the salt crystals in the rocks and mounds.

Quitor Ruins

Just three km north-west of San Pedro, bordering the river of the same name, is the ruin of an Indian fortress built over 700 years ago. From the top of the fortress you can see the whole of the oasis. The turret of this fortress was the residence of the last Indian chief of the area, and the fortress was also the last bastion against Pedro de Valdivia and the Spanish. Archaeologists have rebuilt parts of the ruined walls and it's possible to gauge some idea of what the place looked like originally.

Termas de Puritama

About 30 km from the village, en route to El Tatio, there are some hot springs, the Termas de Puritama. These are well worth a visit and you'll usually have them to yourself.

There are no buses to the springs so unless you have your own transport you have to arrange transport with the drivers of the sulphur-mine trucks. The sulphur mines are past the hot springs and the trucks leave San Pedro every day at around 8 am. You ride in the back of the truck and the journey takes about an hour (it's a fairly cold, rough ride). They'll let you off at a sign for the springs, on the left hand side of the road. The charge for the truck ride varies, but a dollar or two for a couple of people should suffice.

From where you are put down it's a 20-minute walk along an obvious gravel track down into a small canyon. The temperature of the springs is about 33°C and there are a number of waterfalls and pools to choose from. Bring food and drinks with you.

You can stay all night if you like but there's precious little fuel for a fire (and it gets very cold!) though there are a number of ruined stone buildings for shelter. If you don't want to stay, simply get back up to the main track by 1 pm and flag down the first truck which comes by. On the return journey you may be dropped off several km short of San

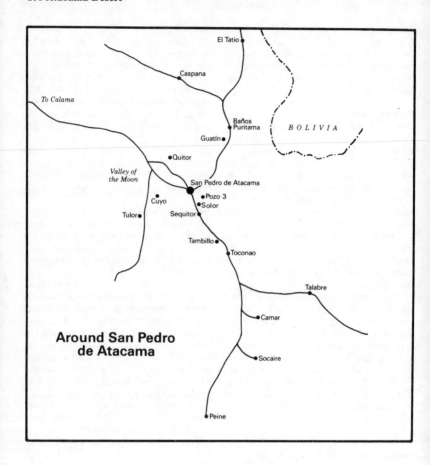

Around San Pedro de Atacama

Pedro, at the mine's crushing plant, so you'll have to walk the rest of the way.

Toconao

If you have time it's worth visiting the village of Toconao, to the south of San Pedro. All the buildings in Toconao are built with volcanic rock. The church in the plaza, with its two-storey bell tower, dates back to the early 1600s. See the Getting There section for transport details.

ANTOFAGASTA

With a population of 250,000, Antofagasta is the largest port and city on the coast of northern Chile. The port handles most of the nitrates and copper mined in the Atacama Desert – in particular the copper from the mine at Chuqui.

The city is also an important import/export centre for Bolivia. Until the War of the Pacific it was actually a part of Bolivia; after the annexation by Chile, Bolivia was given duty-free facilities for the export of its goods.

On a warm evening the centre of the city has a certain understated charm, but there's not much to see or do. For most visitors this city is just a jumping-off point for visits to the Atacama Desert or Bolivia.

Information

Tourist Office The tourist office is at Balmaceda 2786 on the corner of Bolívar, on the sea front. It's a dirty yellow-coloured building. The staff are enthusiastic and eager to help but you have to speak Spanish. They have free maps of the city, of Iquique, and of the surrounding area, as well as bus and train timetables. There's also a municipal tourist kiosk at the junction of Prat and Matta, which has maps of the city.

Bank You may find some street money changers on Prat but don't count on it. The Banco Nacional on Prat between Latorre and San Martín will change US cash, and you may persuade them to change travellers' cheques but, again, don't count on it. The Banco Estado de Chile on the corner of San Martín and Prat seems to be the only bank in town which will change US dollar travellers' cheques and cash.

Post The post office is on Washington between Prat and Sucre, opposite the main plaza.

Consulates The Argentine Consulate (tel 22 2854) is at Manoel Verbal 1632 and is open Monday to Friday from 9 am to 2 pm. Manoel Verbal branches off Grecia which runs along the beach front; the junction of the two is easily identifiable by the small plaza in front of the consulate, with a statue of a naked man (it beats me what he's doing there).

The Bolivian Consulate is at Grecia 563 (Office No 23) (tel 22 1403) and is open Monday to Friday from 8 am to 2 pm. There is another Bolivian Consulate in Calama (see that section for details) so

you can get visas in either place if you're heading to Bolivia.

Things to See

Not much. Have a walk in the area around the railway station (freight only) and the tourist office which is the oldest part of town. There are a number of beaches at the far end of Grecia and further along on Ejército but it's not worth coming to Antofagasta just for them.

Places to Stay – bottom end

Two hotels stand out above the rest for value for money; both are popular with travellers. The first is the *Residencial Paola* at Prat 766, which costs US$2 per person or US$3.65 a double. It's very clean and relaxing; the rooms on the first level are arranged around a central lounge although you'll probably find those on the second level quieter. There's hot water all day and the people are very friendly.

The other is the *Hotel Rawaye*, Sucre 762, which is friendly, clean and excellent value at US$2.50 a single and US$3.30 a double. There's hot water all day in the common bathrooms.

Cheap, but not as good value as the *Paola* or the *Rawaye*, the *Hotel Imperio*, Condell 2736, costs US$2 per person without hot water.

The *Residencial Astor* at Condell 2995 is worth trying. It's clean and it has a pleasant courtyard garden. It costs around US$2.20 per person in a double room. Breakfast is available, and there's hot water in the common bathrooms in the evenings.

The *Residencial O'Higgins* at Sucre 665, is another possibility. Run by a friendly, elderly lady, this is a spacious old building with dimly lit rooms and high ceilings. It's spartan but clean. It's good value at around US$2.50 a single and US$5 a double, although there's only cold water.

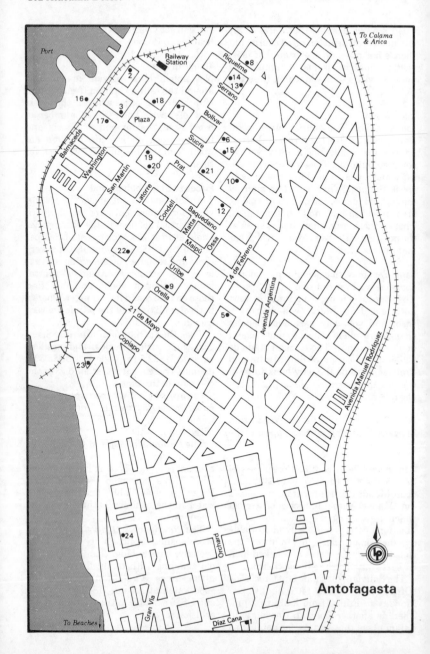

Antofagasta

Places to Stay - middle

On Prat, opposite the Paola, the *Residencial El Cobre* offers very clean and pleasant rooms fronting onto the street for US$5.30 a double. There's gallons of hot water in the common showers. It's a huge place so you'll always find a room.

Try the *Residencial San Marcos* (tel 24124) at Latorre 2946 which costs US$4.70 a single and US$5.30 a double without a private bathroom, and US$6.30 a single and US$7.30 a double with a private bathroom. It's clean to the point of sterility with bright fluorescent lights. There's hot water available in the morning, and a small restaurant attached.

Places to Stay - top end

The pick of the top end hotels is the *Hotel Plaza* (tel 22 2058) at Baquedano 461. Singles start from around US$10, doubles from about US$15, for rooms with a private bathroom and TV. The hotel has its own restaurant and bar, and it seems to be a fairly quiet place.

The *Hotel Antofagasta* (tel 22 4710) on Balmaceda at the junction with Prat has rooms from around US$13 a single and US$17 a double, and rising. Also worth trying, the *Hotel Diego de Almagro* is at the corner of Prat and Condell; singles are around US$14 and doubles are around US$17.

Places to Eat

By far the best place to eat in Antofagasta is the *Sociedad Protectora de Empleados* at San Martín 2544 (opposite the Banco O'Higgins and just off the main plaza). It's very popular with local people at lunch time because of the *enormous* meals; the service is great and the place is spotlessly clean. You're up for several dollars per person but you probably won't get better value anywhere else.

The popular *Apoquindo* at Prat 616 is rather like the Dino's chain you see in southern Chile and serves a good range of drinks, milk shakes, sweets and snacks, but you could end up paying two to three times what a meal costs elsewhere. Other than its long opening hours I can't really understand the reason for its popularity. Another good place for cakes and snacks is *Cari* on Matta between Baquedano and Prat.

For Chinese food try the *Restaurant Chifa Lung Fung* at Sucre 721, where you can get a simple meal for about US$3 per person. Other places which have been suggested are the *Bar Restaurant Los Reyes*, Condell 2540; the *Restaurant Sociedad Italiana*, Prat 730, which offers cheap lunches and slightly more expensive meals in the evenings; and *Café Oriente*, Baquedano 634, which has a mixture of European and Latin American food.

Getting There

Air LAN-Chile is at Sucre 375 facing the main plaza. Ladeco is at Prat 242. Both have flights from Antofagasta to Arica and Iquique (three days a week), Calama (six days a week) and Santiago (daily).

Bus Although there is a central bus terminal at the junction of Díaz Cana and Orchard, to the south of the main part of town, most bus companies appear to shun it and, instead, retain their own terminals in the centre of town.

Many of these companies have buses to Santiago, Arica and intermediate stops. The best company for buses to Calama (and the Atacama Desert) is Tramaca.

Typical fares from Antofagasta are: Arica US$10.50; Iquique US$9.10; Calama/Chuqui US$3.30; and Santiago US$21.70

Bus companies, addresses and destinations are:

Tramaca, Uribe near the corner with 4 de Febrero; 11 or 12 departures daily to Calama and Chuqui; daily to Arica around 9 pm; twice daily to Santiago; daily to Iquique.

Buses Gemini, Ovalle near the corner with Ossa; three times daily to Calama and Chuqui; every Wednesday to Salta in Argentina.

Flota Barrios, Condell between Bolívar and Sucre; double-decker buses to Santiago; daily bus cama to Santiago for a surprisingly cheap US$27.50; daily to Valparaíso and Viña del Mar.

Buses Pacífico Norte, Bolívar 458; to Santiago and Arica.

Fleche Norte, Condell 2243; to Arica, Santiago, Calama and Chuqui.

Chile Bus & Flota Lila, Riquelme 513; to Santiago and Arica. *Transportes Chile*, Latorre 2720; to Santiago and Arica.

Santiago

Looking down on Santiago from the rocky crag of Santa Lucía it's hard to imagine that just six months after the city was founded by Pedro de Valdivia in 1541, it was almost obliterated by the Mapuche Indians. Several Spanish settlers were killed and legend has it that all their supplies were destroyed bar three hogs, two chickens and two handfuls of corn. The faith of Valdivia was not blunted, however. The Spanish troops were gathered on Santa Lucía and plans were made for the rebuilding of the city while they were still surrounded and outnumbered by the marauding Indians.

For two years Santa Lucía was the capital of a tiny fortified country the size of a postage stamp, its houses built of adobe to guard against fire, its inhabitants on the brink of starvation and under repeated attack from the Indians. Not until 1543 did any help arrive from Peru. Valdivia attempted to expand his colony but the new force was still inadequate, and he returned to Peru to seek new troops and supplies. These enabled him to push southwards: Concepción was founded by him in 1550 and Valdivia in 1552.

The new settlements were no more than fortified villages. In Santiago, many of the houses were built around central courtyards, often planted with gardens or fruit trees, although open sewers ran down the middle of the streets. As the settlements gradually became more secure, soldiers formed households with Indian women, and craftsmen like shoemakers, blacksmiths, armorers and tanners moved in to supply the settlers. In their early years the towns served as administrative centres for the new colony and base camps for further bloody forays into Mapuche territory. The majority of the colony's population, however, did not live in the towns but in the countryside,

on the encomiendas or at the mines.

By the end of the 16th century Santiago was a settlement of just 200 houses, inhabited by 500 to 700 Spaniards and mestizos and several thousand Indian labourers and servants. It was occasionally flooded by the Mapocho River; it lacked a safe drinking supply; and communications with, and travel into, the countryside was difficult. Despite their precarious position the wealthy colonists sought to emulate the lifestyle of European nobility, accumulating servants and importing luxury goods from Europe and China. The colony was short on ammunition, weapons and horses, and it had just lost all its territory south of the Bío Bío River to Indian counter-attacks, but in wealthy houses you could find velvet, silk and other luxuries.

Chile remained a backwater of the Spanish empire for the next three centuries, an appendage of the Viceroyalty of Peru, yielding few minerals or metals of any value. As the colonial period drew to a close at the end of the 18th century Chile's population – including the 100,000 or so independent Indians south of the Bío Bío – was maybe 500,000, of which 90% lived in the countryside. Santiago was a backwater town of 30,000 people whose nearest competitors were overgrown villages. The city streets were still unpaved, and the country roads were still pot-holed trails. There were few schools and public libraries. The University of San Felipe, founded in 1758, chiefly as a law school, provided a few intellectuals, but cultural and intellectual life was weak.

It was not until the last quarter of the 18th century that Santiago began to be shaped into a city, with new dykes to restrain the Mapocho River, improved roads between Santiago and Valparaíso

The founding of Santiago, from an old banknote

to handle increased commerce, and various beautification projects. The city became the home for the colonial aristocracy. By the 19th century a railway and telegraph line linked Santiago, now a large town of over 100,000 people, and Valparaíso, a bustling port and commercial centre of over 60,000 people.

Sumptuous houses were built, and adorned with imported luxuries; prestigious social clubs and societies were established; and the very wealthy maintained haciendas as holiday retreats. Social life for the rich revolved around the clubs, the racing season, the opera, or outings to the exclusive Parque Cousino. Chile was governed by gentlemen who valued civility, tradition and good-

breeding, who sent their children to be educated in Europe – but who could always accept new blood and new money into their ranks when they needed it.

From its humble and bloody beginnings, Santiago has grown to be the fourth-largest city in South America. Ask a Chilean where he lives and there's a one-in-three chance it will be Santiago; the metropolitan area and surrounding districts contain something like 4,300,000 people. The growth of the city from its original boundaries to the sprawling mass of the present day is well documented in the Museo de Santiago in the Casa Colorado off Santiago's Plaza de Armas.

Santiago is situated in what is known as the Chilean 'Heartland' or 'Central

Valley'. The valley contains about 70% of the country's total population, provides most of its industrial jobs, and even accounts for a sizeable share of its copper production. At its widest the valley measures only some 70 km between the Andes and the coastal mountains and the sea; only at its southernmost boundary does the flat valley floor extend all the way to the Pacific. Endowed with rich soil and a pleasant Mediterranean climate, the valley is ideal for cereal farming, fruit production, vineyards, and livestock grazing.

For much of Chilean history the central valley has been dominated by a relatively small number of large estates, only a minority of which had taken up modern agricultural practices by the mid-1960s. After 1964, large-scale agrarian reform programmes expropriated the estates from their owners and created co-operatives. After the military coup of 1973 many of the large farms were handed back to their former owners and efforts were made to break up the remaining co-operatives into individual family farms.

The growth of Santiago, and other Chilean cities, is very much a product of the oppression in the countryside. Poverty, lack of opportunity, and the stifling haciendas drove rural workers north to the mines and into the cities in search of work. Between 1865 and 1875, Santiago's population increased from 115,000 to more than 150,000 and Valparaíso's increased from 60 or 70,000 to almost 100,000. The increase was mainly due to domestic migration. The trend continued in the 20th century and by the mid-1970s over 70% of all Chileans lived in cities with over 200,000 inhabitants, most of them in the central valley.

Rapid industrialisation after WW II offered jobs in the cities but there were never enough to satisfy demand. Continued dissatisfaction in the countryside led to further emigration to the cities during the 1960s and this resulted in the growth of squatter settlements (the *callampas* or 'mushroom' settlements) and shanty houses which ringed the major cities of the central valley. Planned decentralisation has managed to ease some of the pressure on Santiago, and housing projects have managed to eliminate many callampas. In stark contrast to the economic depression of the poor and lower-income districts there are the fine houses and suburbs for the rich: El Golf, Vitacura, La Reina, Las Condes and Lo Curro.

As for *el presidente*, work started on his new residence at Lo Curro in 1979 and is estimated to have cost between US$13 million and US$18 million; public opinion has kept him from moving in. In 1984 opposition leaders laid charges of corruption against Pinochet in the Supreme Court, claiming that the land had been obtained for an artificially low price after it had been bought with public money. The government reacted by threatening to sue the litigants for 'injury' to the resident, and the judge ruled that he did not have the constitutional power to try the president. A few days later the litigants appealed and also brought a second case which claimed that Pinochet had defrauded the state of US$30,000 in the purchase of land adjoining his residence at Melocoton on the outskirts of Santiago.

The centre of Santiago is set out in monotonous, right-angled blocks, too narrow for the impatient peak-hour traffic. Seen from the vantage points of Santa Lucía or San Cristóbal, the centre juts out of an immense sea of low, flat roofs, overhung by a thick pall of smog. It's a city which descends, rather than grows, on you. The smog can completely hide the Andes from view.

The central triangle of the city is the home to government and public buildings and some very fine colonial architecture (La Moneda, San Francisco and Santo Domingo Cathedrals, and the Casa Colorado, amongst others). There are many beautifully landscaped parks and gardens, artists' colonies, and impressive views over the city to the snow-capped peaks of the Andes – when the weather and smog permit.

Information & Orientation

Although Santiago covers an immense area, the central core of the city is a relatively small, roughly triangular-shaped region bounded in the north by the Río Mapocho, in the west by the Via Norte Sur and in the south by the Avenida del Libertador General Bernardo O'Higgins. The apex of the triangle is the Plaza Baquedano, where O'Higgins forms a junction with two of Santiago's other main thoroughfares, Avenida Providencia and Avenida Vicuña MacKenna.

The centre of this triangle is the Plaza de Armas, the chief plaza of Santiago, bounded on its northern side by the main post office and on the western side by the cathedral. The streets between the Plaza de Armas and O'Higgins are wall to wall shops, restaurants, snack and fast food bars, cinemas, expensive hotels, and office blocks – this is the heart of Santiago. The Presidential Palace, 'La Moneda' is on Avenida Moneda, facing the Plaza de la Constitución. Near the Plaza de Armas is the National Congress Building – though congress has not sat since the coup.

One of Santiago's main parks – Cerro Santa Lucía – can be found in the triangle, facing O'Higgins. The other main park is Cerro San Cristóbal, a mountain which rises dramatically from the plain, to the north of Avenida Providencia. Between this avenue and the mountain, on either side of the Avenida Pío Nono, is Santiago's Paris quarter.

Tourist Office The tourist office at Catedral 1159 (tel 60474), opposite the National Congress, is open Monday to Friday from 9 am to 5 pm and, in summer, on Saturdays from 9 am to 1 pm. The staff are friendly and helpful and they have a range of good maps and other information including lists of restaurants and bars, transport out of Santiago, hotels, museums, art galleries, and leaflets on other parts of the country. English is spoken.

There is a tourist information kiosk at the junction of Huérfanos and Ahumada which is open on Saturday mornings. There is also a tourist information office at Pudahuel Airport – it's inside the terminal. They're well stocked with leaflets on all parts of Chile; pick up the very useful map *Plano del Centro de Santiago*. English is spoken.

Bank There are a number of *casas de cambio* on Agustinas between Bandera and Ahumada, which will change travellers' cheques and foreign cash. There is a bank and some money exchange offices at the airport next to the tourist office as you exit from Customs.

The easiest way to change money if you have US cash is to walk down Agustinas or Huérfanos in the city centre. There are numerous money changers along these two streets. Once you've agreed on a rate they'll often take you to offices in nearby buildings where the transaction takes place – there's no problem with this and it's much better for both parties. These people usually accept travellers' cheques but the rate isn't so good; it's best to change cheques to US cash at a bank (you can do this in Chile) then change the cash with the money changers.

Take American Express cheques to the American Express International Banking Corporation. Agustinas 1360, where you can get US cash for 1% commission. Pay the commission in Chilean pesos, and then change the dollars on the street.

Thomas Cook has an office at Agustinas 1058 but it only deals with replacing lost and stolen cheques. Go to the Casa de Cambio Andes Ltda, Agustinas 1036, who will change US dollar Thomas Cook travellers' cheques for US cash.

Post & Communications The main post office is on the Plaza de Armas in the centre of the city. The poste restante is also here and is well organised. If you are posting packages and parcels from this office, make sure you read the instructions about how to go about it, otherwise you'll queue up only to be told your parcel is not acceptable (glued brown wrapping paper isn't acceptable – you must use tape). The post office is open Monday to Friday 8 am to 8 pm; Saturday 8 am to 6 pm; and Sunday 9 am to 2 pm.

Long distance overseas phone calls can be made from Entel Chile (Overseas Service) at Huérfanos 1133, which is open Monday to Friday 8.30 am to 10 pm, and Saturdays and Sundays 9 am to 2 pm.

Telegrams and telexes can be sent from the office on Morande, just near the corner with Agustinas facing the Plaza de la Constitución, which is open Monday to Friday 8.30 am to 8.30 pm, Saturday 8.30 am to 5.30 pm, and Sunday 9 am to 1 pm.

Maps The *Plano del Centro de Santiago* is available free from the tourist information office; it covers the central core and inner suburbs of the city and also includes a map of the metro system. It's detailed, clear, readable and easy to use.

The best maps of Chile come from the Instituto Geográfico Militar de Chile, which has a retail outlet at O'Higgins 240, near the Holiday Inn Crowne Plaza Hotel.

Trekking For trekking information and details of refugios in the national parks go to the national parks office at Corporación Nacional Forestal (CONAF), General Bulnes 285.

The Federación de Andinismo de Chile, Almirante Simpson 77, just off Avenida Vicuña MacKenna, caters for those interested in mountaineering in the Andes and the people are very friendly.

Embassies A number of countries have consulates in several Chilean cities, with Peru, Bolivia and Argentina being particularly well represented. Some western countries are represented in smaller cities: Temuco, for example, has consulates from Germany, Spain, France, Holland and Italy. Most other countries have a consulate or embassy in Santiago:

Argentina
    Vicuña MacKenna 41, near the junction with O'Higgins (tel 222 6853)
Australia
    Gertrudis Echenique 420 (tel 228 5065)
Austria
    Barros Errázuriz 1968 (3rd floor) (tel 223 4774)
Belgium
    Providencia 2653 (tel 232 1071)
Bolivia
    Avenida de Santa María 2796 (tel 232 8180)
Brazil
    MacIver 225 (15th floor) (tel 39 8867)
Canada
    Ahumada 11 (10th floor) (tel 696 2256)
France
    Condell 65 (tel 225 1030)
Germany (West)
    Agustinas 785 (7th floor) (tel 33 5031)
Holland
    Las Violetas 2368 (tel 223 6826)
Israel
    Merced 136 (7th floor) (tel 38 4186)
Japan
    Avenida Providencia 2653 (tel 232 1807)
New Zealand
    Isidora Goyenechea 3516
Paraguay
    Huérfanos 886 (Apt 514) (tel 39 4640)
Peru
    Andrés Bello 1751 (tel 49 0045)
Switzerland
    José Miguel de la Barra 563 (tel 32009)
Uruguay
    Pedro de Valdivia 711 (tel 223 8398)
United Kingdom
    La Concepción 177 (4th floor) (tel 223 9166)
United States of America
    Merced 230 (tel 71 0133 ext 255)

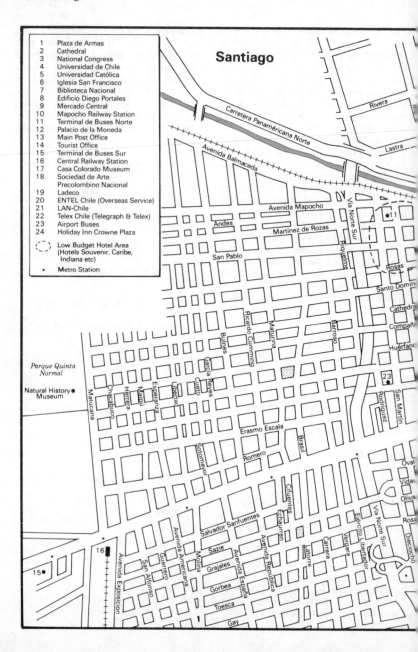

Santiago

1 Plaza de Armas
2 Cathedral
3 National Congress
4 Universidad de Chile
5 Universidad Católica
6 Iglesia San Francisco
7 Biblioteca Nacional
8 Edificio Diego Portales
9 Mercado Central
10 Mapocho Railway Station
11 Terminal de Buses Norte
12 Palacio de la Moneda
13 Main Post Office
14 Tourist Office
15 Terminal de Buses Sur
16 Central Railway Station
17 Casa Colorado Museum
18 Sociedad de Arte
   Precolombino Nacional
19 Ladeco
20 ENTEL Chile (Overseas Service)
21 LAN-Chile
22 Telex Chile (Telegraph & Telex)
23 Airport Buses
24 Holiday Inn Crowne Plaza

⊂⊃ Low Budget Hotel Area
   (Hotels Souvenir, Caribe,
   Indiana etc)

• Metro Station

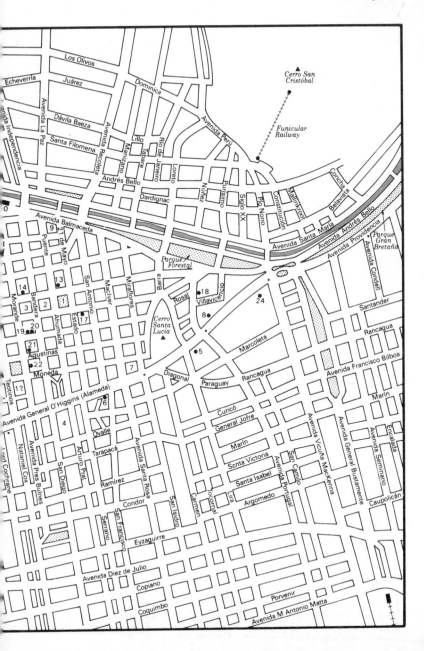

Airlines There are a large number of airlines with offices in Santiago:

Aerolíneas Argentinas
  Moneda 756 (tel 39 3922)
AeroPerú
  Teatinos 335 (tel 71 5035)
Air France
  Agustinas 1136 (tel 72 5333)
Alitalia
  Alameda 949 (tel 698 3336)
Avianca
  Moneda 118 (tel 71 4105)
British Caledonian
  Agustinas 1243 (tel 87538)
Canadian Pacific
  Huérfanos 669 (tel 39 3058)
Eastern Airlines
  Huérfanos 1199 (tel 71 3004)
Ecuatoriana
  Bernardo O'Higgins (tel 696 4251)
Iberia
  Agustinas 1115 (tel 71 4510)
KLM
  Agustinas 802 (tel 39 8001)
Ladeco
  Huérfanos 1157 (tel 71 2960)
LAN-Chile
  Agustinas 1197 (tel 72 3523)
LAP
  Huérfanos 1160 (tel 72 1142)
Líneas Aéreas Paraguayas
  Agustinas 1080 (tel 72 1142)
Lufthansa
  Agustinas 1080 (tel 72 2686)
Lloyd Aereo Boliviano
  Moneda 1170 (tel 71 2334)
Pan American
  Bernardo O'Higgins 949 (23rd floor) (tel 699 0055)
SAS
  Miraflores 178 (15th floor) (tel 39 1105)
Swissair
  Agustinas 1046 (tel 698 1848)
Varig
  Miraflores 156 (tel 39 5976)
Viasa
  Agustinas 1141 (tel 698 2401)

Things to See & Do

You can still find some of the landmarks which Valdivia used to lay out the boundaries of the original city. To the east is the Huelen, today called Cerro Santa Lucía; to the north is the Río Mapocho; to the south is what used to be the San Lazaro Causeway, now the city's main thoroughfare, the Avenida Bernardo O'Higgins.

Cerro Santa Lucía

The Cerro Santa Lucía is a decorated hill in the city centre, honeycombed with gardens, footpaths, plazuelas and fountains and crowned by the remains of a fortress with fine views over the city and away to the snow-capped Andes. Local people will advise you not to walk here after dark as muggings are not unknown, but it's perfectly safe during the day and entry is free. At the foot of the hill, on the Alameda, a large stone is engraved with the text of a letter that was sent to the King of Spain by Pedro de Valdivia extolling the beauty of the newly conquered territories.

Cerro San Cristóbal

The Cerro San Cristóbal is a peak which sprouts from the plain on the other side of the Mapocho River. It's much higher than Santa Lucía and is crowned by a white statue of the Virgin (similar in some ways to Corcovado in Rio). There is a funicular railway, built in 1925, which takes you to the 485-metre summit. The return fare is US$0.55 though you can also buy one-way tickets if you prefer to walk back down or take the minibus. It's in operation every day of the year from around 10.30 am to the late afternoon or early evening (up to 8 pm on Sundays). You board the railway at Plaza Caupolicán, which you get to by heading straight up Pio Nono.

There's also a cable car service to the summit from the Estación Oasis Teleférico on Avenida Pedro de Valdivia Norte (metro station Pedro de Valdivia) which is open the same hours as the funicular railway and costs around US$1.35 return (one-way tickets are also available). Or there's the minibus service for about US$0.35 one-way which can be picked up

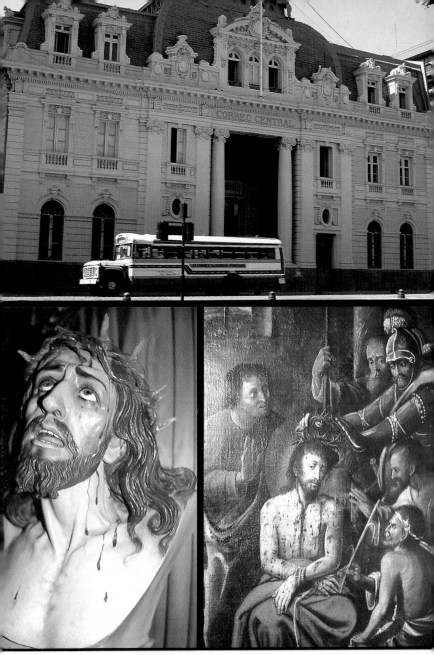

Top: Post Office, Plaza de Armas, Santiago
Left: Statue, Iglesia de San Franciso, Castro
Right: Museum painting, Iglesia de San Francisco, Santiago

Top: One of the oldest churches in Chile, San Pedro de Atacama
Left: Church, Chol Chol, near Temuco
Right: Iglesia de San Francisco, Castro

at Plaza Caupolicán, Avenida Pedro de Valdivia and just about anywhere else on the tortuous road to the summit. Don't bother visiting the depressing zoo.

Museums

There are at least two museums worth seeing to get some feel for the history of this place. The first is the **Museo Precolombiano**, Bandera 361, which catalogues 4500 years of South American civilisation before the arrival of the Spanish. It's open Tuesdays to Saturdays from 10 am to 6 pm, Sundays, 10 am to 1 pm, and entry is about US$0.30.

The second is the **Museo de Santiago** housed in the Casa Colorado, a fine colonial building. The growth of the city from its original boundaries to the sprawling mass of the present day is documented in this museum. It's worth visiting for the building as well as the displays. It's at Merced 860 on one corner of the Plaza de Armas and is open Tuesday to Saturday from 10 am to 1 pm and 2 to 6 pm and on Sundays, Mondays and holidays from 10 am to 1 pm; entry is about US$0.15.

The Tourist Hike

The tourist circuit (and its obligatory 'sights') starts at the northern side of the central triangle with several interesting colonial buildings. Starting at the **Mercado Central** head down 21 de Mayo and take a look at the Posada de Corregidor, the Houses of Velasco and Bernardo O'Higgins and the Iglesia de San Domingo.

The **Posada de Corregidor** is an 18th century colonial building at Esmeralda 732, with a white-washed front and an attractive wooden balcony. It was built in 1780 and is open to the public, although the interior only contains a collection of scenic photos.

Turn the corner at Enrique MacIver and head down San Domingo. Just around the corner is the **Casa Velasco** which is similar to the Posada de Corregidor. Nearby is the **Casa O'Higgins**, home of the first Chilean president. Or head along San Domingo to the **Iglesia de Santo Domingo**, a massive stone church originally built in 1808.

Next is the **Plaza de Armas** which is the centre of the city, flanked by the **Correo Central** (Post Office), the **Museo Histórico Nacional** and the massive **Catedral**. The **Museo Catedral** is on Bandera, and houses collections of colonial religious ornaments; it's only open on Wednesdays from 10 to 12 am and 3.30 to 7 pm.

Between Bandera and Morande stands the **Congreso Nacional** which has not sat since 1973. At the corner of Morande and Catedral is the **Palacio Edwards** which is now used for government administration offices. Immediately behind the Congreso Nacional on Compañía is the **Tribunales de Justicia** (Law Courts).

A short walk westwards along Compañía brings you to a Moorish-style building called the **Palacio de la Ahlambra** at Compañía 1340; this houses paintings and is open Monday to Friday between 11 am and 1 pm and 5.30 to 8 pm. Or head east to the **Museo de Arte Pre-Colombino**.

Leading south from one corner of the plaza is the Paseo de Ahumada which is the main mall of Santiago. It's a street market with dozens of pavement hawkers flogging everything from plywood models of clipper ships to pan pipes and seat belts. Buskers congregate in the evening, and you can hear anything from solo bagpipers to gypsy opera ensembles and Chilean folk groups.

The chief government building is the **Palacio de la Moneda**, a hornet's nest of police and military, set behind the Plaza de la Constitución. It was badly damaged during the coup when it was bombed by air force jets, but it has since been restored.

Turning east up O'Higgins takes you to the **Universidad de Chile**. Next up is the unmistakable **Iglesia de San Francisco** and inside, the **Museo del Arte Colonial**, which houses colonial art and paintings depicting the curing of lepers and bloody representations of the crucifixion. The church is one of Santiago's oldest buildings – originally built in the second half of the 16th century, and later enlarged to its present size. The museum is open every day, except Mondays, from 10 am to 1 pm, and from 3 to 6 pm. Further up on the other side of the road is the monolithic **Biblioteca Nacional** at the corner with Santa Rosa.

Parks

I don't normally rate parks a mention but the **Parque Quinta Normal** at the western edge of the triangle is an interesting one. It's open Tuesday to Sunday from 7.30 am to 8.30 pm. Get there by taking the metro to Estación Central and then catching a bus up Matucana.

On the southern boundary of the park at Avenida Portales 3530 is the **Museo Aeronáutica** (Aeronautical Museum) which is housed in a bizarre building which was built for the Paris Exhibition of 1900, and later installed opposite the Quinta Normal. Even if you're not the least bit interested in aircraft it's worth seeing the building itself – it looks rather like a cross between a Greek temple, the Albert Hall, the Taj Mahal and a beehive. It's open Tuesday to Friday from 9 am to 12 noon and 2 to 5 pm, Sunday 10 am to 1 pm and 3 to 6 pm, and is closed on Saturdays and Mondays.

In the park is the **Museo Nacional de Historia Natural** which is open Tuesday to Saturday from 10 am to 12.30 pm and 2 to 5.30 pm, and Sundays and holidays 2 to 5.30 pm. Exhibits include the body of a 12-year-old child who was sacrificed at least 500 years ago and whose body was preserved in ice at the summit of El Plomo, a 5000-metre peak near Santiago. The body was recovered in 1954 by a team from Chile University. Bone fragments from the milodon (giant sloth) found in a cave near Puerto Natales in southern Chile are also on display.

Near the entrance to the park, opposite the Museo Aeronáutica, there's a collection of steam locomotives; open Tuesday to Sunday 11 am to 2 pm and 3 to 6.30 pm.

Places to Stay – bottom end

How much you like a place often depends on where you stay, and Santiago is no exception. This city is liked by some and hated by others, and the chances are that if you hang out in the dank hotels near the northern bus terminal you'll belong to the second group. Even a bare room with the luxury of a window can make a considerable difference to your attitude.

The main budget-hotel area is around the Terminal de Buses Norte, on the corner of General MacKenna and Amunategui. Most of the hotels are on General MacKenna, Amunategui, San Pablo and San Martín and they're mostly gloomy, Dickensian relics in need of major repairs and redecoration. Toilets and bathrooms leave much to be desired and you should avoid putting any undue pressure on the fixtures since they're likely to part company with the wall and end up smashed on the floor. Locks are flimsy, but luckily this is not Lima or Bogota so baggage is relatively safe. Clean sheets are usually provided but you should enquire whether hot showers are included in the price. If they're not, the price can be pushed up by US$1.30 per person!

The area has something of a reputation for being a rough neighbourhood. Many of the hotels at this end of town double as brothels – the northern end of San Martín is where prostitutes hang out, but they don't hassle you. Lone women should be wary about walking around these streets late at night.

Probably one of the best – which is not saying much – is the *Hotel Caribe* (tel 696 6681), San Martín 851. It's clean and, by Santiago standards, good value at around US$2.20 to US$3 a single and US$4 a double, without your own bathroom, but including hot showers. Rooms are bare little boxes with windows that face onto a passageway, so for the most part the rooms are rather dark. Food and drink is available and the manager is friendly and speaks some English. I found this place rather dingy and depressing but that depends on what room you get; most travellers think it's good value. There are token locks on the doors, but you can leave valuables in the safe, although I'd be reluctant to trust the staff with cash.

The *Hotel Indiana*, Rosas 1334, is similar and costs US$2.60 per person in double rooms without a bathroom, and US$4.60 per person in double rooms with a bathroom. Hot water is included in the price and the hotel is clean and well run, but I thought it was somewhat overpriced for what it offered.

The only other cheapie in this area which can be seriously suggested is the *Hotel Souvenir*, Amunategui 856. To like this place you need to be the sort of person who has a fascination for antediluvian plumbing fixtures, 25-watt light bulbs and undulating wooden stairs and corridors which attest to the carpenter's triumph over earthquakes, riot, civil commotion, and Acts of God. It has clean sheets, hot showers all day (take matches with you to the bathroom to re-light the gas pilot light), it's secure, despite the appearance of the doors, and it costs US$1.60 to $2 a single and US$3.80 a double without a bathroom.

There are a number of other hotels in this area with rooms resembling prison cells. These include the *MacKenna*, MacKenna 1471, which costs slightly more than the Hotel Souvenir. On the same street, the *Hotel Retiro*, MacKenna 1264, has singles for around US$2.70 and doubles for US$4.50 – hot showers cost another US$0.60 per person. It's a reasonably clean place (there's not much to get dirty) and if you're stuck this will probably do. Rubbing shoulders with the Retiro are a number of similar places including the *Hotel Colonial*, MacKenna 1414, and the *Hotel Florida*, MacKenna 1250, both with rooms for around US$2 per person.

Of all these places I'd probably go for the *San Felipe*, MacKenna 1248 which has singles for about US$3.30 and doubles for about US$5.60 – hot showers cost an extra US$1.30 per person. It's outright banditry for the hot water, but at least some attempt has been made to make the cells look half tolerable. Whatever you do, avoid the front rooms of all these hotels; MacKenna is a main street and buses storm down it day and night.

Outside this area there is one place which can be wholeheartedly recommended and is very popular with travellers.

This is the *Residencial Londres* (tel 38 2215) Londres 54, very close to the San Francisco church on O'Higgins (Calle Londres runs down the side of the church). It's great value and worth the walk; costs are about US$2.20 per person in rooms without a bathroom, and US$4.40 a double with a bathroom. There's hot water (no extra charge) all day, the rooms are secure and spotlessly clean, and the staff are pleasant and helpful. There's also a lounge with a TV. Get there as early as possible if you want a room – it's popular with local people too. This is the best hotel in Santiago for the price and the facilities offered. The place looks closed but it *is* operating; just ring the bell at the side of the door and wait for someone to let you in.

If you're only staying overnight in Santiago for less than 12 hours then – if you're a couple – check if the *Vegas Hotel* (tel 38 3225) at Londres 49 is still operating. It's a high-class whorehouse but they have double rooms equipped with huge double beds, crisp, clean sheets, music and soft lighting. Each room has spotless showers, bidets and toilets (towels and toilet paper provided) and carpeted floors and walls (yes, even the walls!). It's a bargain at US$4 per person per 12-hour period especially if you've just suffered a long and tiring journey. Don't overstay the 12 hours or they'll hit you for another US$4 each!

Places to Stay – middle

Santiago hotels don't really come into their own until you get into the mid-range prices – say US$10 a single and US$12 to US$15 a double. At this price you get attractive little rooms with their own bathrooms and toilets, and as you move up a few dollars more there'll usually be a telephone, TV and sometimes even a refrigerator. Places like the Gran Palace Hotel at Huérfanos 1178 and the Hotel Santa Lucía at Huérfanos 779 are typical.

True, if you're a low-budget traveller you probably won't want or need telephones or fridges, but it's worth remembering there *are* alternatives to the shoeboxes near the northern bus terminal. Other mid-range and up-market hotels are listed in a free pamphlet from the tourist office called *Alojamiento – Región Metropolitana*.

One place I'll give an unconditional recommendation is the *Hotel Miami* (tel 71 3112) on Dr Satero del Río 465. This is a small street which runs off Catedral between Teatinos and Morande, just a few blocks down from the Plaza de Armas – so you can't get much more central. Singles are about US$6.70 and doubles are from US$8.70; the rooms are clean and have attached bathrooms, and the manager is friendly and welcomes foreigners. If you want something slightly up-market or can't stand the bottom end of Santiago any longer, this is the place to go.

Otherwise, the cheapest alternative you'll find in the middle of the city is the *Hotel Sao Paulo* (tel 39 8031), San Antonio 357, which has singles from US$5.50 and doubles from US$7.20. Rooms with an attached bathroom only cost about a dollar more. It's a bit dingy but it's extremely well located and, apart from the Miami, you won't get much better in this price range.

Bright and clean, with friendly staff, the *Hotel Cervantes* (tel 67966) at Morande 631, has singles from US$6.70 and doubles from US$10.50 – including a bathroom. There's hot water all day, the staff are friendly and the hotel has its own snackbar and restaurant.

Slightly more expensive, the *Hotel Ritz* (tel 31091) at Estado 248, has been recommended; singles are from US$10 and doubles are from about US$12. Also try the *Hotel Panamericano* (tel 72 3060), Teatinos 320, which is about US$11 a single and US$14.50 a double.

My pick of the hotels in this range is the *Hotel Monte Carlo* (tel 39 2945), Victoria Subercaseaux 209, opposite the Cerro

Santa Lucía. Singles cost from US$12, doubles from US$13.30; they're small rooms, but the place is bright and clean, the staff are friendly, and the rooms have attached bathrooms. If noise bothers you, it may be wise to go elsewhere as there seems to be quite a bit of traffic on this street.

The *Hotel Santa Lucía* (tel 39 8201) Huérfanos 779, is good value at around US$15 a single and US$20 a double: attractive rooms with TV, telephone, refrigerator and attached bathrooms. The staff are friendly. The *Hotel Gran Palace* (tel 71 2551), Huérfanos 1178, is a similar standard but slightly cheaper at US$12 a single and US$15 a double.

Its also worth trying the *City Hotel* (tel 72 4526) Compañía 1063, which has singles for about US$13, and doubles for about US$16; and the *Hotel Libertador* (tel 39 4211) O'Higgins 853, opposite the San Francisco church which has singles for US$12 and doubles US$15.50.

Places to Stay - top end

Santiago has a large number of international class hotels, including most of the well-known chains, equipped with restaurants, cafés and bars. A number of top class hotels also have money change services for their customers.

The *Hotel Tupahue* (tel 38 3810) is at San Antonio 477, and has singles from about US$29 and doubles from about US$35.

The *Hotel Conquistador* (tel 39 6231) is at Miguel Cruchaga 920, which is a small street which runs off Estado near the junction with O'Higgins. Singles with breakfast start from around US$36, and doubles with breakfast from around US$44.

The *Hostal del Parque* (tel 39 2694) is at Merced 294, at the junction with Lastarria and in front of the Sociedad de Arte Precolombiano Nacional. Singles are from US$59 and doubles are from US$70 – plus 20% tax.

The *Hotel Carrera* (tel 698 2011)

Teatinos 180, is one of a matching-pair of monoliths which overlook La Moneda and the Plaza de la Constitución. Singles range between US$65 and US$75, and doubles are from US$75 to US$85.

If external appearances are anything to go by then try the glittering *Hotel Galerías* (tel 38 4011) San Antonio 65; singles are US$65 and doubles are US$75, plus 20% tax.

The *Holiday Inn Crowne Plaza* (tel 38 1042) O'Higgins 136, near the junction with Vicuña MacKenna, has singles which start from about US$74 and doubles from about US$88, including the 20% government tax. A penthouse suite will set you back US$540 a single, or US$600 a double!

The *Sheraton San Cristóbal* (tel 74 5000) Santa María 1742, at the junction with Calle El Cerro, has singles from US$86, doubles from US$97 – plus 20% tax.

Places to Eat

There are a phenomenal number of places to eat in Santiago, especially around the bus stations, the pedestrian streets of Huérfanos and Ahumada, the Plaza de Armas and along the Alameda O'Higgins. You can find Italian pasta, Indian curries, stuffed vineleaves, Chilean *parrilladas* and shoddy imitations of McDonalds. The tourist office has a pamphlet listing many of these restaurants – it doesn't actually tell you anything other than their location and the cuisine served, but it gives you an idea of what's available.

For cheap eats, snacks, drinks and cakes there's a whole string of places shoulder to shoulder in the arcade on Plaza de Armas. Try the *Pollo Montserrat* for cheap fried chicken. The *Chez Henri* in the Plaza de Armas gets rave reviews from travellers. It will cost about US$1.30 for a main meal, a litre of wine is US$0.40 or so, and there's fresh baked bread, and all sorts of ice cream at US$0.20.

Many travellers have recommended the *Bar Central* at San Pablo 1063. It's popular with local people and has good seafood and generous portions, but you may find it relatively expensive. The *Los Alemanes*, Huérfanos between Estado and San Antonio, and close to the Sylvestre, is also recommended for seafood. You can get a huge portion of fish with trimmings plus wine for a few dollars. It's popular with young people so be early if you want a table on the very popular mezzanine. Chicken and steaks are equally good.

The best self-serve place in town is the *Sylvestre*, Huérfanos 956. You can eat enough to last you all day for a few dollars. They dish up ravioli, rice, mixed vegetables, tortillas, fried chicken, deserts and drinks – and they're generous portions. They only serve this sort of food at lunch time; in the evenings it's cocktails and table service.

There's a good Italian restaurant, the *San Marco*, at Huérfanos 618, just near the corner with Miraflores. It's relatively expensive and a full meal including a main course, desert, coffee and drinks will probably set you back US$6 – but if you don't mind the price it's a good choice.

Greasy imitations of McDonalds and Kentucky Fried are well represented in Santiago – like the *Burger Inn* chain recognisable by its hamburger logo sporting two cow's heads. The quality of the food varies, and you can't really call them *fast* food. A cheeseburger in one of these places will cost about US$1; a hamburger with the lot about US$1.20.

There are many places for snacks around the northern bus terminal. Try the *El Paso*, San Martín, opposite the Hotel Caribe, which offers cheap, fixed-menu meals at very low prices. Cheap seafood can be tried at the Mercado Central (Central Market) on San Pablo, east of Mapocho Railway Station. Every conceivable form of marine life is sold and there are dozens of tiny restaurants serving endless plates of sea creatures. Dishes are usually already made up and

displayed in windows and prices are usually shown. You have to be quick to escape the restaurant touts and their machine-gun Spanish. There's not much that costs over US$1.50 a plate, which makes it very cheap. A word of warning: The food is usually served raw, covered in salt and vinegar, and if you're not used to it you could be touring Chilean toilets for the next week. If you haven't got a blast-furnace digestion system I'd give this place a wide berth.

A happy hunting-ground for restaurants is Santiago's 'Paris District' – its main street is Pio Nono which runs north from the junction of O'Higgins and Vicuña MacKenna to Cerro San Cristóbal. One of the best in this region is the lovely *Restaurant Los Chinos de Pío Nono*. A Chinese meal will cost from US$2.50 per person depending on what you eat; they also have very cheap set menus at lunchtime, and two people can eat for about US$3. Other places in this area include the Italian *La Fingarella* at 185, and *La Venezia* at 200. About half-way up the Cerro San Cristóbal, alongside the road and cable car line, is the *Salon Bar Tupahue* which is open daily until midnight; as you might expect, drinks and food are rather expensive.

It's worth checking out the *Pérgola de la Plaza* despite its relative expense. It's in the artist's colony on Victorino Lastarria 305-321, at the back of the Hostal del Parque; there's a bar and restaurant. The surrounding houses have all been renovated and are used as artists' studios. This is also the location of the *Sociedad de Arte Precolombiano Nacional*. The complex is largely a collection of art and handicrafts shops, with a museum taking up a small part of it.

Getting There

As the capital of such a long, skinny country you can't really detour around Santiago, even if you want to. Santiago is either your introduction to Chile or a place you have to pass through.

Air Ladeco (tel 71 2960) is at Huérfanos 1157. Lan Chile (tel 72 3523) is at Agustinas 1197.

Ladeco has flights from Santiago north to Antofagasta, Iquique and Arica (daily), to Calama (about six days a week), and south to Concepción (daily), Osorno and Temuco (three or four times a week), and Puerto Montt and Punta Arenas (daily).

LAN-Chile has flights from Santiago to Antofagasta (daily), Calama (about six days a week), Iquique and Arica (daily), Puerto Montt and Punta Arenas (daily), and Easter Island (see the Easter Island chapter for details).

For fares and details of international services see the Getting There and Getting Around chapters.

Bus - domestic There are two bus terminals in Santiago. The Terminal de Buses Norte, at the corner of General Mackenna and Amunategui, is for buses heading north and to Mendoza in Argentina. There is no metro access to this station.

Southbound buses use the Terminal de Buses Sur, Alameda General O'Higgins 3800. The easiest way to get there is to take the metro to the Universidad de Santiago station – this used to be called the Universidad Técnica. The Terminal de Buses Sur actually consists of two terminals on adjacent blocks – the main terminal and a smaller one known as 'Alameda'. The latter only handles two companies, the main one being Tur-Bus which is a luxury bus company with services to Valparaíso, Viña del Mar and various destinations in the Lake District such as Temuco, Valdivia, Osorno, Villarrica and Puerto Montt.

Sometimes the same bus company will have north and southbound buses, and you can usually buy tickets at either bus terminal – including tickets to other South American countries – but you will have to catch northbound buses from the Terminal de Buses Norte and southbound buses from the Terminal de Buses Sur.

Fares vary from company to company and often special discounts may be offered. Typical fares from Santiago are:

Ancud – US$15.00
Angol – US$6.70
Antofagasta – US$20.00
Arica – US$30.60
Castro – US$16.10
Cauquenes – US$5.00
Chañaral – US$13.90
Chillán – US$5.00
Concepción – US$6.40
Copiapó – US$11.10
El Salvador – US$7.80
Iquique – US$25.00
La Serena – US$7.80
Los Angeles – US$6.40
Osorno – US$11.90
Pucón – US$9.60
Puerto Montt – US$13.60
Puerto Varas – US$13.60
Río Bueno – US$11.90
San Fernando – US$2.10
Talcahuano – US$ 6.40
Talca – US$3.50
Temuco – US$8.60
Valdivia – US$10.60
Vallenar – US$10.60
Valparaíso – US$2.00
Villarrica – US$9.60
Viña del Mar – US$2.00

Journey times can be quite formidable if you try to reach some of these places in one bus trip. Heading north, approximate travel times include: Arica, 27-28 hours; Iquique, 25 hours; and Antofagasta, 15-18 hours. Heading south, approximate travel times include: Concepción, 7-9 hours; Temuco, 10-11 hours; Valdivia, 13-14 hours; Osorno, 14 hours; Puerto Montt 16 hours.

Companies which cover northern destinations include Flota Barrios, Tramaca, Fenix Pullman Norte, Chile Bus, Flecha Norte, Buses Carmelita and Tarapacá.

Companies which cover southern

destinations include Buses Norte, Tas Choapa, Tur-Bus, Cruz del Sur, ETC, Transbus, Igi Llama, Turibús, Pullman Lit, Vía Tur and Nuevo Longitudinal Sur.

Bus - international Amongst the many possibilities available are direct buses to Brazil. The Pluma company runs buses from Santiago to Rio de Janeiro via Mendoza, Rosario, Santa Fe, Paraná, Paso de Los Libres, Uruguaiana, Porto Alegre, Florianopolis, Curitisa and Sao Paulo. The fare to Rio is about US$79 and the trip takes about three days; the fare to Sao Paulo is about US$75 and the trip takes about 2½ days. There are departures about four times a week.

A number of companies run buses to Argentina and typical fares include: Buenos Aires US$48, Mendoza US$16.70, and Bariloche US$31.70. These companies include Fénix Pullman Norte, Chile Bus and Pluma.

There are also taxi colectivos from Santiago to Mendoza; these leave from the Terminal de Buses Sur and cost about US$18.

Rail Trains south to Concepción, Temuco, Valdivia, Osorno and Puerto Montt leave from Estación Central, Alameda General O'Higgins (take the metro to metro station Estación Central). Trains west to Valparaíso leave from Estación Mapocho, Avenida Balmaceda at the junction with Morande (no metro access).

For trains going south you don't need to go right out to Estación Central to book tickets. You can get them at Venta de Pasajes e Informaciones in the Galería Libertador, Alameda O'Higgins 851, Monday to Friday from 9 am to 6 pm and on Saturday from 9 am to 1 pm. This office is at the end of an arcade which runs off the street – look for the yellow sign.

For details of fares and timetables see the Getting Around chapter at the start of this book.

Getting Around

Airport Transport Arturo Merino Bénitez International Airport is at Pudahuel, 26 km from the city centre. The best way to get between the two is to take the Tour Express (tel 71 7380) bus from the downtown terminal at Moneda 1523 just near the junction with San Martín. They leave every half hour (on the hour and the half hour) from 6.30 am to 9 pm from the city centre, and every half hour from the airport (at 15 minutes to and past the hour) from 7.15 am to 8.15 pm. At other times of the day they meet incoming flights as and when they arrive. The fare is US$0.90 and the journey takes about 30 minutes. Buses from the airport leave from in front of the airport terminal; there's also a taxi rank here. The bus will drop you off at the terminal or just about anywhere en route to it.

Metro Santiago has an excellent metro system with two lines presently in operation. It's the most convenient system of public transport, to be used whenever possible (for example, for the Terminal de Buses Sur, Estación Central, and for the embassies – most of which are in Providencia or Las Condes). The metro operates Monday to Saturday from 6.30 am to 10.30 pm and on Sundays and public holidays from 8 am to 10.30 pm. There are trains at approximately three-minute intervals and the fares are a flat rate of US$0.15 per trip (any distance) or US$1.20 for a book of 10 tickets.

You buy your ticket from the ticket offices at each station. The tickets have a metallic strip on the back and you slip the ticket into a slot in the turnstile. Unlike the systems in Hong Kong and San Francisco the turnstile keeps your ticket and does not return it to you; when you get off at your stop you walk straight through the exit gates.

Buses There is said to be a system to Santiago's buses but it seems to be lost under the weight of numbers, though

Santiago Metro

rumour has it that buses to many destinations can be caught from along MacIver. There are three types of buses: the small fast kind called *liebres* (hares), the regular buses, and the large buses marked *expresso*. All have signs in their front windows displaying their destination and fares are flat rates which range between US$0.20 to US$0.30 or so per ride.

Taxis Santiago taxis are black with yellow roofs and are abundant. Fares are around US$1 per km with a flagfall of about US$1. Taxis are metered and most drivers are honest, although a few will try and rip you off.

Car Rental Budget, Hertz, National and Avis Rent-a-car all have offices in front of the airport terminal. City offices are: Hertz (tel 223 7937), Andrés Bello; National Car Rental (tel 223 2416) La Concepción; Dennys (tel 228 7700), Alonso de Cordova 4357; Budget (tel 38 3689), San Francisco 280. Also, try the Automobile Association of Chile (tel 74 9516, ext 254, and for tourist information

tel 74 9516, ext 223), Pedro de Valdivia 195. For details of rates see the Getting Around chapter.

Tours If your time is limited then consider taking a tour of Santiago and the surrounding region. Rahue Tours in the Holiday Inn Crowne Plaza has tours of Santiago for about US$7.70, and tours to Valparaíso and Viña del Mar for about US$15.50. Tour Service at Huérfanos 1307 has similar tours and itineraries. Gray Line, at the corner of Agustinas and Morande, has city tours, tours to Valparaíso and Viña del Mar, and to various other destinations around Santiago including ski resorts and vineyards.

A Santiago city tour takes in places like the Iglesia de San Francisco, Cerro Santa Lucía and Cerro San Cristóbal. There are also half-day tours to Santiago's major museums including the Pre-Columbian Art Museum, the National Museum of Natural History and the Museum of Colonial Art at the Iglesia de San Francisco. Day tours to Valparaíso and Viña del Mar take in the dock and wharf area, the Naval Academy, Santa María University, the Baburizza Museum of Paintings and the Viña del Mar Casino. The tourist office can fill you in on other tours.

VALPARAISO

A more unlikely place for the country's principal port and second largest city is hard to imagine. The commercial and industrial sector is crammed into a narrow strip of land along the sea front with steep mountains rising abruptly behind it. However steep they might be, they're all covered with suburbs and shanty towns connected by tortuous roads, incredibly long flights of steps and *ascensores* (funicular railways) similar to the ones in Salvador, Brazil. There's poverty in these shanty towns – lots of it – and local people will warn you against displaying any conspicuous wealth if you go wandering around up there. The

19th century Valparaíso architecture

commercial centre, on the other hand, is quite safe and has a sort of cluttered charm with its narrow, winding, cobbled streets, attractive buildings and many sailors' bars and clubs.

Information

Tourist information (maps of the city but not much else) can be obtained from either the municipal building, Condell 1490, or from the kiosk on the quay next to the Customs House.

Things to See

Apart from strolling around the city there's not a great deal to do in Valparaíso – mainly because those with money to spend on pleasure and luxuries go to Viña del Mar to empty their pockets. The contrast between the poverty of Valparaíso and the conspicuous wealth of Viña is like the difference between chalk and cheese. But since this is also a naval base you could take a look at the Museo del Mar, Calle Merlet, which was formerly Lord Cochrane's house and which overlooks the harbour.

Places to Stay

The cheapest place is the *Youth Hostel* at Cuarto Norte 636 which costs US$2 per person, but travellers who have stayed there have called it a dump.

There are very few hotels around the bus terminal itself. Most of them are to be found along Serrano, Cochrane and Blanco close to the Plaza Sotomayor. Try the *Residencial Lily*, Blanco Encalada 866 next to the Bar Inglés or the *Hotel Reina Victoria*, Plaza Sotomayor 190. The latter has rooms for around US$3 to US$4 a single, and US$4 to US$6 a double including breakfast; it's an old building in a fine location and there's hot water.

Similarly priced, the *Garden Hotel* at Serrano 501 is opposite one of the funicular railways and just off the Plaza Sotomayor. It has large, clean rooms with good showers and toilets and it's own restaurant.

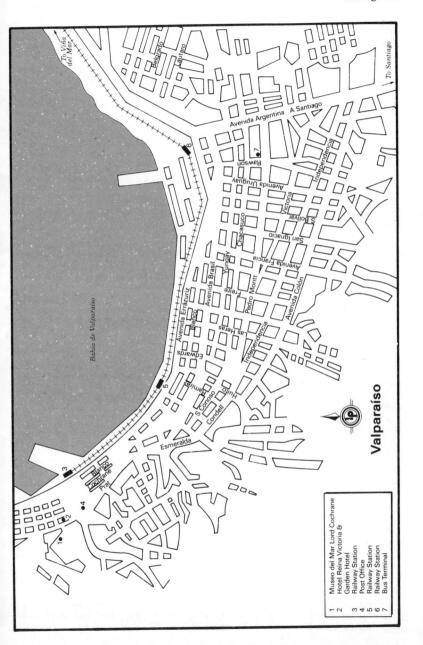

Valparaíso

Getting There

From Santiago the most convenient bus company for Valparaíso and Viña del Mar is Tur-Bus from Santiago's Terminal de Buses Sur. This company has frequent departures every day in either direction from around 6.30 am to 10 pm from Santiago, and from around 6 am to 8.45 pm from Valparaíso and Viña. Some of the buses to Viña go via Valparaíso but others go direct. The two cities are only a few km apart and in any case it's easy to take a local bus between the two. Santiago to Valparaíso takes 1¾ hours, and to Viña about two hours. The fare is the same at around US$2 one-way and US$3.40 return.

The bus terminal in Valparaíso, Terminal Rodoviario, is on Pedro Montt at Rawson. If you're arriving in Valparaíso on a bus which is going to Viña del Mar then you may well be dropped on Avenida Argentina at the junction with Pedro Montt which is one block from the bus terminal.

Alternatively, take the train between Valparaíso and Santiago; it runs along the sea front and through Viña before climbing inland into the hills. There are three or four trains a day between the two cities; they take about three hours and cost US$1.60.

VINA DEL MAR

About nine km round the headland from Valparaíso, Viña del Mar is Chile's premiere beach resort, a sort of Latin American version of Surfer's Paradise or Waikiki Beach. All Chileans with money, and many other wealthy Latin Americans, own houses here. There's even (or there was) a Haitian consulate! Naturally with that sort of clientele you would expect things to be expensive – and they are. The only cheap thing about Viña is getting there. On the other hand, you won't find so much bare flesh roaming the beaches anywhere else in Chile.

Apart from beach-bumming, Viña's other much-touted attraction is the yearly Song Festival, a week-long endurance test akin to the Eurovision Song Contest. Don't bother jetting in especially for the occasion because most of the performers and songs are indistinguishable, even to people with years of musical training. Imagine vacuous cabaret performers, South American folkies especially castrated for the event, and international acts of the calibre of Sheila E (remember Sheila E?), and you get some idea of what you're in for – five nights of rock-solid wanking.

Information

The regional tourist office is at Avenida Valparaíso 507 (3rd floor). There is also a municipal tourist office near the junction of Quillota and Arlegui.

Things to See

The **Museo Naval**, in the castle on the sea front on the Valparaíso side of the Marga Marga estuary, is definitely worth a visit not only for the exhibits (the history of the Chilean navy and especially the War of the Pacific) but also for the building itself. It's open daily from 10 am to 12.30 pm and 3 to 6 pm. Entry is just US$0.10.

The **Palacio Vergara** and the **Museo de Bellas Artes** in the beautifully landscaped Parque Vergara are worth a visit; concerts are performed here in the summer months and this is where the Song Festival is held.

And if you don't have the money to go to Easter Island there's a *moai* (statue) on a traffic island between the Museo Naval and the Hotel Miramar at Caleta Abarca.

Places to Stay

Unless you're lucky enough to meet someone who offers you hospitality at their summer home, then the only cheap place to stay in Viña is the *Youth Hostel* at the Sausalito Stadium. It costs US$0.80 per person but you must have a YH membership card to stay there. Anywhere else is outside the scope of low budget travellers. Viña is an almost entirely modern town with very high real estate values so there are no old centres where you might find budget hotels. If you're determined to spend time in Viña it's much cheaper to stay in Valparaíso and come in everyday on the train or bus.

Getting There
The bus terminal is between Valparaíso and Arlegui one block from Quillota. There are frequent local buses between Valparaíso and Viña del Mar which take about 10 minutes and cost US$0.30; catch them anywhere along Avenida Errázuriz in Valparaíso.

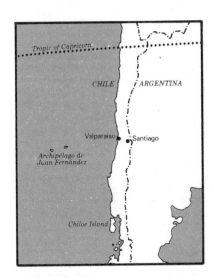

JUAN FERNANDEZ ISLANDS
In search of the real Robinson Crusoe

Robinson Crusoe's name has come to be fairly firmly connected with thoughts of tropical palms, buccaneers, cannibals – and the test of survival. The Crusoe legend has an extraordinary capacity to mirror the reader's ideals – to Rousseau, he was an admirable model for man-in-nature; to Joyce, an English *Ulysses*; to Karl Marx, by contrast, he was a capitalist. Tour companies use his name to promote island holidays (Man Friday undergoing a subtle change, serving cocktails to a suntanned couple). And to the people of the tiny Juan Fernández Archipelago, Crusoe is a cottage industry. He's right there on your ticket from Santiago – goatskins, parrot and all.

It was on these islands, 670 km off the Chilean coast, that the real Crusoe – a Scottish mariner named Alexander Selkirk – was marooned in 1704. The fact that Daniel Defoe set his novel about 5000 km away in the Brazils – leading to counterclaims by Caribbean islands – did not deter the inhabitants of Juan Fernández from happily re-naming their island after Crusoe 15 years ago.

Although Crusoe and Selkirk are quite different men, the similarities between their adventures are striking. Selkirk had himself put ashore from an English frigate after quarreling with his captain. He took along a few supplies, and when these were used up, he made the best of the island's resources. Four year later, when Captain Woodes Rogers chanced across the Scotsman, he was clad in goatskins and could scarcely speak English.

Rogers remarked that Selkirk was in superb physical condition and, having devoted much of his time to Bible-reading, 'he was a better Christian while in this solitude'. It remained for Defoe to explore the philosophical dimensions Rogers had touched upon. Drawing on contemporary accounts of castaways, Defoe spiced his version with a shipwreck, thoughtfully provided an arsenal of ammunition to cover Crusoe's stay of 28 years and, finally, relocated the island to accommodate an Amerindian.

Crusoe's prototype was apparently something of a statistician. He counted the days he'd been kept marooned, and 'he kept an Account of the 500 (goats) that he kill'd while there, and caught as many more which he marked on the ear and let go'. It seems he was involved in an ecological experiment of sorts. Juan Fernández, the Spanish navigator who discovered the islands in 1574, had stocked them with goats for future settlement but, as Rogers explains, other animals ran amok from visiting ships:

'The rats gnaw'd (Selkirk's) Feet and Clothes while asleep which oblig'd him to cherish the Cats with Goats-Flesh; by which many of them became so tame that they would lie about him in hundreds and soon deliver'd him from the Rats.'

Defoe chose to ignore these surreal cat banquets, in keeping with the sober nature of his tale. The Chilean Tourist Board, stretching fact and fiction a little further, offers the following information: 'Visitors to the island today may enjoy many of the sporting activities which allowed the legendary beachcomber to survive.' This refers, of course, to skin-diving: Selkirk's manner of diversion was a little more bizarre.

Because he couldn't stomach the seafood without salt, the mariner's staple was goat flesh. His gunpowder spent, he simply outran the beasts, and discovered the joys of goat-tagging. It could be a dangerous sport: once he stumbled over a precipice clutching the quadruped he had tackled (the goat, luckily, cushioned his fall). The wild sailor demonstrated his great agility by supplying goats for Rogers' crew while they harboured there. He outdistanced Rogers' dogs with ease. Should anyone doubt that Selkirk had the makings of a truly immortal quarterback, there are still enough feral goats on the islands to test the legs against.

There was another sport the hermit indulged in – bull-fighting. In his day, the islands were thickly populated with sea-lions; Rogers sighted one monstrous mammal 20 feet in length and weighing at least a ton. A bull sea-lion like this would charge any intruder interfering with his harem, and could snap a man's leg with his powerful jaw or tail. Selkirk noticed that while these sea monsters were agile enough on land, they had trouble turning around; if he got toward the middle of one, he could despatch it with a matadorial flourish of his hatchet.

Hunting was also a favourite pastime of the buccaneers who put in at the islands; they boiled down the sea-lion's blubber for oil. Between 1797 and 1804 it is estimated that commercial sealers took three million skins, driving the amphibians to the verge of extinction. In Selkirk's time, however, the howling of the sea-lions in breeding season could be heard a mile offshore. Rather than the walls of silence that one imagines for a castaway's island, the air must have been filled with a cacophony of barking sea-lions, bleating goats and wailing cats. Solitude? With the armies of tamed cats and goats around his hut,

and the seal-carpeted foreshores, Selkirk can not have felt *too* lonely.

In fact he came to enjoy his status as absolute monarch. All the same he felt it his duty to get himself returned to civilisation, and regularly hiked up to a look-out point to tend his signal fire – with a singular lack of success. The hardy Scotsman lived roughly where S Juan Bautista is now located; his original cave is close by, and the visitor can retrace his steps to the look-out. Since it first appeared on the map, Robinson Crusoe Island gained a reputation as a health resort for scurvy-wracked crews. Its lush vegetation, temperate climate, abundant wildlife and fresh water attracted Dutch and English pirates. This forced the Spanish to claim the hideaway; the forts they set up have been excavated, along with rusty cannons dating back to 1750. A more recent piece of salvage is the wreck of the German cruiser *Dresden*. The vessel retired to the islands for repairs; when the British bore down on it in 1915, the captain blew up his own magazine.

But, you ask, whatever became of seadog Selkirk? Well, after getting used to shoes, liquor and English voices again, he was given command of a captured galleon. En route to England, Selkirk learned that Captain Stradling, the man who'd let him off at Juan Fernández, had passed four miserable years in a Lima jail after the Spaniards came across his foundered vessel – so Selkirk's fate had not been so bad at all. Back in London, Selkirk was an overnight celebrity – and a rich man with his share of plundered Spanish gold. But, as he confided in an interview, 'I shall never be so happy as when I was not worth a Farthing.' After an abortive attempt to construct a cave behind his father's house in his native Scotland, Selkirk set sail again in 1717 and died aboard ship from a fever in 1723, at the age of 47. He was never to know that his true story would live on for centuries. In his birthplace in Lower Lago, Fife, Scotland, there stands a bronze statue of a mariner with his goatskins and flintlock, hopefully scanning the horizon for a distant ship.

Daniel Defoe, the veteran journalist who so successfully passed off the mariner's story as his own, kept his creditors at bay with his sensational novel. Defoe was a formidable writing machine: in 1719, the year the bestseller appeared, he penned seven other works and contributed to four newspapers. The classic he knocked out in a matter of months has kept critics, artists, editors, scholars and translators busy for the last two centuries. Not to mention hotel owners, advertising men, film directors, souvenir vendors . . . and the present writer.   **Michael Buckley**

Lake District

Chile, your skies spread above you,
So sweet are the breezes that roam
Over fields so richly embroidered with
flowers,
That angels might make you their
home!

– from the Chilean national anthem

There are few areas in the world which can match the Lake District for scenic grandeur. South of the Toltén River and sprawled across the provinces of Valdivia, Osorno and Llanquihue, you'll find everything from snow-capped mountains to deep-blue lakes, smoking volcanoes, forests, glaciers and – in summer – an invigorating northern Mediterranean climate.

Outside the noisy cities like Puerto Montt the loudest sound you're likely to hear is the roar of waterfalls streaming down cliff faces into crystal-clear pools, and the occasional rumbling (and even eruption) of a discontented volcano. Yet had you come this way in the early 17th century you would have found a far less peaceful scene, with all the Spanish settlements south of the Bío Bío River reduced to piles of ash by Indian counterattacks.

Around Concepción, and to the south, the Spanish conquistadores found gold mines, good agricultural land – plus a large potential workforce of Indians. The lands were so tempting that some conquistadores gave up their encomiendas in the Central Valley for grants of land south of the Bío Bío. Despite their optimism, this area was a dangerous frontier for the entire colonial period, its settlements constantly under threat of Indian attack, or some other calamity.

Concepción, for example, was founded in 1550, destroyed in 1554, refounded the following year and then abandoned, re-established in 1558, and destroyed by an earthquake and tidal wave in 1570. Until the end of the 16th century it was nothing more than a military camp; only after 1603, when a large permanent garrison was stationed there, did it take on the appearance of a permanent town. Even then it was the most southern outpost of the Spanish empire in Chile.

Further south, places like Osorno, Valdivia and Imperial were actually the most prosperous towns in Chile – that is until the years 1598 to 1604 when the Mapuche (Araucanian) Indians wiped every settlement south of the Bío Bío off the map. Attempts by the Spanish to wrest this territory back failed dismally and within 20 years the conquerors were reduced to scavengers who made periodic pillaging and slave-hunting expeditions into Indian territory.

In 1641 the Spanish signed a treaty with the Indians and abandoned their settlements. The one exception to this ignominious retreat was the resettlement and fortification of Valdivia in 1645-46. It was a century before the Spanish once again built permanent settlements south of the Bío Bío: Los Angeles was founded in 1741, and Osorno was refounded in the 1790s. It was not until the 1880s, however, that the Mapuche Indians were finally subjugated and the region was made safe for European settlement. The Indians were pushed further south, their land was divided into large rural estates, and the hacienda system was introduced.

Today, the provinces between the Bío Bío River and the Toltén River are still home for the several hundred thousand remaining Mapuche Indians. Deprived of much of their land by Spanish conquerors and, later, by Chilean capitalists and politicians, the Mapuche now make a precarious living from agriculture and crafts. From 1965 to 1973 land reform programmes improved their lot but since the coup the land that was occupied (or 'recuperated') has once again been taken from them. The repression of organised rural militancy – including the murder of Mapuche leaders and farmers – has restored 'peace' to the area.

The most important urban centres in this region are Valdivia, Osorno and Puerto Montt, although about half the population still lives in the country. Tourism plays an important part in the local economy but lumbering, cereal farming, dairy farming and other livestock are also important. Local industries (such as sawmills and leather works) tend to be based largely on rural production.

Many local industries were set up by German immigrants who settled the Lake District in the 19th century. Breweries, tanneries, brick factories, bakeries, machine shops, furniture factories, and mills were all established before the end of the 19th century. The German influence is still evident in places like Valdivia where there are many people of German descent and many central-European-style buildings can be seen. The occupation of Indian lands by European settlers in the 19th century was part of the government's policy, aimed at ensuring the rapid development of the region. Although many Germans, French and Swiss did settle, Chile never attracted settlers in the numbers it needed.

Coming from the north, Temuco (which is actually in the frontier district – the Región de la Araucanía) is the jumping off point for the Lake District. From Temuco you head south-east to Villarrica and Pucón on the shores of Lago Villarrica, from where numerous lakes are accessible. It's possible to wind your way south via Licán Ray and Coñaripe on Lago Calafquén, Panguipulli and Choshuenco on Lago Panguipulli, Futrono on Lago Ranco, to the towns of Valdivia and Osorno on the Santiago-Puerto Montt highway. From here you can visit Puerto Varas and Ensenada on Lago Llanquihue. Then head east to Lago Todos los Santos, the most beautiful lake of them all, crossing it by ferry from Petrohué on its western shore to Peulla on its east.

There are several passes between Argentina and Chile in the Lake District, two of which are open all year round; for details of transport to Argentina see the Getting There chapter at the start of this book.

TEMUCO

This city, of some 220,000 people, arose in 1881 out of the dust of Chile's own version of the American wild west. In the 19th century this was the wild south, the Chilean frontier and the home of the Mapuche Indians. The frontier region is mainly a rural area, though there is a wide range of industrial activity including steel and textile production, coal mining, and the processing of rural products. Only half the population lives in the towns – Concepción and Temuco are the most important.

Spanish fort attacked by Indians

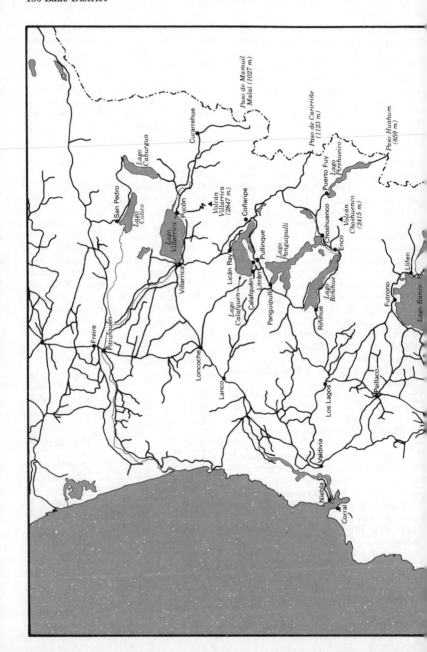

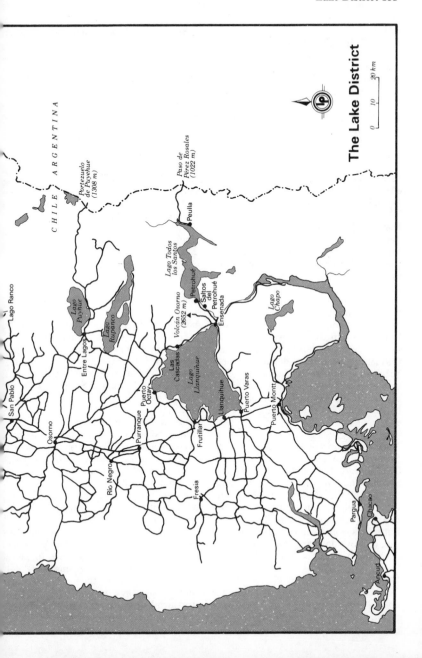

The Lake District

Information
Tourist Office This is at the corner of Bulnes and Claro Solar. The staff are friendly and they have maps of the city and giveaway leaflets. Open daily, 9.30 am to 1 pm, and 3 to 6 pm (tel 34293).

Bank The Banco de Chile is at the corner of Varas and Prat. They'll change foreign travellers' cheques and some foreign cash.

Post & Communications The main post office and Telex Chile are at the corner of Diego Portales and Prat.

Things to See
Temuco itself holds few attractions for the visitor and is mainly a jumping-off point for visiting Mapuche Indian settlements in the surrounding region, or the Lake District. It is also a market town for the Mapuche and *the* place to buy their fine hand-made woollen ponchos, pullovers and blankets. You will see many Indians coming into town with fruit, vegetables and handicrafts. Other than the markets the town itself is a dull place, although it's worth hopping on a city bus to visit the sea of wooden and fibrocement bungalows that comprise the housing estates on the outskirts of the city.

Museum Regional de la Araucanía
Housed in an attractive colonial-style building situated at Alemania 84 this museum has an interesting exhibition recounting the story of the Mapuche Indians before, during and after the Spanish invasion. It's open Tuesdays to Saturdays from 9 am to 1 pm and 3 to 7 pm, and Sundays and holidays from 10 am to 1 pm. Entry is about US$0.30.

The City Market
The main market of Temuco runs for several blocks along Pinto from the railway station to the provincial bus station. Many of the vendors are Mapuche Indians – you'll see them coming into town leading bullocks, and in horse-carts.

The Handicrafts Market
The handicrafts market is at the corner of Diego Portales and Aldunte. Although there's an immense quantity of junk and other mass-produced souvenirs this is also a good place to buy Indian woollen ponchos, blankets and pullovers. Many Indian women also hawk these goods on the streets. Look for jewellery, pottery, polished stone mortars and musical instruments including pan pipes, and drums. The market is open Monday to Saturday from 7.30 am to 7 pm, and Sundays and holidays from 7.30 am to 2 pm.

Galeria Artesanal
The Galeria Artesanal at the junction of Balmaceda and Bulnes sells handicrafts, mainly Indian-made woollen blankets, ponchos and pullovers. Most of the stuff is price-tagged so it could be worth coming here to get an idea of the price before you buy anything at the markets. It's open Monday to Friday from 9 am to 1 pm and 3 to 7 pm; and Saturday from 9 am to 1 pm.

Places to Stay – bottom end
Temuco doesn't have much bottom-end accommodation like Santiago does. Probably the best you'll do is the *Hotel de France*, Aldunte 95 at the corner of Aldunte and Bilbao. Other than the surly manager (distant relative? cleaner?) it's a bright little place with singles for US$5 and doubles for US$8.30.

Cheaper and well worth trying, the rambling *Hotel Terraz* has singles from US$3.90 and doubles from US$6.70, plus 20% tax. Many of its rooms have no windows other than those opening out into passageways, and you may find it worthwhile paying more and taking a room facing the street. There's a fairly cheap restaurant downstairs.

Places to Stay - middle

The *Hotel Emperador* (tel 37124) at Bulnes 853 has pleasant singles for US$7.50 and doubles for US$11 with attached bathrooms. They're friendly people and the place is good value for the price.

Another place I'd recommend is the *Hotel Continental* (tel 3359) which is a rambling wooden building. It's very clean, and the people are friendly. Singles are from US$6.70 and doubles are from US$10.

The *Hotel Espellate* (tel 34255) on Claro Solar 492 is also good. It has singles from US$4.30 and doubles from US$7.20 without attached bathrooms; and singles for US$8.30 and doubles for US$12.80 with attached bathrooms. You could also try the *Hotel Turismo* (tel 32348) at Claro Solar 636 which is similarly priced.

If you're prepared to pay a bit more money my pick of the hotels would be the *Hotel Nicolás* (tel 35547) at General MacKenna 420. It's a new hotel with smallish rooms but they're bright and clean and they've got their own bathrooms and TVs. Singles are US$16 and doubles are US$22.

The *Hotel de la Frontera* (tel 733) at Bulnes 733 has singles from US$14.50 and doubles from US$19.80 The cheapest singles are OK but they're not as good as those in the slightly more expensive Hotel Nicolás.

Although it doesn't look like much from the outside, the *Hotel Aitue* (tel 997) at General Cruz 401, is a pretty good place and reasonable value at US$12 a single and US$18.30 a double.

Places to Stay - top end

Across the road from *Hotel de la Frontera*, the *Nuevo Hotel de la Frontera* (tel 36190) at Bulnes 726 is the biggest, most expensive hotel in town. Singles are US$31 and doubles are US$39.

Places to Eat

There are cheap meals available in the many small restaurants and from the snack places around the Bus Station Rurales. The best value in town, however, is the *Nueva Hosteria Allen Clei* at Manuel Bulnes 902; a full meal with generous servings will only set you back about US$3 per person.

For Chinese food there's the *Long Chinese Restaurant* at Diego Portales 192 where there's a fixed menu for two for about US$5, otherwise, if you eat there alone, you'll be up for about US$4 to US$5 per person. It makes a change from the usual fare although it's nothing to rave about.

Try the spic-and-span *Pizzaria Dino* at Bulnes 563 for pizzas ranging from US$1 to about US$2.70, or check out the *Centro Espanol* at Bulnes 483 – if the food's no good you can go bowling in the three-lane alley in the basement.

Getting There

Air Ladeco (tel 36414) is at Bulnes 375. LAN-Chile (tel 34977) is at Bulnes 398. Only Ladeco flies from Temuco: to Concepción (once a week), Osorno (about three times a week), and Santiago (about four times a week). In the tourist season there is a plane-bus link-up between Santiago, Temuco and Villarrica/Pucón – see the section on Pucón for details.

Bus From Temuco you can head north to Santiago; south to Valdivia, Osorno and Puerto Montt; to Villarrica, Pucón, Licán Ray and Curarrehue in the Lake District; or to Zapala, Neuquén, Mendoza, Bariloche and Buenos Aires in Argentina.

Typical fares from Temuco are: Santiago US$8.30; Valdivia US$2; Zapala US$12.80; Neuquén US$17; Mendoza US$25; Buenos Aires US$53.

The Bus Station Rurales is on Balmaceda by the market. This is where you can get buses to places like Chol Chol in the surrounding districts.

The long-distance and international bus companies have their own terminals around the centre of town, mostly along

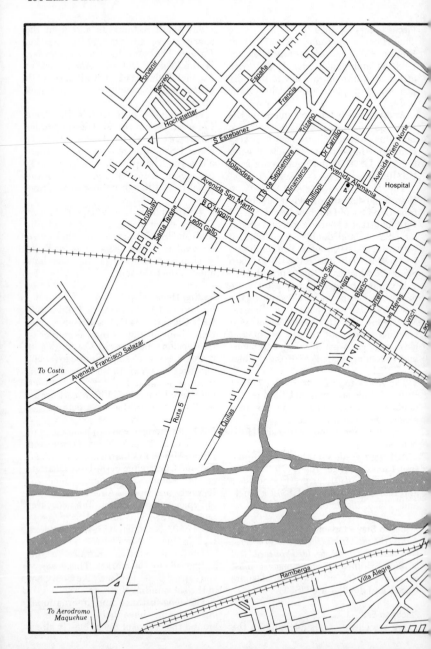

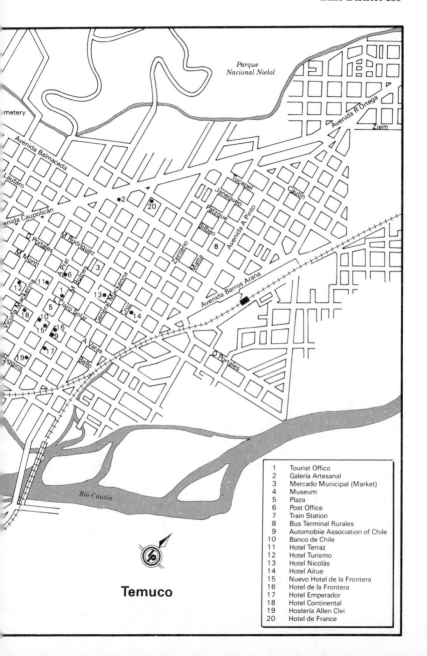

Temuco

1   Tourist Office
2   Galería Artesanal
3   Mercado Municipal (Market)
4   Museum
5   Plaza
6   Post Office
7   Train Station
8   Bus Terminal Rurales
9   Automobiie Association of Chile
10 Banco de Chile
11 Hotel Terraz
12 Hotel Turismo
13 Hotel Nicolás
14 Hotel Aitue
15 Nuevo Hotel de la Frontera
16 Hotel de la Frontera
17 Hotel Emperador
18 Hotel Continental
19 Hostería Allen Clei
20 Hotel de France

Vicuña MacKenna between Varas and Montt, and along Claro Solar between Lynch and Prat.

Bus companies, addresses and destinations are:

Fénix, corner of Lagos and Claro Solar; to Santiago; three times a week to Zapala, Neuquén, Mendoza and Buenos Aires.
Cruz del Sur, MacKenna 761; to Santiago; south to Valdivia, Osorno, Puerto Varas, Puerto Montt, with connections to Ancud, Castro and Quellón.
Longitudinal Sur, MacKenna 650; to Valdivia.
Tas Chopper, Claro Solar 742; to Mendoza, Buenos Aires and Bariloche.
Buses García, Bus Station Rurales; several departures daily to Villarrica and Licán Ray.
Buses Jac, corner of Vicuña MacKenna and Claro Sur; about 16 departures daily to Villarrica; once daily to Curarrehue; twice daily to Licán Ray.

There are other companies around so check the list with the tourist office. The time and frequency of departures is likely to vary throughout the year; during the winter months there are likely to be far fewer buses running.

Getting Around

Temuco is a large town and the railway station and main bus terminal are quite a distance from the centre of town – it can be walked, but not comfortably. There's a city bus system: Bus 1 takes you from the city centre to the train station, and Bus 9 takes you from the city centre to Avenida Alemania.

The Automobile Club of Chile at Bulnes 763 near the corner with Bello has cars for rent from just US$10.60 per day plus US$0.12 per km plus insurance. You could also try Hertz at Bulnes 726, Puig Arrienda Autos at Portales 779, and Auto Car at Montt 411. Renting a car is worth considering since it will give you easy access to the national parks and Indian settlements in the surrounding area.

CHOL CHOL

This is an odd little place of wooden, tin-roofed bungalows, and dirt roads plied by Indian bullock carts and horsemen. It has the peculiar feel of a frontier town where time has either stood still or, at the very least, run slowly.

Buses to Chol Chol depart from Temuco's Bus Station Rurales; there are several departures per day, the fare is US$0.70 and the trip takes about 1½ hours along a gravel road. The bus is likely to be crammed with Indians returning from the market with bags of fruit and vegetables. As you approach Chol Chol you'll see traditional Indian *ruca* houses. From Chol Chol you could take a bus back to Temuco via Imperial, an interesting ride through farming country.

VILLARRICA

Villarrica is one of the chief resort towns of the Lake District, with impressive views of the smoking, snow-covered Volcán Villarrica on the other side of the lake. At night you can sit by the edge of the lake and watch the flames flickering above the throat of the mountain. The volcano smokes for most of the year and, if you're lucky, you may be there during an eruption. White-hot lava pouring out over snow, a relatively frequent occurrence, is quite a sight. The last time this mountain blew its top was in the early 1980s and you can buy photos and postcards of the event from the store-keepers in Villarrica and Pucón, and other resort towns in the area.

Information

Tourist Office The tourist office (tel 22) is on Pedro de Valdivia close to the junction with Acevedo. It's often closed in winter, but in the summer holiday period (January and February) it's open Monday to Friday, 8.30 am to 11 pm, and on Saturday and Sunday, 8.30 am to 3 pm and 4 to 11 pm. They've got a number of useful leaflets and hand-outs, including a list of many hotels and campsites (including prices) in the Lake District.

Post The post office is on Urrutia just near the corner with Muñoz; it's open Monday to Friday, 9 am to 1 pm and 3 to 5 pm, and on Saturday from 9 am to 1 pm.

Things to See

Although the scenery is the main reason for visiting, Villarrica does have a number of other attractions. At the corner of Koener and Pedro de Valdivia there's a reconstruction of a *ruca*, a traditional Mapuche Indian house. It's roughly oblong-shaped with thatch walls and an overhanging thatch roof. There are two wooden burial figures standing outside.

There's an interesting museum near the tourist office, open Tuesday to Saturday from 10 am to 1 pm and 6 to 11 pm, and on Sunday and Monday from 6 to 11 pm (the hours will probably be shorter in winter). Entry costs US$0.30. It has a collection of Mapuche Indian relics including jewellery, musical instruments, and several of their peculiar roughly-hewn wooden masks.

Places to Stay - bottom end

One of the cheapest places in Villarrica is the *Hotel Fuentes* (tel 195), Reyes 665. It's very popular with travellers and hikers and costs about US$2.20 per person for rooms that are pleasant and comfortable, although they're basic. There's hot water in the showers in the mornings (before 9 am). Downstairs there's a bar and cheap restaurant and they'll cook more or less anything for you if you tell them what you'd like in advance. There's usually an open log fire in the restaurant during the winter months and the staff are very friendly. Some people may find this place rather noisy, but at least give it a try.

Volcán Villarrica

To Temuco

Río Toltén

To Loncoche

Isabel Riquelme

L Contreras

J M Carrera

J M Balmaceda

Andrés Bello

M A Matta

Cemetery

1   Buses JAC (Buses to Pucón)
2   Hotel Fuentes
3   Buses Pullman Lit
4   Buses JAC Terminal
    (Buses to Valdivia)
5   Market
6   Buses Rurales Terminal
7   Main Bus Station
8   Residencial Victoria
9   Hostería Ray
10 Residencial Puchy
11 Gran Hotel
12 Banco del Estado
13 Hotel Yachting Club
14 Hotel El Ciervo
15 Hotel Turismo
16 Moteles Melilafquén
17 Museum
18 Tourist Office
19 Telephone Office
20 Post Office

Villarrica

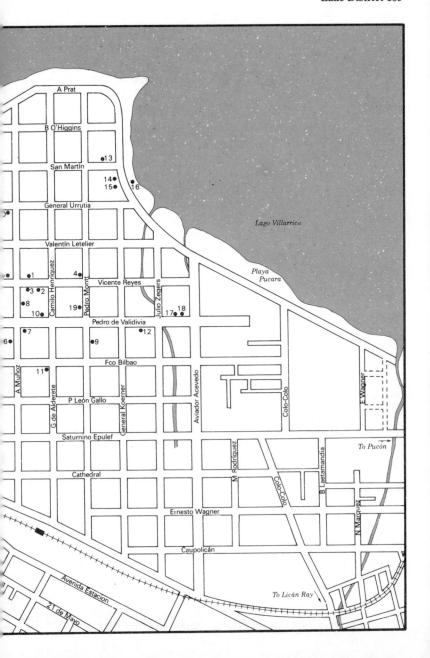

There are a number of cheap hospedajes around town – look for the signs in windows. One that seems to run on a permanent basis is upstairs at Letelier 702. It's run by a local family and is very clean, has hot showers and costs US$3.30 a single and US$5.50 a double. The rooms are pleasant and comfortable and it's a bright little place with a friendly owner.

Another hospedaje worth trying is at the corner of Urrutia and Koerner. It's a decent little place run by a friendly family, and you can get a room for around US$4.40 per person.

The *Residencial Victoria*, Anfion Munoz 530, is also OK, with rooms for US$2.20 per person and hot water for an additional US$0.70 or so. It also has a good, cheap restaurant on the ground floor. Another cheapie is the *Residencial Puchy*, Valdivia 678.

The *Hostería Reyhuen* (tel 271) at Pedro Montt 668, is a beautiful place with hot showers, heating in the rooms and its own restaurant. It costs US$4.60 per person in rooms with attached bathrooms and toilets. It's run by Gualberto Lopez who speaks English.

There's a large number of campsites around the lake, some of them free, others not. You can get a list of sites and prices from the tourist office.

Places to Stay – middle

The *Gran Hotel* at Henríquez 709 is a sizeable hotel in a quiet part of town. Prices may be lower in the off season, but in the tourist season expect to pay about US$10 a single and about US$15.60 a double. This is the place I'd go for if I was after something in this price range.

The *Hotel El Ciervo* (tel 65) at General Koerner 241 is one of three good mid-range hotels at the lake side end of General Koerner. Rooms start from around US$16.60 a single and US$21.70 a double.

Places to Stay – top end

Top of the range in Villarrica, with views across the lake, is the *Hotel Yachting Club* (tel 31) at San Martín 802. Singles are US$35 and doubles, US$53 – including all meals. Singles are US$29 and doubles, US$37 – including breakfast only. It has its own restaurant and swimming pool.

Places to Eat

If you want to eat somewhere other than the Hotel Fuentes or the other hotel restaurants try one or other of the restaurants along Henríquez near the junction with Letelier, and along Valdivia.

The *Club Social Bar-Restaurant* at Valdivia 640 has excellent meals; fish will cost about US$2.20, with generous salads for around US$1 extra. The place is heated in winter. Also try the *Scorpio Café Bar* at the corner of Valdivia and Pedro Montt.

There's a *pena* (folk club) at Acevedo 761 between Bilbao and Gallo which has reasonable prices and the atmosphere is so thick you could cut it with a guitar string. It's open in winter but ask if there are any musicians playing on the night you go.

Getting Around

Although you can get to Pucón on the local buses, to get up to some of the beautiful waterfalls and thermal springs in the nearby hills you really need your own car.

Hertz Rent-a-Car is at the corner of San Martín and Pedro Montt, in the Hotel Yachting Club. The cheapest cars start from about US$10 per day plus US$0.12 per km and insurance.

If you don't want to drive yourself, one guy who may be worth contacting is Aldo Ceballos at Pedro Montt 473. He'll take you on tour in his Suzuki jeep to sites in the surrounding area for about US$19.50 per day plus petrol costs.

Getting There

The main bus terminal is on Pedro de Valdivia at the junction with Muñoz.

There are daily buses to Santiago, other parts of the Lake District, and frequent buses to Mendoza, Zapala, Neuquén and San Martín de los Andes in Argentina.

Typical fares from Villarrica are: Santiago US$9; Temuco US$1.45; Licán Ray US$0.55; Valdivia US$2; and Coñaripe US$0.80.

Typical fares to Argentina are: Zapala US$10; San Martín de los Andes US$11.10; Neuquén US$16.60; and Mendoza US$26.

Bus companies, addresses and destinations are:

Pullman Lit, Fenix, Tur-Bus and *Igi Llaima,* all at the main bus terminal; usually about one bus daily per company to Santiago. These leave around 8 pm to 9.30 pm. *Pullman Lit* also have an office on Reyes, across the road from *Buses Jac.*
Buses Unión del Sud, main bus terminal; to Zapala and Neuquén four days a week.
Fénix, main bus terminal; daily to Mendoza.
Igi Llaima, main bus terminal; to San Martín de los Andes and Neuquén three days a week.
Buses Estrella del Sur, on Muñoz opposite the main bus terminal; daily to Licán Ray, Coñaripe and Liquiñe.
Buses Regional Villarrica, on Reyes, next to the Hotel Fuentes; three buses daily to Pucón and Curarrehue. The late afternoon bus continues on to Puerto Basa.
Buses Jac has two terminals. For buses to Temuco and Pucón go to the terminal on Reyes between Muñoz and Henríquez. During the tourist season there are around 18 buses a day from Villarrica to Temuco; the trip takes about two hours. Buses to Valdivia, Licán Ray and Coñaripe leave from the terminal at the corner of Reyes and Pedro Montt; several departures daily.

PUCON

Apart from windsurfing and building sand-castles there's not much to do in Pucón. This rather drab resort town attracts rich Chileans and their spanking-new Japanese tin-mobiles because of the beautiful waterfalls and thermal springs in the hills outside town. There are also impressive views from the slopes of

Volcán Villarrica, overlooking the lake. There are two fairly crowded, black gravel beaches at the edge of the town, but most of the bare flesh is flabby and frayed. Views of the volcano are better from Villarrica.

Tourist Office There is a tourist office and handicraft centre on Brasil near the junction of Caupolicán but it's usually closed in winter (tel 125).

Places to Stay – bottom end

Finding cheap accommodation in summer is a problem in Pucón, although it's no problem in winter when there are few visitors. Pucón is much more up-market than Villarrica.

The *Residencial La Frontera* is a neat little place at the corner of General Urrutia and Arauco; it has small rooms for US$3.80 a single and US$7.40 a double. The rooms are clean and tidy and are arranged around a pleasant courtyard. The people are reasonably hospitable and I highly recommend the place.

If you have your own bedding, walk the eight-km gravel road out of Pucón to the Parque Nacional Villarrica entrance. At one km and three km from the park entrance there are picnic areas with wooden huts, fireplaces, and good views – there is no charge to stay here.

Places to Stay – middle

The *Hotel La Posada,* at the corner of Lincoyan and Pedro de Valdivia, is a nifty place, rather like the *Fuentes* in Villarrica. Rooms are small but they're clean and bright and cost US$6.60 per person.

The *Residencial Lincoyán,* on Lincoyán between Urrutia and O'Higgins, has rooms without a bathroom at US$8.80 per person. It's rather expensive but it is very clean and the people are friendly. Rates may be considerably lower in the off-season, so ask.

The *Hotel Araucarias,* (tel 54) at Caupolicán 243, is a modern building with rooms from US$6.70 per person. Also

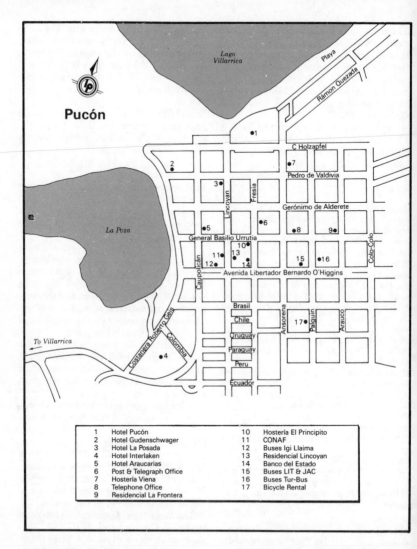

Pucón

1	Hotel Pucón
2	Hotel Gudenschwager
3	Hotel La Posada
4	Hotel Interlaken
5	Hotel Araucarias
6	Post & Telegraph Office
7	Hostería Viena
8	Telephone Office
9	Residencial La Frontera
10	Hostería El Principito
11	CONAF
12	Buses Igi Llaima
13	Residencial Lincoyan
14	Banco del Estado
15	Buses LIT & JAC
16	Buses Tur-Bus
17	Bicycle Rental

worth trying, the *Hostería El Principito*, (tel 123) on Urrutia near the corner with Fresia, is a clean modern building with a restaurant downstairs.

Places to Stay – top end

One of the obvious signs of the German influence in the south is the fine chalet-style hotels to be found in the Lake District. My pick of the up-market places in Pucón is the *Hotel Gudenschwager* at the western end of Valdivia, built like a chalet with interior walls of varnished wood, and front rooms with fine views across the lake. Double rooms with a bathroom are US$27, without a bathroom US$18 – this includes breakfast.

On the beach front at the top end of Fresia is the *Pucón Grand Hotel*, Pucón's biggest hotel. Singles are from US$34, and doubles are from US$52 – including all meals. This place *may* rent out windsurfers.

Alternatively, you could forsake Pucón altogether and head for the Termas de Palguin. This is a hot spring, in the mountains, 30 km (45 minutes drive) from Pucón. There's an attractive chalet-style hotel here originally built by a German in the mid-1940s called the *Hotel Termas de Palguin* (tel 33021). Room and board is about US$16.70 per person per day. Unless you can hitch you'll need your own transport to get here, but there are also day tours from Pucón – see the Getting Around section for details.

There are other places fronting the lake on the road between Pucón and Villarrica, but you'd probably need your own transport to make it worth staying in any of them.

Places to Eat

Apart from the hotel restaurants (which tend to be expensive – like US$3 to US$4 for a mean sliver of meat, a thimbleful of rice and a poisonous fizzy drink) there are quite a few moderately-priced places around the middle of town. A good place for pizzas (as Chilean pizzas go) is the *El Fogón* next to the Jac Bus office. Vegetarians might try the *El Refugio Vegetariano* at Lincoyan 348.

Getting There

Buses Jac handles the Villarrica-Pucón route. They have departures throughout the day from the early morning to the evening, about every hour. The journey takes half an hour and costs US$0.45 one-way. In Pucon most of the bus companies have their offices near the junction of O'Higgins and Palguin.

If you're really in a rush to get to

Villarrica and Pucón then LADECO offers a twice-weekly plane and bus service from Santiago. They fly you from Santiago to Valdivia and from Valdivia you take a bus. The whole trip takes just four hours. These connections may not operate outside the holiday season.

Getting Around

The tourist office runs tours of the area if there are enough people – usually a minimum of five to make up a group. Tours include excursions up to the 12 km mark on the slope of Volcán Villarrica for US$2.20 per person; and an afternoon trip to Termas de Palguin for US$2.70 per person (not including admission to the swimming pool – US$1.40 – or the therapeutic baths) and stopping at several beautiful waterfalls on the way.

Alternatively, you could hire a taxi from the stand on the corner of Ansonena and O'Higgins to do some sightseeing, but the tours are good value.

LICAN RAY

This is a lively, popular resort town on the northern shore of Lago Calafquén, a beautiful lake bounded by mountains and studded with a number of small islands. The town boasts one of the best beaches in the area, a long strip of black sand liberally endowed with bodies (it can get crowded). The tourist strip is on the main street, General Urrutia, where the buses from Villarrica pull in. It turns into something of a carnival at night during the tourist season with overflowing restaurants, hotels, cafés, and a billiard-table shed. Otherwise, this place is like an overgrown village with dirt roads and a curious appearance of underdevelopment despite the tourist hordes.

Information

Tourist Office There's a useful tourist office on Urrutia. They don't speak any English but they do have a list of hotels which is worth checking out. It's open daily, 9 am to 3 pm and 6 to 10.30 pm –

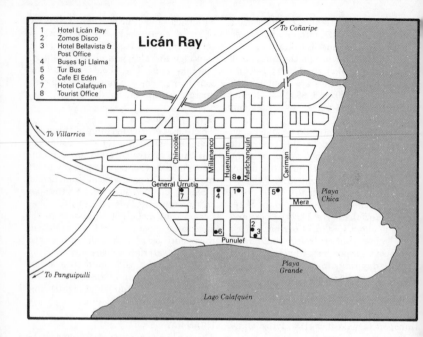

1	Hotel Licán Ray
2	Zomos Disco
3	Hotel Bellavista & Post Office
4	Buses Igi Llaima
5	Tur Bus
6	Cafe El Edén
7	Hotel Calafquén
8	Tourist Office

Licán Ray

To Coñaripe

To Villarrica

Chincolet
Millanenco
Huenuman
Marlchanguln
Cariman

General Urrutia

7   4   1   5   Mera

8

Playa
Chica

6

2
3

Punulef

Playa
Grande

To Panguipulli

Lago Calafquén

the hours will probably be shorter in winter, if it is open at all. They also organise tours to places like Termas de Liquiñe and Inquine.

Post The post office is on Punulef between Cariman and Marlchanguln opposite the Playa Grande (Big Beach). It's open Monday to Friday 8.30 am to 12.30 pm and 2 to 6 pm, and on Saturday from 8.30 am to 12.30 pm.

Places to Stay & Eat

The *Hotel Calafquén*, at the far end of Urrutia, is a good choice since it's away from the crowds. It costs just US$2.80 per person and it's a decent – if very basic – little hotel.

The *Hotel Bellavista*, on Punulef between Cariman and Marlchanguln, is far from the milling crowd of Urrutia and should be fairly quiet at night. The rooms are spartan, but the people are friendly. It

costs around US$10 per person in the tourist season, but that does include all meals and is not bad value for these resort towns.

The *Hotel Licán Ray*, Urrutia 305, is a decent place, but it's right on the main street so don't stay here if you can't put up with a lot of street noise (particularly at night). It costs US$5.70 per person; the rooms are basic but clean, as are the bathrooms. There's a restaurant downstairs.

There are half a dozen cafés and restaurant/bars along the main stretch of Urrutia, as well as several others facing the Playa Grande – like the *Café El Edén* and the restaurant in the *Hotel Bellavista*.

Getting There

You can day-trip easily from Villarrica. Buses Hac have several buses a day for US$0.55 and the journey takes about 45

Top: Volcán Osorno
Bottom: Volcán Villarrica

Top: Shop, Futrono
Left: River front, Valdivia
Right: Street scene, Valdivia

minutes. It's a gravel road, but there are good views of Volcán Villarrica along the way.

The Buses Hac office in Licán Ray is one door up from the Licán Ray Hotel on Urrutia. They also have several buses a day through to Temuco. Buses Igi Llaima has a daily bus to Santiago departing around 8 pm.

There is one bus a day to Panguipulli leaving Licán Ray around 7.15 am (enquire about the time the day before). This is a local bus and it leaves from Urrutia. It takes about two hours since it goes around the back roads picking up passengers, mainly Mapuche Indians.

PANGUIPULLI

This is a quiet little town nestled on the slopes bordering the northern edge of Lago Panguipulli, a beautiful lake with marvelous views towards Volcán Choshuenco. The town itself pales before Villarrica or Licán Ray and can be unpleasantly hot during the summer months, but it's also quieter, slower-paced and less touristy. Just outside the town is a small, uncrowded black-sand beach and you can walk along the edge of the lake away from the town for quite a distance.

Information

Tourist Office There's an office on the main plaza but it's often closed in winter. Pick up their leaflet *Panguipulli – capital de las rosas* which has a useful map of the Lago Calafquén, Panguipulli, Riñihue and Pirehueico region.

Places to Stay – bottom end

There are several hotels and residencials to choose from in Panguipulli but the *Residencial La Bomba*, on the corner of Rozas and Freire, is friendly, pleasant and good value at US$3.30 a single and US$4.40 a double. There are hot showers, and large jugs of water are provided in the rooms. It's a pleasant place with friendly people.

Slightly cheaper, the *Hospedaje El Ciervo* is popular with hikers and travellers. It's on Valdivia between Carrera and Rozas. Singles are US$2.80 and doubles are US$5 – this includes breakfast, but there's no hot water in the showers. Good, reasonably priced meals are available in the restaurant downstairs.

The *Hotel Central*, (tel 331) Valdivia between Carrera and Rozas, is US$3.30 per person. It's a decent place with airy rooms and clean bathrooms (they even have bathtubs) and a hospitable manager. Take an upstairs room, not a matchbox-like downstairs room. There's hot water in the showers.

Places to Stay – middle

Try the *Hostería Quetropillan*, (tel 348) at Etchegaray 381 on the corner with Freire; singles are US$8.70, doubles, US$14.70 – including private bathroom and hot water. It's a quiet location and the staff are friendly.

Places to Stay – top end

If you can afford it, think about staying at the *Club de Yates* at the end of O'Higgins on a beautiful site with great views across the lake, a short walk from town. It has very comfortable rooms with private bathrooms and hot water, which cost about US$19.40 a single and US$22 a double – including breakfast. Winter rates are a bit lower – about US$13.50 a double. In winter there's always an open log fire crackling away in the lounge bar (open to non-residents). In summer they have discos.

Places to Eat

A pleasant little place for breakfast is the *Amanecer*, across the road from the Bus Terminal on Pedro de Valdivia. Just US$0.60 gets you bread, scrambled eggs with bacon, and coffee. The *Restaurant Valparaíso*, on O'Higgins 413, is similar. Other restaurants can be found along Carerra and along Rozas.

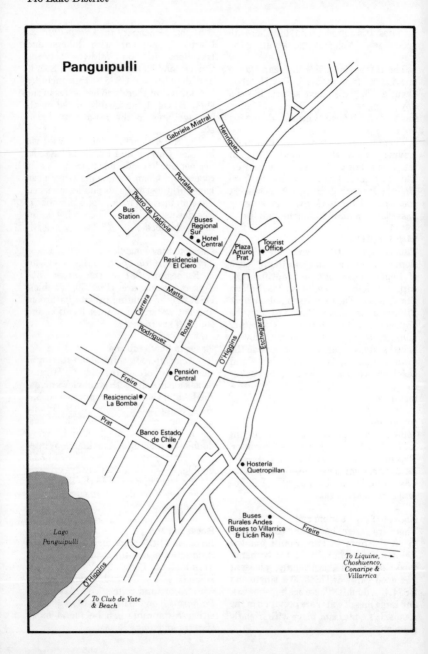

Panguipulli

Gabriela Mistral

Henríquez

Portales

Pedro de Valdivia

Bus Station

Buses Regional Sur

Hotel Central

Plaza Arturo Prat

Tourist Office

Residencial El Ciero

Matta

Carrera

Rozas

Rodríguez

O'Higgins

Etchegaray

Freire

Pensión Central

Residencial La Bomba

Prat

Banco Estado de Chile

Hostería Quetropillan

Lago Panguipulli

Buses Rurales Andes (Buses to Villarrica & Licán Ray)

Freire

O'Higgins

To Club de Yate & Beach

To Liquine, Choshuenco, Conaripe & Villarrica

Getting There

There are two bus stations in Panguipulli. The Bus Terminal on Pedro de Valdivia has buses to Temuco, Valdivia, Santiago, and down the lake to Choshuenco, Neltume and Puerto Fry.

Pirehueico runs several buses a day to Valdivia – the journey takes about 2½ hours. Regional Sur have several departures per day for Temuco (except on Sundays and holidays when there are only two departures per day), and daily departures to Santiago. Chile Neuvo and Valdivia have a couple of buses a day to Valdivia.

Transpacar has a couple of buses per day to Choshuenco, Neltume and Puerto Fry, departing around 3 pm and 3.30 pm.

Fares from Panguipulli are about US$8.90 to Santiago; US$1.50 to Choshuenco; US$1.80 to Puerto Fry; and US$1.80 to Valdivia.

The smaller of the two bus stations is on Freire. It is used by Buses Rurales Andes for its service to Coñaripe, Licán Ray and Villarrica. A bus leaves daily at 3.30 pm, takes about two hours and costs US$1.00 to Villarica.

CHOSHUENCO

Choshuenco is barely more than two streets hemmed in by Lago Panguipulli, farms, and a rocky cliff. It's a tiny settlement, relying for its survival on what it can grow itself, a local sawmill, and a few stray banknotes from the tourists who find their way to its attractive black-sand beach. This place is even quieter and more relaxed than Panguipulli (is there some truth in the rumour that the further south you go in Chile the better it gets?).

There are many fine walks in the surrounding countryside along dirt tracks and roads between the vegetable fields and the grazing land.

If you're heading to Argentina and you're trying to save money you'll probably find that accommodation at Puerto Fry is relatively expensive so it's better to stay at Choshuenco.

Places to Stay & Eat

One of my favourite places in Chile is the *Hotel Rucapillan* next to the beach. It's very clean, with heating units in the rooms, a good restaurant on the ground floor, hot water showers, and friendly people. Singles are US$2.50 and doubles are US$5. They also have some boats for hire.

Another decent little place is the *Claris Hotel* – it's basic but OK – singles are US$2.80 and doubles are US$5. Also worth a mention, the *Hotel Choshuenco* is just US$1.70 a single and US$3.30 a double; the rooms are clean, the people are friendly, and there's a restaurant attached.

The *Hostería Pulmahue* is a beautiful place just a short walk out of town on the road leading to Enco, set amidst a garden overlooking the lake. The dining room is filled with a collection of polished tree roots. Pleasant rooms with attached bathrooms go for a surprisingly low US$8.30 per person. If you can afford it it's a great place to stay.

There are a couple of small shops along San Martín where you can buy fresh fruit and vegetables, as well as some groceries, but they haven't got much to offer.

Getting There

The buses which come through from Panguipulli to Choshuenco carry on to Puerto Fry. They overnight at Puerto Fry and depart early the next morning for the return trip to Panguipulli, coming through Choshuenco about 7 am. Check the times as they could be different in winter.

VALDIVIA

Valdivia was one of the very first Spanish settlements in Chile, but much of its present character is the result of German immigration in the mid-19th century. People used to liken arrival in Valdivia to stepping back in time to Germany before

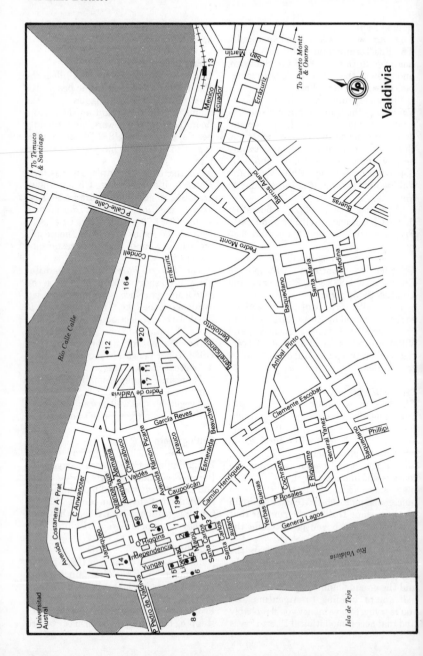

Valdivia

1	Plaza de la República	11	Residencial Ainlebu &
2	Post Office		Residencial Germania
3	Hotel España	12	Bus Terminal
4	Restaurant Palacio &	13	Train Station
	Train Booking Office	14	Hotel Pedro de Valdivia
5	Hotel Schuster	15	Market
6	Tourist Office	16	Torreón del Barro
7	Hotel Unión	17	Hotel Montserrat
8	Archaeology Museum	18	Banco Concepción
9	Hotel Palace	19	Ladeco
10	Banco de Chile	20	Hotel Regional

WW I. Today the comparison is rather a forced one, but the German influence remains in the European-style architecture, and the hotels with German names (Schuster, Germania). There are still many German-speaking people, and people of German descent. When a horse-and-cart plods around the corner in front of the Hotel Schuster it's central Europe and 1905 all over again.

Many of the older buildings were destroyed in the earthquake of 1960 and modern concrete constructions are now the going thing, though off the main streets it's still a town of weatherboard houses and corrugated-iron roofs. There are still many older European-style buildings and fine mansions along Gralle Lagos near the waterfront. There is a university on the river island, Isla Teja, and the large number of students help make Valdivia a lively little town. It's also a major centre for the Lake District and there are buses to scores of small towns further inland.

Information

Tourist Office The tourist office is on Avenida Costanera (otherwise known as Avenida Prat) on the river front between Libertad and Maipú, and is open Monday to Friday but closed on weekends.

Bank You can change money and travellers' cheques at the Banco de Chile on the Plaza de la República, and at the Bank Concepción on Avenida Picarte just up from the Plaza de la República.

Post The post office is on O'Higgins opposite the Plaza de la República. It's open Monday to Friday, 8.30 am to 12.30 pm and 2 to 5 pm; Saturday, 8.30 am to 12 noon; and is closed on Sunday and holidays.

Things to See

Valdivia was rebuilt as a military outpost after the original settlement was reduced to rubble early in the 17th century, and the remains of fortifications can still be seen. There are large Spanish forts at the mouth of the Río Calle Calle at Corral, Niebla and Isla Mancera.

In 1820, during the war of independence, a single ship of the Chilean navy under the command of a mad Scotsman, Lord Cochrane, launched an apparently suicidal, but ultimately successful attack on the forts at Corral. The story goes that having seized a Spanish ship he found in the harbour, Cochrane landed 300 musketeers and took the fort in a surprise assault – no mean feat since it was meant to be defended by more than 700 soldiers and 100 cannon.

Thomas Cochrane had led an equally stormy career in the British navy. He was convicted of fraud and jailed before becoming one of the world's highest-ranking mercenaries and serving with such diverse countries as Chile, Brazil and Greece. Perhaps his exploits redeemed him because in 1842 he was restored to his rank in the British navy and made an admiral in 1854.

The Forts

The **Torreón del Barro** is the turret of a Spanish fort built in 1774, which stands to the east of the bus terminal. A second turret, originally built in the 17th century, stands at the corner of Yerbas Buenas and Yungay facing the Río Valdivia.

Outside Valdivia where the Río Valdivia and the Río Tornagaleones join the Pacific Ocean, there are 17th century Spanish forts at Puerto Corral, Niebla and on the island of Mancera.

The main attractions are the two forts at Corral. The **Fuerte de Corral**, located near the jetty, is the largest and most impressive. It was first built in 1645 and restored and added to in the middle of the 18th century; its battlements and cannon can still be seen.

The second is the **Fuerte Castillo de Armagos** which is about a 30-minute walk from Corral, set on a crag above a small fishing village. There is also a jetty in the village which ferries from Valdivia use.

Niebla is accessible by bus and boat; Corral and Armagos can only be reached by boat. There are buses to Niebla (from the bus terminal) several times daily, in the morning and afternoon, and the fare is about US$0.90.

There are many launches and ferries available for the trip down the estuary between Valdivia and Corral, Niebla and Mancera. The cheapest way to get to any of them is by one of the regular ferries which leave from the Muelle Fluvial on the river front next to the tourist office in Valdivia. The ferries are the *Panguipulli, Duby, Titania* and *Pillanco*. The first departure from Valdivia is around 8 am, then they are hourly until the evening. The first boat departs Corral for Valdivia about 7.30 am and the last about 8 pm. Check times with the tourist office (they keep a timetable) as departure times vary quite a bit from day to day. The journey takes around two to 2½ hours from Valdivia to Corral and costs about US$0.90. The boat runs to Corral via Mancera Island, Niebla and Armagos.

If you prefer a tour which takes you there and back via Corral and Mancera it will cost considerably more. The Motonave boats, *Río Calle Calle* and *Neptuno*, both offer similar half-day tours between 1.30 and 6.30 pm which include visits to Corral and Mancera. They cost around US$8 to US$9. For reservations on the *Río Calle Calle* contact the Hotel Villa del Rio (tel 6292), España 1025. For the *Neptuno* telephone 3235 or make arrangements down at the river front. There are other launches but they're luxury trips which cater to idle minds and deep-sea fishermen (no connection implied).

In Corral there are a couple of places to eat on the waterfront, like the *Restaurant Español* which dishes up an enormous plate of mussels, sausages, potato and chicken for just US$2.

Museum of History & Archaeology

This is one of the most beautiful museums in Chile, housed in a fine timber mansion near the river front on Teja Island. There's a large collection of Mapuche artefacts, and household items from the early days of German settlement. To get there, walk across the bridge over the Río Valdivia, turn left at the first street and it's about 200 metres on the left.

Places to Stay – bottom end

Valdivia isn't a particularly cheap town to stay in. Most of the private houses which offer rooms are full of students from Valdivia University for most of the year so there's no point wasting your shoe leather by trying to find one. Many owners of the cheap hospedajes are also very reluctant to let rooms to short-stay visitors.

One traveller wrote to say that the *Casa de Estudiantes*, Camilo Enrique 792, will take short-stay visitors if there is room. It costs about US$2.50 per person, including breakfast, and is very clean and friendly.

During the vacations you might have more luck so it may be worth strolling down Camilo Henríquez, Cochrane and

Aníbal Pinto where most of the cheap hospedajes are located. At these times try the places at Cochrane 375, Aníbal Pinto 1335, and Henríquez 648.

One of the cheapest places to stay is the hospedaje at Baquedano 670 (tel 4549), run by Señor Edgardo Quiróz, which costs around US$3.20 per person (less in winter) and has hot water and central heating. Edgardo speaks English.

The hospedaje at Carlos Anwanter 802 is a real gem. It's run by a very friendly old lady and is popular with young people. It's as clean as a new pin, very pleasant, has hot water and heating in the rooms and costs US$3.35 per person, either in dormitory-style rooms or doubles.

Another which is very pleasant is the *Hospedaje Pensión Estudiante*, Casa 377, in a small alley off Chacabuco. It's clean, has a homely lounge with an open fire and hot water, but there's no heating in the rooms. It costs US$4.65 a double.

On the other side of town, the *Hotel Regional*, Ramón Picarte 1005, is worth trying. It's a white building opposite the bus station. There are rooms for US$2.80 per person and they have hot water. It's a fairly basic place, but clean, and the people are friendly; there's a small restaurant attached. If this fails, try the *Residencial Picarte* right next door. The Picarte really can't be highly recommended, but if you're on a tight budget, well, it's there. It costs US$2.20 per person.

The *Residencial Germania*, Ramón Picarte 873, is a very decent place which costs US$4.70 a single, and about US$9.40 a double (a bit less for a room with a double bed), including breakfast (toast and coffee). There's hot water in the showers, heating in the rooms and meals are available. The owners are friendly and speak German.

Next door to the Residencial Germania is the rather cheaper *Residencial Ainlebu* which goes for around US$3.40 per person, including breakfast. There are hot showers and meals are available.

One place I'd highly recommend is the *Hotel Montserrat* at Ramón Picarte 849, just a few doors from the Residencial Germania, heading towards the city centre (it's set back from the street so look for the sign). The people are friendly, the rooms are small, but bright and very clean; singles are US$4.20 and doubles are US$5.80, including breakfast.

The *Hotel España* (tel 3478) at Independencia 628, has a good, central location. Singles are US$3.30 and doubles, US$5.60, and there's hot water.

If you'd like to stay right on the river front check out the *Hotel Unión*, (tel 3819), Prat 514, opposite the tourist office. Costs are US$4.40 a single and US$8.30 a double that does not include breakfast, and the rooms do not have attached bathrooms. It's an old place overlooking the river; the rooms and bathrooms are clean, the staff are friendly and there's a bar downstairs.

For some olde worlde charm try the *Hotel Schuster*, (tel 3272) at Maipú 60. It's a rambling old timber hotel with very clean, spacious rooms and the manager speaks both German and English. Rooms without bathrooms are US$4.70 a single and US$6.25 a double; with a bathroom, US$7.20 a single and US$8.60 a double – plus 20% tax. There are hot showers all day and the rooms are heated, there's a bar on the ground floor, and breakfast is available. This is my pick of the hotels in Valdivia.

Places to Stay - middle

Try the *Hotel Palace*, (tel 3319) Chacabuco 308, which costs US$10 a single and US$12.20 a double for rooms with a bathroom and including breakfast. They're smallish rooms but it's a good hotel in an ideal location.

The *Moteles Raitue*, (tel 2503) Lagos 1382, has cabins for one or two people for US$10, for three people US$12, and for four people US$15.

Places to Stay - top end

The *Hotel Pedro de Valdivia*, (tel 2931) at Caranpangue 190, is surprisingly cheap at US$27 a single and US$35 a double, including breakfast. It's a fine hotel with a mezzanine floor in the foyer and a pleasant garden and lawn at the rear.

Places to Eat

There are some good restaurants on Arauco between Caupolicán and García Reyes, on the right-hand side as you walk away from the river. They're popular with the local people and the food is very good. The large market facing the river has many cheap restaurants.

For coffee and snacks check out the *Restaurant Palacio*, on the corner of O'Higgins and Arauco, which is popular with young people, especially on Saturday mornings.

For some up-market eating try the *Restaurant El Conquistador* on O'Higgins, facing the Plaza de la República. Downstairs there's a simple café and bar (good for morning empanadas), and upstairs there's a restaurant with white table cloths and candles with a balcony over-looking the street and plaza. You'd be looking at about US$6 per person for a complete meal here.

For the best cakes and pastries in town try the *Establecimientos Delicias* at Camilo Henríquez 372. Eat elsewhere and then come here for drinks and deserts. Across the road, the *Cheers Restaurant* serves pizzas, pasta dishes and an innumerable variety of drinks, and has big green cushioned couches you can disappear into.

Other places that could be worth checking out are the *Fuente Alemana* next door to the Cheers Restaurant; the *Centro Español* on Henríquez near the Plaza de la República; and the *Bomba Bar & Restaurant* at the corner of Arauco and Caupolicán.

Getting There

Air Ladeco is on Caupolicán, just near the corner with Arauco. There are three flights a week between Valdivia and Santiago via Temuco.

Bus The bus terminal is on Munoz below the junction of Anwanter and Picarte. All long-distance buses to the Lake District depart from here. It's well organised and there's a huge direction indicator at the entrance which lists destinations, journey times, distances, and bus companies. Enquire about student discounts on ticket prices – Igi Llaima offers them.

The large cities (Santiago, Temuco, Osorno and Puerto Montt) are covered by a number of companies including Tas Choapa, Buses Norte, Nuevo Longitudinal Sur, Turibús, Cruz del Sur, ETC, Lit, Vía Tur, Transbus, Igi Llaima, and Pullman Sur.

Departures to Santiago are all in the evening and fares are around US$10, or about US$18 for a bus cama.

Heading south, there are usually several departures daily from early morning to late at night: to Puerto Montt (US$2.20), Osorno (US$1.70) and Temuco (US$2). Some, like Buses Norte, have departures almost every hour throughout the day. There are also regular buses direct to Ancud (US$4.20) and Castro (US$4.70) on Chiloé Island – try Pullman Sur.

Buses Norte have buses from Valdivia to Punta Arenas, via Argentina. The route goes via Bariloche, and south along the Argentinian coast to Río Gallegos. There are one or two buses a week to Punta Arenas and the trip takes about two days and costs US$60. Also try Turibús – they have bus cama.

Buses Norte also have a daily service as far as Bariloche for around US$18. For other buses to Argentina try Igi Llaima which also has buses to Bariloche, to Zapala for around US$16 and to Neuquén for around US$20. Tas Choapa has buses three times a week to Bariloche, and daily to Mendoza and Buenos Aires. Buses Chiloé also has buses to Bariloche.

Typical fares to towns in the Lake District are: San José (US$1), Lanco (US$1.65), Panguipulli (US$2), Malalhue (US$1.80), Villarrica (US$2), Pucón (US$2.30). Companies and the destinations they service in the Lake District are:

Buses Chile Nuevo to San José, Lanco, Panguipulli, and Malalhue several times daily, Monday to Friday, but only once or twice on Saturdays and Sundays. Also try them for buses to Futrono – several departures daily except on Sundays.
Buses Pirehueico to San José, Lanco, Malalhue and Panguipulli several times daily.
Buses Oriente to Panguipulli once a day, and to Niebla about eight times daily.
Buses Futrono to Futrono, with departures about three times a day Monday to Saturday, but none on Sundays; the trip takes about 2½ hours, via Paillaco.
Buses Rinihue to Los Lagos and Paillaco about eight times daily in either direction.
Buses Niebla to Niebla several times a day; and to Panguipulli, several departures daily Monday to Saturday, and once on Sunday.
Buses Jac to San José, Lanco, Lancoche and Villarrica; daily departures, twice in the morning and once in the afternoon, except on Sundays when there's one morning and one afternoon bus. The afternoon bus carries on to Pucón.
Buses Valdivia to Panguipulli via Lanco, Purulon, Malalhue, Melefquen and Huellahue, six times daily.

Rail Valdivia lies on the Santiago-Puerto Montt railway line. The train station is quite a long way from the centre of town on Ecuador which branches off Ramón Picarte. Get a local bus or taxi into the centre. To book tickets for the train you don't have to go all the way to the station; there is a booking office in the centre of town at the junction of O'Higgins and Arauco. For details of timetables and fares see the Getting Around chapter.

Getting Around

Valdivia is too large to depend entirely on walking so you'll definitely need some help from the bus network. The buses all have signs in their front windows indicating their destinations.

From the bus station or the train station any bus marked 'Plaza' will take you to the Plaza de la República. Coming in from the bus station the buses run up Ramón Picarte and then turn down Chacabuco; for the plaza you get off at the corner of Chacabuco and Henríquez. The bus then continues over the bridge to the Isla Teja. There's a flat fare of about US$0.20 per trip.

Heading away from the plaza towards the bus station the buses go down Arauco before turning down Ramón Picarte. There's a taxi rank outside the bus station, and at the corner of Letelier and Henríquez at the Plaza de la República.

FUTRONO

This is a dusty little town set on the slopes overlooking Lago Ranco. There's nothing to the town, but the island-studded lake with its low hills and mountains on one flank is a pretty sight. At the edge of the town a track leads down to a black-sand beach, and you can swim in the calm, clean water. Although it is a tourist resort, relatively few people visit so you'll find Futrono quiet, peaceful and much underrated.

Places to Stay

People often camp out by the lake, alongside the beach. A lovely spot if you've got your own tent.

Otherwise, the cheapest place to stay is the hospedaje on the main street at No 90, next to the gas station. It's a clean, neat place with friendly people and it costs US$2.50 per person – breakfast is an extra US$0.80.

Without a doubt one of the best places in Chile to stay is the *Hostería El Rícan Arabe*, just off the main street on the edge of town as you come in from Valdivia. It's situated on a hill overlooking the lake, and has its own swimming pool and restaurant. What makes it special however, is the exuberant (if a bit weird) personality of its proprietor, Yelila Osman, the daughter of a Palestinian couple who emigrated to Chile in the 1940s. She dishes up some extraordinary (and enormous) Arabic meals, including rack of lamb, stuffed vine leaves and cucumbers, accompanied by wine and Arabic songs. Rooms are around US$5.30 per person, or US$6.70 per person including breakfast. If you can afford it then this place is really worth it! The hostería is only a half-hour walk or so from the lake.

Places to Eat

Apart from Yelila Osman's hostería there are several small restaurants on the main street and some supermarkets and food shops in the vicinity of the bus terminals. For ice-cream, sandwiches, and snacks try the *Fogón Negonta* on the edge of town on the road heading back to Valdivia – it's a pleasant place with cane furniture and, on some nights, a disco.

Getting There

The two bus companies operating from Futrono both have terminals on the main street. Buses Futrono have departures about three or four times a day to Valdivia via Paillaco. Across the road is another company with about three departures a day for Valdivia. The fare is US$0.80.

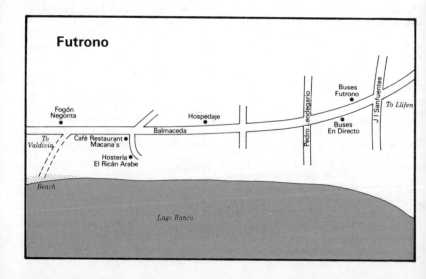

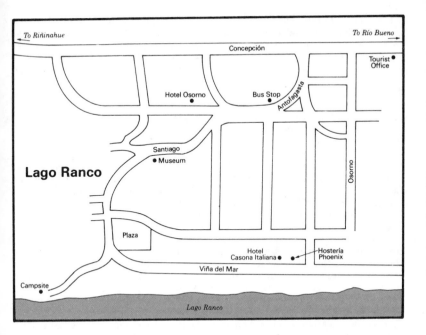

Buses from Valdivia to Futrono carry on as far as Llifen, 20 km further on, and some go as far as Arquilhue. There are probably no buses with either company on Sundays.

LAGO RANCO

On the southern shore of Lago Ranco, this little town stands out from all the others in the Lake District for its remarkable ugliness. The best views of the place are as you come over the hills from Río Bueno – a pretty trip through cattle-grazing country – and the place to turn around and start heading back to Futrono. Generally, the surrounding countryside is quite beautiful, so if you can keep away from the town it's worth coming this way.

Information

Tourist Office The tourist office has a give-away map of the town, and a very detailed map of Lago Ranco hanging on the wall. They also have all sorts of leaflets on places further south if you're heading that way. There is a small museum, on Santiago in the middle of town – mainly an exhibit of Mapuche pottery.

Places to Stay & Eat

The one saving grace of this place is the *Hotel Casona Italiana* on the shore front at Viña del Mar 145. It's clean and bright with friendly people and a decent view overlooking the lake. US$14 a per person includes three meals a day; or US$7.20 includes breakfast only. Almost next door, the *Hostería Phoenix* at Viña del Mar 141, is slightly cheaper than the Casona Italiana.

The *Pensión Osorno*, Temuco 103, is a neat, spartan little place, and the people are friendly. Rooms are US$6.70 including meals, or US$2.80 including breakfast only.

Meals at the *Hotel Casona Italiana* are good and they're available to non-residents. There are a couple of other places to eat – like *La Cabaña* on Santiago which has a friendly manager.

Getting There
Since there are no direct buses between Futrono and Lago Ranco you have to take the daily bus from Futrono to Paillaco first. From Paillaco you take another bus south to Río Bueno, which is 47 km from Lago Ranco. From the bus terminal at Río Bueno there are several buses per day to Lago Ranco.

Alternatively, catch a taxi colectivo to Lago Ranco from outside the Río Bueno bus terminal – these cost US$1.40 per person and seat four or five people. The train line which used to run between Lago Ranco and Río Bueno is now derelict.

From Lago Ranco there are two buses a day direct to Osorno – one in the morning and one in the early afternoon. Otherwise simply go to Río Bueno. This is on the Temuco-Puerto Montt road so there are numerous buses each day from Río Bueno to Osorno and Valdivia, and regular buses to Puerto Montt, Temuco and Santiago.

OSORNO
Osorno is one of the largest towns in southern Chile. It has a population of over 100,000 and is a major transport centre for buses and trains to the Lake District, especially to Lagos Puyehue and Rupanco and to the Parque Nacional Puyehue. Like Valdivia there are many people of German descent and many are bilingual.

Information
Tourist Office The tourist office is on the second floor of the bus terminal. The staff are very helpful and have a wide range of literature and maps (all of them free) including a map of the town.

Bank The quickest and most convenient way of changing money is to go to

Comercial Real at Ramírez 1079 between Cochrane and Freire. It's an electrical and white-goods shop. There's no fuss and it's all done within a few minutes. They take cheques and cash. Exchange rates are favourable. Otherwise try the Banco de Santiago at Matta 624 and the Banco Osorno at Ramírez 902, but they might only change US cash.

Things to See
Osorno is really just a transit stop on the way to somewhere else, but if you've got a few hours to spare this *is* an interesting place to wander around. First and foremost there's the Catholic Cemetery on Rodríguez at the southern end of Eduvijes, with massive, ornate family crypts, far surpassing any others in Chile.

The most interesting part of the town is the old district between the Plaza de Armas and the railway station. There is a profusion of buildings left over from the early part of this century, including old factories and numerous weatherboard houses. On the outskirts of the town, particularly as you come in from Valdivia, you will see many slum dwellings.

Like Valdivia, Osorno also has its Spanish fort, the **Fuerte Reina Luisa** which was built in 1793 on the orders of the Governor of Chile, Don Ambrosio O'Higgins, father of Bernardo O'Higgins. The fort guards the river entry to Osorno, stands to the west of the new railway station, and has been restored.

Places to Stay – bottom end
Most of the cheapies in Osorno seem to be owned by hard-faced sharks who quote the first price which comes into their heads. For the flea pits which most of them offer it's outright banditry. Some people may find this description too harsh, but the fact is that there are only a few good cheap places in Osorno and a lot of crumbling hovels which command no less than US$4 per person – and that's if

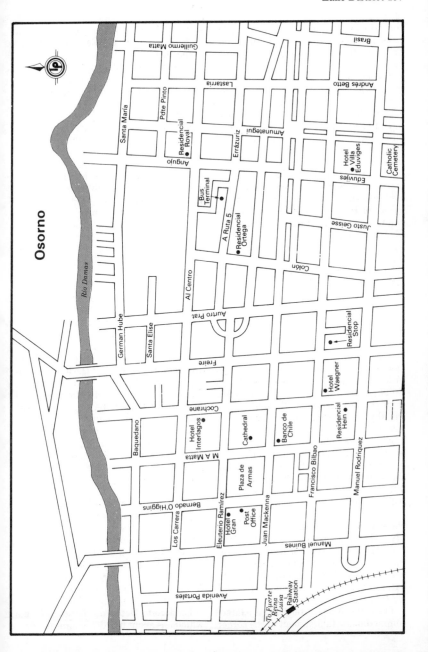

Osorno

you're lucky! This is unlike the rest of the Lake District where you can generally find something decent for a reasonable price.

The one cheapie I'll give an unequivocal recommendation to is the *Residencial Ortega* at Colón 602, just near the corner with Errázuriz. It's US$3.30 per person, including breakfast. The rooms are clean and the common bathrooms have hot showers and even bathtubs. It's run by a friendly, elderly lady.

Other than that there's not much worth mentioning. Some travellers recommend avoiding the *Residencial Stop*, on the corner of Bilbao and Freire, but if you can't find anything it may do for a night. Shoe-box sized rooms with paper-thin walls cost US$3.30 per person; the bathrooms are OK and have hot water.

The *Residencial Hein*, Cochrane 551 between Bilbao and Rodríguez, is a real rip-off at US$5.50 per person (including breakfast) and you don't even get a peek at the room before you sign up – most unusual in Chile.

Places to Stay – middle

One which can be recommended is the *Villa Eduvijes Hotel*, (tel 5023) at Eduvijes 856, just a few minutes walk from the bus terminal. It's good value, friendly and clean, with constant hot water, and costs US$5.30 a single and US$8.60 a double with a private bathroom. Breakfast is an additional US$0.80 per person. It's rather expensive by shoestring-budget standards but it's difficult to find anything cheaper that's still habitable.

Places to Stay – top end

My pick of the top end is the *Hotel Gran* (tel 2171) facing the Plaza de Armas in the centre of town. Simple, clean and neat rooms with a telephone and private bathroom are US$10.60 a single and US$16 a double.

The *Hotel Waegar* (tel 3722) is a large, commodious establishment at the corner of Cochrane and Bilbao. It has singles from US$12.20 and doubles from US$21.10 – and there's a restaurant downstairs.

Also try the *Hotel Inter Lagos* (tel 2684) at Cochrane 551, which has singles for US$15.60 and doubles for US$23.30.

Places to Eat

The *Club Social Ramírez*, Eduvijes, almost next door to the Eduvijes Hotel, has good cheap food and generous portions. There are a couple of small snack bars along this street – good for empanadas. Fresh fruit and vegetables are available from the market at the corner of Errázuriz and Augulo. In town there's a *Dino's* at the corner of Matta and Eleuterio Ramírez facing the plaza – good for drinks, snacks, grills and ice-cream.

Getting There

Air LAN-Chile (tel 4355) is at MacKenna 110. Ladeco (tel 4419) is at MacKenna 1010. Ladeco has flights about three times a week from Osorno to Valdivia, Temuco and Santiago.

Bus From the bus terminal in Osorno you can get buses to most of the larger towns in the Lake District – Temuco, Valdivia, Puerto Varas and Puerto Montt – as well as some of the smaller ones like Lago Ranco and Puerto Octay.

Going north, there are buses to Valdivia and Temuco by Pullman Lit, Transbus, Cruz del Sur, Igi Llaima, Vaftur, ETC and Buses Norte. Fares from Osorno include Temuco for US$3.10 and Valdivia for about US$1.70.

Going south, there are buses to Puerto Varas and Puerto Montt by Cruz del Sur, Igi Llaima, Buses Chiloé, ETC and Varmontt. Some of these companies have direct buses to Ancud and Castro on Chiloé Island. Fares include Ancud for US$3.30, Castro for US$3.90, Puerto Montt for US$1.70, Puerto Varas for US$1.70.

For Puerto Octay use Buses Turismo which has about five departures per day,

Monday to Friday, four on Saturdays and three on Sundays. Vía Tur has buses twice a day to Lago Ranco for US$1.70.

You can also get buses to the Argentinian destinations of Bariloche, Mendoza, Zapala, Neuquén, Rosario and Buenos Aires with Igi Llaima (several days a week to Zapala, Neuquén and Bariloche), Turismo Lanin (five days a week to Bariloche), Buses Norte (daily to Bariloche), and Tas Choapa (to Buenos Aires, Bariloche and Mendoza). Fares to Bariloche are US$17.80, to Mendoza, US$28.30, and to Buenos Aires, US$56.

Turismo Lanin also has salón cama buses once a week from Osorno, through Argentina to Punta Arenas. Buses Norte has a bus once a week to Punta Arenas.

Most of the above lines, plus Turibús, Transbus, Vía Tur and Tur-Bus, have daily departures to Santiago and Valparaíso, with some going through to Viña del Mar. The fare is around US$15. Try Cruz del Sur for salón cama coaches to Santiago.

Rail Osorno is on the Santiago-Puerto Montt train line. The railway station is at the western end of town on Portales. For details of time-tables and fares see the Getting Around chapter.

PUERTO OCTAY

Puerto Octay is a peaceful, picturesque little town situated on the low hills bordering Lago Llanquihue. One of my favourite towns in the Lake District, Puerto Octay is reminiscent of a European village with many European-style buildings and people of German descent.

Things to See

There's a museum on Independencia. It seems like the whole town contributed to the displays by digging up their old farm machinery, and rifling through attics and cellars for their pioneer grannys' favourite porcelain, rusting irons, forgotten gramophone records and steam-driven telephones. It's open Monday to Friday, 9 am to 12 noon and 1.30 to 6.30 pm, and on Saturday 9 am to 12 noon.

Places to Stay – bottom end

Near the the lake, next to the large

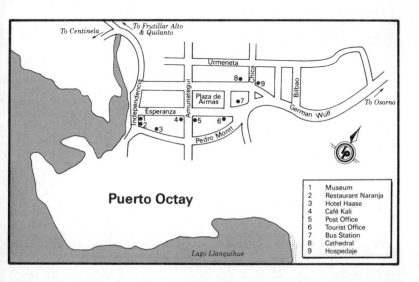

1	Museum
2	Restaurant Naranja
3	Hotel Haase
4	Café Kali
5	Post Office
6	Tourist Office
7	Bus Station
8	Cathedral
9	Hospedaje

Puerto Octay

Lago Llanquihue

church, there's an upstairs hospedaje at Wulf 712. It costs US$2.80 per person, including breakfast, and although spartan, it's clean, the people friendly and there are hot showers. It's a fairly quiet place too. The same people run the *Restaurant Cabaña* across the road.

The *Hotel Haase*, (tel 3) on Pedro Montt, is an amazing place run by an elderly German lady who will probably give you a guided tour of the whole establishment, with its spacious interiors, high ceilings and no less than *three* dining rooms. If you can afford to stay here then do so – it's unique! Singles are US$6.70 and doubles are US$10. Only a few rooms have their own bathrooms.

Just before you get to the Hotel Centinela on the Centinela Peninsula there's the Playa La Baja and the *Hostería La Baja* where rooms start from around US$3.60 per person; full board is around US$7 to US$8 per person.

There are two campsites: one on the beach, and one just before it on the right, as you come in from the town.

Places to Stay – top end

The *Hotel Centinela* (tel 22) is at the end of Andrés Schmoelz, the road which runs from the town through a grove along the Centinela Peninsula. It's a massive timber chalet; it has simple rooms, a fine view across the lake and a large restaurant. Doubles with a private bathroom cost US$14, including breakfast; doubles without a bathroom cost US$12.20, including breakfast; and singles with breakfast are US$11.10. It's worth the money if you want something somewhat different to run-of-the-mill accommodation. It takes about an hour to walk from the town to the hotel.

Places to Eat

Aside from the hotels, the *Café Kali*, opposite the plaza, is a good place for breakfast, drinks and cakes. For morning empanadas there's the *Restaurant Naranja* on Independencia.

Getting There

There is a bus from Puerto Octay to Osorno about five times a day Monday to Friday, four times a day on Saturdays, and three times a day on Sundays. Monday to Friday there is one bus in the early morning from Puerto Octay to Purranque. There is one bus in the late afternoon, Monday to Friday, from Puerto Octay to Las Cascadas.

LAS CASCADAS

Las Cascadas is a tiny town so named because of the nearby waterfalls. The bus ride from Puerto Octay provides you with grand view of Volcán Osorno, and takes you through dairy country with many small farms and little, shingle-walled churches (all painted yellow with red corrugated iron roofs). Las Cascadas fronts onto a decent black sand beach and there are good views across the lake.

Places to Stay & Eat

You may be able to get a room at the *Hostería Irma*, one km out of town on the road to Ensenada, on the left. Don't count on it however; although the family is friendly don't expect them to put you up just because you land on their doorstep. They'll charge about US$2.80 per person, and they have a bar and serve food as well (for an extra charge).

Diagonally opposite the hosteria, alongside the lake, there's a quiet and peaceful campsite. Another 3½ km down the road from the Hostería Irma, towards Ensenada, there's a second campsite which charges a few cents per person. There are several small shops in the town where you can stock up on food.

Getting There

There is one bus per day, Monday to Friday, between Las Cascadas and Puerto Octay. There is no bus service further south between Las Cascadas and Ensenada so you have to walk or hitch between the two. The bus from Puerto Octay gets into Las Cascadas about 7 pm,

Top: Petrohué
Bottom: Chol Chol, near Temuco

Top: Indian bullock cart, Chol Chol, near Temuco
Left: Waterfall, near Pucón
Right: Indian grave monument, Villarrica

if it's on time. Unless you want to hitch at night you'll have to stay in Las Cascadas.

The distance between Las Cascadas and Ensenada *is* 20 km, although various people and depraved tourist leaflets will tell you it is less. This is four hours solid walking if you can't get a lift – and there's not much traffic even in the summer holidays.

ENSENADA

Ensenada lies in the shadow of the 2660-metre, snow-capped Volcán Osorno, on the shore of the biting-cold Lago Llanquihue; there's a good black-sand beach and beautiful views of the perfectly conical volcano across the misty lake. To the south is the jagged, demolished cone of Volcán Calbuco which must have blown its top off with a massive burp. Ensenada is on the road to Petrohué and Lago Todos los Santos, the most beautiful lake in the entire district. The hotels, campsite, and restaurants are all spread along Ensenada's single street.

Places to Stay – bottom end

A few minutes walk from the Hostería Ruedas Viejas (see Places to Stay – middle) there's an unsignposted hospedaje – a two storey, wooden house. It's clean and tidy and only about US$3.30 per person, which is great value for Ensenada. Don't count on getting in though, it's very likely to be full.

The cheapest place to stay is the *Boy Scout Lodge* on the main street, though this place seems to lodge just about anyone, including teams of little children. Could be fun, in a way ...

The *Teski Ski Club* has a mountain refuge outside Ensenada with excellent views over the lake; it's a good base for climbing Volcán Osorno. It's worth making the effort to get there. Take the Ensenada-Puerto Octay road and turn off about three km from the town (signposted) and continue nine km up the side of the mountain (but below the snow line). It's open all year, has a warden who

looks after the place, a log fire and hot water.

Places to Stay – middle

The *Hostería Ruedas Viejas* has rooms for US$7.50 including breakfast – singles and doubles are the same price. You stay in cosy individual cabins each with a double bed, private toilet and shower (cold), and a small wood-burner for heating. The restaurant here is not exactly cheap but the servings are huge and well worth the money.

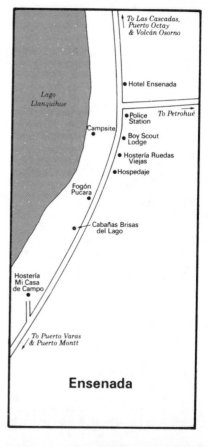

The *Fogón Pucara* has rooms for US$11 – singles and doubles are the same price. The main attraction of this place is the restaurant with its barbecue. Even in summer you'll welcome the chance to sit around the cosy fire. The *Cabanas Brisas de Lago* has cabins at US$7.80 per person.

Places to Stay – top end

Top of the list is the *Hotel Ensenada* (tel 2363), the first large building you pass as you trudge in from Las Cascadas. It's a fine place, similar to the Centinela in Puerto Octay. It has a large restaurant decorated with odd bits of ironwork, and even machinery. There's a bar and a fireplace amongst the scrap metal. If you can't afford to stay here come in and have a drink. Singles cost from US$16, and doubles from US$16.40 (more expensive rooms have private bathrooms).

Something of a hike out of town on the road to Puerto Varas is the *Hostería Mi Casa de Campo* – you'd probably need a car to enjoy staying here. There's cabin accommodation for about US$19.40 per cabin and each cabin fits up to four people. There's a moderately-priced bar and restaurant.

Getting There

From Ensenada to Las Cascadas you have to walk or hitch, and from Las Cascadas you can catch a bus to Puerto Octay; see the Las Cascadas and Puerto Octay sections for details.

There is now a daily bus to Petrohué which comes through Ensenada from Puerto Varas and Puerto Montt around 11 am; in Ensenada it pulls in briefly at the Hostería Ruedas Viejas. The fare from Ensenada to Petrohué is about US$0.80. For more details see the section on Petrohué.

Heading west to Puerto Varas or Puerto Montt you can either catch this bus on its way back from Petrohué or try and flag down one of the tour buses that comes through in the afternoon (you probably won't have much luck). There's supposed to be another bus company which operates a twice-daily service between Puerto Montt and Ensenada, so ask around about that one. Otherwise, try hitching.

PETROHUE

Petrohué is not much more than a hotel and a CONAF base but it's one of the biggest tourist destinations at this end of the Lake District – mainly for day-tripping tour groups who get bussed in and packed on boats for a spin around the lake. Lago Todos los Santos, its skyline completely overwhelmed by Volcán Osorno, is the climax of the Lake District. The most dramatic views of the volcano are from the lake, a narrow body of water hemmed in on every side by high, forested hills. Peeking over the hills is Volcán Puntigudo.

Information

CONAF CONAF has built an exhibition hall in front of the Hotel Petrohué, with exhibits on the Parque Nacional Vicente Pérez Rosales which includes Volcán Osorno and Lago Todos los Santos, including descriptions of its fauna and flora, geography, geology and the formation of the volcanoes, glaciers and lakes. It's well set out, but the captions are only in Spanish.

Post There is a small post office at Petrohué, by the boat dock. It's open Monday to Friday, 8.30 am to 12.30 pm and 2 to 6 pm, and on Saturday, 9 am to 1 pm.

Things to See

From the Hotel Petrohué you can walk along a dirt track to the Playa Larga, a large black-sand beach which is much better than the one near the hotel, and less crowded. Follow the road through the CONAF campsite and then look for the sign which points to the beach. It's half an hour from the hotel.

There is a daily tourist boat from

Petrohué which will take you to Isla Margarita and back. It leaves at 3 pm during the summer months only. If you're not going to Peulla you really must take this trip for the striking views of Volcán Osorno. Margarita is a strangely beautiful island with one small farm on it. The trip lasts about two hours and costs US$2.20 per person.

Places to Stay & Eat

There are very few cheap places but try the Kuscher family's house as they regularly rent out rooms in summer and may do so in winter too. They're on the other side of the river and you'll have to hire a rowboat (from beside the pier) to get over there. You can also camp out in their grounds. Rooms cost about US$2.80 per person. It makes an interesting change from ordinary hotels and camp-sites and they are friendly people.

There is a campsite on the beach on the shore of the lake a few minutes walk from the Hotel Petrohué. It costs US$2.80 per tent per day, and US$1.70 per person per day.

The large *Hotel Petrohué* is the only hotel. It's comfortable and has its own restaurant. Singles are US$8.30 and doubles are US$13.90, all with private bathrooms, so it's good value. The manager speaks fluent Spanish, English and German. Contrary to popular belief this hotel was *not* built especially for the visit of England's Queen Elizabeth and her sundry hangers on.

There are no shops or stores selling food in Petrohué so the hotel is the only place to eat. This gets moderately expensive by the time you put together a decent meal. If your budget's tight, bring supplies from Puerto Varas. You will have to do this if you camp or stay with the Kuschers.

Getting There

Bus There is now a daily bus (except Sundays) which goes through from Puerto Montt, via Puerto Varas and Ensenada to Petrohué where it arrives about 12 noon.

This includes a short stop at Los Saltos del Petrohué where the water of the river surges through narrow channels in the rock – it can be very dramatic. Unfortunately this bus gets you to the lake after the ferry to Peulla has left, so you have to stay at least one night in Petrohué if you're heading to Peulla or on to Argentina. The bus remains at Petrohué for about half an hour or so before returning to Puerto Varas.

Boat Two ferries depart Petrohué for Peulla, daily at around 11 am. They depart Peulla for Petrohué at 5.30 pm and 7 pm. The trip takes two hours.

The *Esmeralda* is the ferry which runs all year round. If you're going to Argentina this is the one to take since it will probably connect with buses in Peulla to take you straight out (enquire about this). It's also the faster of the two boats. The disadvantage is that it has only one small deck for everyone to try and stand on – so most of the time your views are from inside the cabin.

The launch run by Transporte Lagos del Sur is the better of the two since it has more deck space to stand on and allows you to enjoy the views. It costs US$4.70 for the return trip. It departs Petrohué at 11 am, and departs Peulla for the return trip at 5.30 pm.

If you take the second ferry (it only runs in summer when there are tourists to fill it) you can get the buses to Argentina from Peulla which leave about 2.30 pm. These take you the first leg of the journey to Bariloche, a trip which includes more boats rides. You get to Bariloche that night at about 7.30 pm or 8.30 pm. The fare to Bariloche is US$28 including boat trips. Chilean customs is at Peulla. Buses do not run on Sundays.

Tours Transporte Lago del Sur runs day excursions from Puerto Montt and Puerto Varas to Petrohué and Peulla and back, but not during winter. A number of other bus companies also have tours to Petrohué and Peulla originating in Puerto Montt; see the Puerto Montt section for details.

PEULLA

Todos los Santos changes colour as you approach Peulla – you pass through a narrow stretch of deep-blue water which changes to emerald-green before Peulla. Peulla has a hotel, customs post, school, post office and that's about it. Despite its size it's a busy place in summer with numerous tourist groups passing through between Chile and Argentina.

Things to See

Cascadas Los Novios is a waterfall just a few minutes walk uphill from the Hotel Peulla and is a good picnic spot. Transporte Lagos del Sur have a bus trip from Peulla which takes you 17 km up the road towards Argentina to the lookout point for Volcán Tronador which is an immense extinct volcano with a huge glacier rolling down one side. It lies on the Chilean border – one peak belongs to Chile, the middle one marks no-person's land and the other is Argentinian. The bus ride takes you to within seven km of the Argentinian border. The road from Peulla follows a river which has its source in the volcano's glacier.

Places to Stay & Eat

One km from the dock is the *Hotel Peulla* (tel 3253). It's a large place with singles for US$18 and doubles for US$25, including breakfast. It's run by a Chilean and his Californian wife. There is nowhere to eat in Peulla except at the hotel restaurant. There is a tiny store behind and to one side of the hotel but it doesn't sell very much food so bring your own.

There's a campsite opposite the CONAF office. It may be possible to get a room with one of the local families, but don't count on it, and be prepared to stay at the hotel or camp. According to some reports, staying with a family is excellent value – dinner, bed and breakfast, a warm, cosy bedroom with embroidered sheets – although it can be on the expensive side. Ask around.

Getting There

For details of transport between Peulla and Petrohué, and Petrohué and Puerto Varas, Ensenada and Puerto Montt see the Petrohué section.

PUERTO VARAS

Puerto Varas is a friendly, if ordinary town on the south-eastern shore of Lago Llanquihue. There's not much of interest and the town is really just a transit point. From Puerto Varas you can leave the Lake District and make your way south to Puerto Montt, head east to Lago Todos los Santos and Argentina or north towards Osorno, Valdivia, Temuco and Santiago.

Tourist Office There is a tourist office at Santa Rosa 340 (tel 278) which has brochures about the entire area.

Places to Stay – bottom end

Puerto Varas is a large town with a population of about 23,000 and it's a tourist destination, so there's no problem finding accommodation.

The *Residencial Unión* at San Francisco 669 opposite the bus terminal, is basic but clean and has hot showers. Singles are US$2.80 and doubles are US$5.60 – this includes breakfast and there's a cheap restaurant on the ground floor. The *Residencial Hellwig*, at the corner of Portales and San Pedro, is also cheap and recommended.

Places to Stay – middle

The *Hotel Playa Ltda*, (tel 338) Del Salvador 24, is a large, rambling hotel with spartan rooms, but the place has a good atmosphere about it and the manager is friendly. The front rooms have fine views across the lake. The cheapest singles are US$4.30, doubles, US$8.70. Rooms with private bathrooms

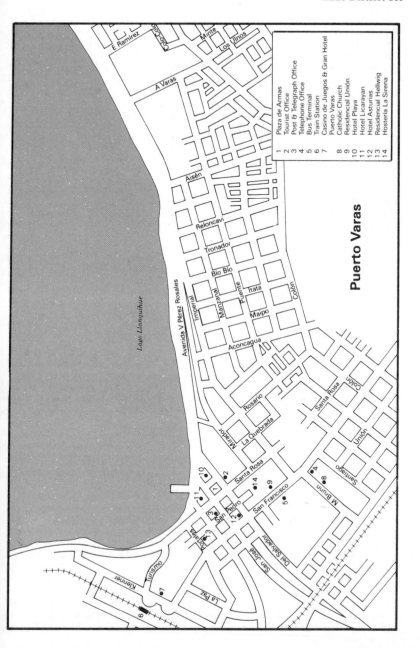

Puerto Varas

Lago Llanquihue

1 Plaza de Armas
2 Tourist Office
3 Post & Telegraph Office
4 Telephone Office
5 Bus Terminal
6 Train Station
7 Casino de Juegos & Gran Hotel
8 Puerto Varas
9 Catholic Church
10 Residencial Unión
11 Hotel Playa
12 Hotel Licarayan
13 Residencial Hellwig
14 Hostería La Sirena

start from US$7.20 a single and US$13 a double. There's a good restaurant downstairs but you'd be looking at about US$6 per person for a full meal.

The next best of the mid-range places is the *Hostería La Sirena*, Santa Rosa 710, which is on a hill overlooking the whole town. You get there by walking up Santa Rosa (not San Pedro as it may appear from the map – it's a dead end). Singles are US$11.10 and doubles are US$22.20, including breakfast and a private bathroom.

Places to Stay – top end

The *Gran Hotel Puerto Varas*, (tel 524) Klenner 351, looks like a grand concrete bunker from the outside – it's instantly identifiable by the huge, illuminated 'CASINO' sign. Singles are US$27.50 and doubles are US$33.90. Admission to the casino (they take your money before you've even started losing it) is US$2.80 and you can play roulette, bingo and the poker machines (Ch$15, Ch$30 and Ch$50 tokens).

You could also try the *Hotel Licarayen* (tel 305) overlooking the waterfront, with singles and doubles for US$26.70; and the *Hotel Asturias*, (tel 446) Del Salvador 322, which has singles for US$32 and doubles for US$36.

Getting There

The bus terminal is on San Francisco and a number of bus companies have their offices in it.

The best company for buses north to Santiago or south to Puerto Montt is probably Buses Varmontt; they have daily buses to Santiago, and about 30 buses a day to Osorno and Puerto Montt. Buses to Puerto Montt depart about every half hour from 8.30 am to around 8.30 pm. Apparently there is also a local bus line which has buses to Puerto Montt all through the day from around 6.15 am to 7.45 pm.

A number of bus companies have their offices in the town centre. Igi Llaima is at Del Salvador 237 between Santa Rosa and San Pedro, with daily buses to Santiago, and a couple of departures a day for Temuco. Tur-Bus Jedimar has an office in the Hotel Asturia and LIT is at the corner of San Pedro and San Francisco.

Fares from Puerto Varas are: to Santiago US$26.10; Temuco US$6.30; Valdivia US$3.80; Osorno US$1.80; Puerto Montt US$0.40

Try Andina del Sur at Del Salvador 243 and Buses Norte at the corner of Del Salvador and San Francisco for buses to Bariloche in Argentina.

There is a daily bus to Petrohué via Ensenada and Puerto Varas coming through from Puerto Montt. The company running this bus has its office and terminal in Puerto Varas at the Residencial Hellwig, at the corner of Portales and San Pedro.

Getting Around

Check the bus companies for tickets northwards and also for excursions to Petrohué, around Lago Llanquihue and even south to Chiloé Island. Typical prices for day tours in the local area are US$8 for Petrohué, US$11 for Ancud (on Chiloé Island) and US$12 for a circuit of Lago Llanquihue.

PUERTO MONTT

This is one of the largest towns in southern Chile and there are still many reminders of its German-influenced past. The area was settled by Germans in the mid-19th century and many houses are of northern-European design, faced with unpainted shingles, high-pitched roofs and quaint, ornate balconies. Weatherboard houses probably make up the majority of dwellings, but Puerto Montt's pioneer image has long since faded – the inner city is too big, too ugly, too congested. The cathedral on the main square, built in 1856 entirely of redwood, is the oldest building in the city, an important reminder of the early days.

Today Puerto Montt is the gateway to the southern end of the Lake District, to the island of Chiloé and to Chilean Patagonia. It's the transport hub for buses, trains, planes and boats going north, east and south.

Information

Tourist Office The tourist office is in a kiosk on Vargas in the large public square and gardens which face the sea front. The staff are very helpful and have a range of literature including a map of the town. There's also an office in the railway station but it only seems to open when trains arrive.

Bank The Banco de Chile is at the corner of Urmeneta and Rancagua, and will change cash and travellers' cheques.

Post The post office is at Rancagua 126; it's open Monday to Friday, 8.30 am to 7 pm, and on Saturdays, Sundays and Public Holidays, 8.30 am to 12 noon.

Argentine Consulate The Argentine Consulate, 2nd floor, Cauquenes 94 near the junction with Varas, is open Monday to Friday from 9 am to 2 pm. The consul is extremely pleasant and helpful and speaks perfect English. If you have a British passport and need a visa then this

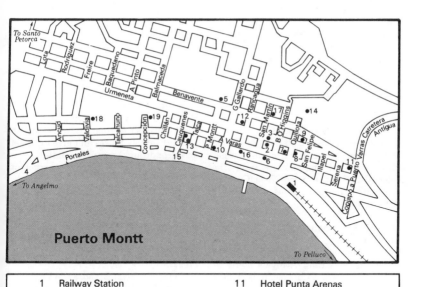

Puerto Montt

1	Railway Station	11	Hotel Punta Arenas
2	Plaza de Armas	12	Banco de Chile
3	Cathedral	13	Hotel Colino
4	Bus Terminal	14	Hotel Panorama
5	Hotel Central	15	Argentine Consulate
6	Tourist Office	16	Hotel Vincente Pérez Rosales
7	Hotel Montt		& Ladeco
8	Hotel Royal & Museum	17	LAN-Chile
	Vicente Pérez Rosales	18	Residencial Embassy
9	Residencial Urmeneta	19	Raul Arroya's House
10	Hotel Burg		

is the best place in South America to get it. This man will do his level best to get you one within 15 days (it's at least a month anywhere else) but *don't* count on him being able to do so.

Angelmo

Probably the biggest attraction in the area is the fishing village and market of Angelmo about three km west of the town centre along the Portales. There are frequent local buses between the two which cost a few cents. The real attraction, however, is the row of craft shops on Calle Angelmo just before you get to Angelmo itself, selling a range of goods including sweaters, handmade boots, curios, copperwork, ponchos, woollen hats and gloves. Underneath the tourist junk there are some fine handicrafts.

There is also a row of seafood cafés along the sea front at Angelmo itself where you can eat very well (that is, if your stomach can stand the idiosyncratic custom of not cooking seafood) for around US$2.

Museo Vicente Pérez Rosales

This museum has a collection of curios, small cannon and firearms and other implements of destruction from the colonial era and the period of German settlement. The museum is at the corner of Varas and Quillota.

Places to Stay – bottom end

Most visitors to Puerto Montt stay in rooms in private houses and the best of these places is Raúl Arroya's house at Concepción 136. Concepción is a very short street and this house is right at the end, round the corner, up against the bottom of the hill. Raúl and his family will make you very welcome. He'll probably find you before you find him since he often goes to meet incoming buses and checks out the tourist office for travellers. The rooms are very clean and pleasant and cost around US$2.80 per person. There are hot showers and

breakfast is included in the price. Raul can arrange evenings meals for you (very reasonable prices and excellent food) if you give him advance notice. Highly recommended and popular with travellers.

The house at Aníbal Pinto 328 has also been used by travellers for many years. Some people like it a lot saying it's warm, clean, friendly and good value at around US$2.80 per person (with hot showers), but others don't seem to be so impressed. Check it out for yourself. If it's full they may recommend another house you can stay in.

The *Hotel Central* at Benavente 550, costs US$3.30 per person – including breakfast and hot water, and some of the rooms have their own showers. The place is OK if, and only if, you avoid the rooms on the 1st floor (the same level as the dining room) which are ridiculously noisy! Upstairs rooms are OK though the toilets could be kept much cleaner. Hans, the owner, also offers rooms in his own house for a bit less than the hotel rate. He's a friendly, interesting man who speaks Spanish, German and some English – unfortunately I just can't give his hotel an unconditional recommendation.

The *Hotel Royal* near the corner of Quillota and Varas is a good place to try. Despite the name it's just US$4.20 a single and US$7.80 a double, including breakfast. Another good place is the *Residencial Urmeneta* on Urmeneta between Quillota and San Felipe, which is just US$2.80 per person including breakfast.

The *Residencial Embassy* on Valdivia, just up from Varas is a decent place. Singles are US$2.80, doubles are US$5.60, and there's hot water.

Places to Stay – middle

My pick of the hotels in this price range is the *Hotel Montt* (tel 3651) at the corner of Varas and Quillota. It has small but cosy rooms from US$8.30 a single and US$13.90 a double without private bathrooms, and

US$21.10 a single and US$25 a double with private bathrooms.

Another good place is the *Hotel Colino* (tel 3501) at the corner of Talca and Portales which has doubles from US$14.40. The *Hotel Panorama* (tel 4049) is also worth trying. It used to be very cheap but its insides and its prices have both been renovated; it's up on the hillside above the junction of Benavente and San Felipe. You can't miss it as there are huge signs.

The *Hotel Punta Arenas* (tel 3080) near the corner of Copiapó and Varas, diagonally across from the Varmontt bus terminal, could be worth checking out. Singles are US$6.70 and doubles are US$11.10.

Places to Stay - top end

Try the *Hotel Burg* (tel 3813), a comfortable hotel at the corner of Pedro Montt and Portales. Singles are US$26.40 and doubles are US$28.50, all with attached bathrooms.

The *Hotel Vicente Pérez Rosales* (tel 2470) is the city's top hotel. Singles are US$39 and doubles are US$42.

Places to Eat

Perhaps the best restaurant in Puerto Montt is the *Bar Restaurant Savoy*, Rancagua 256, on the junction with Rengipo. It's an excellent place with a very pleasant atmosphere and friendly staff. The food is tasty, the servings generous and the prices very reasonable. A fish dish and a vegetarian dish both with separate salad, a bottle of wine and two hot drinks cost about US$5.

The *Restaurant Bodegón* at Varas 931, is popular with local people and sometimes has live music in the evenings, but it tends to close early. The *Club Alemán*, Varas 264, is also popular, especially as a drinking spot, though they do offer meals too; it's somewhat more expensive than most other places but you often run into travellers. *La Nave*, on the corner of Varas and Ancud, is also very good. For drinks, snacks and cakes try the *Café Central* at Rancagua 117, opposite the post office.

Getting There

Air Ladeco is at Varas 449 and is open Monday to Friday, 9 am to 1 and 2.30 pm to 6.30 pm, on Saturdays from 9 am to 1 pm. LAN-Chile is at the corner of San Martín and Benavente; its open Monday to Friday, 8.30 am to 7.30 pm, and Saturday, 9 am to 1 pm.

Ladeco has flights to Santiago (daily), to Concepción (twice a week) and to Punta Arenas (daily). LAN-Chile has daily flights to Punta Arenas and Santiago. LAN-Chile *may* have flights between Puerto Montt and Coyhaique.

Bus There's a huge central bus terminal on Portales.

Companies with daily buses to Santiago include Tur Bus, Cruz del Sur, Turibús, Buses Lit, Vía Tur, Bus Norte, Varmontt, Igi Llaima and Tas Choapa. They all leave from the central bus terminal in the evening between about 4.30 and 8 pm.

Some companies run express buses to Santiago with meals included, for around US$15. Others have salón cama buses. There are also buses to Valparaíso and Viña del Mar.

Some companies, like ETC, only go as far north as Temuco, but there are usually numerous departures throughout the day along this stretch, particularly as far as Osorno.

Typical fares northwards from Puerto Montt are: Valparaíso US$15.30, Santiago US$13.30, Valdivia US$2.80, Río Bueno US$1.90, Osorno US$1.70, Puerto Varas US$0.40, Llanquihue US$0.70, and Frutillar US$1.05.

To Ancud, Castro and Quellón on Chiloé Island there is a choice of companies. Cruz del Sur has around nine buses daily to and from Ancud and Castro. Some of the buses continue on to Quellón. Trans Chiloé has around six departures per day in either direction to

Ancud and Castro in the summer months, but only once daily in either direction in the winter months. In summer they have one or two buses daily to Quellón. Fares and journey times are the same for all companies: to Ancud US$1.90 (two hours), Castro US$2.80 (3½ hours), Quellón US$4.40.

You can also get to Bariloche in Argentina with Bus Norte (daily departures) and Turismo Lanin (departures five days a week). The fare is around US$17.70. All these buses go via Osorno and Puyehue.

Buses Andina del Sur at Varas 437 have daily departures in both the summer and winter months for Bariloche via Ensenada, Petrohué and Peulla (on Lago Todos los Santos). This costs US$38 but that includes all transport, two meals and an overnight stay in a hotel. They offer this trip throughout the year – it can be a problem getting to Argentina via Lago Todos los Santos in winter by any other means.

Buses Norte have buses from Puerto Montt through to Punta Arenas via Argentina. There are about two departures a week costing around US$58. Also try Buses Frontera Austral.

Rail There are daily trains to Santiago from Puerto Montt. The railway station is on the waterfront at the eastern end of Avenida Portales. For details of fares and timetables see the Getting Around chapter at the start of this book.

Boat A road, now being built in the south of Chile, will eventually extend all the way from Puerto Montt to Villa O'Higgins. Until this is completed the only way to get further south is to fly, take a bus through southern Argentina, or take a ship or bus/ship combinations from Puerto Montt.

Using ships and bus/ship combinations it's possible to journey from Puerto Montt to Chiloé Island, the Región Aisén including Chaitén, Puerto Cisnes and Coyhaique, the far southern towns of Puerto Natales and Punta Arenas; and truly remote places like the village of Puerto Eden and the Laguna San Rafael glacier. For full details see the Getting Around chapter at the start of this book.

Getting Around

Budget Rent-a-car is in the LAN-Chile office at the corner of San Martín and Benavente; if you want an easy way to circumnavigate Lago Llanquihue and push on to Petrohué on Lago Todos los Santos then hiring a car is definitely worth considering.

There is a local bus between the airport (El Tepuel) and the bus terminal which connects with all outgoing and incoming flights.

Several bus companies, including Turimontt, have day excursions to Ensenada, Petrohué and Lago Todos los Santos, which could be worth checking out if you only have limited time. Try Excursiones Turimontt in the Hotel Asturias, and Varastur at Varas 437. The latter has tours to Petrohué about three times a week in the summer months for US$9.50 per person, and to Peulla daily for US$14.50 which includes lunch. Andina del Sud, also at Varas 437, has daily excursions to Peulla for around US$10.30 and to Petrohué for US$5.60, lunch is extra. Also try Turismo Angelmo at Talca 77. Some of these companies have city tours of Puerto Montt which cost about US$3 per person.

Chiloé & Aisén

About 180 km long by 50 km wide, Chiloé is one of South America's largest islands. It has a comparatively temperate climate – that is by comparison to the forbidding archipelago of islands and fjords immediately to the south. The climate enabled Indians to settle on the island at an early date and grow potatoes in its fertile, volcanic soil. In the interior there are huge virgin forests, while the rest of the land is turned over to wheat, vegetables, and cattle grazing. Fishing is also important. It's sparsely populated – there are only about 115,000 people and most of them live within sight of the sea. Sixty per cent of them make a living from agriculture.

The Spanish took possession of Chiloé in 1567 and the following year founded Castro. The Jesuits dug themselves in, and early in the 17th century, refugees from the Indian counter-attack on the Chilean mainland also established settlements. The Spanish remained in Chiloé during the War of Independence, resisting attacks in 1820 and 1824 until they were finally defeated in 1826. The island was their last Chilean stronghold, and one of their forts can be seen in Ancud.

Chiloé has a kind of romantic, brooding quality to it, in some ways similar to the Scottish Hebrides. The difference is that instead of stone crofts, the houses are clapboard with corrugated-iron roofs. It's a very relaxing place to visit. For much of the winter months the island is enveloped by mists and rain, but when the sun does break through the clouds it can be spectacularly green and beautiful, with views across the gulf to the snow-capped volcanoes of the mainland.

There are only two towns of any size on the island: Ancud and Castro. Chonchi and Quellón, two smaller places, are of interest since they are the ports for ferries to the mainland.

Apart from the towns there are also small villages with distinctive churches that are up to 200 years old. In all there are about 150 churches on the island, of which nine have been declared national monuments. Those built in the 18th century are at Achao, Chonchi (the most readily accessible), Quilquico, Quinchao and Villipulli; those at Dalcahue, Nercon and Rilán were built in the 19th century; and the garish Iglesia San Francisco de Castro in Castro was built this century.

Chiloé also has some distinctive fishing villages, or *palafitos*. These are made up of rows of houses built over the water on stilts so that fishermen can park their boats underneath when the tide comes in; these can be found at Ancud, Castro, Quemchi, Chonchi and other ports.

Typical Chiloé church

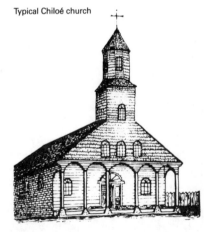

Getting There

There are daily buses from Puerto Montt to Ancud, Castro and Quellón which involve a ferry crossing between Pargua, on the mainland, and Chacao, on the northern tip of Chiloé. Buses go on the

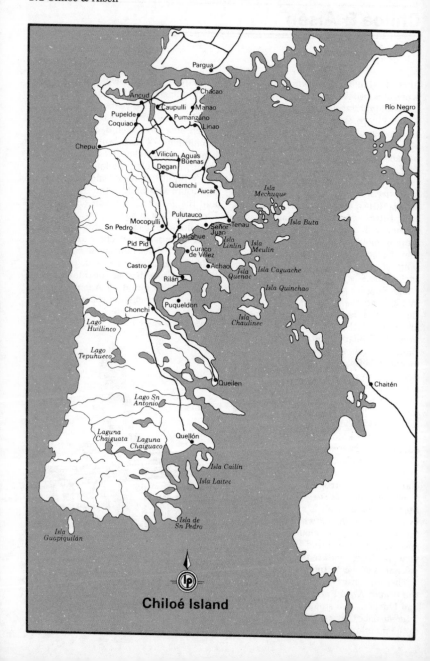

Chiloé Island

ferries so there's no need to change or to wait in Pargua or Chacao. For details on the buses see the section on Puerto Montt.

The Aisén region can be reached by taking a ferry from Chiloé to either Chaitén (from Chonchi) or Puerto Chacabuco (from Quellón). Puerto Chacabuco is the disembarkation point for Coyhaique.

From Coyhaique you can enter Argentinian Patagonia via Balmaceda. Alternatively, you can carry on south to Puerto Ibáñez, cross Lago Carrera (known on its unworldy-looking Argentinian side as Lago Buenos Aires) to the peculiar fruit-growing district of Chile Chico and enter Argentina from there.

Chiloé Island to the Mainland There are three connections between Chiloé Island and the mainland. The first is with the Cruz del Sur ferries which operate between Chacao at the northern tip of the island, and Pargua across the straits on the mainland.

The second and third connections are made by the Transmarchilay Ltda ferries which operate between Chiloé and Chacabuco and Chaitén. Transmarchilay Ltda has offices at Libertad 669, Ancud (tel 317); 21 de Mayo 417, 2nd floor, Coyhaique (tel 21 971); Pedro Montt 265, Quellón (tel 290); O'Higgins, Puerto Chacabuco (tel 144); O'Higgins 243, Chaitén (tel 272); Costanera, Chonchi (tel 66); and Angelmo 1668, Puerto Montt (tel 4654).

Quellón-Chacabuco The *El Colono* sails between Quellón and Puerto Chacabuco. It departs Quellón on Tuesdays, Thursdays and Sundays at 3 pm and Puerto Chacabuco on Mondays, Wednesdays and Fridays at 3 pm. The trip takes 18 hours. Aside from cabins there are three classes on the Quellón-Chacabuco ferry:

1. Reclining aircraft-type seats (*Pasajes Pullman Proa - asiento reclinable*). There is a

snack/drink bar and a TV in this class and quite cheap meals are served during the voyage. The fare is US$14.

2. Reclining bus-type seats (*Pasajes Pullman Popa - asiento reclinable*). The fare is US$13.60.

3. Tourist Class with fixed seats (*Pasajes Turistas - asiento fijo*) costs US$8.60. There are actually two divisions within 'Tourist Class'. The first, *asiento fijo*, allows you to take a place indoors in a large room with tables and upright bench seats. The second is referred to as 'without accommodation', *sin acomodación*, and means deck class, or trying to find a space to squat in a corridor.

Take my advice and forget about camping out on deck, even in the summer months. Regardless of how warm it may be in Quellón it's bitterly cold when you're out on the open water! Unless you've got the necessary equipment to camp on the cold bare metal of a ship's deck with rain pissing down all night, it would be a good idea to forget about being a heroic traveller and get a seat for the night!

The upright bench seats would be almost as formidable a proposition as the deck, so if you actually want to enjoy the trip and get some sleep then take a reclining bus-type seat (*Pasajes Pullman Popa*). This is actually better than 1st class since there is no bar or TV set and you don't get the constant stream of people passing through.

Chonchi to Chaitén *La Pincoya* sails between Chonchi and Chaitén. It departs Chonchi on Tuesdays, Thursdays and Fridays at 8 am and Chaitén on Tuesdays, Thursdays and Fridays at 3 pm. The fare is US$3.60.

ANCUD

Ancud was founded in 1765 as a fort town designed like the other Spanish outpost, Valdivia, to defend the Chilean coastline from foreign intrusion. Today it's the largest population centre on the island, a

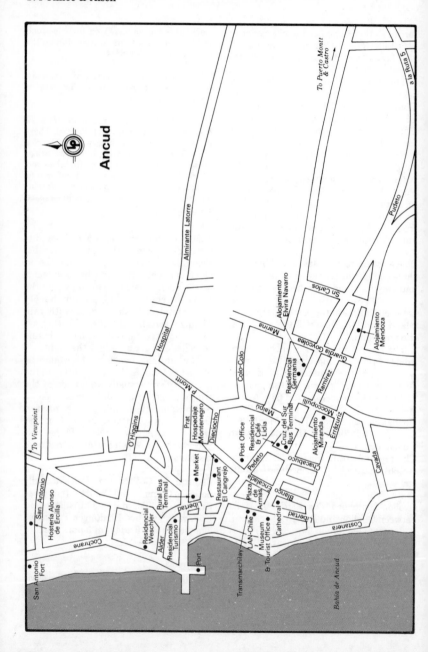

Ancud

picturesque fishing and agricultural town built on a series of small hills overlooking a bay to the north. It doesn't look like much when you first come in on the bus from Chacao, but don't be swayed by first impressions.

Information

Tourist Office The tourist office is on Chorrillos at the junction with Ramírez at the corner of the Plaza de Armas. The office is part of the museum, which is also worth a visit. Maps of the town and up-to-date information about all the hotels and residencials is available.

Books If you can read Spanish there is a good bookshop next to the Café Grill Lydia on Chacabuco which has a number of interesting books on Chiloé Island.

Things to See

Ancud is a place for strolling around and relaxing, popping into cafés and talking with local people. There's a peculiarly amiable feel to the place quite distinct from the feel in other Chilean towns, particularly during the holiday season when many Chilean tourists and backpackers come this way.

Museum

Built with towers and battlements like a small fort, this building houses a very fine collection of exhibits concerning the early history of Chiloé and southern Chile. It's open Monday to Saturday from 9 am to 8 pm, and Sunday, 10 am to 7 pm.

Exhibits include a rough wooden hut originally used by early European settlers, and erected in 1815 just 20 km from Ancud. The first fire-engine to arrive in Chile from Europe – it was built in 1851 and arrived in Valparaíso the following year – is also here. Rather more historically significant is the *Goleta Ancud*, a tiny sailing ship which braved the Chilean fjords and sailed to the Straits of Magellan in 1843 to claim the southern peninsula for Chile.

San Antonio Fort

A short walk up Cochrane brings you to the remains of the San Antonio fort. Built in 1770, the fort dominates Ancud's harbour and its cannon still stare over the battlements. This was the last bastion of the Spanish in Chile, but has now been turned into a park. Follow the coast road to get there; it's on the edge of town a short walk from the centre.

Places to Stay – bottom end

For some reason, a number of the owners and staff of the hospedajes and residencials seem to have won fortunes on the national lottery and then lost them on the dogs. Many not only appear to be hostile, but are hell-bent on extracting as much money out of you as possible – a stark contrast to the rest of the population who are very friendly and helpful. Not all the owners are like this, but a disproportionate number are, and in any case you can still easily end up paying a surprisingly high price for very basic accommodation.

The hospedajes are the cheapest places to stay, and these may or may not be indicated by a simple sign in the window. The *Alojamiento Elvira Navarro*, Pudeto 361, costs US$2.35 per person including breakfast; the *Alojamiento José Santos Miranda*, Mocopulli 753, has hot showers and costs US$2 per person without breakfast or US$2.35 with breakfast; and the *Alojamiento Natalia Mendoza*, Errázuriz 430, is the same price as the *Santos Miranda*.

The *Hospedaje Montenegro*, Blanco Encalada 541, quotes US$2 a single and US$4 a double without a bathroom, but the final bill escalates to US$4 per person and can only be brought down with much head-banging.

The *Residencial Germania* at Pudeto 357, is also relatively cheap at US$3.30 a single and US$6.70 a double; the rooms and bathrooms are clean and there are hot showers. The people are friendly enough and I'd highly recommend it.

The *Residencial Turismo* (once called

the *Residencial El Viajero*), Bellavista 491, has little boxes for rent for US$3.30 per person. There's a bar and restaurant downstairs and the people seem friendly.

Places to Stay – top end

Ancud's top hotel is the *Hostería Alonso de Ercilla* (tel 340) at San Antonio 30, overlooking the sea and the San Antonio Fort. It's a beautiful place that looks like a giant log cabin, and even if you can't afford to stay you should at least have a drink at the bar in the lobby. Double rooms (there are no singles) go for US$14, triples for US$16.70, which is bloody good value!

The *Residencial Weschler* (tel 318) at Cochrane 480 used to be a very cheap place, but it seems to have been renovated and now costs from around US$13.60 for doubles with private bathrooms. They're very comfortable rooms and it's an attractive place. They don't seem to have single rooms, but ask, just in case.

Places to Eat

One of the cheapest places is the *Cocinería Real* behind the Municipal Market; good food is available for about half the price of the other restaurants in the market.

For a splurge go to the *Restaurant El Cangrejo* at Dieciocho 155. This is a seafood restaurant and judging from the business cards and other scrawls on the walls it seems just about every visitor to Ancud has eaten here. A full meal with generous servings will cost around US$4 per person. Try their *paltina de mariscos* if you want a change from fish – it's a meal in itself. The staff are very friendly and the service is great.

Despite its appearance, the *Café Grill Jardín* is also relatively cheap and dishes up enormous slabs of meat – you're looking at US$3 to US$4 for a meal, but it's worth it.

For good coffee and cakes try the *Café Lidia*, Chacabuco 650, next to the *Cruz del Sur* bus office.

Getting There

Cruz del Sur, Chacabuco 672, has about 10 buses a day to Puerto Montt, 10 to Castro, four direct to Osorno, Valdivia and Temuco, and three to Chonchi and Quellón.

Trans-Chiloé has several buses per day to Castro and Puerto Montt. A couple of the buses to Castro carry on to Chonchi and Quellón, so you can connect with the ferry crossings to Chaitén and Puerto Chacabuco; check departure times.

There are a number of other bus companies with offices at the bus terminal. Local rural buses have their terminal at the junction of Prat and Libertad.

Transmarchilay (the company which operates the Chonchi-Chaitén and Quellón-Puerto Chacabuco ferries) has offices at Libertad 669 overlooking the Plaza de Armas. If you're heading further south, confirm ferry times here.

CASTRO

Castro is the capital of the province of Chiloé. Although a very old town its principle attraction – the bizarre wooden cathedral in front of the main plaza – was only built this century. Like Ancud this is a resort town during the holiday season with large numbers of Chilean tourists.

Information

Tourist Office The tourist office is on the Plaza de Armas, beneath the stage of a small pavilion which looks like a cross between a bomb shelter and a prop from *Close Encounters*. It's open 9 am to 10.30 pm in the tourist season, but probably has shorter hours the rest of the year. Maps of the town are available, and there's information about the surrounding area; they're a very friendly, helpful lot. Also ask them about tours to Dalcahue, Curaco and other places of interest; boat trips to the small islands are sometimes organised if there are enough people.

Things to See

Dominated by its unusual cathedral, Castro has a lively feel about it. It's an interesting town with some intriguing architecture. At first glance it may not look like much but it's actually a very likeable place, at its best in the summer evenings when the streets are filled with people.

Iglesia San Francisco de Castro

Built in 1906 and the centrepiece of Castro, the cathedral is a lurching monstrosity painted in a dazzling shade of orange. The interior is varnished wood and is rather attractive. The cathedral houses some incredibly bloody represent-ations of the crucifixion. There are even weirder statues, but I'd hate to spoil the surprise . . .

The Palafitos

At the junction of Gamboa and Pedro Montt there are a number of fishermen's houses built on stilts over the edge of the river. When the tide comes in the fishermen park their boats between the stilts. From the street they look no different from other houses. Several other *palafitos* can be found in the vicinity of Castro.

The Market

On Lillo, this market is good for buying fine woollen ponchos and pullovers, gloves and caps, and also basketwork. Bundles of dried seaweed and chunks of peat are also sold.

Regional Museum

Go out and ransack all the old farms in the district and this is what you come up with: an extraordinary collection of Indian relics, farming implements from the early days of settlement, even a rough wooden bicycle only used for travelling downhill. The museum is at Blanco 261.

Places to Stay – bottom end

The *Hotel Splendid* (tel 362) at Blanco 266 is not exactly splendid with its bare, spartan rooms, but it is fairly clean (there's not much to get dirty) and very cheap at US$1.70 per person. The friendly manager speaks quite good English and there's a good cheap restaurant on the ground floor.

The *Hotel La Bomba* (tel 300) at Esmeralda 270 has simple rooms for US$2.80 per person, and it's a brighter, airier place than the *Splendid*. There's hot water available.

The *Hotel Plaza* (tel 5109) is on Prat, facing the main plaza and opposite the tourist kiosk. It costs US$2.80 per person, including breakfast and common bath-room; or US$11.10 for a double with breakfast and a private bathroom.

The *Hotel Costa Azul* (tel 440) is above the *Restaurant Octavio* at Lillo 67. Singles are US$2.20 and doubles are US$4.40 – small rooms, but it's a clean, decent place and the people are friendly. The restaurant is good and cheap.

Places to Stay – top end

The *Hostería de Castro* (tel 301) at Chacabuco 202 is easily identified by its high sloping roof. It's at the corner of Thompson and Chacabuco. Singles are US$23.30 and doubles are US$30.

Getting There

The Bus Terminal Rurales is just off San Martín near the junction with Sergio Aldea. Buses Arriagada depart from here for Dalcahue, Curaco and Achao, daily at 7 am, 12 noon and 4 pm. Each of these returns to Castro the same day. Check the departure times, but don't expect any more than about three departures per day.

Buses Cruz del Sur is at San Martín 681 and has about 10 or 11 departures a day to Ancud and Puerto Montt, four per day to Osorno and Valdivia, and three per day to Chonchi and Quellón.

Buses Chiloé is at Esmeralda 252 and

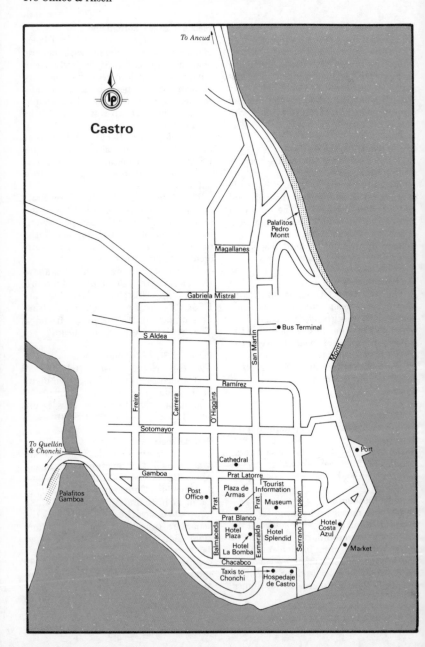

Castro

has about seven departures a day to Puerto Montt, three per day to Quellón, three per day to Queilén, and one per day to both Puqueldon and Quemchi.

CHONCHI

Chonchi is the jumping-off point for the ferry to Chaitén. It's memorable for the impressive Iglesia San Carlos de Chonchi, at the junction of Centenario and Pedro Montt, with its tall three-stage spire and archways at the front. Jesuits founded the town, and the original church was constructed in the 18th century. The structure you see today dates to the middle of the last century; its size was completely out of proportion to the small population of the time.

Information

Tourist Office The tourist office is at the corner of Candelaria and Centenario. There's another tourist office at the end of Centenario by the port; they have some useful maps and leaflets.

Places to Stay

The *El Sacho Hotel* (tel 42) at Centenario 102, has singles for US$5.60 and doubles for US$6.70, all including breakfast. It doesn't look like much from the outside but it's an enormous place with spacious, if simple, rooms. The manager is amiable and there's a good, fairly cheap restaurant on the ground floor.

Getting There

The best way to get to Chonchi is with a taxi colectivo from Castro. These leave from Chacabuco just around the corner from Esmeralda. In Chonchi they leave from Pedro Montt which is opposite the cathedral. The fare between Castro and Chonchi is US$0.70 per person and they stuff in five or six people. There are buses from Castro about three times a day with

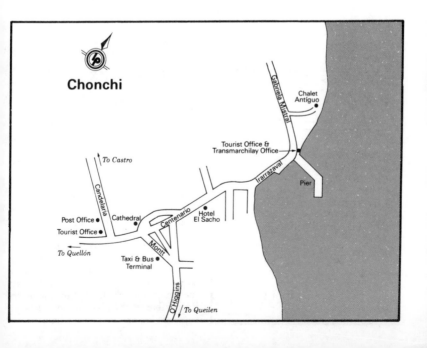

Cruz del Sur. In Chonchi the Transmarchilay office is at the end of Centenario by the port.

QUELLON

Not to be confused with Queilén, Quellón is the most southerly port of Chiloé, a rather drab little town from which the Transmarchilay ferries sail to Puerto Chacabuco.

Places to Stay

A few doors from the Transmarchilay office on the waterfront is the *Hotel Playa* (tel 278) at Pedro Montt 255. It's a decent little place with rooms for US$2.80 per person. There's hot water available and there's a good cheap restaurant.

The *Pensión Vera*, Gómez García 18, is US$1.70 per person. Despite it's tatty appearance from the outside it's quite OK inside. It's very spartan, but it does have hot water.

The *Hotel La Pincoya* (tel 285), La Paz 64, is a comfortable place with friendly people, and hot water. It costs US$5 per person, including breakfast.

Getting There

The bus ride from Castro to Quellón takes about two hours – the road is mainly gravel so it may take longer. There is a lot of roadwork going on so it's possible the road will soon be surfaced. To be on the safe side though, take an early bus. The fare from Castro is US$1.70. The ferry runs to a timetable but it is often late to leave, depending on how long it takes to get all the cars and trucks on board.

In Quellón, the Buses Cruz del Sur office is at Aguirre Cerda 52 around the corner from the pier. The Transmarchilay office is on the waterfront at Pedro Montt 261, in front of the pier.

Aisén

South of Chiloé and Puerto Montt, Chile is wild and beautiful, quite unlike anywhere else in the world, with the possible exception of Norway. A road is being built to link Puerto Montt with Coyhaique and Villa O'Higgins but it is not yet complete. Only the stretch from Chaitén to Coyhaique and from Coyhaique to Puerto Chacabuco and Puerto Ibáñez is presently open.

The natural scenery of the *Región Aisén del General Ibáñez del Campo* in southern Chile (of which Coyhaique is the capital), is built on monolithic proportions. The road edges its way along cliffs that drop into immense river valleys; walls of water stream down huge rock faces; ravines open up into vast valleys; lakes change colour half way across; and in the distance the Andes form a continuous barrier gashed by glaciers. On a clear day the short stretch from Coyhaique to Puerto Ibáñez provides some of the most eye-boggling panoramas in Chile.

Quellón

Pier

Pedro Montt

Hotel Playa   Transmarchilay Office

Pension Vera

Buses Cruz del Sur

A Gómez García

P Aguirre Cerda

La Paz

Ladrilleros

Hotel La Pincoya

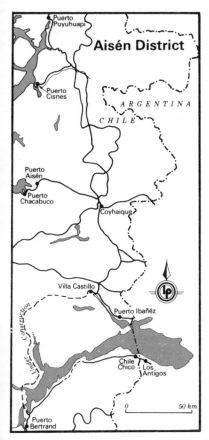

Aisén District

ARGENTINA

CHILE

Quellón, on Chiloé, and lies at the eastern end of a very narrow fjord. Puerto Chacabuco is a tiny settlement of no great interest; just up the road on the way to Coyhaique is Puerto Aisén, which has a silted up harbour and is no longer a port.

Places to Stay
If you do want to stay in Chacabuco there two small hotels just outside the harbour compound on the road leading to Coyhaique.

Getting There
Buses from Coyhaique meet the ferry and will take you straight from the harbour to Puerto Aisén and Coyhaique. It's a 2½ hour trip by bus along a gravel road from Chacabuco to Coyhaique. The road, for most of the way, follows the river along the base of a deep, rocky gorge. There are waterfalls and vast walls of steep rock; great sheets of water stream down from high above to the river below. Eventually the road climbs up the gorge and passes through a narrow man-made tunnel (officially opened by President Pinochet in early-1986). Soon Coyhaique can be seen, nestled in a valley far below and backed by a huge range of barren mountains. It is one of the most impressive bus rides in Chile. See the Coyhaique section for more details of transport between Coyhaique and Chacabuco.

CHAITEN
A port town of just 2500 people, Chaitén is connected to Chiloé by a Transmarchilay ferry from Chonchi. You can also get to Chaitén on the Empremar ferry from Puerto Montt. For details of these ships see the Getting There section at the start of this chapter. For somewhere to stay try either the *Hotel Mi Casa* or the *Hostería Schilling*.

PUERTO CHACABUCO
This is the terminus for the ferry from

COYHAIQUE
Coyhaique is a fairly sizeable, neat and tidy town with a floating population of around 37,000 people. Despite its remote location – it was founded as recently as 1929 – this is one of the largest towns south of Puerto Montt, and is largely a military and government administration centre. It's a popular centre for hiking in the area and is connected by road to Puerto Aisén and Puerto Chacabuco in the west, to Puerto Ibáñez in the south, and to Chaitén in the north.

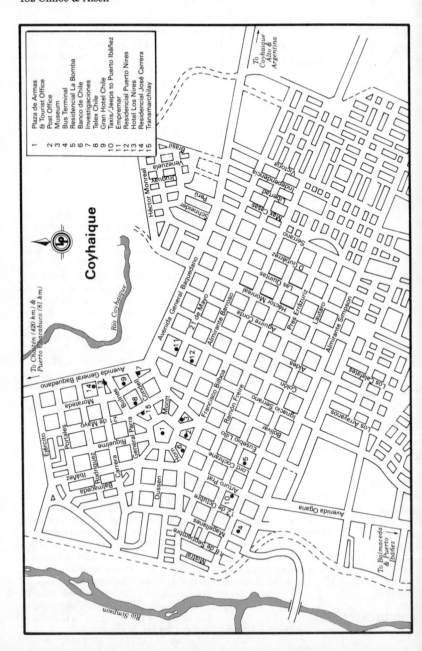

Coyhaique

To Chaitén (420 km) & Puerto Chacabuco (81 km)

Río Coyhaique

Río Simpson

To Coyhaique Alto & Argentina

To Balmaceda & Puerto Ibáñez

1 Plaza de Armas
   & Tourist Office
2 Post Office
3 Museum
4 Bus Terminal
5 Residencial La Bomba
6 Banco de Chile
7 Investigaciones
8 Telex Chile
9 Gran Hotel Chile
10 Taxis/Jeeps to Puerto Ibáñez
11 Empremar
12 Residencial Puerto Nires
13 Hotel Los Nires
14 Residencial José Carrera
15 Transmarchilay

Information

Tourist Office The tourist office is a small kiosk in the main plaza. It's open Monday to Friday, 10.30 am to 1 pm and 3 to 7 pm, and Saturday, 9.30 am to 1 pm. They're quite helpful and have a useful map of the city.

Post & Communications The post office is at Cocane 202, next to the main plaza. It's open Monday to Friday, 8.30 am to 12.30 pm and 2.30 to 6 pm, and Saturday, 8.30 am to 12 noon. Telex Chile is at 21 de Mayo 472 and is open Monday to Friday, 8.30 am to 8 pm, Saturday, 9 am to 2 pm, and Sundays and holidays, 9 am to 1 pm.

Investigaciones This is the plain-clothes police force office. You may have to come here to get your passport stamped if you intend leaving Chile for Argentina either from Coyhaique or from further south at Chile Chico. It's at the corner of Condell and Baquedano. It's open Monday to Friday, 9 am to 12 noon and 3 to 6 pm, Saturday, 9 am to 12 noon and 6.30 to 7.30 pm, and Sunday, 10 am to 12 noon.

Places to Stay - bottom end

One of the cheapest places is the residencial at José Carrera 33. If that's full, try the *Residencial La Bomba* (tel 22 518), Cocane 532, which has singles for US$1.70 and doubles for US$3.30. It's OK though the room partitions are thin (you may find it quite noisy), and there are no locks on the doors. There are hot showers.

The *Residencial Puerto Varas* (tel 21 212), Ignacio Serrano 168, is also reasonable value at US$2.80 per person, US$3.90 per person for room and breakfast, or US$7.80 per person for full board. There's hot water and heating in the rooms and common areas, and there's a restaurant attached.

Places to Stay - top end

Try the *Gran Hotel Chible* (that's Chible, not Chile) on José de Moreledan. Singles are US$21.70 and doubles are US$32.50, including breakfast. There is a restaurant on the ground floor.

The *Hotel Los Nias* is at the corner of Baquedano and Carrera. Singles are US$13.90 and doubles are US$19.40 including breakfast, and a private bathroom. It's a fine place with a large restaurant and bar downstairs.

Places to Eat

Prat is the street to visit if you're looking for restaurants; there's a string of places from Lautaro all the way down to the plaza. The *Samoa* is a cosy little bar and restaurant with dishes from US$1.40 to US$3.30 – it also serves snacks like humitas and empanadas.

The *Café Restaurant Ricer* is a nifty little snack and drink bar on Horn (the street which becomes Prat) by the main plaza. Other places worth checking out include the *Tranquera 77* (at the corner with Lautaro) and the *Café La Moneda de Oro* on the other side of this corner towards the plaza.

Getting There

Air Ladeco and LAN-Chile have agents at the corner of General Parra and 21 de Mayo. Ladeco has flights to Balmaceda which is to the south of Coyhaique and connected to it by bus. There are flights to Puerto Montt, Punta Arenas and Santiago three days a week.

Another airline worth investigating is TAC at Eusebio Lillo 315; apparently they have flights to Puerto Montt, and also fly Coyhaique-Chile Chico-Cocane three days a week.

Bus The bus terminal is at the corner of Lautaro and Magallanes. Buses Artetur has buses to Chaitén, via Amengual, Puerto Cisnes, Puyuhuapi, La Junta, and Santa Lucía. The fare is US$19.40 and the trip takes about 16 hours. Currently there's only one departure per week, but check this as improvements to the road may soon change all bus schedules on this route.

Also ask at Buses Artetur about buses to Puerto Ibáñez. Buses BAP has buses to Puerto Ibáñez (US$5, three hours).

For buses to Puerto Aisén and Puerto Chacabuco there are two companies: Expreso Las Cascadas and Transportes Don Tito.

Colectivos There are colectivo taxis and jeeps to Puerto Ibáñez from Coyhaique. Taxis will cost about US$8.30 per person and jeeps about US$6.70 per person. These leave from the corner of Prat and Lautaro, but they'll pick you up from your hotel if you arrange beforehand with one of the drivers. It takes about three hours by bus and about 2½ hours by taxi or jeep to reach Puerto Ibáñez, along a gravel road which takes you through farmland and some of the most dramatic scenery in Chile.

Boat Transmarchilay (tel 21 971) is upstairs at 21 de Mayo 417. It's open Monday to Friday, 9 am to 1 pm and 2.30 to 6 pm, and Saturday 9 am to 1 pm. They run ferries from Puerto Chacabuco to Quellón on Chiloé Island. Empremar (tel 22 586) is at 21 de Mayo 758 and has ships to Chaitén and Puerto Montt. For details of these ships, see the Getting There section at the start of this chapter.

PUERTO IBAÑEZ

This port is named after the president who initiated the settlement of this area. Puerto Ibáñez is a tidy little place on the shores of an emerald-green lake, walled in by barren mountain ridges and lightly vegetated hills. From here you cross the lake to Chile Chico and cross the border to Los Antigos in Argentina.

Places to Stay

There are at least two places to stay here, both opposite the ferry dock. The *Residencial Ibáñez* is at Buenos Aires 201, at the corner with Dickson. Rooms

are US$1.90 per person and there's a cheap restaurant downstairs. Breakfast is an additional US$1.10

On Dickson, next to the Residencial Ibáñez is the *Hotel Monica* which also has a restaurant and costs US$1.90.

Getting There

Some of the most spectacular scenery in Chile can be seen on the short journey from Coyhaique to Puerto Ibáñez. The road winds through beautiful sheep and cattle grazing country set in deep valleys, flanked by immense mountain ridges. As you approach Puerto Ibáñez the Andes can be seen spreading across the horizon. The mountain tops are covered in snow and to one side there are jagged peaks with a massive glacier spilling down between them. The best views are in the morning before the clouds roll in – so if you're going to catch the ferry you'd be better off taking an early morning taxi.

Buses & Colectivos There are buses and taxi colectivos to Puerto Ibáñez from Coyhaique. See the Coyhaique section for details. These link up with the ferry to Chile Chico.

Ferries From Puerto Ibáñez there is a ferry which takes you to Chile Chico. This departs Puerto Ibáñez three times a week: Tuesday at 9 am, Thursday at 9 am and Saturday at 11 am. The ferry is run by Transmarchilay, so check departure times at their office in Coyhaique. This is a car ferry. The passenger fare from Puerto Ibáñez to Chile Chico is US$1.40. The ferry from Chile Chico to Puerto Ibáñez departs on Sundays at 4 pm, Wednesdays and Fridays at 5 pm.

CHILE CHICO

Founded in 1928 by immigrant fortune-seekers including Brazilians, Argentinians, Chileans, Germans, Italians and French (a row of flags on a hill crest above the town represents each nationality) Chile Chico's early prosperity was based on a copper mine. You can still see blue-tinged copper ore in the rocky hills that lie behind the town, separating it from the Argentinian pampas on the other side.

You can imagine the optimism and hopes of the first settlers, but there is now only one indication of the great city that was expected to rise: the dusty main street, built as wide as any in Chile to accommodate the streams of traffic and trucks that never came. When the mine was exhausted the town began to decline, and only fruit-growing has kept it from disappearing in recent years.

Chile Chico means 'little Chile' and for some reason it has a micro-climate which is especially warm and sunny almost year round, and quite different from the colder climes you find around Coyhaique. Fruit-growers produce apples, pears, red and yellow plums, guinda (a cherry-like fruit) of a quality equal to the fruit produced in the Chilean heartland. Most of the locals live in mud-brick houses surrounded by alamo trees, the tall and very dense trees which are used as windbreaks around the fruit tree plantations.

But life is ebbing from the town. Families move away, and houses are abandoned and fall into ruins. Government houses remain unoccupied because there is no work and no one to fill them. Fruit growing is not profitable. The farmers cannot sell their produce to Argentina because the Argentinians ship their own fruit right up to the border. Nor can they sell to Coyhaique because transport fees, a 20% tax on their profits, plus other taxes (apparently designed by the government to protect fruit-growers in the Chilean heartland) mean they cannot make a profit. Instead, they attempt to make a living selling their fruit in the town itself, or to tourists. Otherwise the fruit falls off the trees, rots on the ground, or is fed to pigs

Because the town has no other industry many people have left Chile Chico and gone to work in Argentina. One estimate puts the population of the town at 6000 in the 1960s – today it is only about 2200. The remittances of the expatriate workers, or those who have gone to work in other parts of Chile, seem to be the

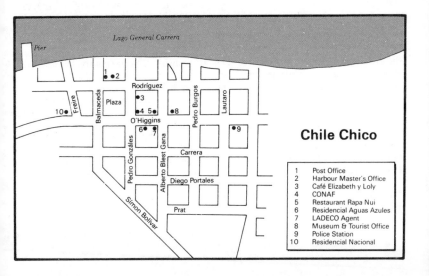

Chile Chico

1	Post Office
2	Harbour Master's Office
3	Café Elizabeth y Loly
4	CONAF
5	Restaurant Rapa Nui
6	Residencial Aguas Azules
7	LADECO Agent
8	Museum & Tourist Office
9	Police Station
10	Residencial Nacional

major source of income for the town. The government provides a subsidy to some of the farmers but that only amounts to US$20 per month per adult. Others make a living catering to the small tourist trade, and the passing traffic in Chileans and Argentinians who cross the unbridged river which marks the border.

Information

Museum & Tourist Office There's a tiny museum with Indian skeletons and artefacts at the corner of O'Higgins and Gana. The spherical stones on display were used in slings for hunting. There is also a tourist office at the museum which has a give-away map of the town.

Post The post office is at the corner of Rodríguez and Balmaceda; open Monday to Friday, 8.30 am to 12.30 pm and 2.30 to 6.30 pm, and Saturday, 9 am to 1 pm.

Police The police station is at O'Higgins 506, at the corner with Lautaro. They keep a record on who's going to Argentina so they may be able to help fix you up with some transport if you can't find anything else.

Places to Stay & Eat

The residencial and restaurant at O'Higgins 41 has some small rooms out the back for US$5.60, full board. The meals are good, the helpings are generous, the people are friendly and there's hot water.

Try the *Residencial Nacional* (tel 265) which is next door on Freire. Another decent place is the *Residencial Aguas Azules* (tel 320), Rodríguez 252, which has rooms at US$2.20 per person or US$6.70, full board.

For snacks and drinks there's the *Café Elizabeth y Loly* on Gonzáles, opposite the plaza, which is good for cakes and drinks. Also try the *Restaurant Rapanui* at the corner of O'Higgins and Alberto Blest Gana.

Getting There

Boat From Puerto Ibáñez there is a ferry which takes you to Chile Chico. This departs Puerto Ibáñez three times a week: Tuesday at 9 am, Thursday at 9 am, and Saturday at 11 am. The ferry is run by Transmarchilay, so check departure times at their office in Coyhaique – this is a car ferry. The passenger fare from Puerto Ibáñez to Chile Chico is US$1.40. The ferry from Chile Chico to Puerto Ibáñez departs on Sundays at 4 pm, Wednesdays at 5 pm, and Fridays at 5 pm.

Crossing to Argentina From Chile Chico you can cross to Argentina. The Argentinian border town is Los Antigos, just four km from Chile Chico. You can walk, hitch or find someone to take you by jeep (try the owner of the residencial on the corner of O'Higgins and Freire).

The problem is that there is a wide, unbridged river between the two towns. It is possible to walk across it – at least in the summer months – and many people do, but it is very wide and there is no distinct route across. You can't even see the Argentinian border post on the other side (look for a communications aerial) so it may be better to hire a jeep, which will probably cost about US$3 per person.

The Chilean checkpoint is at the edge of the river about a km out of Chile Chico, and the Argentinian one is on the other side just before entering Los Antigos. From Los Antigos you can hitch or get a bus (twice a week) to Perito Moreno and Caleta Olivia.

Southern Patagonia

Patagonia was given its name by Magellan. Whatever romantic visions it may conjure up, it's actually said to be derived from the Spanish word *patagones* which means 'big feet'. This is possibly a reference to a race of large Indians who inhabited these parts and who wrapped their feet in animal skins, making them seem disproportionately large. An Italian, Antonio Pigafetta, who survived the Magellan expedition and made it around the world, recounts seeing giants in Patagonia and describes one as:

... so tall that the tallest of us only came up to his waist; however he was well built ... When he was brought before the captain he was clothed with the skin of a certain beast, which skin was very skilfully sewed ... This giant has his feet covered with the skin of this animal in the form of shoes ... The captain named this kind of people Pataghom ...

There is another story that Magellan named the land after *Gran Patagón*, a monster in a contemporary Spanish tale. Whatever, *Patagonia* is the name that has stuck, and with the Indians literally cleared out of the picture it became a stamping ground for explorers, outlaws, missionaries, eccentrics, mountaineers, oilmen, ranchers, *gauchos* (Argentinian cowboys), businessmen and finally, tourists.

The name refers to the huge area of land occupying the southern cone of South America, generally considered to be the area south of the Río Colorado and north of the Straits of Magellan, the strait which separates the island of Tierra del Fuego from the mainland. Most of it belongs to Argentina. On the other side of the Andes is a thin and geographically very different slice which belongs to Chile.

Unless you fly or take a ship, the only way you can get from central Chile to the far south (Tierra del Fuego and Magellanes Province) is to overland through Argentinian Patagonia, since there is no road on the Chilean side. What makes the detour so interesting is the striking contrast between the land on the eastern and western sides of the Andes.

HISTORY

The Spanish came to Argentina in search of silver – they even named the place after it. The Italians who flocked here in the 19th century, and who now make up its largest ethnic group (even outnumbering those of Spanish descent) dreamed of picking money off the streets of Buenos Aires. Like Chile, Argentina is something of an oddity in Latin America – a European nation a long way from home, as is sometimes said. Cattle, sheep and wheat (never silver!) contributed to Argentinian prosperity. Another saying is that the soil is so rich on the Argentinian pampas that if you poke your finger in the ground for more than five minutes it will begin to sprout!

The country is four times larger than Texas, about five times larger than France, and stretches from Antarctic wastelands in the south to tropical jungles in the north, bordered by the massive Andes in the west. There are well over 30 million Argentinians; 10 million of them live in Buenos Aires, the third largest city in Latin America. The rest are spread across Patagonia, the mountain valleys of the northwest, the lowlands of the north-east, and the fertile plains of the pampas. Like Chile it is a heavily urbanised country: less than 20% of Argentinians make their living on the land. Despite this, the major exports are not the industrial products of the cities and towns but beef, mutton, hides, wool and maize.

On the borders with Bolivia, Chile and

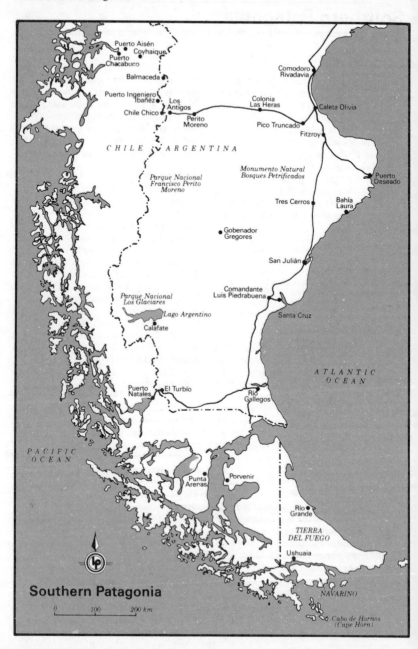

Southern Patagonia

0   100   200 km

Paraguay there are still a few Indians left, but the Argentinians are even more racially homogeneous than the Chileans; some 85% of Argentinians are of direct European descent.

Argentina wasn't regarded by the Spanish as a particularly important part of their colonial empire. The first attempt to settle the south bank of the Río de la Plata was made by Juan de Solis in 1516, but after he was killed by the Indians the expedition was abandoned. Another attempt in 1536, by Pedro de Mendoza, met much the same fate, but not before part of the expedition was despatched north, where they founded Asunción (in what is now Paraguay). There were no further attempts to settle the La Plata area until 1580 and it was not until the turn of the 17th century that Buenos Aires became secure from Indian attack. Meanwhile, other Spanish expeditions launched from Peru and Chile, resulted in the foundation of Argentina's oldest cities such as Jujuy, Salta, Tucumán and, further south, Mendoza and Córdoba.

Independence from Spain was gained in 1816 but the new nation was still a good deal smaller than it is now. The whole of Patagonia and a good slice of the pampas remained firmly under Indian control right up until the middle of the 19th century.

The Indians at the southern tip of the continent, the *Patagones*, lived by hunting the rhea (a bird similar to an ostrich or emu), the seal, and the guanaco (a variety of llama) with bow and arrow and by collecting shellfish from the rocky shoreline. Their homes were mere windbreaks, their clothes were furs, their implements were made from seashells, stone or wood. In the 16th century several nomadic Indian hunting groups occupied northern Patagonia and the pampas. If there ever was a race of giant Indians in Argentina, they disappeared (along with most of the other Argentinian Indians) in the exterminations of the 19th century. In

1833 the naturalist Charles Darwin came to Patagonia on the voyage of *HMS Beagle* and recorded in his diary the destruction of the native people. In one instance he records the massacre of Indians by a force of 200 soldiers:

They first discovered the Indians, by the dust of their horses, in a wild mountainous country ... The Indians were about 112, women, children and men, in number. They were nearly all taken or killed, very few escaped. The Indians are now so terrified, that they offer no resistance in body, but each escapes as well he can, neglecting even his wife and children. The soldiers pursue and sabre every man. Like wild animals, however, they fight to the last instant. One Indian nearly cut off with his teeth, the thumb of a soldier, allowing his own eye to be nearly pushed out of the socket. Another who was wounded, pretended death, with a knife under his cloak, ready to strike the first who approached ... Every one here is fully convinced that this is the justest war, because it is against Barbarians. Who would believe in this age in a Christian civilised country that such atrocities were committed ... Great as it is, in another half century I think there will not be a wild Indian in the Pampas North of Río Negro ...

Today Argentinian Patagonia makes up a quarter of the country's land area, yet contains only a few per cent of the population. This is an arid land. Most of the few cm of moisture it gets each year falls in the form of snow in the winter, but for the most part the climate is moderate. Only in the far south does the temperature dip below freezing during the winter months of June, July and August. The prevailing westerly winds leave a haze of dust in the air as they sweep incessantly across the plain.

For centuries Patagonia seemed too remote and barren to warrant settlement or even exploration by the European settlers further north. Occasionally, Jesuit missionaries made forays into hostile Indian territory, but it wasn't until a group of Welsh immigrants set themselves up at Chubut in 1865 that any large settlement was established. Two decades later, after the extermination campaigns had removed the Indians, sheep herders began to move southward to the good, short grazing grass of the plateaus and the water of the streams and canyons.

The border with Chile was finalised in the 1880s, Argentinian military outposts were established, railroads were built, crop farming and cattle grazing gained a foothold along the Río Negro and the Río Colorado and sheep grazing expanded into Patagonia. Pedigree cattle were imported from Britain and, following the introduction of refrigerated ships in 1877, the export of fresh beef began in earnest. The agricultural expansion in Argentina in general created prosperity for many, provided the basis for commercial, industrial and urban growth, and built Argentina into a leading Latin American power by the end of the 19th century; the future was guaranteed by exports of meat, grains, wool and hides.

Sheep raising is still the major occupation of Patagonia, with huge ranches, covering thousands of square km, altogether pasturing millions of animals, but only employing a handful of men.

The other major occupations are oil and natural gas extraction at places like Comodoro Rivadavia on the east coast, coal mining at Río Turbio near the Chilean border in the far south, and iron-ore mining at Sierra Grande. These industries have their origins during and after WW I when Argentina found itself short of metallic ores and cheap sources of power.

The Great Depression and WW II also reduced imports to Argentina and encouraged Argentinian industrial expansion to fill the gap, but for the most part the country was unable to satisfy its need for industrial products and agriculture continued to be the mainstay of the country.

The potential profits from mining were constantly overshadowed by the dazzling investment opportunities in agriculture and livestock on the pampas. With long and costly freight hauls to the coast, legal wrangles surrounding all mining claims, and an inadequate supply of capital, machinery and trained workers, it seemed simpler and cheaper to buy coal and metals from Europe, and oil and kerosene from the USA. Neither the ruling elite of Argentinians, nor the British capitalists who had massive investments in Argentina, saw much point in exploiting the country's coal, mineral or oil wealth.

Despite being the second largest country in South America and the eighth largest in the world, Argentina has always fallen short of establishing itself as the major power which its size, current range of industries, and enormous capacity for stock-raising suggest it could be.

There are many reasons for this. One is a string of corrupt military governments; the most recent held power from 1976 to 1983 until it collapsed after Argentina's defeat in the Falkland's War. Another is bad economic management, such as the elimination of tariffs in the mid-19th century which led to the collapse of Argentinian industry as foreign goods – principally British – poured into the country. Another was the domination of the agricultural and grazing land, on which Argentinian prosperity depended, by large *estancias* (estates) owned by just a minority of the population.

One writer, comparing the development in Argentina to the development of diverse industries and agriculture in the USA, noted that the situation in Argentina was as if:

... long before the Civil War, the South had emerged as the dominant and only area of United States expansion ... an economy based entirely on cotton exported to British mills, and an oligarchy composed of plantation owners and merchants.

It was not until after WW II that the industrialisation of Argentina really got underway, this time under President Juan Perón who held power from 1943 to 1955. The economic policies introduced during Perón's presidency resulted in the establishment of of a rail link between the coal reserves of Río Turbio near the Chilean border and the port of Río Gallegos. A natural gas pipeline from Comodoro Rivadavia to Buenos Aires was completed in 1946, leading a new era in the exploitation of Argentinian oil and gas reserves. Patagonia became an area of great economic importance.

After Mexico and Venezuela, Argentina is now Latin America's largest petroleum producer, although all its natural gas and almost all its oil is used for domestic consumption. A large percentage of its oil production comes from the Comodoro Rivadavia and Chubut fields in Patagonia. The rest comes from the vicinity of San Sebastián in Tierra del Fuego and from the Mendoza fields 50 km south of the city of Mendoza, among other areas. Coal production is restricted to the Río Turbio district, but by 1960 these mines provided the country with almost a fifth of its coal needs.

Patagonia offers some of the most monotonous scenery in Latin America, but also some of the most spectacular. The Moreno Glacier near Calafate stretches a km across a lake and stands 50 metres high. At the huge wildlife sanctuary on the Valdés peninsula you can see colonies of penguins, sea elephants and sea lions. Guanacos and rheas are abundant.

Geographically Chilean Patagonia is quite unlike Argentinian Patagonia. The coastline of southern Chile is a wild and beautiful area unlike anywhere else in the world with perhaps the exception of Norway. It's a land of virtually unspoilt mountains, glaciers, forests and lakes, with many national parks, including the spectacular Torres del Paine park near Puerto Natales.

From Río Gallegos in the far south of Argentina you can head west to Río Turbio and then over the mountains to the Chilean town of Puerto Natales. Alternatively, head direct to Punta Arenas and cross the Straits of Magellan to Porvenir on the island of Tierra del Fuego.

VISAS

Visas for Argentina are required by everyone except citizens of most West European countries, Canada, Japan and a number of Latin American countries. Australian, US and French citizens do require visas. The visa is valid for three months and allows you to exit and re-enter the country as often as you like within the time period of your visa. It's renewable for three months.

The visa costs almost US$17 and in Chile you can pay for it in Chilean pesos. You may require a letter of introduction from your embassy when applying for an Argentine visa, so you should try and sort all this out with the Argentine embassy in Santiago. There are also Argentinian consulates in Punta Arenas, Puerto Montt, Arica and Antofagasta.

As a result of the Falklands (oops, Malvinas) War, British and New Zealand passport holders are still on what might be called the 'undesirable tourists' list and should expect major problems when applying for visas. These problems differ from place to place but it's generally true to say that the nearer you are to the Argentine border and the busier the border crossing, the easier it is. In San Francisco, USA, for instance, the Argentine consulate is barely even civil and will tell you that visas are not available except to businessmen and then only after a two or three month wait. In Santiago you'll be told it takes a month or two – though there are no problems otherwise. In Montevideo, Uruguay, it will take about two weeks but you have to pay for a telex to Buenos Aires (about US$8 to US$9).

In Puerto Montt, Chile, the Argentine consul is not only a very intelligent and sympathetic man who understands that not all Brits support their government's absurd stand on the Malvinas but he'll do his best to get you a visa. He'll tell you that officially it takes 15 days but that he can't guarantee it in less than three weeks. He also speaks perfect English.

Obviously there's no telling how long these problems will go on, so don't believe this book – check before you go!

If you don't require a visa for Chile your three-month tourist pass starts all over again each time you re-enter the country. If you need a Chilean visa you should check that it's good for multiple entry, otherwise you'll have to pick up another Chilean visa in one of the Chilean consulates in Argentina (there is one in Río Gallegos if you're in the south). Otherwise you can hop back and forth between Chile and Argentina as often as you like, within the time limit of your Argentine visa.

CUSTOMS

Officially you're allowed to import 400 cigarettes and 50 cigars, two litres of alcoholic beverages, gifts and souvenirs. In practice you'll probably find customs checks fairly cursory. Going from Argentina to Chile they'll probably check your bags to make sure you're not taking fruit into Chile.

MONEY

The unit of currency is the Austral (A) which replaced the peso in mid-1985 as part of an economic package designed to stabilise the economy and get inflation under control. Currently the exchange rate is around US$1 = A0.85 but in some places you can get about A0.90 to the dollar.

When the new currency was first introduced the old notes continued to be used – some stamped with their new designations. It is planned to gradually phase out the old notes and replace them with new notes. Currently the notes used are A10, A5, A1, A0.50 and A0.10. There are no coins.

Hotels and travel agents usually give the best exchange rates, and it's generally possible to exchange US cash just about anywhere you go.

HEALTH

No vaccinations are required to enter Argentina from any country. There is a malaria risk from October to May in a tiny piece of Argentinian territory in the far north of the country bordering Bolivia.

GETTING THERE

There are several cross-over points between Chile and Argentinian Patagonia and Tierra del Fuego. The main ones are: Coyhaique to Comodoro Rivadavia; Chile Chico to Caleta Olivia via Perito Moreno; Río Gallegos to Puerto Natales via Río Turbio; Río Gallegos to Punta Arenas; Ushuaia to Punta Arenas; Puerto Williams to Ushuaia. Transport details are given in the relevant sections.

GETTING AROUND

Patagonia, you may soon discover, pales very quickly. Distances are immense and the scenery becomes monotonous after the initial novelty wears off. If you intend doing a lot of travelling then it can be worth allowing some money for plane flights, particularly if you have to do any backtracking.

Air

Líneas Aéreas del Estado (LADE), Austral Líneas, and Aerolíneas Argentina have extensive networks in this part of the country and their fares are often the same or, in some cases, even cheaper than the bus fare! The only snag with these flights, as you might well imagine, is that there's *heavy* demand for tickets and they are often booked out two weeks in advance. If so, get yourself on the waiting list as there are always cancellations.

Typical fares in southern Patagonia and Tierra del Fuego are: Ushuaia to Río Gallegos, US$18; Ushuaia to Río Grande,

Top: Milodon Cave, near Puerto Natales
Bottom: Penguins, near Punta Arenas

Top: Mural of the Falklands (Malvinas) War, Caleta Olivia, Argentina
Bottom: Southern Patagonian landscape, Argentina

US$11.80; Perito Moreno to Río Gallegos, US$14.50; Perito Moreno to Ushuaia, US$21.30.

Fares from Punta Arenas are: to Río Grande, US$34.60; Río Gallegos, US$41.70; Comodoro Rivadavia, US$60.30; Buenos Aires, US$124.

If you go to Buenos Aires, get hold of a copy of the companies' schedules and fares. Their addresses are LADE, Calle Perú 710 (tel 34 7071); Aerolineas Argentinas, Perú 2 (tel 362 5008/6008). These airlines also have offices in Santiago, Chile – see the Santiago chapter for details.

Airport departure tax in Argentina is US$4 for international flights and US$1.40 for internal flights.

Bus

Argentinian buses are similarly organised and of much the same standard as buses in Chile. Most of the buses in Argentina are modern, comfortable and fast – but they are not particularly cheap, especially in Patagonia and Tierra del Fuego! Most large towns and cities have a central bus terminal though some bus companies operate from their own private terminals. Buses are few and demand is heavy in some parts of Patagonia; be prepared for some slow travelling in this region, perhaps even being forced to wait a few days for the next bus or for a vacant seat.

Rail

There is an extensive network of railways in northern Argentina with frequent service between towns. There are, however, no passenger railways in Patagonia and the main forms of transport are the buses and planes.

Hitching

Hitchhiking is fairly easy in Argentina and you'll rarely be asked to pay for a lift, unlike in some Latin American countries where it is a recognised form of public transport. This applies as much in Patagonia and Tierra del Fuego as in the more developed northern part of the country, though in the former areas you may have to wait *much* longer for a lift as fewer people live there. I met one Australian who had taken three days to

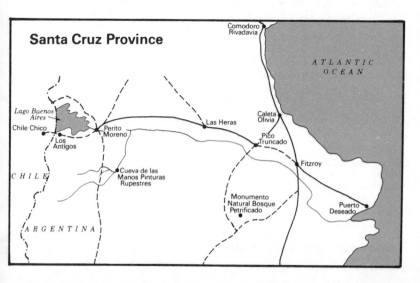

hitch the 300 km or so from Ushuaia to the Argentine/Chilean border at San Sebastían in Tierra del Fuego. If you do intend hitching then make sure you have warm, *wind-proof* clothes!

COMODORO RIVADAVIA

This oil and petro-chemical town of 100,000 people is one of the largest in Patagonia, and the oil wells to the west and south supply around 30% of Argentina's crude oil. There's not much of interest for travellers, but you may find yourself staying overnight on your way to or from the southern tip of the country.

Information

The tourist office is in the bus terminal. The Chilean Consulate is at Sarmiento 936. The Banco Regional de la Patagonia will change travellers' cheques and charges the smallest commission.

Places to Stay

One of the cheapest places is the residencial at Sarmiento 264. If it's full, try the *Comercio* at Rivadavia 341, near the bus station – it's friendly and has hot showers. Also try the *Hospedaje Belgrano* at Belgrano 546, which is a clean place with hot water.

Places to Eat

Meals at most restaurants tend to be pretty expensive. The *Comercio* does good meals for around US$6 and there are several *rotiserías* in the 400s of Rivadavia in the municipal market where you can eat cheaply.

Getting There

There are regular buses south to Caleta Olivia. There may be direct buses between Comodoro Rivadavia and Coyhaique, otherwise you may have to go to Balmaceda and take a daily bus from there. Aerolíneas Argentinas has flights two days a week from Comodoro Rivadavia to Río Gallegos, Río Grande and Ushuaia.

LOS ANTIGOS

Reminiscent of Chile Chico, Los Antigos is a dusty little town set on the shores of the beautiful Lago Buenos Aires. In the setting sun the soft colours on this vast lake, rimmed by the distant mountains, make it look quite unworldly. Los Antigos is on the other side of the border from Chile Chico, on one of the more obscure cross-over points between Chile and Argentina. From here you can head east to Perito Moreno, catch a bus to Caleta Olivia on the coast and then turn south to Río Gallegos and Tierra del Fuego.

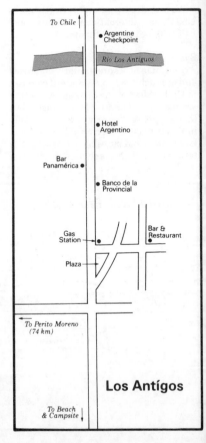

Los Antígos

Places to Stay

The *Hotel Argentina* appears to be the only hotel in town. It's a fairly new building and though quite basic it's spotlessly clean, and has a bar (with pool tables) and restaurant attached. Singles are US$8 without a bathroom, or US$10 with a bathroom. Doubles are twice the price. You can pay in US cash if you have no Argentinian currency and they will also change your US dollars for Argentinian currency.

Other than that there is a campsite at the end of 11 de Julio by the beach. It's an attractive place and there are a few cabins if you don't have your own tent; worth checking out.

Getting There

To get further south from Los Antigos you must first go to Perito Moreno, from where you catch another bus to Caleta Olivia and then head down the coast to Río Gallegos. It's a strange and beautiful ride from Los Antigos to Perito Moreno, with the Andes range in the background rising up above the dusty, yellow-green sea of scrub. It's a gravel road the whole way and there are few cars so hitching would be difficult.

The bus company Transporte Co-mi has a bus every Monday and Thursday from Caleta Olivia to Perito Moreno and Los Antigos. It returns from Los Antigos to Caleta Olivia on Tuesday and Friday. The departure days may change but don't expect any more than two buses a week on this route. If you miss the bus or don't want to wait and around Perito Moreno or the other towns you'll have to hitch.

Fares are: Los Antigos to Perito Moreno about US$4.10; Perito Moreno to Caleta Olivia, US$8.60. Tickets in Perito Moreno can be bought from the Hotel Argentina, which is also where the bus leaves from. Tickets in Caleta Olivia are available at the bus terminal. Perito Moreno to Caleta Olivia takes about 6½ hours along a surfaced road, and includes a few rest stops.

PERITO MORENO

You can tell you're getting closer to civilisation at Perito Moreno – the main roads in this town are paved. The last reminders that this was once a frontier town are the elderly gauchos, still dressed in their riding boots and enormous baggy trousers called *boleadoras*. Over 2000 people live in Perito Moreno, but most of them a seem a sullen lot, contrasting markedly with the people of Chile Chico.

Information

Tourist Office The tourist office is at the corner of San Martín and 12 de Octubre. It's open Monday to Friday, 9 am to 8 pm. They're a friendly and helpful lot and they have a good map of the town.

Bank The Banco Provincia and the Banco Nación are both on San Martín, and are open Monday to Friday, 10 am to 4 pm. Don't count on either of them changing money or travellers' cheques. If you have US cash (make sure you bring some!) you can change it at the Hotel Belgrano.

Post Office The post office is on Buenos Aires. It's open Monday to Saturday, 10 am to 6 pm.

Places to Stay – bottom end

The *Hotel Argentina* on Buenos Aires charges about US$4.70 per person. It's run by a rather absent-minded old man, has fairly clean spartan rooms (there's nothing to get dirty), and the bathrooms leave much to be desired! Still, it's about as cheap as you'll get and the people are friendly. There are no locks on the doors so don't leave valuables in your room.

The *Hotel Fénix* at the corner of San Martín and Mitre is a cheap and nasty place. The rooms are US$4.70 per person.

Worth trying is the *Hotel Santa Cruz* on Belgrano, just around the corner from the Hotel Argentina. It's the same price as the Hotel Argentina and they have hot showers.

Possibly the best place to stay is the

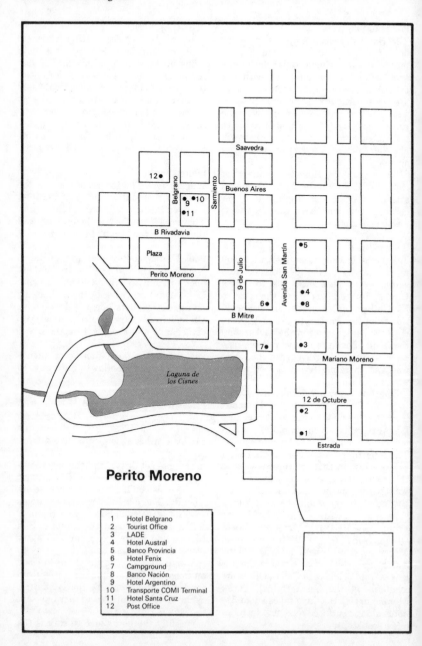

Saavedra

12●

Belgrano

9● ●10
●11

Sarmiento

Buenos Aires

B Rivadavia

Plaza

Perito Moreno

9 de Julio

Avenida San Martín

●5

●4
●8

6●

B Mitre

7●

●3

Mariano Moreno

Laguna de los Cisnes

12 de Octubre

●2

●1

Estrada

Perito Moreno

1	Hotel Belgrano
2	Tourist Office
3	LADE
4	Hotel Austral
5	Banco Provincia
6	Hotel Fenix
7	Campground
8	Banco Nación
9	Hotel Argentino
10	Transporte COMI Terminal
11	Hotel Santa Cruz
12	Post Office

campsite in front of the Laguna de los Cisnes – on Mitre, almost at the corner with San Martín. You can pitch a tent for about US$0.90 or take a cabin for just US$5.90.

Places to Stay - top end

The *Hotel Austral* on San Martín is a newish, up-market hotel with singles for US$14.10 and doubles for US$22.40. Breakfast is an additional US$2.40.

Also up-market, the *Hotel Belgrano* on, San Martín at the corner with Estrada, has singles for US$14.10 and doubles for US$22.40. They'll also change your US dollars for Argentinian currency.

Getting There

From Perito Moreno you either head west to Los Antigos and cross over to Chile Chico in Chile, or you head east to Caleta Olivia on the coast and then either turn north to Comodoro Rivadavia, or south to Río Gallegos.

Air LADE, and its glum staff, is at the corner of Mariano Moreno and San Martín. The airline flies Fokker F-27s from Perito Moreno to Ushuaia via Calafate, Río Gallegos and Río Grande. There are flights every Thursday.

Bus For details of buses on the Los Antigos, Perito Moreno, Caleta Olivia route see the Los Antigos section.

CALETA OLIVIA

Like Comodoro Rivadavia the first thing you notice about this place is the heavy stench of oil. The city has a backdrop of wall murals commemorating the Falklands War, monuments to the hardy oilmen, concrete-block housing estates and ravaged streets and footpaths, political graffiti and fading posters holding up crumbling walls.

This is a way-station on the road to the south or on an escape to the north. A town of few redeeming features, about the most interesting thing you can do is translate the political slogans, sit in a restaurant watching 'Sesame Street' in Spanish, or wander up the side-streets and poke your nose in the window of the local Communist

Oilman in Caleta Olivia

Party headquarters. If that comes as a surprise you've spent too long in Chile and you need to get your brain in gear.

Places to Stay & Eat
Hotels are either scant or well camouflaged. The only one that cares to advertise its presence is the *Hotel Robert* on San Martín, a few minutes walk from the bus station. Look for a large sign saying 'HOTEL' – you can see it from the bus station. Singles are US$14, doubles are US$21.20 – with attached bathrooms. It's a new hotel and is very clean and comfortable.

There are many restaurants in the vicinity of the bus station, most of them fairly cheap. The bus station also has a café snack-bar open until midnight.

Getting There
The main bus station is in the centre of town at the junction of San Martín and Independencia – easy to find since it's the same junction where the gigantic statue of the oilman stands. A number of bus companies have their offices here.

Buses from Caleta Olivia run to Río Gallegos via Fitzroy, Puerto San Julián and Piedra Buena, through monotonous plains. Caleta Olivia to Piedra Buena costs around US$16.50, and takes about 8½ hours; Piedra Buena to Río Gallegos is US$9.80, 4½ hours. It should be possible to get a bus straight through from Caleta Olivia to Río Gallegos, but buses seem to fill up quickly so you may have to wait a few days for a seat (lucky you).

Transportadora Patagonia runs buses to San Julián, Piedra Buena and Río Gallegos, with departures three days a week in the *very* early morning.

Transporte Co-mi has a bus every Monday and Thursday from Caleta Olivia to Perito Moreno and Los Antigos. Departure days may change but don't expect any more than two buses a week. Fares from Caleta Olivia are: Perito Moreno about US$8.60; and Los Antigos about US$12. Perito Moreno to Caleta Olivia takes about 6½ hours along a surfaced road, and includes a few rest stops in dreary outback towns. Expect the bus to be crowded – you may not get a seat for the whole journey.

Transporte La Unión has buses to Comodoro Rivadavia and Puerto Deseado.

RIO GALLEGOS
Close to the southern tip of the Patagonian peninsula, Río Gallegos is the jumping-off point for trips both to Calafate and to Ushuaia in Tierra de Fuego. There's nothing much to see and it's an expensive town, but if you're heading for Chilean Tierra del Fuego you need to come through here. One thing worth checking out is the museum on Perito Moreno and its sizeable collection of fossils and Indian artefacts.

Information
Tourist Office There's a tourist office on the corner of Perito Moreno and Zapiola. They have some good maps of the city and

1 Tourist Office	11 Hotel Comercio
2 Post Office	12 Hotel Punta Arenas
3 Police Station	13 Hotel Covadonga
4 Esmeralda Hotel	14 Hotel Puerto Santa Cruz
5 Hotel Alfonso	15 Residencial Nachan
6 Residencial Internacional	16 Hotel Colonial
7 Hotel Ampeuro	17 Chilean Consulate
8 Hotel Río Turbio	18 Buses Pingüino
9 Hotel Entre Ríos	19 Transportadora Patagonia
10 Museum	20 Hotel Central

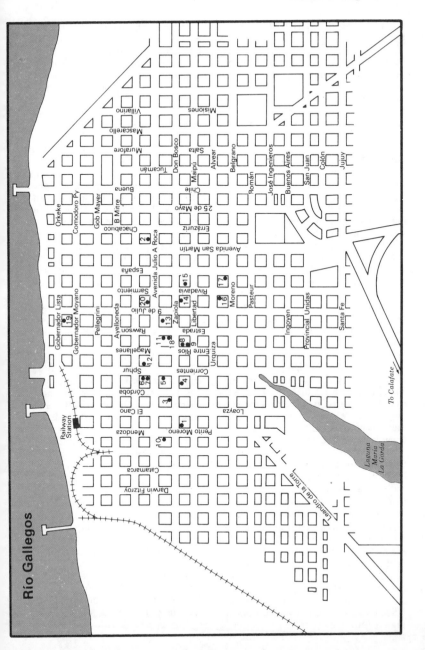

are useful for information, if you speak Spanish.

Bank Change US dollars and Chilean pesos at the Cambio El Pingüino at Zapiola 469, a door or two up from the Buses El Pingüino office. There are a number of other change-houses and banks around the centre of town where money can be changed.

Consulates The Chilean consulate is at Mariano Moreno 155 and is open Monday to Friday from 9 am to 1 pm and 3 to 5 pm.

Places to Stay – bottom end

Río Gallegos is an expensive city for accommodation and like other towns at this end of Argentina the cheapest places are often permanently full. You may have to visit several hotels or residencias before you find anything even mildly cheap. Most levels of accommodation are pretty basic, but most of the buildings are fairly new so even the cheaper places are usually in good condition.

One place you should be able to get a room at, and one I'd highly recommend, is the *Hotel Colonial* at the corner of Rivadavia and Urquiza, a short walk from the centre of town. Clean, comfortable rooms are US$5.90 per person – there are hot showers and the people are *very* friendly. There's a bar attached.

Also recommended is the large *Hotel Central*, upstairs at Roca 1127, also US$5.90 per person. They've got hot water, the manager is friendly and the place should be quiet since the rooms are set back from the main street.

Another good place is the *Residencial Nachan* at Rivadavia 122 which has rooms for around US$7 per person, and fairly hospitable people. Similar is the *Residencial Internacional* on Federico Sphur near the corner with Roca – friendly manager and rooms are only US$5.90 per person, but you may find it's always full.

Another cheapie is the *Esmeralda Hotel* at Zapiola 636 which has rooms for US$4.10 per person. Apparently, during the summer months you can sleep for free in the classrooms at the Salesian College in the centre of town (but don't quote me!).

Places to Stay – middle

Try the *Hotel Puerto Santa Cruz* on Zapiola near the corner with Rivadavia. Singles are US$8.80 and doubles are US$11.20, all with attached bathrooms.

A comfortable place is the *Hotel Río Turbio* (tel 2155) at Zapiola 486 on the corner with Entre Ríos. There are rooms from around US$11.20 a single and US$18.80 a double without bathrooms, and US$17.60 a single and US$27.60 a double with bathrooms. The people are friendly, but you may get quite a bit of traffic noise on this intersection.

The *Hotel Punta Arenas* (tel 2743) at Federico Sphur 75 near the corner with Roca, is similar – a good, mid-range place with singles for US$10.60 and doubles for US$16.50.

The *Hotel Ampuero* , Federico Sphur 178, at the corner with Julio Roca, has singles for US$11.80 and doubles for US$15.30 and is a pretty good place with friendly people, but even by Río Gallegos standards it's rather overpriced.

If that's too much try the *Hotel Entre Ríos* on Entre Ríos between Zapiola and Libertad, which is also good with rooms for US$8.20 per person.

Places to Stay – top end

The *Hotel Alfonso* (tel 2414), Corrientes 33, is worth trying and has singles for US$17.60 and doubles for US$27, with attached bathrooms. Slightly more expensive, the *Hotel Comercio* is at the corner of Roca and Estrada.

Top of the list, however, is the *Hotel Covadonga* (tel 8190), Roca 1244, which is a good place with doubles for US$29.40 and some cheaper singles.

Places to Eat

Both the cosy *La Casa de Miguel* at Roca 1284, and the larger *Restaurant Díaz* at Roca 1157, serve very good inexpensive seafood. Also try the nifty little *Restaurant Montecarlo* at Zapiola 558.

Getting There

From Río Gallegos you can head west to Río Turbio and then cross the mountains to Puerto Natales in Chile; or head south-west to the Chilean city of Punta Arenas, from where you can cross the Straits of Magellan to Tierra del Fuego. The other alternative is to take a bus from Río Gallegos to Lago Argentino for a look at the Moreno glacier; if you want to continue on to Chile, however, you will first have to backtrack to Río Gallegos since the road from Calafate to Chile is not yet open.

Air LADE is at Fagnano 53; Aerolíneas Argentinas is at San Martín 545; and Austral Líneas Aereas is at Zapiola 122. With Aerolíneas Argentinas and LADE you can get to Comodoro Rivadavia, Río Grande and Ushuaia (several flights each week); with LADE to Perito Moreno and Calafate (one flight per week); with Aerolíneas to Punta Arenas (two days a week). There's no bus for the 7½ km trip from the airport to the centre; a taxi costs around US$2.50.

Bus El Pingüino ('The Penguin'), Zapiola on the corner with Rawson, has buses to Punta Arenas about five or six days a week for about US$10.50 . They also have departures for Río Turbio twice daily for about US$9.80.

Buses San Ceferino, Entre Ríos 371, has buses to Río Turbio four days a week.

Ruta 3, San Martín 470, has daily buses to Puerto Santa Cruz, Piedra Buena and San Julian.

Transportadora Patagonia, Gobi Lista 330, has buses to Río Turbio (US$10.60), Calafate (about US$13, taking about six hours) and northwards to Caleta Olivia (US$26.20) via San Julian and Piedra Buena. From Caleta Olivia you can pick up buses to Buenos Aires.

Along with Transportadore Patagonia, other companies to try for buses to Calafate are Interlago Turismo at Fagnano 35, and Los Lagos at España 54.

Ship There are no direct buses between Río Grande and Río Gallegos although there is another ferry crossing between Punta Delgada and Primera Angostura. The ferries are operated by ENAP (Chilean oil boats) and generally leave every two hours between about 7.30 am and 9.30 pm (don't quote me) except if it's too rough to cross. There are no buses along this route so you have to hitch-hike. If you miss the boat there is nowhere to stay in either of these places and you may get stuck.

CALAFATE

If you've made it to this part of the world, then you can't miss Calafate on the shores of Lago Argentino. It's in the Parque Nacional de los Glaciares that you'll find the spectacular Moreno glacier. The glacier itself is a km wide and 50 metres high, and descends to the surface of the lake. It's a tremendous sight! Huge pieces of ice break off occasionally and thunder into the water to float off as icebergs, often creating large waves in the process. The glacier has almost cut the lake in two and has blocked off the outlets with a wall of ice.

There's a second glacier – the 30 metre high Upsala glacier – at the end of the lake which can be visited by motorboat. In addition to the glaciers, there are many possibilities for walking and trekking in the mountains.

Information

There is a tourist office on San Martín, and a national park office opposite the ACA Motel in Calafate. Travellers' cheques and cash can be changed at the Banco de la Provincia de Santa Cruz.

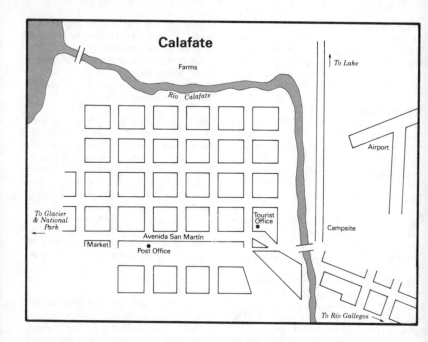

Good maps of the area are available from the national parks office.

Places to Stay & Eat

The cheapest accommodation, apart from camping, is a room in a private house. Try the one at San Martín 989. Apart from this there are a dozen hotels to choose from in Calafate (see map) but most of them are quite expensive. The only one which falls into the budget category is the *Amado* on San Martín.

There's a municipal campsite in Calafate which costs around US$1. There are two others, one about five km from town in the national park and another eight km from the Moreno glacier. Before you can use these last two you need a permit from the *guardaparques* hut at the park entrance. There are also a number of refugios in the park which are free and generally provide firewood and heating. For details about these enquire

at the national park office in Calafate. Four-person tents (US$2) and four-berth cabanas (US$3 per person) can be hired at the tourist office.

If you'd like to stay at the Moreno glacier itself, the *Motel ACA* has a number of bungalows which will each sleep four people, but they're often booked up at certain times in summer. Cooking isn't allowed in the cabins and there's often no food for sale so take your own supplies.

There's not much choice of restaurants in Calafate and very few could be described as cheap. If you stay with a family it would be best to eat with them.

Getting There

Río Gallegos is the jumping-off point for buses to Calafate; see that section for details. Hitching in the summer months is fairly easy as the national park is a popular holiday destination for Argentinians. If you're hitching, you have a choice of coming from Río Gallegos or Santa Cruz further north. There's also a new road connecting Calafate to Puerto Natales in Chile which goes through the Torres Del Paine national park but there are no buses as yet. LADE flies from Ushuaia to Perito Moreno one day a week, via Río Grande, Río Gallegos and Calafate.

The Moreno glacier is about 80 km from Calafate. In the summer season – November to February – there is a daily minibus to the edge of the glacier which sets off early in the morning and returns in the afternoon for US$13 return. It's also possible to get a lift in the national park truck which leaves most mornings at about 8 am, but you need to be there by 5 am at the latest. A taxi to the glacier will cost at least US$25 per person return.

In the winter local people drive tourists out to the glacier. A large station wagon which will hold up to eight people and costs about US$65 to hire is usually available from the Residencial Avenida on San Martín.

In the summer months it's also possible to visit the Upsala glacier by motor boat. The boats go from Punta Bandera, 45 km from Calafate (a bus from Calafate costs US$8) at 8 am and return at 4 pm. The travel agents, Turista Lacustre, also offer the complete trip (to Punta Bandera by bus and the boat trip to the glacier) for US$19 return.

RIO TURBIO

After a long drive across the plains, with rheas bounding across the road in front of the bus, and just before you cross the hills into Chile, is Río Turbio. It lies in a valley, and even though it has existed for several decades it still looks like a real frontier town, with a drab collection of bungalows, hovels, converted army barracks, concrete bunkers and coal dust (it's not bad compared to the even uglier settlement half an hour out on the road to Río

Gallegos). Coal mining is the reason for Río Turbio's existence, and many Chileans also work in the mines – you'll meet them on the bus as you cross the border to Puerto Natales.

Places to Stay

The *Hotel El Gato Negro* is on Roque Saenz Pena and costs US$9.40 per person for a room with wash basin. It's very clean, and by the standards of southern Argentina it's good value for money.

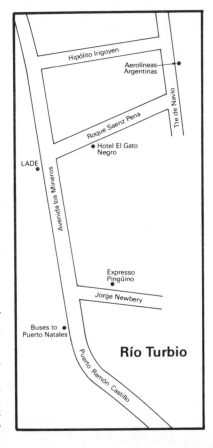

Getting There

Air Aerolíneas Argentinas is on Castillo, at the junction with Hipólito Irigoyen. LADE is at Mineros 375.

Bus The bus ride from Río Turbio to Puerto Natales takes about 1½ hours in all. One bus takes you to the Argentinian customs post (about US$0.50) where you transfer to a Chilean bus which takes you to Puerto Natales (about US$1.40). Buses leave Río Turbio from the junction of Avenida de los Mineros and Ramón Castillo. Customs only checks that you're not importing fruit into Chile, and they're usually fairly speedy. You no longer need permission from the police in Río Gallegos to cross into Chile. However you may need permission from the Chilean police (*investigaciones*) to cross into Argentina – so check first in Puerto Natales if you're coming the other way.

Río Turbio to Río Gallegos takes six hours to 6½ hours along a gravel road cutting through grassland grazed by sheep and dotted with large estancias.

El Pingüiino bus line has its office and terminal on Jorge Newbery, near the corner with Avenida de los Mineros; they have buses to Río Gallegos daily at 6 am and an additional bus at 1 pm on Tuesdays, Thursdays and Saturdays.

Buses San Ceferino also runs buses to Río Gallegos; they're on Castillo, at the junction with Hipólito Irigoyen. The fare from Río Turbio to Río Gallegos is around US$9.80.

Magallanes

The brief civil war of 1831 delivered Chile into the hands of the landed aristocracy of the central valley. Three conservative presidents came to office during the next 30 years, each of whom served two five-year terms: Joaquín Prieto in the 1830s, Manuel Bulnes in the 1840's and Manuel Montt in the 1850s. But the strong man of the period was Diego Portales, who ranked no higher than a cabinet minister yet ruled as a virtual dictator until he was assassinated in 1837, having just fought a successful war against Peru and Bolivia.

Pride in the nation's military prowess matched by triumphs at home gave the Chilean upper class a certain satisfaction. Trade was booming, Valparaíso was developing into the major port on the west coast of South America, mines were being opened, the old families were finding new wealth and a class of nouveau riche arose. Chilean nationalism, spurred by the successful war, led to a wave of expansion which embroiled Chile in conflict with Argentina.

In 1843 President Bulnes laid claim to the territory around the Straits of Magellan, Tierra del Fuego and much of southern Patagonia. In that year the first Chilean stake in Patagonia was established with the founding of Fuerte Bulnes on the Straits of Magellan, and five years later the city of Punta Arenas was founded nearby. The Lake District to the south of Valdivia was also opened for settlement, despite the tentative hold of the Mapuche Indians on this area, and German immigrants began to arrive in the late 1840s.

Fuerte Bulnes and Punta Arenas might have remained nothing more than token gestures had it not been for three things: the discovery of gold in California in 1848, the industrial age in Europe, and the development and increasing use of steamships in the second half of the century. Since the Panama Canal had not yet been built, one way of getting from eastern USA to the goldfields in the west was a five month wagon ride across the continent. The other was to sail to Panama, cross the isthmus by mule, then sail to California. Cheaper, and potentially quicker, was to sail via the tip of South America, a journey which could take anything from three to seven months.

Ferdinand Magellan

Punta Arenas became a port of call for giant sailing ships, and a coaling stop for steamships. Migrants were not the only cargo. By the 1880s these ships were also transporting Chilean nitrates, Australian meat and American wheat, oil, and petroleum to Europe. Tools were transported from Europe to Australia, and machinery, railroad tracks and iron from Europe to America. When the Americans dug their trench across Panama, shipping around the Horn declined dramatically and the Chilean ports on the western coast of South America were bypassed. The golden age of Punta Arenas was over.

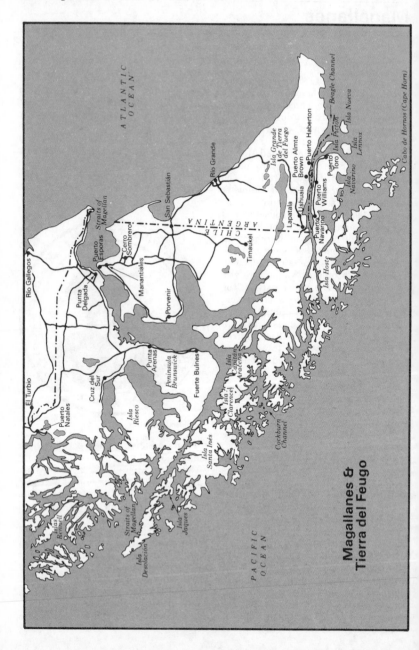

Magallanes &
Tierra del Feugo

PUNTA ARENAS

Situated at the very end of the Chilean mainland looking across the Straits of Magellan to Porvenir and Tierra del Fuego, Punta Arenas is a city of some 80,000 people. It once resembled Puerto Montt and the towns of Chiloé Island with its wooden buildings, but these have mostly been replaced with concrete and brick. Much of its recent development has been fuelled by the discovery of oil in the region, and Punta Arenas is a surprisingly large and well-developed city and an important Chilean naval base.

Information

Tourist Office The tourist office is at Waldo Seguel 689 (tel 24435) at one corner of the main plaza. They have maps of the city and the staff are really friendly and helpful. There's also a tourist information kiosk on the nature strip at the junction of Magallanes and Colón; that's open Monday to Saturday, 10 am to 7 pm and Sundays, 9 am to 1 pm. The office in the city centre is open in the morning but may be closed in the afternoon.

Bank There are several places around the centre of town where you can change Chilean and Argentine currency. Try La Hermandad, corner of Roca and Lautaro Navarro; Sur Cambio, corner of Pedro Montt and Lautaro Navarro; Casa Stop, Nogueira 1170. The Banco de Chile on Roca, between Lautaro Navarro and 21 de Mayo, will change US dollars and US dollar travellers' cheques; however you will get about a 10% better exchange rate from the exchange houses. Different exchange houses give different rates, so if you're changing a lot of money shop around!

Post & Communications The main post office is at the corner of Menéndez and Bhories one block up from the Plaza de Armas; open Monday to Friday from 8.30 am to 12.30 pm and 2 to 6.30 pm, and

Saturday, 9 am to 12.30 pm. Long-distance phone calls can be made from the telephone office at the corner of Fagnano and Nogueira diagonally opposite the plaza; open Monday to Friday, 8.30 am to 8 pm; and Saturdays, Sundays and holidays, 9 am to 10 pm.

Consulates There is an Argentinian consulate at 21 de Mayo 1878 which is open Monday to Friday from 10 am to 2 pm.

Investigaciones Investigaciones is at Errázuriz 911 (tel 21 714). It used to be the case that before you went to Argentina you had to report here and have your passport stamped. This is no longer necessary but regulations could change as relations between the two countries fluctuate. It could be worth checking before you get turned back at the border at San Sebastián on Tierra del Fuego.

Things to See

All around Punta Arenas there are reminders of bygone days. Monuments are lined up like beads on a string along Bhories, including memorials to the early Yugoslav settlers and to hardy farmers who pioneered the area. The enormous cemetery on Bulnes contains many large family crypts and numerous tombstones and graves of early British and Yugoslav settlers.

Magallanes Regional Museum

Though once mainly a city of wooden buildings with corrugated tin roofs, the many gracious mansions of the city centre betray the early importance of Punta Arenas on the trade route round South America. One of the finest mansions ever built, belonging to what was once one of the city's most important families – and whose name still crops up in the higher circles of both Chilean and Argentinian society – is now referred to as the Centro Cultural Braun-Menéndez and houses the Museum Regional

Magallanes. The owner of vast areas of Patagonia and Tierra del Fuego at the turn of the century, the family eventually moved to Buenos Aires due to a combination of expropriation and the opening of the Panama Canal.

The displays depict the European settlement of Punta Arenas and Tierra del Fuego. The front rooms of the house are preserved as they were when the family lived here, and the furnishings are the originals – almost every piece imported from Europe (mainly France) to produce a house no less palatial than any in Santiago at the time.

The museum is situated on Magallanes just off the Plaza de Armas. It's open Tuesday to Saturday, 11 am to 4 pm, and holidays, 11 am to 1 pm.

Salesian College

A curious museum in the Colegio Salesiano describes the geography, fauna and flora of southern Patagonia, and harbours a collection of stuffed animals and the relics of dead Indians. Large dioramas depict the Indian way of life before the coming of the white man, but depressing before-and-after photos (before the whiteman and after the whiteman) hardly require captions or explanations. Ten thousand year-old droppings and unidentifiable fragments of the giant ground-sloth uncovered in the Milodon Cave near Puerto Natales are also on display. All else aside, this is probably the best place to come if you want a concentrated overview of the natural history of southern Chile.

The museum is at the corner of Bulnes and Sarmiento. It's open daily from 3 to 6 pm, and entry is about US$0.30. Photography of the exhibits without permission is prohibited – this rule *is* enforced.

Patagonian Institute

At the Instituto del Patagonia there's an extraordinary collection of old farming machinery, including steam tractors built in England or Europe and used in Tierra del Fuego and Magallanes in the 19th and 20th centuries. Other vehicles include a wooden wagon used by the early settlers before permanent houses were built, horse-drawn wagons and coaches, early petrol-engine farm tractors and vintage cars. More surprising are the simple wooden horse-drawn ploughs used in southern Patagonia and Tierra del Fuego until the 1930s. There is also a reconstructed settler's house from the Punta Arenas area dating back to 1875-80 and a tiny zoo with several condors and pumas.

The easiest way to get to the Institute is with a taxi colectivo from the front of the Museum Regional de Magallanes, on Magallanes just off the plaza. They cost about US$0.30 and drop you off right in front of the institute.

Zona Franca

Across the road from the institute is the Zona Franca (Free Zone) where duty-free goods are sold – everything from Walkmans to sacks of rice and Dodge trucks. It's worth a look, but check prices in the city before you buy anything as some things are more expensive in the Zona Franca!

The Penguin Colony

The best sight outside Punta Arenas is the *pingüineros*, the penguin colony. This is rather like a colony of hobbits, with burrows dug in the shoreline's soft, sandy soil – into which the penguins disappear 'when large stupid folk like you and me come blustering along'. Like hobbits they're surprisingly amiable, although they will bite if you prod them too closely. Penguin beaks, by the way, can inflict a nasty cut.

Try and go with only a small group of people if you visit the colony. Large groups frighten them and they'll hide in their burrows. Otherwise, they stand around in little herds and you can get to within a few feet of them. The drive to the

Top: Fuerte Bulnes, near Punta Arenas
Bottom: Balmaceda Glacier, near Puerto Natales

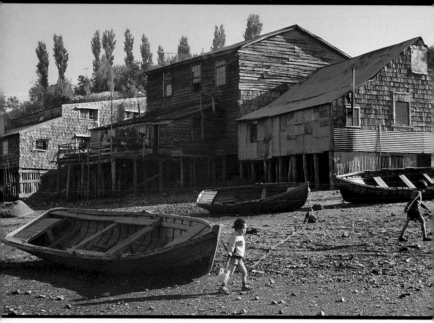

Top: Torres del Paine National Park
Bottom: Fishing village, Castro

penguin colony takes you through sheep-grazing country, also inhabited by wild guanacos, rhea and ibises. For details of how to get there (you'll either have to hire a car or go on a tour) see the Getting Around section.

Fuerte Bulnes

Although Bernardo O'Higgins may have planned to annex the southern tip of South America for Chile, it was not until 1843 that the Chileans finally claimed the place. In October of that year the first rude buildings of Fuerte Bulnes were slapped up from logs, thatch and mud and the lonely outpost was given the respectable status of a fort by the addition of cannon and a fence of pointed stakes. The fort – 55 km from Punta Arenas – has been partly restored and is now a national monument. For details of how to get there see the Getting Around section.

Places to Stay - bottom end

Like many towns in southern Chile, the best deals in accommodation are offered by private houses. Two of those which have been recommended are at Calle Boliviano 238 and Calle Boliviano 366. The second, which is run by a friendly woman, charges US$2.80 per person, which includes breakfast.

In the centre of town on Nogueira, in the same building a few doors up from the Plaza de Armas, are the *Hotel Turismo Plaza* and the *Residencial París*. The *Turismo Plaza* is the more expensive of the two with its cheapest rooms (without attached bathrooms) from US$8.60 a single and US$11.10 a double; more expensive rooms have their own bathrooms. It's spotlessly clean, bright, and the front rooms have good views looking out onto the town. The *Residencial Paris* has rooms without bathrooms from US$5.60 per person, though that includes breakfast. It's a very spartan place, but it's clean and has a rather jolly female proprietor. There are no locks on the

doors, so don't leave valuables lying around. A few of the rooms have no windows.

If these are full then there's the *Residencial Roca* at the corner of Roca and Emilio Korner, which is a decent place and somewhat cheaper at only US$4.20 per person (including cups of coffee). They're friendly people and the place appears to be popular with travellers.

The *Hotel Monte Carlo* at Ecuatoriana 18 has also been recommended as a good, cheap place to stay.

Places to Stay - middle

The *Hotel Ritz* (tel 24422), Pedro Montt 1102, is recommended without hesitation. It's clean and comfortable but fairly quiet, with friendly people. Singles start from around US$9 and doubles from about US$11. If you can afford it then it's good value. There's also an attached restaurant.

Places to Stay - top end

The *Hotel Los Navegantes* at Menéndez 647 is the place to go if you want top-end accommodation; it's much better than the illustrious *Cabo de Hornos* which faces the plaza. Rooms at *Los Navagantes* are US$30 to US$38 per person, including breakfast.

Places to Eat

This side of the Argentine border most people's idea of a pizza is a large potato chip smothered in baked cheese. One exception is the *Roka Pizza* at Bhories 546, near the corner with Mejicana. A medium-sized pizza *with the lot* will cost around US$2.50 – and by the looks of the cards and the writing on the walls it seems just about everyone who's been through Punta Arenas has eaten here. It's a favoured hang-out for young Chileans.

For Italian food don't go past the *Bar Ristorante Peppino* at O'Higgins 1134 near the waterfront; along with pizzas they've got fairly cheap but decent-sized

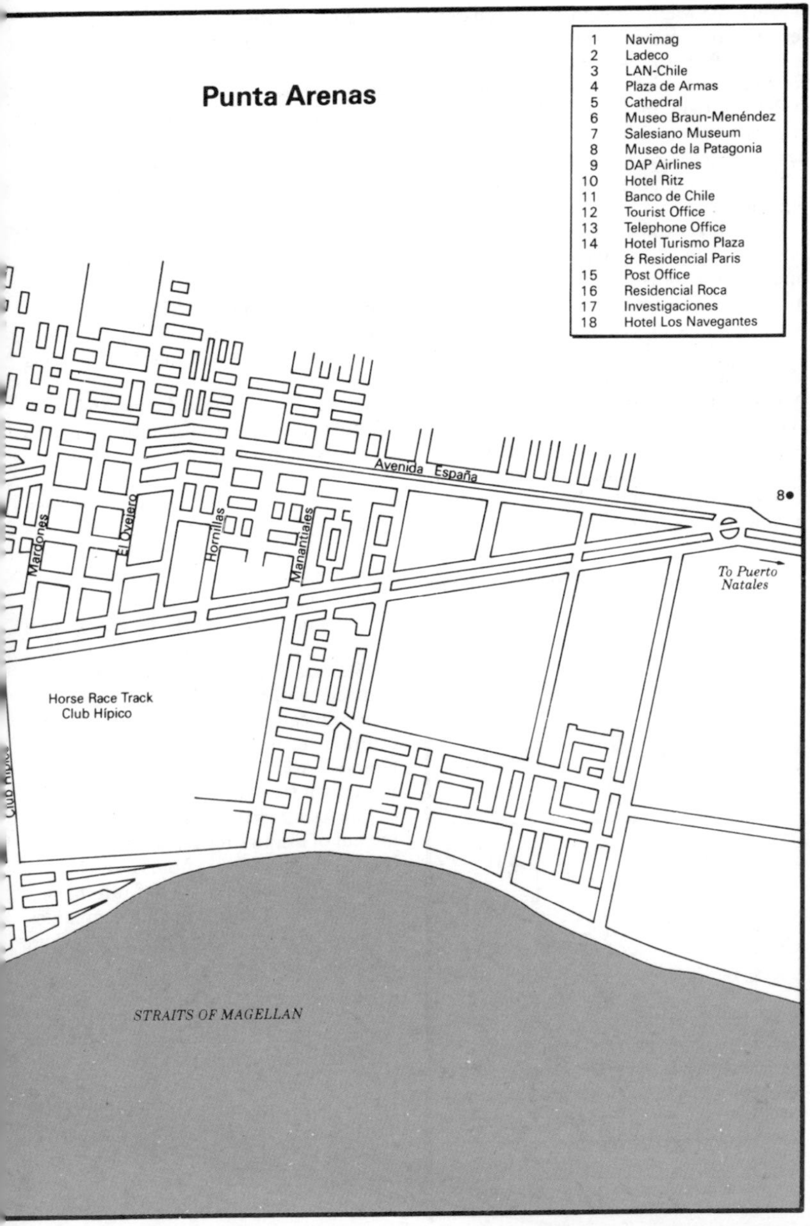

Punta Arenas

1	Navimag
2	Ladeco
3	LAN-Chile
4	Plaza de Armas
5	Cathedral
6	Museo Braun-Menéndez
7	Salesiano Museum
8	Museo de la Patagonia
9	DAP Airlines
10	Hotel Ritz
11	Banco de Chile
12	Tourist Office
13	Telephone Office
14	Hotel Turismo Plaza
	& Residencial Paris
15	Post Office
16	Residencial Roca
17	Investigaciones
18	Hotel Los Navegantes

Avenida España

8●

To Puerto
Natales

Macdones

El Ovejero

Hornillas

Manantiales

Horse Race Track
Club Hípico

Club Hípico

STRAITS OF MAGELLAN

servings of lasagna, spaghetti bolognaise, fettucini and other pasta dishes.

Next door to Peppino's is the *Bar Restaurant Sotitos* for some up-market Italian seafood. Investigate the impact of the raw sea urchin on your digestive system right here. Otherwise it's a lively place with amiable waiters – but it is expensive!

Other places worth trying include the *Nandu Café Grill*, Waldo Seguel 670, opposite the tourist office, which is more a bar than a restaurant – not bad. There are a number of sailor's bars along the harbour. The *British Club* at Roca 858, above the Chamber of Commerce, has a homely pub atmosphere and good billiard tables.

If all else fails there is a terrific smorgasbord restaurant in the Zona Franca – in the first building on your right as you enter the compound. A big plate of

cannelloni, chips, dessert, bread and soft-drink will cost under US$3.

Getting There

The tourist office keeps a list of all road, sea and air transport out of Punta Arenas, Puerto Natales and around Tierra del Fuego, including connections to Argentina.

Air LAN-Chile (tel 23460) is at the corner of Pedro Montt and Lautaro Navarro. Ladeco (tel 22665) is at Roca 924. DAP (tel 23958) is at Ignacio Carrena Pinto 1022. Aerolíneas Argentinas (tel 21247) is at Gamero 1013.

DAP connects Punta Arenas to Tierra del Fuego. It flies from Punta Arenas to Puerto Williams and back every Tuesday, Thursday and Saturday; the fare is US$37. DAP also has daily flights between Punta Arenas and Porvenir; the fare is US$9.50. You may have to take the flight if the sea is too rough for the ferries.

Ladeco flies from Punta Arenas to Concepción (two days a week), and Santiago and Puerto Montt (daily). LAN-Chile flies from Punta Arenas to Santiago and Puerto Montt (daily).

Aerolíneas Argentinas has flights from Punta Arenas to Buenos Aires via Río Grande, Río Gallegos and Comodoro Rivadavia (two days a week).

The Aeropuerto Presidente Ibáñez is 20 km out of Punta Arenas. DAP has its own bus to take passengers from the city to the airport. Ladeco and LAN-Chile have a deal with one of the regular bus companies, so when you buy your tickets ask where you catch the bus.

Bus There are direct buses between Punta Arenas and Río Gallegos in Argentina. Alternatively, you could take a bus to the Chilean town of Puerto Natales, from where you can cross the border to Río Turbio and carry on to Río Gallegos. You can also get buses which will take you all the way through to Puerto Montt via Argentina. Bus companies, their addresses

---

SOTITOS – BAR

Restaurant de Turismo
José y Fanor Soto Alvarado Ltda.
O'Higgins 1138 – Fono 23565   N° 129306
RUT.:   84.602.900 - 1
Punta Arenas

Mesa N° _____ Garzón N° _____

Punta Arenas, 21 de 922010 de 198 _

Señor: _____

BOLETA DE VENTA
Imprenta ARCOIRIS · San Nicolas 1011 · Fono 512844 · San Miguel

en in wi	3.0
Perzop. op	55,
2 e .	3,0
i & e	4.0
TOTAL $	230

AGRADECEMOS SU VISITA   CLIENTE

and some of their fares and destinations are:

Buses Sur, Menéndez 565, has daily departures to Puerto Natales around 3 and 7 pm. They take about four to 4½ hours and the fare is about US$6.70.

Buses Fernández, Chiloé 930, has buses to Puerto Natales departing daily about 9 am and 6.30 pm. They run three-day tours to the Torres del Paine park departing every Tuesday and Friday (probably only in the summer months). Also ask about tours to the penguin colony and to Fuerte Bulnes.

Buses Río Gallegos, Lautaro Navarro 971, runs buses to Río Gallegos. There are daily departures, usually either at 9 am or 12 noon, but check first. The fare from Punta Arenas to Río Gallegos is around U$9.50.

El Pingüino, Lautaro Navarro 971, has buses to Río Gallegos about five days a week, leaving at either 9 or 11 am. Also try *Buses Mancilla* at Menéndez 55.

Buses Ghisoni, Lautaro Navarro 971, has a weekly bus from Punta Arenas to Osorno and Puerto Montt. Also try *Buses Norte*, at Gamero 1039 and *Turibus* at Menéndez 647. Punta Arenas to Puerto Montt costs about US$60.

Boat There are regular passenger ferries between Punta Arenas and Porvenir in Tierra del Fuego. Passenger shipping services from southern Chile to Puerto Montt and intermediate destinations leave from Puerto Natales; for full details see the Puerto Natales section and the Getting Around chapter at the start of this book.

In Punta Arenas, for ships to the north enquire at Empremar, Lautaro Navarro 1338 (tel 21608); and at Navimag, Independencia 830 (tel 26600/ 21608). Both these companies *may* have passenger accommodation on their ships but don't count on it. If you want assured passages on ships going north then you'll have to go to Puerto Natales from where Navimag have passenger/cargo ships to Puerto Montt, three times a month.

There are regular ferries across the Straits of Magellan between Punta Arenas and Porvenir. A ferry leaves at 9 am daily from Punta Arenas (except Sunday when it leaves at 11 am) and 6 pm daily from Porvenir (except on Saturday when it leaves at 3 pm). The journey takes about three hours, and the fare is US$1.80. Vehicles can be transported on these ferries and I've even seen people take horses across.

In Punta Arenas the ferries to Porvenir leave from Puerto Trente about a km past the Zona Franca – take a local bus or a taxi colectivo. A hired taxi from the city centre to the port will cost you about US$2.80. Taxis meet the incoming ferries.

Getting Around

Taxi colectivos in Punta Arenas are about US$0.22 on weekdays, and about US$0.30 on Sundays and holidays. Buses are US$0.15 all week. Fares and destinations are posted on the outside of each bus and taxi. Although much of Punta Arenas is small enough to walk around you'll need the buses and colectivos to get to places further out like the Patagonian Institute and the Salesian College.

There are a couple of car rental firms around: Hertz Rent-a-car at Lautaro Navarro 1064, has cars from about US$19 per day (rent plus daily insurance costs) plus US$0.15 per km plus 20% tax. You can also rent for three-day periods (if, for example, you want to head off to Puerto Natales and the Torres del Paine National Park) for around US$100 plus 20% tax, including 600 km free.

For tours to the penguin colony or to Fuerte Bulnes try Turismo Patagonia LTDA at Roca 886. They usually run morning tours to the fort for about US$10, and afternoon tours to the penguin colony for slightly less per person. These trips are quite expensive but they're worth it – particularly the penguin colony. They also have three-day tours to the Torres del Paine National Park.

Ask at the travel agents and the Hotel Cabo de Hornos about plane rides over the surrounding region. They're likely to be expensive but they take you over Tierra del Fuego, the Marinelli Glacier, the Beagle Channel, Puerto Williams and even as far south as Cape Horn. Flights last about four hours.

PUERTO NATALES

Puerto Natales is a cool and tidy town of timber and corrugated iron houses. It's the last town of any size on the southern Chilean mainland, save for Punta Arenas on the Straits of Magellan. While unspectacular in itself, some of the most astonishing sights in southern Chile can be found in the vicinity of Puerto Natales. It's very popular with trekkers and climbers during the summer months as it's the gateway to the spectacular Torres del Paine National Park. It's also the jumping-off point for the Balmaceda Glacier and the Milodon Cave. Ships to Puerto Montt leave from Puerto Natales, and you can also take a bus over the mountains to Río Turbio in Argentina.

Information

Bank There are a number of casas de cambio in Puerto Natales where you can

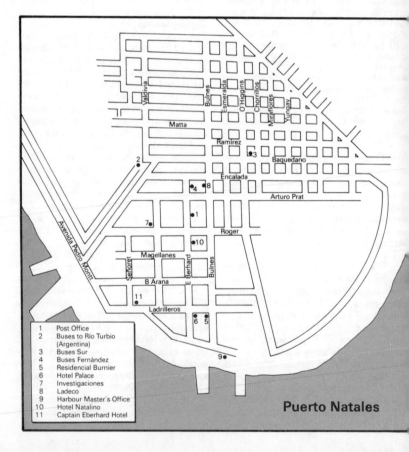

1 Post Office
2 Buses to Río Turbio (Argentina)
3 Buses Sur
4 Buses Fernández
5 Residencial Burnier
6 Hotel Palace
7 Investigaciones
8 Ladeco
9 Harbour Master's Office
10 Hotel Natalino
11 Captain Eberhard Hotel

Puerto Natales

change Argentinian currency for Chilean currency (and vice-versa). Try the one at Encalada 226, at the junction with Eberhard. There doesn't seem to be anywhere to change travellers' cheques or even US cash – you will have to do this in Punta Arenas.

Post & Communications The post office is on Eberhard, facing the main plaza. It's open Monday to Friday, 8.30 am to 12.30 pm and 2.30 to 5 pm, and Saturday, 8.30 am to 12 noon. Telex Chile is in the same building, and is open Monday to Friday from 8.30 am to 1.30 pm and 2.45 to 6.30 pm, and on Saturday from 8.30 am to 1.15 pm.

The Meat-Packing Plant

The miniature steam engine now set up in the Plaza de Armas was built in Bristol, Britain in 1920. It was used at the British-owned meat-packing and tanning factory, which was established early this century, just outside Puerto Natales. The meat and hides were taken from the factory along a railway line laid along a pier, and loaded onto ships.

The factory still operates, though the scale of operations is much smaller than it was during its heyday when several thousand sheep were being slaughtered weekly. At that time some of the sheep ranches in the area each ran as many as 80,000 to 120,000 sheep. Some of the land now included in the Torres del Paine park was once a sheep ranch, owned by a Chilean-Italian up until the early part of the 1970s. No more sheep are grazed in the park now; instead there are herds of guanaco and flocks of rheas and pink flamingo. Rheas are now a protected species; their meat is said to taste like turkey.

The meat processing plant is just outside Puerto Natales, by the road leading to Torres del Paine. Much of the original steam-driven machinery is still there but is no longer used. These days the compressors used to freeze the meat

are electrically powered. Only a few hundred sheep a week are now processed at the factory. The wooden buildings in front of the plant are used to dry the hides. Narrow spaces are left between the slats of their walls to allow air to circulate.

The Balmaceda Glacier

This impressive glacier slides down a mountain right into one of the many estuaries and fjords which make up the jagged southern Chilean coastline. Huge blocks of ice break off and wallow around in the lagoon in front of the glacier wall.

The glacier lies to the north-east of Puerto Natales. During January and February (and perhaps March) a boat called the *21 de Mayo* takes groups to the glacier almost every day; the cost is about US$16 per person. It leaves from the pier at the end of Bulnes around 8.30 am and returns in the late afternoon.

If the boat is not docked, enquire at the house of Señor Alvarez at Cadilleros 91, at the corner with Eberhard. You'll only be able to go when there are tour groups to fill up the boat. Bring something to eat – drinks are provided but no food unless you're with a tour group

The tub is about 40 or 50 years old and the pioneering spirit is maintained by the provision of two inadequately sized lifeboats and two life-preservers; there are no life-jackets. The winds that roar through the narrow channel leading to the glacier can be so strong that sometimes the boat has to turn back or does terrifying rolls in the choppy sea. Console yourself with the knowledge that it has done many successful trips. Small waterfalls, condors and bands of seals can be seen on the voyage. At the glacier the boat pulls into a small jetty and you can get off and walk up along a trail very close to the glacier itself. The Torres del Paine can be seen in the distance.

The Milodon Cave

The milodon was a Giant Ground Sloth,

rather larger and more ferocious looking than a full-grown bull, and of a class unique to South America. Towards the end of the 18th century the bones of an even bigger relative of the Giant Ground Sloth were sent from Buenos Aires to the King of Spain. This creature stood some five metres high – an enlarged version of the ordinary insect-eating sloths that hang upside down by their tails in trees. Darwin also found the bones of a milodon in South America and sent them back to England. The animal was so big that rather than putting it in a tree, zoologists of the day imagined it rearing up on its haunches and using its long, extendable tongue to scoop up leaves and grubs.

The Milodon Cave forms an enormous cavity in a mountain at the back of what was once a sheep ranch on Last Hope Sound. It was settled in 1893 by a Prussian, Herman Eberhard, who found his way to Chile via a pig farm in Nebraska, a whaling station in Alaska, and piloting ships in the Falklands. He rowed up the Sound with two British naval deserters and established a farm. The story goes that in early 1895 he took a look at the giant cave and found a human skull and a piece of skin sticking out of the floor. A year later a Swedish explorer visited the cave and found more skin as well as the eye-socket of an enormous mammal, a claw, a human thighbone of giant size and some stone tools.

As pieces of the animal and other milodon bones found their way to England and Europe, the inevitable conclusion was drawn: some species of giant sloth had managed to survive into recent years! Hoping that some might still be around – for there were Indian stories and traveller's tales of grotesque creatures inhabiting South America – a British expedition was launched to find one, but had no success.

Meanwhile the cave was excavated. In the uppermost layer were the remains of human settlement; in the middle were the remains of the now-extinct American horse; and in the bottom layer were the remains of the milodon. One excavator even devised the bizarre theory that the milodon was a domesticated beast, kept by the Indians at the rear of the cave like a horse in a corral, and suggested it's name should be changed to *gryptotherium domesticum*. The modern verdict is that the Giant Sloth lived about 10,000 years ago. Indians may have killed it in a battle for possession of the cave but, sad to say, they did not keep it as a pet.

The cave is not far from Puerto Natales, and is just off the road to Torres del Paine. Entry to the cave is about US$0.30. A full-size model of the creature stands in the cave. For a run-down on the history of the cave and the discovery of the creature's remains see Bruce Chatwin's book *In Patagonia*.

Places to Stay – bottom end

Very spartan and a bit dilapidated, the *Pensión La Busca* is at Valdivia 845 (there's no sign but it is there). There are hot showers downstairs. Basically it's OK and probably the cheapest you'll find in this town at just US$2.50 per person.

The *Residencial Burnier* at the corner of Bulnes and Ladrilleros is also worth trying. It's another fairly spartan place, but the rooms are large and have heaters, and there's an attached restaurant and general store. It costs US$3.60 per person. There are no locks on the doors, so don't leave valuables in your rooms when you're away. The people are friendly.

Places to Stay – middle

The *Hotel Natalino* on Eberhard, near the corner with Tomas Rogers, has got to be the best value in town, if not one of the best little hotels in Chile. It's very clean and comfortable, with heaters in the rooms, and it's run by a lively, friendly woman. Rooms without private bathrooms are US$5.30 a single and US$10 a double; with private bathrooms they're US$8 a single and US$14 a double. Prices include breakfast, but all you get is toast and coffee – the hotel's one shortcoming.

Another fine place is the *Austral Hotel* at Valdivia 955, with singles for around US$4.20 and doubles for about twice that. It's clean and comfortable, with a friendly manager and a restaurant downstairs.

Places to Stay – top end
One of Puerto Natales' most commodious hotels is the *Hotel Palace* near the corner of Eberhard and Ladrilleros. Singles are US$18, doubles are US$24. The town's No 1 hotel would probably be the *Captain Eberhard Hotel* on the waterfront at the corner with Senoret; US$36 a single and US$41 a double.

Places to Eat
The *Restaurant Midas* at Thomas Rogers 169, facing the main plaza, is a fine place for seafood – despite its appearance it's surprisingly cheap and a full meal will come to around US$4 per person.

A few doors down from the Midas is *Bianco's Pizza*. Also worth a try, the *Café Tranquera* is at Bulnes 579.

The very best in town is Eduardo Scott's *Restaurant Río Serrano* at Captain Eberhard 261, which specialises in fish and other seafood dishes such as crab and shellfish. Make sure you try his *sopa de marina* which is a piping-hot, thick broth of seafood – a meal in itself. The restaurant is also something of a gathering place for foreigners.

Getting There
Air Ladeco have an office at Bulnes 530, open Monday to Friday, 9.30 am to 12.30 pm and 3.30 to 8.30 pm. There are no flights out of Puerto Natales – the nearest airport is at Punta Arenas – but you can make bookings for the Ladeco flights at this office. If you don't want to visit Punta Arenas you can arrange for the bus coming through from Puerto Natales to drop you off at the Punta Arenas airport.

Bus Bus Sur at Baquedano 534 has buses twice a day to Punta Arenas. Buses Fernandez at Eberhard 555 has buses

twice a day to Punta Arenas. The fare with both is US$6.70 and the trip takes about four hours.

For buses to Argentina try Buses Alvaro Gomez and San Ceferino at Baquedano 244. They appear to have buses direct from Puerto Natales to Río Gallegos via Río Turbio – about three departures per week.

Alternatively, to get to Río Turbio (where you can catch another bus to Río Gallegos) go to the corner of Phillippi and Baquedano and get one of the local workers' buses. There are departures about every half hour, or hour, every day from early morning to early evening.

Boat The Navimag office is at the port of Puerto Natales. They have passenger ships about three times a month to Puerto Montt. For details see the Getting Around chapter at the start of this book.

PUERTO EDEN
The south coast of Chile, with its hundreds of islands, looks like a demolished jigsaw. On the way between Puerto Montt and Puerto Natales is Puerto Edén, one of the most isolated settlements

in the world. The ship may pull in briefly (otherwise ask the captain if it would be possible to do so – if sufficient people want to see the place he may stop, even if he is not scheduled to).

Perhaps 500 people live in Puerto Edén, making a living solely by fishing and selling some of their catch to ships that call in. They have chickens but there are no other animals. The soil is clay so they cannot grow crops of any kind. There is at least one policeman and – even in this remote place – the inevitable bust of the naval hero Arturo Prat!

TORRES DEL PAINE NATIONAL PARK

The Towers of Paine, huge granite pillars of metamorphic rock thrust up and folded by intense heat and pressure, make a sudden and dramatic appearance on the horizon in the midst of a flat, dry, windswept plain – they're so extravagantly beautiful that superlatives soon fail you. This is – despite the almost constant cold wind – some of the finest trekking country in Chile. It is endowed with mountains, lakes, waterfalls, glaciers, as well as herds of guanaco, flocks of pink flamingo, condors and the large Patagonian hares, amongst much other wildlife.

The park was originally established in 1959 as the Parque Nacional Lago Grey. Prior to this, shepherds grazed their flocks here, and their fires occasionally burnt out of control. You can still see the devastation that was wrought near Lago Grey, with large areas of burnt-out forest and charred logs extending up the hillsides as far as the snowline. Even after all these years the land has still not fully recovered.

More land was added to the park in 1962 and the name was changed to its present one. It is said that the towers and park were named after a woman climber or settler (or both) named Paine, although *payne* is also an Indian word for 'blue'. Estancia El Paine, a sheep grazing property, was added to the park around 1974.

With a bit of planning trekkers could spend weeks exploring the park, but it's possible to see a good deal of it on a day trip from Puerto Natales. A rough but motorable track extends up to Lago Grey, and you can see enormous blue icebergs which have broken off from the glacier at the other end of the lake and floated down. Some of the lakes are also accessible by road and the towers – when not shrouded by low cloud – are always present in the background.

The entrance fee to the park is about US$1.30 – you pay at the entrance on the road up from Puerto Natales.

Maps

If you intend camping or trekking you'll need a map of the area to find out where the refugios are located. These are simple mountain huts, some of them with basic facilities, where you can find shelter for the night.

A good map to get hold of is the CONAF (Corporación Nacional Forestal) map called Parque Nacional Torres del Paine. This has all the refugios, roads, tracks, ranger stations and picnic areas marked on it. It was available from the CONAF office in Puerto Natales but this seems to have disappeared. You can get it from the CONAF hut at the entrance to the park.

Eduardo Scott at the Restaurant Río

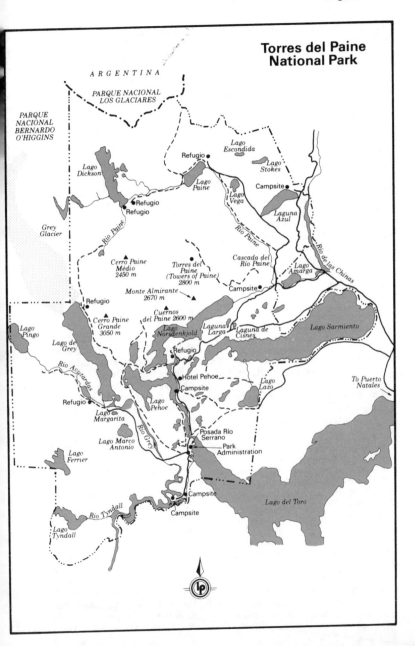

**Torres del Paine
National Park**

Serrano in Puerto Natales sells good photostat copies of a map which is even clearer and more detailed than the CONAF map – definitely worth getting.

Books

If you intend trekking you should go to the park armed with Eduardo Scott's map and a copy of Hilary Bradt's and John Pilkington's *Backpacking in Chile & Argentina* which includes a chapter on the park.

Warning

Take warm clothes with you even if you're not trekking! The weather can be stormy right through the summer months (though there are also beautiful days of warm sunshine and light wind). At Lago Grey, where the wind sweeps off the glacier, it can be very cold! You must have rain and wind protection and a change of clothing.

Places to Stay & Eat

There are two hotels in the park. The *Hotel Pehoe* is located on an island in Lago Pehoe and connected to the shore by a footbridge. It faces the towers across the lake – one of the most beautiful settings in the park.

The other is the *Posada Río Serrano* which is near Lago del Toro at the start of the road leading to Lago Grey. Single rooms are about US$9.40 and doubles, US$13.90; breakfast is an additional US$2.20 and dinner is US$5.40. Camping in the hotel grounds, with the use of hot water, is US$4.20 per person. There is a small shop in the hotel where you can stock up on food although it may be an idea to bring essentials from Puerto Natales.

There are refugios, campsites and shelters in the park. These are free. For their location get one of the maps already mentioned. If you intend trekking you must bring all your own food as there is none available in the park other than what is available at the two hotels.

Getting There

Getting to the park can be a bit of a haphazard affair, but don't worry – you'll make it somehow!

If your time is limited or if you don't have the equipment or the urge to trek and camp out, then consider taking a tour to the park. Eduardo Scott, a Falklander who speaks both Spanish and English, is the guy to contact for tours of the surrounding area and especially of the Torres del Paine park. He takes people for day-trips to the park in a mini-van, and charges about US$11 per person – although you may have to pay a bit more if the van is not full (it *is* worth it!). He can also arrange a visit to the old meat-packing and tanning factory just outside of Puerto Natales. Contact him at the Restaurant Río Serrano (tel 193) in Puerto Natales. Very informative and knowledgeable, he used to work on the Estancia El Paine, so he knows a lot about that particular region. If you want to go trekking and camping in the park you can go up with one of his groups and get dropped off in the park. I've been on a tour with him to the park and recommend him highly!

Buses Sur at Baquedano 534 in Puerto Natales has tours to the park in the summer months. Generally, you go up to the park on the first day and overnight at the Hosteria Cisne de Cuello Negro; tour the park the second day and overnight at the Posada Río Serrano; then return the third day with a visit to the Milodon Cave on the way down. The itinerary depends on whether you take a bus starting from Puerto Natales or coming through from Punta Arenas; if the latter bus is full you don't get on. The whole trip, including bus, meals and accommodation will cost around US$55 to US$70 per person. These buses depart Punta Arenas for the park every Monday and Friday during the summer months.

Buses Fernández at Eberhard 555 in Puerto Natales has tours about twice a week in summer to the park. These buses come through from Punta Arenas and will invariably be full, so don't expect to be able to get on board unless you've booked ahead. You're probably better off trying to start these tours in Punta Arenas rather than trying to pick them up in Puerto Natales.

If you don't want to go on a tour then Bus Sur has a bus which is timetabled to go from Puerto Natales to the park on Tuesdays and Saturdays at 7 am, and to depart the park on Wednesdays and Sundays at 8.30 am. The return fare from Puerto Natales is around US$10. The return fare from Punta Arenas is about US$24. However, check all these fares and departure times as they seem to be completely imaginary, or depend on whether they get enough people to fill up the bus.

You may be able to get to the park on one of the tour buses and then go your own way, but don't count on it. Tour buses may be full, or they may be cancelled if there are not enough people going. They may not run at all outside the summer months.

It's sometimes possible to get a lift in a parks administration vehicle to the entrance (if you can find the vehicle). During the rest of the year – and even during the summer – you'll have to hitch. There are very few vehicles outside summer and quite a bit of competition for rides during summer. If there's a large group of you (say eight to 12) it's often cheaper and more convenient to hire a minibus to take you from Puerto Natales to the park entrance.

A day-trip in a hired taxi from Puerto Natales to Torres del Paine will cost you about US$70. If you can get a few people together it's not an impossible proposition, and it does have the advantage that it would be easier to stop the vehicle and take photographs when you want to – particularly if you want some close-ups of the guanaco herds that wander up to the roadside.

A new road connects Puerto Natales with Calafate in Argentina but there are no buses along this route. If it does open, and if you don't have the time or the equipment to go trekking, this is one way you could see something of the park.

Penguins

Contrary to popular belief penguins are not confined to the Antarctic; several species can be found in the tropics and one variety lives right on the equator. There are some 18 living species of penguins. The easiest place to see penguins in Chile is at a colony near Punta Arenas in the Región de Magallanes in the far south.

The first reliable record of a penguin-sighting by a European appears in the diaries of the Italian Antonio Pigafetta, a member of Magellan's round-the-world voyage (1519-1522). Exactly where this sighting was made is debatable; some think it was in the Straits of Magellan which divide Tierra del Fuego from the South American mainland; others that it was somewhere on the coast of Patagonia in Argentina.

Exactly how the penguin gained its name is something of a mystery. One theory is that it derives from the Welsh name *pen gwyn* which means 'white head'. More far-fetched guesses suggest the name comes from the Latin *pinguis* which means 'fat' or even from the English 'pin wing'. It seems probable that before the name 'penguin' was applied to the birds of the southern hemisphere it had already been applied to a similar species of bird which once inhabited parts of the North Atlantic. For reasons still unclear these birds became extinct by the middle of the 19th century, but it seems likely that the name 'penguin' (whatever the origins) was first applied to them and only later transferred to the southern birds.

One of the earliest records in which the term 'penguin' is applied to the southern birds is in an account of Thomas Cavendish's voyage around the world in 1586-88. Why the name pops up here is unknown, but it was perhaps a logical connection made by English (or Welsh?) sailors familiar with the North Atlantic and the similar species of bird found there.

In any case, penguins considerably antedate the European mariners – by about 45 million years. The first fossil penguin bone ever discovered was found last century about 1858 or 1859 on the South Island of New Zealand.

The bone was from a penguin variety much larger than any living now; this variety probably reached a maximum height a bit under 1½ metres.

The penguin is marvelously well-adapted to its environment. In a sense these flightless birds do 'fly' – but in the water. Their webbed feet are actually used as rudders, not for propulsion, and they propel themselves in the water using their wings which move in unison (as in usual flight) and are as heavily muscled as those of aerial fliers. Unlike ostriches and other flightless running birds the breastbones of penguins have high keels for the muscle attachment. Their wings are long, narrow and pointed and, like their bodies, streamlined and covered in feathers. Penguin feathers are reduced in size to small, scale-like things which reduce drag without losing their ability to insulate.

Unlike aerial birds their bodies are relatively heavy, solid and dense. They generally weigh only a bit less than the volume of water they displace, and need expend little energy to remain submerged (as they pursue their food) or to stay on the surface. But unlike seals or whales they cannot, or at least do not, remain submerged for long periods. All penguins feed exclusively on marine animals and mostly on those found at shallow depths in the ocean – such as crustaceans, fish and squids. The depth and duration of a dive varies from species to species but in general it lasts for no more than a few minutes and reaches a depth

of no more than 20 metres. Because their food has such a high salt content penguins have developed a pair of specialised salt-secreting glands to deal with the problem; these are so efficient that a penguin can even drink sea-water without any harmful effects.

Although their individual feathers seem insignificant, they are ideal for retaining heat. When the feathers lie flat the exposed parts overlap and form a shield which is almost impermeable to wind and water. On the shafts below are tufts which form an insulating layer. Penguins also have a thick layer of insulating fat or blubber over most of their body beneath their skin. Oddly enough, despite the cold environments in which most species live, they do have problems keeping cool. They keep cool by ruffling their feathers (which reduces insulating power and exposes skin) or by spreading their wings to expose more body surface to the air.

Although they're more at home in the water, penguins do need to spend periods on land. Their eggs must be incubated on land (or ice) and it is some time after hatching before the chicks can feed themselves or until they lose their fluffy plumage (which would become waterlogged if they went swimming) and develop adult feathers. Until then they must be fed by their parents. Both the male and female parents take part in incubating the eggs and feeding the chicks.

A number of animals feed on penguins or their eggs, although this depends on the location of each species of predator. In the antarctic and sub-antarctic regions large birds like giant petrels take eggs and occasionally chicks. Leopard seals attack them in the water, and killer whales will prey on larger species like the emperor penguins but tend to leave the small ones alone. There seems to be no predator which feeds entirely on penguins or needs them as an essential element of their food supply. The Indians of Tierra del Fuego once hunted penguins for food and for their skins, and the Maori of New Zealand may once have eaten them, but it was not until the arrival of the Europeans that penguins were hunted on any large scale – by sealers and whalers who killed them and boiled down their blubber for oil. Today penguins are a globally protected species.

The penguin you see near Punta Arenas is the *Spheniscus magellanicus*, which is named for the Straits of Magellan where it lives (not

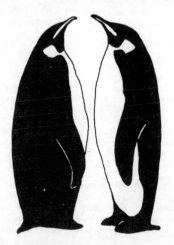

after Magellan himself). The common name is 'magellanic penguin' or the 'jackass penguin' because it brays. All species of *spheniscus* bray, but the term is more frequently applied to the *spheniscus demersus* which is an African species and a champion brayer. The magellanic penguin nests in burrows which they dig themselves near the shoreline. When alarmed they can run on all fours using their flippers as front legs, dashing into the safety of their burrows and then glaring out at the intruders. This species breeds from near the 42°S latitude in Patagonia (that is, from the Valdés Peninsular southwards) around the tip of South America and up the Pacific side to about the latitude of Valparaíso – mainly on islands, including Tierra del Fuego and the Falklands (Malvinas). They spend roughly April through to August at sea (during which time they move northwards) and September through to March at or near their breeding grounds.

Tierra del Fuego

When Magellan came to the great island at the tip of the American continent he observed the Indian campfires and called the island *Tierra del Humo* – the Land of Smoke. Later his patron, the King of Spain and Emperor of the Holy Roman Empire, Charles V, reasoned that there could be no smoke without fire and renamed the island *Tierra del Fuego* – the Land of Fire.

Ferdinand de Magellan did not circumnavigate the world, nor did he ever intend to. When he and his ships left Spain he had a very different purpose in mind. In 1518 this Portuguese sailor was awarded a charter by the King of Spain to command a Spanish fleet which would voyage to the legendary Spice Islands – now known as the Maluku (Moluccas) Islands of Indonesia and at that time the only source for a number of valuable spices – and claim them for Spain. It was the intention of the Spanish to get several ships into the Pacific Ocean, sail them west to the Spice Islands, and having taken spices on board to head back through the north Pacific to Panama, where the goods would be carried over the isthmus to the Carribean and shipped to Spain. The ships were to stay in the Pacific and form a permanent Spanish fleet for trade between the Spice Islands and central America.

Having sailed across the Atlantic, in October 1520 the fleet entered the Strait separating the mainland of South America from what is now known as Tierra del Fuego. It took 38 days to get through this tempestuous strait, with its nightmarish seas, into the Pacific. The fleet headed west and finally came to the Philippines where, as fate would have it, Magellan was killed in a minor skirmish with some of the indigenous inhabitants.

It is possible Magellan (when he was in the East Indies and Malaya) had picked up some ideas from Chinese or Malay navigators about crossing the north Pacific using the Asian monsoon winds, but he had not revealed the secret to anyone else. Since no one else on the voyage would risk returning through the terrible Straits of Magellan they pushed on westwards. The dismal voyage not only caused Magellan's death but also the deaths of most of his crewmen. Three years after the voyage had begun just one ship of the original five, the *Victoria*, limped into Spain with a few survivors. In a voyage akin to Homer's Odyssey, they had inadvertently become the first people to sail around the world. Only some 30 men survived the expedition.

Magellan's ships had found a western route to Asia, but they may not have been the first to sail through the Straits of Magellan. That honour may actually be due to a Portuguese expedition which may have sailed through the strait and back in 1514, or even to Egyptian sailors who may have come this way in the first and second centuries AD. Most probably, however, the prize should be awarded to the Indians who have lived in Tierra del Fuego since about 7500 BC.

The Straits of Magellan cut Tierra del Fuego off from the rest of South America. Tierra del Fuego is, in fact, not one island but a whole archipelago. The largest of the islands is the Isla Grande de Tierra del Fuego and is usually the one which is referred to when one speaks of this region. The other inhabited islands of the archipelago are Navarino and Dawson, the three islands at the mouth of the Beagle Channel (which separates Isla Grande from Navarino) and the eastern-most tip of Hoste Island.

When Magellan came by, the archipelago was home to four distinct groups of Indians. The oldest of these groups was the *Haush* who were pushed to the eastern tip of the island by the more numerous *Ona* and *Yahgan*. Like the Ona, the Haush hunted guanaco with bows and arrows, dressed in guanaco skins, and lived in huts made of sticks, branches and sometimes skins. Like the Yahgan they used spears and harpoons to fish and also gathered mussels from the beaches at low tide. The nomadic Ona were similar to the Haush, but were much more numerous and ranged over most of Isla Grande in search of guanaco which provided them with all their needs.

Further south, along the beaches of the Beagle Channel and the islands southward to Cape Horn, lived the Yahgan. This group was also nomadic but they lived by spearing otters, fish and seals from canoes, and using slings and snares to catch birds. Their canoes were made from bark and their clothes were made from seal skin.

The fourth group were the *Alacaluf* who ranged from Puerto Edén, in the forbidding fjords of southern Chile, to the Beagle Channel. They were similar to the Yahgan, but their language was different. They also used bows and arrows, and they had sails on their canoes. Unlike the Indians further north, none of the Fuegian Indians had chiefs, or organised religion.

When Charles Darwin came to Tierra del Fuego in 1834 he described some Indians he found at Woollaston Island which lies to the south of Navarino:

... naked and uncovered from the wind, rain & snow in this tempestuous climate, sleep on the wet ground, coiled up like animals. In the morning they rise to pick shell fish at low water; & the women, winter & summer, dive to collect sea eggs; such miserable food is eked out by tasteless berries & Fungi. They are surrounded by hostile tribes speaking different dialects; & the cause of their warfare would

17th century map of Tierra del Fuego

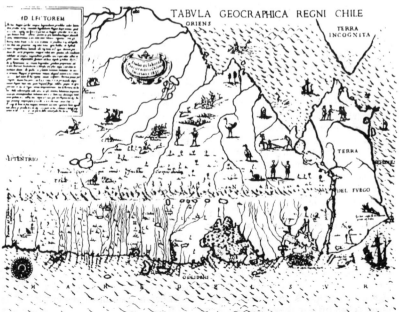

TABVLA GEOGRAPHICA REGNI CHILE

appear to be the means of subsistence. Their country is a broken mass of wild rocks, lofty hills & useless forests, & these are viewed through mists & endless storms. In search of food they move from spot to spot, & so steep is the coast, this must be done in wretched canoes . . .

The 18th century French philosopher Jean Jacques Rousseau might have found some place for the Fuegian Indians in his fanciful 'noble savage' theories which contend that only the so-called primitive peoples have retained the qualities of nobility bestowed by the Creator. Darwin, however, found the Indians a less pleasing sight:

I never saw such miserable creatures; stunted in their growth, their hideous faces bedaubed with white paint & quite naked. One full aged woman absolutely so, the rain & spray were dripping from her body. Their red skins filthy and greasy, their hair entangled, their voices discordant, their gesticulation violent and without any dignity. Viewing such men, one can hardly make oneself believe that they are fellow creatures placed in the same world . . . how little must the mind of one of these beings resemble that of an educated man. What a scale of improvement is comprehended between the faculties of a Fuegian savage & a Sir Isaac Newton!

Today there are no 'pure-blooded' Fuegian Indians although there are some mestizos, such as those at Puerto Williams on Navarino Island. Many of the Indians were killed by the white settlers, in fights amongst themselves, or more commonly by measles, tuberculosis and other diseases brought by the whites. It is hard to say when the last 'full-blooded' Fuegian Indians died. For all practical purposes the latest any of them lived according to their old ways was around 1915 to 1920. The last sizeable groups of 'full bloods' were those who worked on the estancias in Chilean and Argentinian Tierra del Fuego in the 1930s, and in any case most of these knew or practised little of the old ways.

Magellan's voyage brought on what for those days was a veritable stampede; Spanish, Dutch, French and English ships passed through the strait. To keep these interlopers out the Spanish contemplated building forts on the straits, as early as 1580. Although this plan didn't come to fruition, in 1584 two colonies were established on the north side of the strait, only to be wiped out by famine. Voyages of exploration, scientific expeditions, English pirates sailing through the straits and up the west coast of South America to attack Valdivia and, by the end of the 18th century, increasing numbers of sealers and whalers, all came this way occasionally skirmishing with the Indians or introducing European diseases. It was not until the early 19th century, however, that a real attempt was made to settle these regions.

In 1843 Chile (in the guise of the Englishman John Williams) officially took possession of the Straits of Magellan and founded Fuerte Bulnes on its western shore near the present-day city of Punta Arenas. Had it not been for the discovery of gold in California this settlement might well have remained a distant outpost at the end of the earth. But the same metal that drove the Spanish to South America now provoked an enormous migration to North America. Punta Arenas which was founded on the west side of the strait was suddenly an important port on one of the world's busiest shipping routes.

In 1843 Chile also laid claim to southern Patagonia. The renunciation of this claim and the division of Tierra del Fuego between Chile and Argentina was made in 1881 when Chile was fighting the War of the Pacific with Bolivia and Peru. This war made it imperative for Chile to keep the peace and finalise her borders with Argentina. It was not until 1899, however, that the northern boundaries of the two countries were settled, and it was 1902 before the southern boundaries were finalised. This 'perpetual accord' inspired the famous statue of Christ which was erected on Mount Aconcagua to celebrate the decision and symbolise peace between the two countries.

The first farms were opened up on Tierra del Fuego in the 1880s and from here on the history of the island is one of who owned the turf. In the years to come, less and less of it was owned by Yahgans, Onas, Haush and Alacalufs and more and more by foreigners. The first white residents were English missionaries who stayed on as farmers to be followed by Germans, Argentinians, Chileans, Yugoslavs, Italians and other immigrants. For a few years the island even had a Rumanian dictator, who printed his own money and stamps, and maintained his own goldmines and a private army until his death in 1893.

The Indians, meanwhile, were forced to prey on the settler's livestock as the herds of guanaco and other animals which they hunted became increasingly scarce. The settlers arranged punitive expeditions against the Indians, and eventually bounties were placed on Indian heads with the result that they were hunted down like animals. Others were simply wiped out by imported diseases. An epidemic in 1864 killed half the Yahgans; a measles epidemic in 1884 reduced their numbers to just a few hundred, and more died in 1891 during an epidemic of typhoid, smallpox and whooping cough. Many Ona were rounded up and placed in missions, only to be almost exterminated in 1925 by a measles epidemic.

Sawmills, meat-salting and tallow-making plants, whaling stations, meat warehouses, and crab and mussel canning industries were all established on the island from the 1880s to the 1920s. For many decades sheep held body and soul together; by the middle of the second decade of the 20th century there were over 780,000 sheep on the island, outnumbering humans by 300 to one. Ushuaia and Río Grande (with just 150 people) were the only towns and almost the whole population was spread across the estancias. Along with oil, sheep farming is still the main industry on the island, but cattle are also big business. The estancias are enormous properties because of the large amount of land required to graze even small numbers of stock.

History, however, continues to repeat itself and the latest fires in the Land of Fire are those that flicker from the the oil fields; the San Sebastián refinery was completed in 1975 and produces liquified petroleum gas. Oil prospecting began back in 1938 but it wasn't until 1959 that the first commercial well was drilled by the Tennessee Argentina Company. Today, Río Grande is a large town, dependent on the petroleum industry, meat exports and farming. During the last decade or so tourism has also boomed in Tierra del Fuego. Aided by its magnificent trekking country and the duty-free status of the biggest town Ushuaia, the island is a favoured holiday resort for Argentinians.

Altogether the archipelago covers an area slightly smaller than Ireland, and about 70% of this belongs to Chile. The border between Chile and Argentina on the Isla Grande is a straight line running north to south and then along the Beagle Channel. The northern part of the island is a windswept land of rolling hills and vast plains bare of trees; sheep grazing and oil extraction are important. The central region includes mountains which are covered in snow from April to November and is too rugged for farming or grazing. The Beagle Channel separates Isla Grande from Navarino; the narrow strip of land on Isla Grande bordering the channel has a *comparatively* mild climate with cool summers and snow in winter (this usually melts quickly). The channel never freezes and there are no icebergs.

The eastern part of the island has less snow and ice, but much more rain and cloudy weather; in the west the climate is sub-Antarctic with fierce winds, cloudy skies and frequent rain. These distinct climatic areas influence the type of fauna and flora found on the island. In the north are tree-less plains. The mountains and shores of the Beagle Channel are covered in forest and swampland which merge to the east and to the west with the 'rain-forests' of the even wetter areas. Cape Horn and the other outer islands have a sub-Antarctic flora of hardy bog plants and dwarf trees and bushes, but only in sheltered places. Tierra del Fuego is home to several of the world's largest birds, the rhea (akin to an ostrich or emu), the condor and the albatross, and to large animals such as the guanaco (which is the most commonly seen), otters and several varieties of seal and sea-lion.

The chief settlement on the Chilean side is Porvenir from where you can get a ferry to Punta Arenas. On the Argentinian side Río Grande and Ushuaia are two large, well-developed towns. The main crossing point between the two halves is at San Sebastián on the road between Río

Grande and Porvenir. As the Germans settled in Valdivia, the British and Yugoslavs settled in Tierra del Fuego and there are still sizeable populations of their descendants in the area. Immediately to the south of Tierra del Fuego, separated by the narrow Beagle Channel, is the Chilean island of Navarino. Puerto Williams is a Chilean naval base. It's the only settlement on Navarino and can be visited.

PORVENIR

The sign at the Punta Arenas dock says it all; you're now 18,662 km from Yugoslavia. With some 4500 people, Porvenir is the only settlement of any size in Chilean Tierra del Fuego and its predominant ethnic group – in case you haven't guessed – is of Yugoslav descent.

Places to Stay & Eat

There are a number of good, reasonably cheap pensiones including the *Residencial Camerón*. Ask around for others – it's a

Sign at Porvenir, Tierra del Fuego

Distancias			
Por Puyehue	kms		kms
Arica	5.299	Talca	2.990
Iquique	5.091	Concepción	2.734
Antofagasta	4.615	Temuco	2.573
Copiapó	4.050	Valdivia	2.408
La Serena	3.718	Osorno	2.302
Valparaiso	3.367	P. Montt	2.404
Rancagua	3.161	Castro	2.573
	Santiago 3.248 kms		

Yugoslavia 18.662 Kms

very small town. For somewhere to eat – most pensiones offer full board – try the *Yugoslav Club*, which does good lunches for a few dollars. The *Restaurante Puerto Montt* is also good for seafood.

Getting There

Air If rough weather forces the cancellation of the ferries to Punta Arenas, there is the possibility of flying. DAP (tel 23958) have daily flights to Porvenir from Punta Arenas costing about US$9.40.

Bus Transporte Senkovic is at Carlos Bories 201, near the waterfront but at the opposite end of the harbour from the pier where you catch the ferry to Punta Arenas. This company runs buses between Porvenir and Río Grande in Argentinian Tierra del Fuego. There are buses every Wednesday and Saturday from Porvenir departing around 2 pm; the fare to Río Grande is around US$8.90 and the trip takes about 7½ hours.

Boat There is a daily ferry from Porvenir to Punta Arenas, departing Porvenir around 2 to 2.30 pm. It's about a two to three hour trip to Punta Arenas (depending on the weather) and it costs US$2 per person – buy your ticket on the ferry. The company running this ferry is called Transbordador Broom Ltda and has an office in Porvenir at Roca 924.

This is a car ferry, and it will even take horses (some people have been known to hire them). If you're given to sea sickness then try not to eat anything beforehand. Even in summer the weather can turn foul and the seas can be furious and almost frightening with spray crashing right over the front of the boat and drenching the top decks. A fierce wind blows constantly. There are two small compartments with bench seats for passengers and if the weather is bad, use them – otherwise you'll freeze your ass off!

RIO GRANDE

On the east coast of Tierra del Fuego, Río Grande sits on a flat, windswept plain and is a shepherds' town and oil refinery centre. It's of little interest to the traveller except as a halfway house between Punta Arenas or Río Gallegos and Ushuaia. It's a surprisingly large and well-developed town (if rather ugly) but the bus ride from Ushuaia is impressive.

Places to Stay

It's not always easy to find a room in Río Grande because most of the cheapies are occupied by men working on the oil installations. You may have to check quite a few before you find something and even then, if you want somewhere cheap, you may have to take a dormitory bed. If not, you'll have to opt for the places in the middle price range.

Places to Stay – bottom end

The cheapest place you're likely to find is the *Hospedaje Argentina* on San Martín, between 11 de Julio and Libertad, which is only US$2.90 for a dormitory bed.

The *Hospedaje Irmary* at Estrada 743 (near the corner with San Martín) is very clean and pleasant and is conveniently located two blocks from the *Buses Senkovic* office. It's about US$6 per person in a two-bed room.

The *Residencial Rawson* at Estrada 750 (opposite the *Irmary*) is a good place, if rather sterile, but it costs around US$9 per person.

Try the *Hotel Anexo Villa* at Piedrabuena 641. It's a decent enough place but it's likely to be permanently full. Beds cost about US$5 per person. Also try the *Hospedaje Rayenfray* at San Martín 236; it used to be called the *Hotel Shelkman*.

Places to Stay – middle

Possibly the best hotel in the whole city is the *Hospedaje Miramar* at the corner of MacKinley and Belgrano. Singles are US$7.60 and doubles are US$15.30 with-

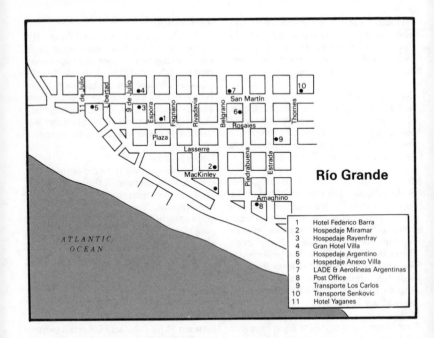

1	Hotel Federico Barra
2	Hospedaje Miramar
3	Hospedaje Rayenfray
4	Gran Hotel Villa
5	Hospedaje Argentino
6	Hospedaje Anexo Villa
7	LADE & Aerolíneas Argentinas
8	Post Office
9	Transporte Los Carlos
10	Transporte Senkovic
11	Hotel Yaganes

out attached bathrooms, or US$9.40 a single and US$18.80 a double with bathrooms. The manager is friendly, and the hotel is very clean, and has heating in both the rooms and passageways making it an exceptionally warm and cosy place. Since it's a bit more expensive than the other places there's a good chance they'll have a room.

The *Gran Hotel Villa* at San Martín 281 is also good. Singles are US$13, doubles are US$16.50 without bathrooms; singles are US$17.60, doubles are US$23.50 with bathrooms. It's clean, surprisingly quiet, and the people are friendly. There's a good, cheap restaurant downstairs.

Places to Stay – top end
The *Hotel Yaganes* is on Puy, at the junction with Belgrano. Singles are US$29 and doubles US$39 – including breakfast. The top hotel in town is the *Hotel Federico Barra* on Rosales, facing the main plaza; singles are US$29 and doubles are US$36.50

Places to Eat
The *Confitería Piano Pub* on Fagnano, near the corner with Rosales just up from the plaza, is a cosy, almost romantic little place.

Other places worth checking out are the *Restaurant La Cantina* on Lasserre, near Belgrano; and the *Restaurant El Castor* which is a parrillado place on Lasserre near the corner with Fagnano. Otherwise you'll find the meals at the *Gran Hotel Villa* to be fairly cheap and very filling.

Getting There
Air LADE and Aerolíneas Argentinas are at the corner of San Martín and Belgrano.

Bus Buses Senkovic at San Martín 959 have buses for Porvenir at around 6 or 6.30 am every Wednesday and Saturday. The trip takes about 7½ hours, the fare is about US$11.80 and the bus connects with the ferry to Punta Arenas. The road from Río Grande to Porvenir is a poor, unsurfaced one, passing through oil fields and flat, sheep-grazing country.

Negotiating both the Argentinian and the Chilean customs checkpoints at San Sebastián is a rather slow process (it has been known to take up to two hours to clear a bus load through Argentinian customs alone) although otherwise it's fairly straight-forward.

If you're hitching, don't count on being able to pick up the bus at San Sebastián. It seems – officially anyway – that the only people allowed on the bus are those who bought their tickets in Río Grande. These people have been included on the list of passengers – copies of which are dispensed at the checkpoints for eventual inclusion in the great Argentinian bureaucracy's filing cabinets. However, that depends on who's in charge at the checkpoint, so always ask! It's very unlikely you won't be allowed on the bus, but allow for the small possibility that you'll have to continue hitching.

When you arrive in Porvenir the bus pulls into the Senkovic Terminal. From here you have to take a taxi colectivo (about US$0.55 per person) to the ferry dock on the other side of the harbour (it's too far to walk).

Buses Los Carlos are at Estrada 568. They have two buses daily from Río Grande to Ushuaia, the first bus departing in the morning or early afternoon and the second at 7 pm. Buses are less frequent in winter – once a day on Monday, Wednesday and Friday. The trip takes about five hours and costs US$8.70.

USHUAIA

The world's southernmost town began, not with a brave band of hardy colonisers, but with a prefabricated mission hut put up in 1869 by an Anglican bishop who lived there for six months alongside the huts of the Yahgan Indians. The following year an Anglican minister named Thomas Bridges, together with his wife and baby daughter, set up a mission here and became Tierra del Fuego's first permanent white settlers. Perhaps his greatest achievement was the compilation of a large dictionary of the Yahgan language which described the phenomenal complexity and the wide-ranging use of metaphor which these people employed.

Anglican Christianity, vegetable gardens and the Indians thrived for 16 years, until the Argentinian navy paid a visit and the Indians dropped dead of imported pneumonia and measles. After its time as a naval base, Ushuaia was used as a convict station, with a jail masterfully built from stone and concrete.

Ushuaia has been called a 'romantic kind of place' but it would have to be a bitter love affair. Some people find the area reminiscent of parts of Canada, while others liken the mountains, the drizzle and the biting wind to Scotland. You can forget any images you have of some isolated backwoods town inhabited by weather-beaten frontiersmen; the city at the end of the world is a modern, duty-free port of concrete houses, sprawling up hills overlooking the Beagle Channel and whipped by cold winds that sweep in from every side. This is a tourist resort town, a sort of Antarctic version of Cairns or Brighton, and a good place to base yourself to explore the many tranquil lakes and mountains of Tierra del Fuego.

Ushuaia is actually the second last resort – from here you can travel south to Puerto Williams, the Chilean naval base and the most southern settlement in the world barring those in Antarctica. Or you can head from Ushuaia to Punta Arenas in Chile, via Río Grande, Porvenir and the stormy straits that separate Tierra del Fuego from the mainland.

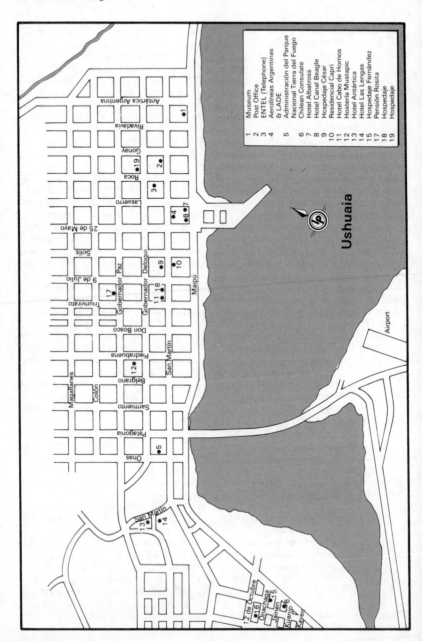

Ushuaia

1   Museum
2   Post Office
3   ENTEL (Telephone)
4   Aerolíneas Argentinas
    & LADE
5   Administración del Parque
    Nacional Tierra del Fuego
6   Chilean Consulate
7   Hotel Albatross
8   Hotel Canal Beagle
9   Hospedaje César
10 Residencial Capri
11 Hotel Cabo de Hornos
12 Hostería Mustapic
13 Hotel Antártica
14 Hotel Las Lengas
15 Hospedaje Fernández
16 Pensión Rosita
17 Hospedaje
18 Hospedaje
19 Hospedaje

Information

Tourist Office The tourist office is at San Martín 524, Office No 2/3, just near the corner with Lasserre. The staff are friendly and speak communicable English, and there's plenty of information about hotels and prices. It's open daily from 9 am to 3 pm. You can't miss it – it's the office with the stuffed seals in the window. If you're stuck for accommodation (and chances are you will be) they'll telephone around families who put lodgers up and try and find a room or a bed for you.

Books For a round-up of Tierra del Fuego get *Tierra del Fuego* by Rae Natalie; it's in both English and Spanish and can be bought in the book shops in Ushuaia for about US$12. Also, preferably before you get here, get hold of a copy of *Backpacking in Chile & Argentina* by Hilary Bradt and John Pilkington (Bradt Enterprises), which has an excellent description of the treks in the area.

Other The post office is at the corner of San Martín and Godoy. The Chilean consulate is at the corner of Maipú and Alapa.

Things to See

Most of what there is to see around Ushuaia demands time and reasonable funds. There are few marked trails and you need appropriate equipment, but the area is a trekker's paradise. A trek to the Martial Glacier (the Martial Mountains overlook Ushuaia) is one possibility.

For details of trekking possibilities, enquire at the tourist office; it's also been suggested you try Onas Tours, which is on 25 de Mayo just off the main street – they're very friendly.

If you don't intend trekking there are tours available to various places of interest in the surrounding area. Try the tourist office, the travel agency at San Martín 216 or the other travel agents for details.

During the summer months, daily boat trips are available to visit the sea-lion colony on the Isla de los Lobos. The trip costs US$14 and takes six hours in all. There are also nine-hour trips which take you to Gable Island at the mouth of the Beagle Channel, and day-trips to Río Grande which include visits to an estancia and a meat-processing plant.

It's even possible – at least during summer – to charter yachts on a weekly basis and cruise around the region, even as far south as Cape Horn. Half-day yacht trips are also possible at about US$35 per person, and full-day trips are about US$60 per person.

Places to Stay – bottom end

It's worth trying to find somewhere to stay in a private house in Ushuaia especially during January and February. The tourist office has a list of these places and will telephone around to try and find a room or a bed for you – but don't expect too much. Chances are that at the height of the tourist season you'll wind up sharing someone's bunk-bed in a match-box-sized attic crash-pad – no kidding! It may not be palatial accommodation but it will certainly beat sleeping out!

All prices listed are what you can expect to pay in the tourist season. Things may be cheaper during the off-season, but don't count on it since Ushuaia is also a ski resort.

One place that's been recommended is the hospedaje at Deloqui 395 which is US$4.70 a bed; the people are friendly and there are cooking facilities you can use.

Another good place is the *Pensión Rosita* on Paz between 9 de Julio and Triunvirato. It costs just US$6.20 per bed and it's run by a friendly woman. Recommended.

It's also worth trying the hospedaje in the same building next to the Don Antonio Jazz Bar, at the corner of Maipú and 9 de Julio. They have short and long term rates; it's about US$8.20 per person per night, or US$47 per person per week. This place is likely to be full during the tourist season.

There is a similarly priced hospedaje at San Martín 845. This one has a downstairs restaurant – it's not terrific food by any means but it is fairly cheap and you do get decent-sized portions and friendly service.

In desperation try the *Las Goletas* at Maipú 857 (there's no sign but it's on the waterfront) which is one of the cheapest places in town – and you'll see why when you get there. There may be better rooms on the top floors but the dormitories on the ground floor look like flop houses. You may have to sleep on the floor of the lounge if the place is full. Rumour has it that there are hot showers, if that's some consolation.

Try the *Estrella de Torres* at Avenida Kayen 137; you may get a single here for as little as US$5 but don't count on it.

Places to Stay – middle

One of the cheaper hotels is the *Residencial Capri* (tel 91833), San Martín 720, between 9 de Julio and Solis. It has bunk beds and hot water, is fairly clean, but is often full of long-term residents. Try and get an upstairs room away from the booming TV set, but if there's only a room next to the booming TV set then take it – you may not get anything better anywhere else. Singles cost about US$13.90 and doubles about US$18.50 (highway robbery anywhere else, bloody good by Ushuaia standards).

Another reasonably cheap place is the *Hospedaje Fernández* (tel 91453) at Ochanaga 68, which is very friendly, has hot showers and meals. Singles are US$15.30 and doubles are US$21.

One place that's been recommended is the *Hospedaje Malvinas* (tel 92626) at Deloqui 609, with singles for US$15.30 and doubles for US$21.20 – the people are said to be friendly and helpful. Another traveller quoted prices here as US$10 a single and US$14 a double, with break-

fast and attached bathroom – so it may be worth bargaining.

Other places in this price range include: the *Hospedaje César* (tel 91460), San Martín 753, which has singles for US$17.60 and doubles for US$25.50; the *Hostería Mustapic* (tel 91718), Piedrabuena 230, with singles at US$21.20 and doubles at US$35.30; the *Hotel Maiten* (tel 92 745), 12 de Octubre 140, with singles for US$18.80 and doubles for US$23.50.

Places to Stay – top end

Top of the range is the *Hotel Canal Beagle* (tel 91 117) at the corner of Maipú and 25 de Mayo on the waterfront. Singles are US$29.40 and doubles are US$38.80 – which includes breakfast.

Only very slightly cheaper, the *Hotel Albatross* (tel 92 504) is next door at the corner of Maipú and Lasserre. About the same price as these two, the *Hotel Cabo de Hornos* (tel 92 187) is at the corner of San Martín and Triunvirato.

Places to Eat

The *Don Antonio Jazz Bar* at the corner of Maipú and 9 de Julio is the best of the lot in Ushuaia. It serves drinks and snacks and has music some nights of the week. Also try the *Sloggert Pub* (yes, that's what it's called) on Godoy between Maipú and San Martín.

The appropriately-named *Cafetería Ideal* at the corner of San Martín and Roca is an ideal – if expensive – little place to eat. A main course of giant mussels (*cholga*) with potatoes plus drinks and dessert will set you back about US$6 to US$7, but it's sort of worth it. They also have pretty good pizzas – served whole or by the portion.

Getting There

Ushuaia is not a recognised international port for arrival by air, although you are allowed to arrive by boat from Puerto Williams. To arrive by air in this part of Argentina you have to land at Río Grande, which means that each time there's an international flight the customs officials (who live in Ushuaia) must travel up to Río Grande to meet it. Or so the story goes!

From Ushuaia you can take the ferry to Puerto Williams in Chile, and from there fly to Punta Arenas; or take the bus to Río Grande and carry on to Punta Arenas via Porvenir; or fly out of Ushuaia to Río Grande and beyond.

Air LADE is at San Martín 542; it's open Monday to Friday from 8 am to 6.30 pm, and Saturday from 9 am to 12 noon. Aerolíneas Argentina is at San Martín 528; it's open Monday to Friday, 9.30 am to 12 noon and 2.30 to 6 pm, and Saturday, 9.30 am to 12 noon.

If you want to head back up to Río Gallegos it works out cheaper to try and get on a flight between Ushuaia and Río Gallegos than to take a bus. Ushuaia to Río Gallegos costs US$18. Try both LADE and Aerolíneas Argentinas. There are several flights a week but they're heavily booked.

LADE also has a weekly flight from Ushuaia to Perito Moreno via Calafate, and Aerolíneas has a weekly flight to Punta Arenas.

Ushuaia's airport is on the other side of the harbour to the town – it's too far to walk! To get there take a local bus or a taxi. A taxi will cost about US$5. The local buses run down Maipú before heading out to the airport.

Bus Buses Los Carlos are at the corner of San Martín and Triunvirato. In the summer months they have daily buses to Río Grande at 12 noon and 7 pm. The fare is about US$8.70 and the trip takes about four to 4½ hours. You get a short refreshment stop at the Hotel El Kaiken on Lake Fagnano, before finally passing out of the mountains onto the plains where flocks of sheep and many large estancias can be seen. It's a dirt road all the way from Ushuaia to Río Grande.

The travel agency at San Martín 216

has a direct minibus to Punta Arenas in Chile every Saturday. This costs US$80 one-way and US$111 return. This bus only seems to run during the January and February tourist season.

Boat Information and tickets for the ferry to Puerto Williams are available from the office of Turismo Tierra del Fuego, corner San Martín and the 25 de Mayo. During the summer tourist season the ferries go on Wednesdays and Sundays around 8 am, returning in the late afternoon. The fare is US$29 return, or about half that one-way. There may be ferries on other days of the week if there are tour groups going over. As for the frequency of these boats during winter I don't know.

PUERTO WILLIAMS
For over 30 years Puerto Williams on Navarino Island has been waving the Chilean flag at the toenails of Argentina. Established in 1953 as a naval base – which it still is today – the forerunner of this settlement was the world's most southerly sawmilling concern. Spread along the shores of the Beagle Channel it's an admirable setting. The last people of identifiable Yahgan Indian descent can be found here and there is a fine museum.

Trekking is limited since there are few trails and only two roads. Other than that the flight from Punta Arenas is spectacular on a clear day, and if you've come as far as Tierra del Fuego you can hardly turn back now . . .

Information
The settlement has a central block of shops and offices. The DAP agent is in the Casa Stop (look for the sign). The Agencia de Viajes Avenoger Loda sells tickets for the ferry to Ushuaia and will also change US dollars for Argentinian and Chilean currency. The post office is open Monday to Friday, 11.30 am to 1 pm and 5 to 7 pm, and Saturday, 1 to 2.30 pm.

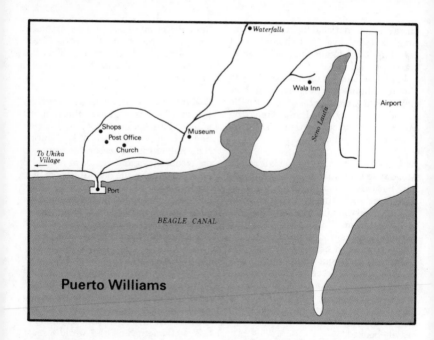

Puerto Williams

Things to See

The museum (Museo Martín Gusinde) is open Tuesday to Friday from 10.30 am to 1.30 pm and 3 to 6 pm, Saturday from 3 to 6 pm, and Sunday from 10.30 am to 1.30 pm and 3 to 6 pm. Most of those times are rather hopeful, and probably don't apply in winter at all. There are fine exhibits on the natural history of the region, on the Indians who once lived here, and on European exploration and settlement.

The last people of Yahgan Indian descent live in a small enclave of several houses called Ukika, by the road a short distance east of the town. Further along you can – on a clear day – get good views across the Beagle Channel to Gable Island and the mountains to the north. West of town, a branch road runs about four km to a waterfall.

Places to Stay & Eat

In the central block just behind the gymnasium (a large green building) is a small hotel which also has a restaurant. Its a spartan little place but clean and decent. Rooms are US$6.70 per person with full board – which is remarkably cheap. It's run by a friendly woman. There's a another small restaurant beside it.

The *Hostería Walo* is on the road in from the airport. It's surprisingly comfortable, with a good restaurant and blazing fireplace, and it costs US$25 a single and US$30 a double. The food is quite expensive; *curanto* for lunch will set you back US$10, and even a simple breakfast is US$4.20. They run tours to the museum, waterfalls and the Ukika village (these tours are worth taking if it's a cold, wet day).

There is a supermarket next to the post office; open 10 am to 1 pm and 4 to 7 pm.

Getting There

Air DAP flies Puerto Williams to Punta Arenas on Tuesdays, Thursdays and Saturdays. The fare is US$38. Tickets are available in Puerto Williams from the DAP agent at the Casa Stop.

Boat Ferries run between Puerto Williams and Ushuaia every Sunday. There are more boats running when tour groups are being brought over – there's usually an additional boat on Wednesdays. The fare from Ushuaia is about US$29 return and about half that one-way. The boat leaves Ushuaia at about 8 am and takes about 2½ to three hours. It leaves Puerto Williams around 4 pm. Departure and return times may vary so always check. In Puerto Williams, information and tickets are available from the Agencia de Viajes Avenoger Loda.

Once a month the ship *M/N Argonauta* does the Punta Arenas to Puerto Williams journey. The fare is US$83. Tickets and information are available from the Agencia de Viajes Aventour in the Hosteria Walo.

Easter Island

How the world's most isolated island was discovered by early seafarers is as baffling a problem as how these people were able to carve hundreds of enormous statues from hard volcanic basalt, transport them several km from quarry to coast, and erect them on great stone platforms.

All sorts of theories have been concocted about who the original Easter Islanders were: ancient Egyptians, red-haired caucasian North Africans on their way to the Pacific via South America, Greeks, Hindustanis, Andean Indians, Melanesians, Polynesians, or the survivors from a sunken continent. Some say the statues were moved by the magical powers of a now extinct race of priests, others believe they were moved using aerial ropeways, or with the aid of extra-terrestrial construction workers!

Polynesia versus America

Easter Island has been known by a number of names: San Carlos (after King Carlos III of Spain) was given to it by the first Spanish to land on the island; Davis Island was given to it when it was confused with another island that was named by an English buccaneer in the 17th century; and Rapa Nui was the name given to it by Polynesians – and is the name by which it is often referred to today. But you only need to climb to the top of Terevaka, the islands highest point, and scan the sea in all directions to understand why the natives of Easter Island called it *Te Pito o Te Henua* – the Navel (Centre) of the World.

The island is just 117 square km and there is no inhabited land within a radius of some 2000 km, so the chances of just finding the island in the first place seem exceedingly small. The South American coast lies over 3000 km to the east. Some 2000 km to the west lies Pitcairn Island,

which was once inhabited by Polynesians but was abandoned or depopulated prior to the arrival of the first group of Europeans (mutineers from the *Bounty*) in 1790. The nearest inhabited islands to the west are the Mangarévas which are 2500 km away and the Marquesas which are 3200 km away.

Unless they were spontaneously generated on the island, from where did the original Easter Islanders come? If they came from the east then they must have had their origins in South America. Traditional stories told on Easter Island describe the original homeland as a place where, during certain seasons, the burning sun scorched and shrivelled plants – which fits in very well with the formidable climate of northern Chile and the coastal plains of Peru, but which does not fit any possible points of embarkation to the west.

At the time of the Spanish invasion the Indians of Peru had some knowledge of the existence of distant islands in the Pacific. Centuries before, their ancestors had sailed to some of these islands, and it is possible the location of Easter Island was known to them. In 1947 the Norwegian adventurer and archaeologist Thor Heyerdahl proved that such voyages were possible when he and his companions sailed the *Kon Tiki*, a balsa log raft designed according to what was known of these early vessels, from South America to Raroia in the Tuamotu Archipelago of Polynesia.

A European mariner on a voyage from Chile, who sailed past Easter Island in 1828 and 1834, described the strong southern branch of the Humboldt Current which, he said, could speed sailing ships from the coast of northern Chile and southern Peru towards this island even with vague winds. He therefore recommended that all sailing ships

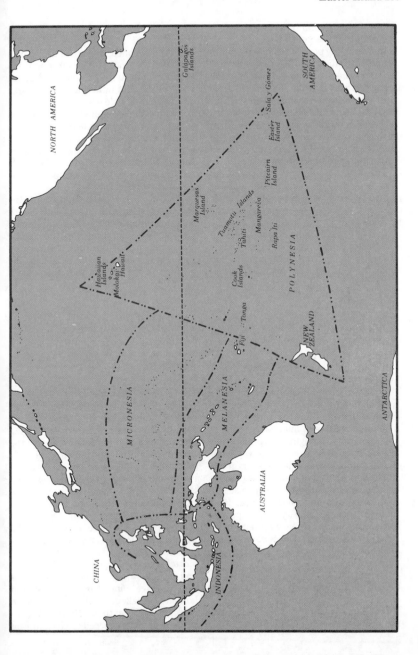

follow this particular route on a voyage to the islands of the South Seas.

It is certainly *possible* that early South American Indian mariners were carried to Easter Island on their rafts. It has been argued, however, that if voyagers from South America did reach Polynesia, they did so by deliberate voyages of exploration rather than by allowing their rafts to drift with the winds and ocean currents, and that the chances of finding Easter Island by the latter method are almost nil.

The other possibility is that the island was populated by Polynesians coming from the west. These people somehow managed to spread out over a multitude of islands, covering a gigantic triangle with its apexes at New Zealand, Hawaii and Easter Island, together with a scatter of small islands deep in Melanesia, and along the southern border of Micronesia. There have been many theories about the origin of the Polynesians: some thought they were survivors from a lost continent reduced to rubble by some immense catastrophe, others that they came from the Middle East, India, South-East Asia, Indonesia or the Americas.

It's probably fair to say that orthodox opinion within the academic world is currently in favour of an Asian origin for the Polynesian peoples, and that it was Polynesians who built the Easter Island monuments. Details may vary, but it is now generally thought that migration into the Pacific region got underway some 40,000 years ago when the ancestors of the Australian Aboriginals and New Guinea highlanders first crossed the open sea to settle Australia and New Guinea. It is thought that Papuan-speaking people settled the islands of New Britain, New Ireland and perhaps the Solomons, no later than 6000 years ago and perhaps much earlier.

The settlement of the Pacific islands beyond the Solomons was the achievement of a different ethnic group – the Malay-Polynesian speakers who had colonised the western islands of Micronesia, Fiji,

Samoa and Tonga by about 1000 BC. It is thought that a distinctive Polynesian culture developed on Samoa and Tonga and that the final Polynesian migration probably started from Samoa and Tonga early in the first millennium AD. Large double canoes, able to carry the food and domestic animals required for colonisation sailed eastwards to settle the Marquesas Islands around 300 AD and perhaps as early as 100 AD. From the Marquesas, Easter Island was settled by about 400 AD, Hawaii by 800 AD or earlier and New Zealand by 900 AD.

Whatever, it seems that both the Polynesians to the west and South American Indians to the east did launch voyages of exploration into the Pacific Ocean in search of new land. It also seems that they were able to establish the position of the islands they discovered, record the information, pass it on to others and revisit the same locality. Interestingly, traditional stories of Easter Island tell of the arrival of *two* different peoples – the first from the east and the second from the west – and of the division of the islanders into 'Long Ear' and 'Short Ear' groups.

The Legend of Hotu Matua

Generally speaking, the traditional history of Easter Island falls into three distinct periods. First there is the arrival of King Hotu Matua and his followers, and the period of initial settlement. This is followed by a period of rivalry between two groups of people, the 'Long Ears' and the 'Short Ears' which ends with the extermination of the Long Ears. Lastly there is a more recent tribal war between the people of the Tuu region and the people of the Hotu-iti region.

Hotu Matua ('the prolific father' – *matua* is a Polynesian word for 'ancestor' and means 'father' on Easter Island) is said to have come from the east and landed at Anakena on the island's north coast. According to tradition, 57 generations of kings succeeded Hotu Matua

Top: Statues, Rano Raraku quarry, Easter Island
Bottom: Unfinished statues, Rano Raraku quarry, Easter Island

Top: Ahu Ko Te Riku, Easter Island
Bottom: View from Rano Raraku, Easter Island

on Easter Island – from which it is estimated that Hotu Matua landed on the island around 450 AD. A second group of immigrants is supposed to have arrived later, coming from the west and led by a chief called Tuu-ko-ihu.

The problem is that by the early part of the 20th century, European visitors were bringing back different versions of the story. A number of different starting points for Hotu Matua's voyage were now proposed: the Galapagos Islands to the north-east, the Tuamotus Islands roughly to the north-west, Rapa Iti to the west, and the Marquesas to the north-west. Some versions of the story even have Tuu-ko-ihu arriving on Hotu Matua's boats.

Trying to date events by working with genealogies is fraught with problems. A number of lists of the kings descended from Hotu Matua have been collected – all of them different. One estimate, working on a figure of 20 to 30 generations of kings descended from Hotu Matua until the last died after a slave raid in 1862, concludes that Hotu Motua arrived at Easter Island as late as the 16th century.

Long Ears & Short Ears

In the old stories there is a sudden leap from the arrival of Hotu Matua to the division of the islanders into Long Ear and Short Ear groups. It has been suggested that the Long Ear immigrants may have come from some part of Polynesia, where the custom of ear lobe elongation was practised. But since no one knows the actual direction from which the original inhabitants of the island came it's equally possible that the custom was brought by Indian immigrants from Peru, where ear lobe elongation was also a custom.

It has also been tempting to speculate – in order to fit the old stories in with theories of migrations from both South America and Polynesia – that the Long Ears arrived with Hotu Matua from the east to be followed by Short Ear arrivals

under Tuu-ko-ihu from the west. Some theories suggest that the Long Ears were the first to build the great *ahu* (altars) and that the Short Ears began to carve the *moai* (statues) and placed them on the ahu. Other stories hold that the Long Ears began to carve the statues and that the Short Ears helped them.

At some time though, there appears to have been a war between the two groups which resulted in the extermination of the Long Ears, bar one solitary survivor. Counting back the generations from the Easter Islanders who claimed descent from the last Long Ear (who had married a Short Ear woman after the end of the war) one estimate puts that survivor as having lived in the second half of the 17th century. Oddly enough, the islanders are known to have practised ear lobe elongation into this century, possibly because the religious or class barriers to it were removed once the original Long Ears were done away with.

The Toppling of the Statues

After the victory of the Short Ears over the Long Ears there is said to have been a long period of peace, but dissensions arose between different families or clans, bloody wars and cannibalism broke out and many of the stone statues were toppled from their platforms. The only statues which stand today have been restored this century. According to one account, the tribes or clans each had their own area and were proud of their statues, so an enemy tribe would topple the statues to insult and anger the owners.

The Dutch Arrival - 1722

Spanish ships began entering the Pacific from South America in the 16th century, but it was the members of a Dutch expedition under the command of Admiral Jacob Roggeveen which, in April 1722, became the first Europeans to land at Easter Island, having sailed from Chile. Their observations are recorded in Roggeveen's log and in a narrative

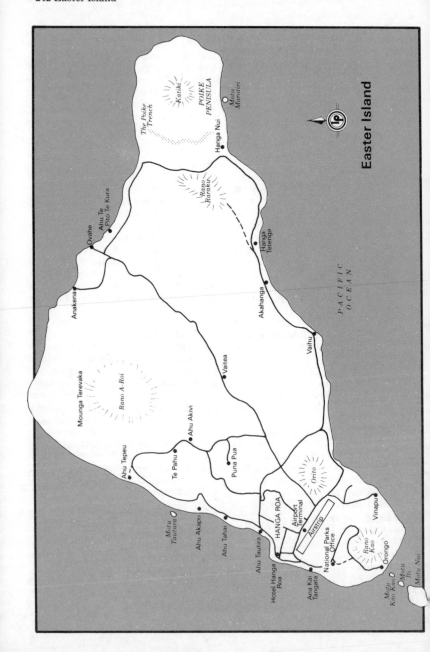

Easter Island

published by one of his companions, Carl Behrens. The island was named in honour of the day of its discovery, Easter Sunday.

The Dutch found the native inhabitants friendly, and living primarily on agricultural produce, the island being very extensively and neatly cultivated. But what baffled the Europeans were the great stone statues, which they thought had some religious significance. Roggeveen writes:

What the form of worship of these people comprises we were not able to gather any full knowledge of, owing to the shortness of our stay among them; we noticed only that they kindle fire in front of certain remarkably tall stone figures they set up; and, thereafter squatting on their heels with heads bowed down, they bring the palms of their hands together and alternately raise and lower them.

Behrens records that the natives:

relied in case of need on their gods or idols which stand erected all along the sea shore in great numbers, before which they fall down

Islander, Cook's 1774 visit

and invoke them. These idols were all hewn out of stone, and in the form of a man, with long ears, adorned on the head with a crown ...

Behrens mentions how some of the natives wore a block of wood or a disk in their artificially extended ear lobes. Some were so long that, after taking out the plugs, the natives often hitched the rim of the lobe over the top of their ear to stop it from wobbling during work. Behrens concluded that those who wore the wooden blocks or disks were probably priests because they paid more reverence to the gods than the others did, and could also be distinguished by their shaven heads. Roggeveen noted that those who did not cut their hair wore it long, either hanging down the back or else plaited and coiled on the top of the head.

The Spanish Expedition - 1770

It was not until 1770 that another European ship came to Easter Island, this time a Spanish expedition from Peru led by Don Felipe Gonzalez de Haedo who claimed the island for Spain and renamed it San Carlos.

They found that the male Easter Islanders were generally nude, wearing only plumes on their heads, whilst a few wore a sort of coloured poncho or cloak. The women usually wore hats of rushes, a short cloak around the breasts and another wrap from the waist downwards. Most of the natives dwelt in underground caves whilst others lived in long, boat-shaped reed houses (probably of the type seen by the Dutch). The islanders' only weapons appeared to be sharp-edged stones (probably made of obsidian, the hard, black volcanic rock found on the island) but there were no metal implements and the natives had no goods which suggested that there had been any trade with the outside world. Plantations of sugar cane, sweet potatoes, taro and yams were being grown. An officer of the expedition recorded that the islanders appearance:

does not resemble that of the Indians of the Continent of Chile, Peru or New Spain in anything, these islanders being in colour between white, swarthy and reddish, not thick lipped nor flat nosed, the hair chestnut coloured and limp, some have it black, and others tending to red or a cinnamon tint. They are tall, well built and proportioned in all their limbs; and there are no halt, maimed, bent, crooked, luxated, deformed or bow legged among them, their appearance being thoroughly pleasing, and tallying with Europeans more than with Indians.

Captain Cook's Arrival - 1774

After the Spanish, the next European ships to visit the island were those under the command of the Englishman Captain James Cook, in 1774. Cook, already familiar with the inhabitants of the Society Islands, Tonga and New Zealand, concluded that those on Easter Island were of the same general origin. Later accounts also suggested a Polynesian origin. In 1864 Eugene Eyraud, the first missionary on the island, wrote:

These savages are tall, strong, and well built. Their features resemble far more the European type than those of the other islanders of Oceania. Among all the Polynesians the Marquesans are those to which they display the greatest resemblance. Their complexion, although a little copper-coloured, does neither differ much from the hue of the European, and a great number are even completely white.

Cook concluded that whatever the statues may have been at the time of the Dutch visit they were no longer regarded as idols but appeared to be used as burial places for certain tribes or families. It appeared that the statues were still held in some sort of veneration and Cook thought that they were erected in memory of former kings.

But most importantly it is mentioned for the first time that though some of the statues were standing and still carrying their topknots, others had been toppled and the platforms on which they stood had been damaged. Cook found the islanders in a poor and distressed condition, describing them as small, lean, timid and miserable. It therefore seems possible that some great war had raged on the island since the Spanish visit in 1770, reducing the population to misery and causing a number of the statues to be overturned. Another theory is that no such decimation of the

Ahu drawn during La Perouse's 1786 visit

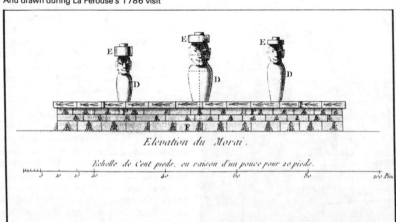

Elevation du Morai.

Echelle de Cent pieds, en raison d'un pouce pour 20 pieds.

population had taken place at all, and that most of the islanders had become wary of foreigners and hidden themselves from Cook's sailors in underground caves. It's also possible that a number of statues had already been toppled at the time of the Spanish and Dutch visits but that sailors from these ships did not visit the same sites Cook did.

Only one more European ship called at the island in the 18th century, that of the Frenchman La Perouse whose two ships crossed from Chile in 1786. They found the population of Easter Island a happy one with what seemed a prosperous economy, suggesting that if some great catastrophe had struck the island just before Cook's landing then the people had recovered very quickly.

There were a number of visits by European vessels in the early 19th century, and from the visit of a Russian ship in 1804 it is known that at that time over 20 statues were still standing, possibly including some of those at Vinapu on the south-west coast. Accounts from visitors over the following years suggest that another period of statue overturning began about this time and that perhaps only a few statues still stood a decade later.

Colonialism in the Pacific

If the native inhabitants of Easter Island had indeed fallen into a period of self-inflicted havoc and bloody wars, then their discovery by the outside world resulted in almost total annihilation.

The first catastrophe was the Peruvian slave raid of 1862 which directly or indirectly led to the death of most of the island's inhabitants. This was followed by a brief and violent period which involved the transportation of many islanders to foreign mines and plantations, the assaults of diseases previously unknown on the island, emigration induced by missionaries and a substantial disintegration of Polynesian culture on the island.

The Peruvian raid came at a time when European and American entrepreneurs were beginning to enter and loot the Pacific, hard on the rudders of the initial European voyages of discovery in the late 18th century. First came the whalers – many of them North American – who ranged the Pacific from Chile to Australia. Then came the planters who set out to build up a fairly long-term source of income by supplying the growing demand in the western world for tropical agricultural products like rubber, sugar and coffee. This usually resulted in the indigenous people becoming wage labourers on what was once their own land, and foreign labour being imported where local labour proved insufficient, inefficient or difficult to control.

Then came the slaving ships which either kidnapped Polynesians or – to give the trade in human bodies an aura of legality – compelled or induced them to make contracts committing themselves to work in foreign lands as far afield as Australia and South America. Many died due to the rigours of hard labour, poor diet, disease and ill-treatment.

Missionaries also entered the Pacific, introducing their own variations of Christianity to the islanders, importing European-American culture and morality, and breaking down and degrading local culture.

What happened on Easter Island in the 19th century was not so different from what was happening in other parts of the Pacific at this time.

The history of Easter Island since the 1860s can be split into three periods: the first when the island was ruled by a French sea captain; the second from 1888 to 1952, when almost the entire island was leased to a Chilean-Scottish sheep grazing concern; and the third is the ongoing control by Chile.

The Peruvian Slave Raid

There were raids on Easter Island by slavers in the first half of the 19th century and other violent incidents associated with the visits of European and American ships (even the first Dutch visit left several islanders dead or wounded) but these were nothing compared to the Peruvian raid.

About a thousand islanders were kidnapped in this raid – including the island's king and nearly all the *maori* or learned men – and taken to work on the Chincha Islands off the coast of Peru. Protests by Bishop Jaussen of Tahiti to the French representative at Lima resulted in the Peruvian authorities ordering the return of the islanders to their homeland. But by that time disease and hard labour had killed about 900 of them. Smallpox killed most of the others on the return voyage and only about 15 made it back to Easter Island. These 15 brought a smallpox epidemic to the island which resulted in the decimation of the surviving population, leaving perhaps only a few hundred survivors.

The first recorded attempts at Christianising the island occurred in the wake of this disaster. Eugene Eyraud, from the Chilean branch of the French Catholic *Societe de Picpus*, which was charged with the Christianisation of the Eastern Pacific, landed on the island. Eyraud met with a hostile reception and was badly treated by the islanders. He left the island in 1864 but returned in 1866, and with the assistance of other missionaries the islanders were converted to Christianity within a few years.

The Dutroux-Bornier Period
The first attempt at commercially exploiting the island began in 1870 when a French sea captain, Jean-Baptiste Dutroux-Bornier, settled at the site of the old Mataveri settlement at the foot of Rano Kau. Setting up as a sheep rancher, his intention was to turn the whole island over to grazing and ship the excess islanders off to work on the plantations of Tahiti. The missionaries – who planned to ship the islanders to mission lands in

southern Chile or the Mangaréva Islands – stood in the way of his claims to ultimate sovereignty over the island and its people.

Bornier armed his own native followers and raided the missionary settlements, burning houses and destroying crops, probably leaving a number of dead and injured, and eventually forced the missionaries to evacuate the island in 1870 and 1871. Most of the islanders were induced to accept transportation to Tahiti (others went to the islands of the Gambier archipelago) leaving about 100 on the island. Easter Island was ruled by Bornier until he was, apparently, killed by the remaining islanders in 1877.

Annexation by Chile
Spain had not kept up much interest in its original 1770 annexation and, in any case, lost most of its possessions in South America the following century. Chile officially annexed the island in 1888 during a period of aggressive Chilean expansion.

With its vigorous and effective naval force, Chile had the capability to expand into the Pacific. Easter Island was valued for its agricultural potential (real or imagined); for use as a naval station; for its location on what was perceived to be the major future trading route between South America and east Asia; to prevent its occupation by a hostile power which might use it as a base to attack the Chilean coast; and no doubt for the prestige of having overseas possessions – *any* possessions – in an era of colonialism.

The Williamson & Balfour Company
Attempts to colonise the island after the annexation came to nothing, and with no clear government policy about the future of the island it had, by 1897, come under the control of a single sheep grazing company run by Enrique Merlet, a businessman from Valparaíso who had bought up or leased the land. Control

soon passed into other hands, however.

In 1851 three Scottish businessmen founded S Williamson & Company in Liverpool, England, with a view to shipping goods to the west coast of South America. Williamson, Balfour & Company officially came into being as the Chilean branch in 1863, by which time a shipping fleet had been built up and the company had expanded its interests into an incredible range of products and countries. They took over Merlet's holdings on Easter Island in the first decade of the 20th century and controlled the island through their Compania Explotadora de la Isla de Pascua (CEDIP), under lease from the Chilean Government. The company effectively became the government of the island and until the middle of the 20th century continued profitable sheep grazing and wool production.

How the indigenous Easter Islanders actually fared under this system depends on which reports of the period you choose to believe, but it seems that there were several uprisings of sorts by the islanders against the company. One interesting result of foreign control was the fairly rapid elimination of the Easter Islanders as a pure-bred race, as other immigrants inter-bred with them. By the 1930s it was estimated that about three-quarters of the population of several hundred islanders were of mixed descent, including North American, British, Chilean, Chinese, French, German, Italian, Tahitian or Tuamotuan stock.

The company's lease was finally revoked in 1953, at a time when the Chilean Government was seeking to extend its control over its far flung and rather unwieldy territories. In place of the company the Chilean Navy was put in charge of the island, thus continuing the authoritarian (some would say dictatorial) rule to which the islanders had been subjected for 50 years.

Chilean Colonialism

The island continued under military rule until the mid-1960s. After that a brief period of civilian government followed until the military coup of 1973 when the island once again came under the direct control of the military. Since December 1984 the island's governor has been Sergio Rapu; Rapu is a civilian, a native of Easter Island and a professional archaeologist who was trained in the USA.

During the 1960s the island was as much a colony as any other. The islanders' grievances included unpaid labour, travel restrictions, confinement to the Hanga Roa area, suppression of the indigenous language, ineligibility to vote (universal suffrage in Chile did not extend to Easter Island) and arbitrary decisions on the part of the navy administration against which there was no appeal. Coupled with this were increased opportunities for contact with the outside world, and in 1967 the opening of a regular commercial air link between Santiago and Tahiti, via Easter Island. Perhaps because of the islanders' unrest, international attention drawn to the island, the potential of the tourist industry, increased immigration from the mainland, feelings of guilt after 80 years of neglect, or the coming to power of President Frei, the Chilean Government did undertake some improvements on the island during the 1960s and 1970s. These included improvements to the water supply, medical care, education and electrification.

Although livestock are still grazed on the island, the chief industry seems to be tourism – a fairly recent phenomena which only got going with the institution of regular air services between Easter Island and mainland Chile. Tourism will certainly have some sort of long-term impact on the island, but the really substantial changes to the island occurred under the onslaught of inter-tribal wars, slavers and foreign looters.

There may, however, be one more radical change to the island this decade. In August 1985 President Pinochet approved a plan allowing the USA to use

Easter Island as an emergency landing site for the space shuttle. The plans – and they should have been put into effect by the time this book is out – involve the extension of the island's airstrip out into the sea. Others believe that Easter Island is to be turned into a US military base (the US already has a number of major bases in the Pacific region – including communication bases, missile testing ranges, and air and naval bases). This would inevitably make the island, and possibly mainland Chile, a nuclear target in the event of war. There is opposition both in Chile and amongst the people of Easter Island to the establishment of this base, but the island is still treated like a colonial outpost by the military government and the indigenous people have no say in major decisions such as these.

GEOGRAPHY

Easter Island is a small, hilly island of volcanic origin, roughly triangular in shape with a volcano at each corner, none of which are active. The total area of the island is just 117 square km; its maximum length is 24 km and maximum width 12 km.

The largest volcano, Terevaka, rises 600 metres above sea level in the northern corner of the island and makes up the largest mass of the island. Katiki, about 400 metres high, forms the eastern headland known as the Poike Peninsula. Rano Kau, about 410 metres high, forms the south-west corner of the island. There are several smaller craters, including Rano Raraku from whose hard basalt rock (the chief type of rock found on the island) the giant statues were carved. Puna Pau, from whose red rock the statue's topknots were carved, is a small crater on the flank of Terevaka. Orito is another volcanic cone where black obsidian, an extremely hard volcanic rock which was used to make spearheads and various types of cutting tools, was quarried.

The craters of Rano Kau and Rano Raraku both contain freshwater lakes. Rano Kau's lake is about one km in diameter and is partly covered by a thick floating bog of reeds and peat. The surface of the lake is about 120 metres above sea-level and is bounded by crater walls which rise 400 metres above sea-level on the inland side, with a lower saddle on the southern edge facing the sea.

For the most part the slopes of all these volcanoes are gentle and covered in grass, except where cliffs have been formed either by the action of the sea (as at Rano Kau) or by quarrying (as at Rano Raraku). In contrast, the larger stretches of the island are covered in very rugged lava fields. There are several areas where there is thick soil suitable for cultivation; these are mainly in the Hanga Roa and Mataveri areas of the west coast, Vaihu on the south coast, the plain south-west of Rano Raraku, and inland at Vaitea.

There are numerous caves formed by volcanic action, many of them located in the cliffs by the sea. Some of the caves extend for considerable distances into the lava rock, and generally consist of large and small rooms connected by tunnels through which a person can barely squeeze. Some of these caves were used as refuges in time of war, others as secret storage or burial places, and others appear to have been used as long-term homes.

There are no coral reefs around Easter Island, although some areas of coral occur where the water is sufficiently shallow. This means, without the protection of the reef, that the action of the sea has produced huge cliffs in parts of the island, some of them rising to heights of over 300 metres. Those cliffs composed of lava are usually lower but are also extremely hard, torn and rugged. There is no natural sheltered harbour on the island, and Anakena on the north coast is the only wide, sandy beach although there are a few shallow bays.

Some theories have it that the island

Volcanic crater and lake, Rano Kau, Easter Island

once belonged to a much larger land mass, home of an advanced civilisation which sunk into the ocean through some catastrophic volcanic eruption – like a Pacific version of Atlantis. Though the island rests on a platform some 50 or 60 metres below sea-level, at about 15 to 30 km off the coast the platform ends and the ocean bottom drops off to between 1800 and 3600 metres, reaching over 7000 metres as the coast of South America is approached. It also seems to have been very stable geologically, and was pretty much its present shape and form when the great statues were carved. In any case, most of the statues were erected around the coast, suggesting little change in the shape of the shoreline since.

There are three tiny islands just off Rano Kau: Motu-nui, Motu-iti and Motu-kaokao. Motu-nui is the largest and has more level ground than any of the others. It is (or was) the nesting ground of thousands of sea-birds and, along with the ceremonial village of Orongo on the crest of Rano Kau, became the focus of a peculiar 'birdman' cult which persisted until the middle of the 19th century.

There is sufficient rainfall on Easter Island to maintain a permanent covering of coarse grasses, but the volcanic soil is very porous and the water quickly finds its way underground. There are no permanent streams on the island and water for use by people and livestock is drawn either from the volcanic lakes or from underground. It seems possible that the island vegetation was once much more luxuriant – perhaps including forests with palms and conifers and species no longer found on the island – but much of it was cut down by the inhabitants long ago. Most of the trees you see on the island today, like the eucalypts, were only planted within the past century.

Like other isolated islands whole families of both plants and animals are completely absent, whilst other species appear to be unique to the island. Small animals like chickens and rats were originally brought by the original immigrants. The Norway (or ship's) rat was brought by European ships; horses and other large animals were also introduced by Europeans, initially by missionaries in the 19th century.

CLIMATE

Although Easter Island lies just to the south of the Tropic of Capricorn – or on the same latitude as central Queensland, Australia – its subtropical climate is profoundly influenced by winds and ocean currents.

The hottest months are January and February, and the coolest are July and August. The average maximum summer temperatures are around 28°C and the average minimum is around 15°C, but these figures belie what can often be a fierce sun and formidable heat.

The average maximum winter temperatures are around 22°C and the average minimum around 14°C – but it can, apparently, get very cold when Antarctic winds lash the island with rain.

Light showers are the most common form of rainfall; the wettest month is May but heavy tropical downpours can occur during all seasons.

GETTING THERE

LAN-Chile is the only airline which has commercial flights to the island, flying once a week Santiago-Easter Island-Tahiti and return. This means that coming from Australia or New Zealand you can take a Melbourne/Sydney-Tahiti flight with Qantas or an Auckland-Tahiti flight with Air New Zealand and then change to LAN-Chile for the onward flight to Easter Island and Santiago. This may involve a stopover in Tahiti. For details of fares see the Getting There chapter at the start of this book.

Coming from the east, the one-way flight to Easter Island from Santiago by LAN-Chile will cost US$303, return US$369 (you can pay for this in Chilean pesos because it's an internal flight). The outward flights are on Wednesdays and the return flights are on Saturdays – but check this as it may change.

This makes the prices fairly hefty, especially if you're trying to travel South America on a shoestring, but if you have any interest at all in Easter Island you'd be mad not to visit!

BOOKS

One of the most substantial works on the island is *Reports of the Norwegian Archaeological Expedition to Easter Island & the East Pacific – Volume 1 – Archaeology of Easter Island* (George Allen & Unwin, London, 1962). This was the expedition led by Thor Heyerdahl in 1955 and 1956. It's fully illustrated and gives a detailed description of all the important sites, although none of them had been restored when the expedition did its work on the island. Copies of reports on the restoration of certain sites are sold by one of the shops at the Hanga Roa's Mataveri airport.

Father Sebastian Englert's *Island at the Center of the World* (Charles Scribner's Sons, New York, 1970) relates the history of the island according to some versions of the Easter Islanders' traditional stories. A Bavarian, Englert was the island's priest from 1935 until his death nearly 35 years later. If you can read Spanish then get *La Tierra de Hotu Matu'a* (Editorial Universitaria, Santiago, 3rd edition 1983) which is his main book about the island and was first published in 1948. Also in Spanish is his *Idioma Rapanui* – Gramatica y Diccionario del antiguo idioma de la Isla de Pascua (Universidad de Chile, 1978). Both books can be bought in Santiago.

To add colour to mystery you can't go past Thor Heyerdahl's *Aku-Aku – The Secret of Easter Island* (George Allen & Unwin, London, 1958). Written rather like a detective story this is his popular account of Easter Island and the work of the Norwegian expedition.

There are a number of accounts of early expeditions and visits to the island. The first archeological expedition was a private venture in 1914 headed by the English woman Katherine Routledge; all the scientific notes of the expedition were lost but she did write *The Mystery of Easter Island* – the story of an expedition, first published in 1919. Other interesting accounts include J MacMillan Brown's *The Riddle of the Pacific* (published in 1924); and *Easter Island* (published in 1957) by the French archeologist Alfred Metraux who first went to the island on a French-Belgium expedition in the 1930s.

If Easter Island is the navel of the world then it's also the centre of the Polynesian versus South American Indian debate – from which direction was the Pacific colonised and who built the enormous statues on Easter Island? Thor Heyerdahl's *American Indians in the Pacific – The Theory Behind the Kon-Tiki Expedition* (George Allen & Unwin, London, 1952) is an enormous book which makes a comparative study of American Indian and Pacific cultures, legends, religious ideas, stone sculpture, boat building, physical characteristics and cultivated plants. It includes a discussion on Easter Island. For the story of the Kon Tiki expedition read his book *Kon Tiki* (Rand McNally, Chicago, 1952).

Computer simulations have been done of both drift and navigated voyaging in the Pacific in an attempt to explain the distribution of the Polynesian people. One of these is *The Settlement of Polynesia – A Computer Simulation* (Australian National University Press, Canberra, 1973) by Michael Levison, R Gerard Ward and John Webb.

It is now generally thought that the original Easter Islanders were Polynesians who arrived at Easter Island from the west by way of the Marquesas. For a general review of current thinking on the migration of people across the Pacific try *The Peopling of the Pacific* (in *Scientific American*, Nov 1980, vol 243, No 5) by Peter Bellwood. For more reading try *Man's Conquest of the Pacific* (Oxford

University Press, New York, 1979) by the same author, which also includes a lengthy section on Easter Island and the Polynesian-American argument, although you may find his conclusions rather shaky. Despite the book's title, presumably some women also went along for the ride.

The other alternative to the Polynesian-American debate is not to go sideways, but upwards. Erich von Daniken's theories about the origin of the island's statues can be found in his book *In Search of Ancient Gods* (Souvenir Press, London, 1974).

The Peruvian slave raid on Easter Island was not an isolated incident. The first few years of the 1860s saw many Polynesian islands raided and their populations decimated by the Peruvian slavers; for the story behind the slave trade read Henry Maude's *Slavers in Paradise – the Peruvian labour trade in Polynesia, 1862-1864*, (published in the Pacific by the University of the South Pacific, Fiji; in Australia by the Australian National University Press; and in the USA by the Stanford University Press).

Largely ignored, as if it doesn't have one, is the modern history of Easter Island. For a blow-by-blow account of the island's history from the mid-1800s until the late 1970s try *The Modernization of Easter Island* (University of Victoria, British Columbia, Canada, 1981) by J Douglas Porteous.

Photo Books

If a picture book is what you want then perhaps there is none finer than *Isla de Pascua* by Michel Rougie, published by the National Tourist Service of Chile. The beautiful photos record all the major sites and the text is in Spanish, French and English. A general store called the Establecimiento McKay on the main street of Hanga Roa stocks this book but they sell it for US$50! It's sold for half that price in bookshops in Santiago.

Maps

There are several souvenir shops in Hanga Roa which stock a large map of the island called *Isle de Pascua Rapa Nui* published several years ago by the National Tourist Service of Chile. It can be useful but it has – like most maps of Easter Island – a number of errors, and does not show clearly how to get out of Hanga Roa to the various sites. Look around for maps on tourist leaflets – these are often much more useful than maps in books about the island.

Perhaps the best map available on the island is a relief map housed in the island's museum; it shows the town, all the roads, volcanoes, and archaeological sites and is very good for getting your bearings.

If you really need a detailed map of the island you might try the *Instituto Geografico Militar* which has a retail outlet in central Santiago (see the section on Maps in the Facts for the Visitor chapter).

HANGA ROA

Just a few thousand people live on Easter Island. About 70% are Polynesians (they think of themselves as Polynesian, not as Chileans or South Americans) and the rest are mainly immigrants from the Chilean mainland. Almost the whole population lives in the township of Hanga Roa on the west coast of the island. How people make ends meet in this place is something of a mystery to the casual observer; there are a few fishermen and there is some cattle and sheep-grazing, but there seems to be no agriculture other than small vegetable, banana and papaya gardens on the outskirts of the township. Government offices, general stores, a bank and post office soak up a fraction of the labour supply, but scraping money off the tourist trade seems to be the main industry.

Information

Tourist Office There is a tourist office at the airport and in Hanga Roa on Tuu Maheke (tel 55). The tourist people usually speak Spanish, French and English. The airport office has a list of local families who rent out rooms. The airport office is only open when planes arrive or depart. The tourist office in town is open Monday to Friday, 9 am to 2 pm.

Bank The Banco del Estado de Chile is next to the tourist office and will change some foreign currency and travellers' cheques, but they charge a hefty 10% commission on US dollar travellers' cheques! Otherwise, US cash can changed readily with the locals in Hanga Roa, and can be used to pay for anything from hotel bills to toothpaste. The bank is open Monday to Friday from 9 am to 2 pm.

Post The post office is on the road leading to Ahu Tautira. It's open Monday to Friday from about 9 am until 2 pm.

LAN-Chile The airline has an office in the Hotel Hanga Roa; open daily from about 9 or 10 am to 1 pm.

Film Bring as much of this stuff as you need! Film is scarce and expensive on the island. You may be able to find some Fujicolor and Ektachrome 35 mm transparencies, and perhaps some Kodak 110 but don't expect much else. Look in the general stores in Hanga Roa and at the two large hotels.

Places to Stay

Easter Island, you will soon discover, ain't cheap, and accommodation is particularly expensive – don't worry, the rest of Chile is *not* like this! Room prices on the island are more or less fixed, although you may have some leeway for bargaining if a place is half empty. If you want to keep costs to minimum you will have to stay away from the two large hotels – the Hotel Hanga Roa and the Hotel Hotu Matua – and find a room in

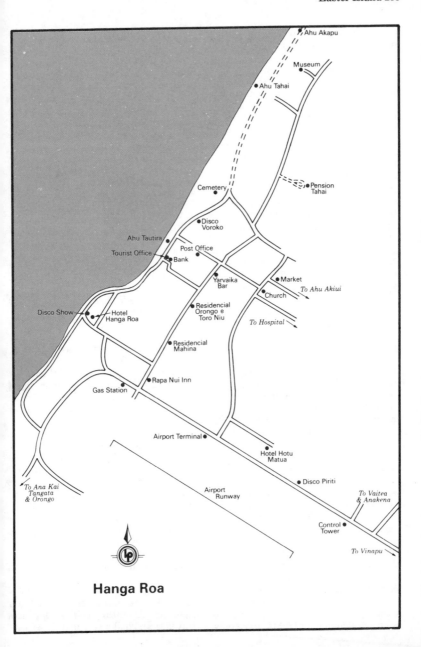

Ahu Akapu

Museum

Ahu Tahai

Pension
Tahai

Cemetery

Disco
Voroko

Ahu Tautira

Tourist Office

Post Office

Bank

Market

To Ahu Akiui

Yarvaika
Bar

Church

Disco Show

Residencial
Orongo e
Toro Niu

To Hospital

Hotel
Hanga Roa

Residencial
Mahina

Rapa Nui Inn

Gas Station

Airport Terminal

Hotel Hotu
Matua

Disco Piriti

*To Ana Kai
Tangata
& Orongo*

Airport
Runway

*To Vaitea
& Anakena*

Control
Tower

To Vinapu

Hanga Roa

one of the many residencials or with a family. You are *expected* to pay your bill in US cash.

The cheapest rooms you'll get in a residencial will be about US$15 a single and US$25 a double per night including bed and breakfast, or US$20 a single and US$40 a double per night, full board. Occasionally someone meets the incoming flights at the airport with something cheaper to offer – say US$10 per person for bed and breakfast, or US$15 per person, full board – but don't count on it.

There are only a few places at the bottom end of the price range. The majority of residencials in Hanga Roa charge US$30 to US$45 a single, and US$40 to US$65 a double with full board. Next up is another group which charge about US$45 to US$50 a single, and US$70 to US$80 a double with full board.

The best way to find a place is to check out what's available at the tourist office at the airport. The locals and hotel proprietors flock there to meet the incoming flights and to rake in a tourist or two. The advantage of this is that you can find out which hotels and residencials have spare rooms and this saves you tramping all over Hanga Roa looking for a place. You also get transport into the town which is useful – Hanga Roa is so spread out that just the walk from the airport to a place like the Residencial Tahai would take you an hour.

If you don't like what you get you can always move the following day; the tourist office on Tuu Maheke should help you find a cheap place. Most residencials are not sign-posted.

Places to Stay – bottom end

One place to stay which has been enthusiastically recommended is the *Pension Tahai* run by Maria Hey. She charges US$10 per person, room only, or US$20 per person, full board. You may even get a double for US$15, room only,

with a bit of bargaining. You stay in a very clean bungalow with an attached dining room, lounge and bathroom (cold water only) set amidst a large garden. Great meals too. She's not as aggressive as the other punters at the airport so she doesn't scoop up the clientele that she ought to. Her place is a bit out of town on the road leading up to Ahu Tahai; it's very quiet and relaxing.

Another good place is the *Rapa Nui Inn* (tel 228) near the corner of the main street and the airport road. It's a good location and the hotel has an amiable manager. Singles go for US$10 including breakfast, or US$30, full board. Doubles are twice that. You get a big, clean room with a large double bed, and your own bathroom.

Also try the *Residencial Mahina* which is set in a palm tree garden on the main street just down from the Rapa Nui Inn. Singles are US$30, doubles are US$50 with full board.

Camping is allowed on the island, but officially only at Anakena and Rano Raraku. Rangers are stationed at Orongo, Rano Raraku, Ahu Tahai and Anakena. Apparently camping out other than in the official campsites is frowned upon – but I imagine if you did so in some of the more remote areas, nobody would see you or come looking for you.

Places to Stay – middle

The *Residencial Orongo E Toro Niu* is on the main street and has a good, central location. It's set in a pleasant garden and has basic but clean and tidy rooms with their own bathrooms. They serve up excellent meals (make sure you ask for the seaweed dish) and the people are friendly. They charge US$45 a single and US$75 a double with full board. It's quiet at night and if you can afford it then it's good value!

It's suggested you avoid the *Hostal Apina-Nui* (tel 92). We had a long letter from an American and a Japanese traveller who had a very bad time there.

The owners were described as exceptionally rude (once the deposit had been paid) and they refused to stick by the conditions which they had offered at the airport. They advertise their rates as US$25 a single and US$45 a double, with breakfast, or US$45 a single and US$75 a double, full board. They may also cater for camping in their grounds.

Places to Stay – top end

The *Hotel Hanga Roa* (tel 99) on Avenida Pont is a rather lengthy walk from the middle of town, but it does have a swimming pool, a bar and restaurant, and several souvenir shops (the shops are usually only open when there's a fair number of tourists around). Rooms go for a devastating US$75 a single and US$95 a double, including continental breakfast; and US$116 a single and US$163 a double, full board. If you forgo full board then breakfast (American style) is an additional US$10 and lunch is US$20. You can pay in US dollars or in Chilean pesos.

Rather cheaper and perhaps just as good is the *Hotel Hotu Matua* which is a much more reasonable US$56 a single and US$94 a double, full board. It's also a rather long way out of town – much too far to walk so you'll really need your own transport if you want to stay here. The locals sometimes stage hula dances for tour groups at these hotels.

Places to Eat

Some residencials are prepared to rent you a room only but there isn't any advantage in doing this unless you're going to put your own food together with what you can buy at Hanga Roa market. Food at the few restaurants in Hanga Roa will cost you as much as it does at a residencial, and in any case the restaurants are more like snackbars and the food is not particularly sustaining.

You can bring in canned food from outside but fresh fruit and vegetables are *not* allowed – your bags will be checked at the airport to ensure you're not bringing any in, whether you're coming from Tahiti or from Chile.

The island's water supply is safe to drink. It's all bore water and has a heavy mineral content, and it can take an appalling couple of days to adjust. Make it more palatable by squeezing in some orange juice or buying some flavouring from one of the general stores.

Probably the best place for a snack and drink is the *Yarvaika Bar* on the main street, with its pleasant little front yard with tables, tree-stump chairs and shady trees. They serve up hamburgers, cheeseburgers, pizza slices, roast chicken and other snacks. The proprietor is friendly.

If you want to camp out or cook your own food there's no trouble getting enough provisions to do so. There are a couple of general stores and bread shops on the main street where you can buy canned food, bottled drinks (coke, soft drinks, wine, beer) as well as fresh vegetables, fruit and eggs. You can also buy fresh fruit and vegetables at the market (Mercado Municipal).

Things to Buy

There are a number of souvenir shops in Hanga Roa, most of them on the main street, and on the street leading up to the church. You can buy small stone replicas of the statues, *moai kavakava* which are the small famished-looking figures with protruding ribs, replicas of wooden rongo-rongo tablets, and fragments of obsidian from Mt Orito. T-shirts with Easter Island motifs (rongo-rongo writing, statues) cost about US$10 – some of the tackier models are made in the People's Republic of China.

The Hotel Hanga Roa has a number of stalls set up by local souvenir sellers (if she's still on the island, look for the work of a Chilean woman who makes cloth rubbings of the birdmen and rongo-rongo petrogylphs). Obsidian ear-rings are good, cheap souvenirs – they sell for about US$1.50 to US$2 a pair. The locals set up a small market at the airport when planes arrive or depart, selling souvenirs and handicrafts.

Getting Around

The town centre is about a 20-minute walk from the airport, but to get much beyond the town you really need your own transport. Just how long you take to get around the island is going to depend on what sort of transport you take and how long you want to spend at each site. A week is certainly enough to take in all the major sites, but there are many minor places of interest on the island and if you're really into this sort of thing you could easily spend weeks and weeks studying the place.

Rented horses, motorbikes and cars are your main transport options. Some books say you can walk around the island in two or three days or so. Theoretically it's possible but there are some good reasons why you should *not* walk around Easter Island: it is fiercely hot in summer; there is almost no shade or water supply outside the settlements; and distances quoted from one site to the next are often grossly misleading. Maps and tourist leaflets often show distances to places of interest from Hanga Roa – but these are sometimes as the crow flies, not the distance you actually have to walk, ride or drive to get there.

If you ride a horse or a motorbike around the island you *will* need a day-pack. A shoulder bag stuffs up your balance too much and is very uncomfortable in the heat. Saddle bags for horses and pack-racks or panniers for motorbikes are nowhere to be seen, so if you intend riding with more gear than you can carry in a small daypack it could really be worth bringing them with you.

Bring sun-block with you! Regardless of how good a tan you got on the beach before you arrived you need a powerful sun-block, otherwise you'll spend your time sheltering in a hotel room watching your skin erupt in blisters and peel off in

great sheets. Use the sun-block liberally on everything that's exposed – including the back and sides of your hands if you're riding a horse or motorcycle. There is no pharmacy on the island (a few general stores sell sun-block but not the strength you really need) but you can go to the hospital if you get badly burnt.

Bring a long-sleeved shirt with you, sunglasses, and a large hat or headgear which will cover your face and neck. For a day trip bring at least two litres of water per person in summer – and always carry a water bottle at places like Rano Raraku where you have to do a lot of walking and where there's no shade other than that provided by the statues. Head-hunting is hot work!

Horses Horses can be hired for US$10 a day, but beware – they will rent you *any* horse. And if it isn't dead when you get it then it may well be by the time you've finished with it. Most horses hired from locals (some will approach you on the street, if not, ask at your hotel or residencial) will only have a rope for the reins and another holding on the stirrups and nailed to the saddle. That latter arrangement can be quite dangerous if you ride too fast and put too much pressure on the stirrup – the stirrup flies off and so do you. The Hotel Hotu Matua or the Hanga Roa seem to organise horse-riding excursions for groups but may be able to get you a horse with proper stirrups and reins. Horses are good for visiting sites close to Hanga Roa like Ahu Tepeu, Vinapu, Ahu Akivi and Orongo, but to get to places like Rano Raraku and Anakena you really need some motorised transport, unless you've got the time to take things slowly.

Motorbikes & Cars The locals will rent their motorbikes for about US$30 to US$35 a day – or if you need someone to drive you, for about US$40 per day. Motorbikes can be rented from the Hotel Hanga Roa for US$30 per day. Cars can

Top: Toppled statues, Vaihu, Easter Island
Left: Statue, near Ahu Tahai, Easter Island
Right: Squatting statue, Rano Raraku quarry, Easter Island

Top: Ahu Nau Nau, Easter Island
Left: Statue designs, Ahu Nau Nau, Easter Island
Right: Long-eared statue, Ahu Nau Nau, Easter Island

be rented from the Hotel Hanga Roa for US$72 per day. The cheapest car rental on the island is about US$60 per day; ask at the residencials and at the tourist office to see if they can fix you up with something. All the roads on the island are unsurfaced – beware of potholes, rocks and ruts if you're on a motorcycle.

If you've never ridden a motorbike but need a convenient way to get around town then ask the manager at the Hotel Hotu Matua to fix you up with one of the small 70 cc bikes you often see here. These will cost you about US$20 per day. They're small three-speed bikes with no handle clutch control, so it's easy to ride them if you've never ridden a fully-fledged motorbike before. All you have to operate is a hand brake, foot brake, an accelerator on the same handle as the hand brake, and a gear shift operated with your foot. Simple, once you get the hang of it. Find out what range it's got before you do any long-distance driving.

Tours There are a couple of people running tours around the island in minivans. If you're only in transit on the way to Tahiti or to the Chilean mainland then Anakena Tours often has a half hour tour which takes you from the airport up to the impressive Ahu Tahai site and then back to the airport. Your passport is held by immigration until the tour is finished.

THE ARCHAEOLOGICAL SITES

Giant, brooding stone statues buried up to their necks in dirt and rubble are the images that Easter Island brings to mind. But there are, in fact, several types of stonework found on the island. Apart from the statues (*moai*) some of the other important sites include altars (*ahu*) or large platforms on which the statues were erected, burial cairns which are basically large piles of rock in which bodies were entombed, and the stone foundations of unusual boat-shaped village huts.

Although many of these structures

were partially demolished or rebuilt by the original inhabitants and the statues were toppled during inter-tribal wars many years ago, a good deal of damage was done during the rule of the CEDIP. Many ahu, burial cairns, house foundations, and other structures were ripped apart and used to make the piers at Hanga Roa and Hanga Piko as well as stone fences to wall off sheep-grazing areas Windmills were constructed over the original stone-lined wells to provide a water supply for sheep, cattle and horses.

Not only have many of the ancient monuments been destroyed but much has been pillaged. Only a few moai were carried off but wooden *rongo-rongo* tablets inscribed with a forgotten script, painted wall tablets from the Orongo ceremonial village houses on the edge of the Rano Kau crater, small wood and stone statues, weapons, clothing, skulls and other artefacts have been taken from the island and can now be found in foreign museums and inaccessible private collections in Chile and elsewhere. Some sites, like the Orongo village, were wholly or partially dismantled by the islanders for use as building material.

A number of sites have been restored within the last 30 years or so including Ahu Tahai, Ahu Akivi, the Orongo ceremonial village, and Ahu Nau Nau. Others, such as Ahu Vinapu and Ahu Vaihu, lie in ruins but are nonetheless impressive sights.

It's possible to take in all the major sites on three loops out of Hanga Roa. This is a convenient way to see the sites with a minimum of back-tracking, and a description follows.

The South-West Route

This takes you from Hanga Roa up the road leading to the top of the Rano Raraku crater and the Orongo ceremonial village. You backtrack to the township, then follow the road along the northern edge of the airstrip to Mt Orito which is the site of the old obsidian quarries.

From here you head southwards to Ahu Vinapu with its impressive, finely-cut stonework.

The Northern Loop

This route takes you from Hanga Roa to Puna Pau which is a volcanic crater from whose red-coloured rock the statue's topknots were cut. From here you continue inland to Ahu Akivi which has been restored and its seven statues re-erected. From Ahu Akivi you follow a track to Ahu Tepeu on the west coast which is said to be the burial site of Tuu-ko-ihu. You then head southwards to Hanga Roa, stopping off at Ahu Akapu, Ahu Tahai and Ahu Tautira which have all been restored and their maoi re-erected. Because of the vagueness of the trail between Ahu Akivi and the coast it's probably easier to go from Hanga Roa to Ahu Akivi and then cut cross-country to Ahu Tepeu rather than the other way round.

The Island Circle

This route takes you from Hanga Roa along the southern coast stopping off at the ruins at Vaihu and Akahanga with their massive ahu and giant toppled statues. From Akahanga you continue west and detour inland to the Rano Raraku crater from whose hard basalt rock most of the statues on the island were cut, and where statues in all stages of production can still be seen. Leaving Rano Raraku you follow the road west to Ahu Tongariki which is a ruined ahu whose statues and masonry were hurled some distance inland by a massive tidal wave after the Chilean earthquake of 1960. From here you follow the road to the north coast to Ahu Te Pito Kura which boasts the largest statue ever erected on an ahu. Continue east to the beach at Ovahe, and then to Anakena which is the island's main beach and the site of two more restored ahu; excavation and restoration of Ahu Nau Nau at Anakena showed that the statues once had inlaid eyes and were not 'blind'.

Distances

Approximate distances to the important sites by road from Hanga Roa are:

Mt Orito – 2 km
Vinapu – 5 km
Vaihu – 9½ km
Akahanga – 12½ km
Rano Raraku – 18 km
Ahu Tongariki – 20 km
Ahu Te Pito Kura – 26 km
Ovahe – 29 km
Anakena – 30 km
Ahu Tahai – 1.5 km
Ahu Tepeu – 2 km
Ahu Akivi – 10 km
Puna Pau – 2 km
Orongo – 7 km

AHU TAUTIRA, TAHAI, AKAPU & TEPEU

Lined up along the west coast of the island are four large ahu complexes. Ahu Tautira is next to Hanga Roa's small pier; northwards to Ahu Tahai, which is connected by another track along the coast to Ahu Akapu and Ahu Tepeu.

There are some 245 ahu on the island (the number differs according to various classifications) most of them forming an almost unbroken line along the coasts except for some high cliffs around the Poike Peninsula and Rano Kau, though there are some by the cliff edges in other places. The ahu tend to be sited around good landing places and areas which are favourable for human habitation, although only a few were built inland.

There are several varieties of ahu, built at different times for different reasons, but the most impressive type is the ahu moai or the platforms on which the statues are placed. Each ahu moai is essentially a mass of loose stones held in place by retaining walls, and paved on the upper surface with more or less flat stones. Each structure has a perpendicular wall on the seaward side and usually around each end. The statues which were erected on these platforms range from two to almost 10 metres in height, although even larger statues were under construction in the quarry at Rano Raraku when work came to a sudden end.

Usually gently sloping ramps paved in various ways – often using rounded beach boulders or closely placed slabs of irregular stones – are built against the landward sides of the platforms. Adjacent to the ramps there are usually large flat plazas which may have been artificially levelled. In a few cases these are outlined by earth embankments forming rectangular or irregular enclosures. Sometimes there are small rectangular platforms built on the plazas which may be altars, and large circles paved with stones. Sometimes a bit further inland there were boat-shaped thatch-houses in which members of the priesthood which served the altars may have lived. It is known that the original Easter Islanders used one and two-person reed boats, and it's likely that much larger reed boats were launched from the stone ramps (*apapa*) leading into the sea by the side of the ahu.

Not much is known about the ceremonies once associated with these ahu complexes. One theory is that the statues represented ancestors of the clan owning the ahu, and that the ceremonies were part of a clan ancestor cult. Ahu were also a place of burial; originally bodies were buried in stone-lined tombs constructed in the ahu ramps and platforms. However, it seems that later on, after the statues had been toppled, the bodies were placed around the fallen statues and on other parts of ramps and covered with stones. Other bodies were cremated at the ahu sites, but whether these were bodies of deceased members of the clan or the remains of human sacrifices is unknown, though traditional stories do tell of human sacrifice by burning.

The large plaza in front of Ahu Tahai has been restored and there are several interesting features including the foundation stones of the houses once used by the islanders, and which were probably the main type of housing right up until European-style houses were introduced. Long and narrow, the general appearance of this house has been likened to an upturned canoe. The floor shape is outlined by shaped rectangular blocks or curb stones having small, cup-shaped depressions on their upper surfaces. A single narrow opening at the middle of one side served as the doorway. To form the walls and the roof, the ends of thin poles were inserted into the cup-shaped sockets of the stone foundations. These poles were arched across the centre of the structure and, where each opposed pole crossed with another, lashed to a ridge pole. As the space to be covered narrowed progressively toward the ends, the roofing poles decreased in length, thus lowering the roof level and producing a house shaped like an overturned canoe. A crescent-shaped, boulder pavement often covered the ground in front of the house. The size of these dwellings varied enormously; some were capable of housing over 100 people, while others could house only about six.

Ahu Tautira

Ahu Tautira stands by Hanga Roa's tiny port which is only used by a few tiny fishing boats. The torsos of two broken statues have been re-erected on the ahu.

Ahu Tahai & Ahu Akapu

Although 'Ahu Tahai' seems to be commonly used in reference to the entire site, there are actually three restored ahu here – the work was done in 1968 under the direction of the American archaeologist, William Mulloy. The large, solitary statue wearing its topknot stands on Ahu Ko Te Riku. Regardless of its appearance this is a relative light-weight – about a quarter of the weight of the giant at Ahu Te Pito Te Kura on the north coast of the island. Ahu Akapu with its solitary statue stands on the coast further to the north of Ahu Tahai.

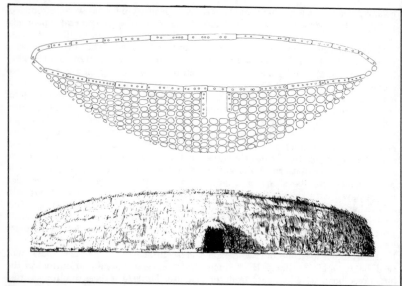

Floor plan and profile of a boat-shaped house

Ahu Tepeu

This ahu is situated on the west coast of Easter Island between Hanga Roa and the North Cape. To the north-east rises Terevaka, the highest point on the island, while to the south is a large grassy plain over a jagged lava sheet. To the west the sea breaks against jagged cliffs which in parts are 50 metres high.

The seaward side of the large ahu is the most interesting feature of the structure. It has a wall about three metres high near the centre composed of large vertical slabs of stone. A number of statues once stood on the ahu but these have all been toppled. Immediately to the east of Ahu Tepeu is an extensive village site marked by the foundation stones of several large boat-shaped houses and the walls (consisting of loosely piled stones) of several round houses.

AHU VINAPU

Although the original structures at Ahu Tahai appear to belong to the earliest period of building on Easter Island, the restored complex looks something like the second last chapter of an unfinished mystery novel with the clues pieced together but the puzzle unsolved. To shed some light on how, why and when the statues were carved you have to begin in the south-west corner of the island at Ahu Vinapu, situated in a small valley facing the coast.

To get to Ahu Vinapu you follow the road from Hanga Roa along the northern edge of the airstrip. At the end of the airstrip you'll see a road heading south between the airstrip and the large oil containers. Follow this road past the containers until you see an opening in a stone fence and a sign pointing the way to Ahu Vinapu, which is nearby.

There are two ahu next to each other on the valley floor. Both once supported statues but these have all been over-turned, and most of them are broken and lying with their faces in the dirt and rubble in front of the platforms. Accounts by 18th and early 19th century visitors to the island suggest that the statues were not all overturned at once, although they were all tipped over by the middle of the 19th century – some by undermining the foundation stones on which they stood, while others may have been pulled down with ropes.

An interesting find at the Vinapu site, which now stands in front of one of the ahu, is a long brick-red stone, shaped something like a four-sided column. It's obviously not one of the standard statues found on the island, but if you look closely you can see that it is in fact a statue of some sort with hands and arms, but minus its head. It also has short legs, unlike most other statues on the island which have no legs. It's rather reminiscent of pre-Inca column statues in the South American Andes.

Ahu No 1, with its perfectly carved and fitted stonework, is the most interesting ahu of the group and is usually referred to

as 'Ahu Vinapu' although the name originally seems to have referred to the entire area and the ahu itself once went under a different name. Ahu No 2 has walls made of cut stone but is not as finely worked as Ahu No 1.

The Vinapu stonework is so reminiscent of the fine stonework of the Incas of the Cuzco Valley in Peru, and to that of the pre-Inca civilisation which once had its capital at Tiahuanaco near Lake Titicaca in Bolivia, that it was suggested that the Easter Island stonework had its origins in South America. However, it was generally accepted that the Easter Islanders could have developed the techniques to produce such perfectly carved blocks independently of South America, and that Vinapu represented the last and most advanced phase in the development of stone-carving on the island.

This theory was upset when the Norwegian expedition's excavations at Vinapu found that the central wall of Ahu No 1 – with its finely carved stonework –

Stonework, Ahu Vinapu

belonged to the very oldest building period. They concluded that the ahu had twice been rebuilt and added to by builders who were no longer capable of reproducing such stonework. From this and other evidence it appeared that there had been three clearly separate periods in the island's history: Early, Middle and Late.

During the Early Period, ahu were built of large stone blocks which were carved and fitted together without a crack or hole between them. No burials seem to have been placed in the structures and there were no statues standing on them. Carbon 14 dating of remnants of fires and other material found at various sites suggests that the Early Period began sometime before 400 AD and ended about 1100 AD.

During the Middle Period most of these structures were altered or pulled down. A paved slope was built up against the wall of the ahu which faced inland and giant stone figures carved at Rano Raraku were erected on the platforms which now often contained burial chambers. Less care was taken with the stonework of the ahu itself since the emphasis was now on the production of the statues. It is thought that this second period finished towards the end of the 17th century.

Then, for some unknown reason, the island entered into a period of bloody war and cannibalism and the production of the statues came to an end. During this Late Period, boulders and shapeless blocks were flung together to make funeral mounds along the walls of the ahu. The statues – all of which had been toppled by the middle of the 19th century – were often used as improvised roofs for new burial vaults. Many of the ahu were modified into semi-pyramid shapes by packing stones over and around the fallen statues, and the dead were buried amidst the mass of stones.

Others, however, did not find these categories quite so conclusive. Over two decades ago, just by re-interpreting the

findings of the Norwegian expedition, it was argued that Ahu No 2 at Vinapu (which does not have the same finely cut stonework as Ahu No 1) was actually built earlier than Ahu No 1. This suggests that Ahu No 2 could have been a development of the *marae* platforms found on other Polynesian islands. Eventually masonry skills improved so much that it was possible for descendents of the original Polynesian immigrants to produce the finely worked stones of Ahu No 1 – independent of any influence from South America. It's generally accepted that the main function of the ahu differed for each period, apparently serving as an altar in Early Period, a base for statues in the Middle Period, and a burial place in the Late Period. However the change from one to the other appears to have been more gradual than previously thought.

RANO RARAKU

Otherwise known as 'the nursery', it was from the hard basalt rock of the Rano Raraku volcano that the statues were cut. The mountain is littered with statues in all stages of completion – in quarries on both the exterior and interior sides of the southern slope, as well as along the crater rim. Coming in from the south you'll see the slope of the volcano studded with statues, most of them standing upright but up to their shoulders or necks in the earth so that only the heads gaze across the grassy slopes. The volcano is bounded by a stone fence and from the entrance gate a trail leads up the slope. Going straight up brings you to a 21-metre giant – the largest statue ever built. Follow a trail to the right to several other large statues still attached to the rock, or turn left along the trail which leads over the rim and into the interior of the crater.

Inside the crater stand about 20 statues, a number of fallen statues and a number only partly finished – making a total of some 80 figures in all. Outside on the mountain stand about 50 statues. Below them, at the foot of the mountain and on the plain towards the sea lie almost 30 more, all of which have fallen and, with a few exceptions, lie face downwards. In the quarries above, there are something like 160 unfinished statues. That means that when work came to a stop some 320 statues were in the process of being carved or had been completed but not yet erected on ahu. The total number of statues made at the Rano Raraku quarries would appear to be well over 600.

Although all the statues are of a uniform type, contrary to popular belief they are not all identical. The standard Rano Raraku statue has its base at about the level of the hips. Arms hang stiffly at the sides and extended hands with long, slender fingers are turned toward each other across the lower part of a protruding abdomen. The heads are elongated and rectangular with heavy brows and prominent noses. The mouths are small with thin lips. Chins are prominent. The ear lobes are elongated and some are carved to show inserted ear ornaments. Hands, breasts, navels and facial features are clearly shown, and the backs are sometimes carved to represent what may be tattoos. It is interesting to speculate where the makers of the statues got their models from, since the features of the statues – long straight noses, tight-lipped mouths, sunken eyes and low foreheads – seem to be very un-Polynesian. Large stone statues have also been found on the Marquesas, Raivavae and other islands of eastern Polynesia, but they can also be found in western South America.

Since the quarry shows all the stages of carving a statue it's easy enough to see how this process was conducted. Most were carved face up, and in a horizontal or slightly sloping position. A channel large enough to accommodate the workmen was excavated around and under each statue leaving the statue attached to the rock only by a narrow keel along its back. Almost all the carving of the figure – including the fine detail – was done at this stage. The statue was then detached from its keel, and by some means transported down the mountain – a task which sometimes required transporting them down a perpendicular wall and avoiding statues on which work was still proceeding on a ledge below. At the foot of the cliff the statues were raised up into a standing position in trenches; the sculptors then carved the finer detail on the back and decorated the waist with a belt surrounded by rings and symbols. When the carving was finished they were then moved to their ahu on the coast.

Modest statues can be found next to giants; some of the smallest are as little as two metres in length whilst the biggest is just under 21 metres. Overall there are few statues here under three metres long, and the usual length is between 5½ and seven metres. The 21-metre colossus is unique; the face alone is just over 9 metres long; it measures just over four metres across the shoulders, and the body is about 1½ metres thick. The story goes that it was destined for Ahu Vinapu but it is hard to believe that it could ever have been moved. Work has been completed on the front and both sides of the statue but it has not been freed from the rock beneath it.

The carving was done with basalt tools called *toki*, literally thousands of which have been found discarded at the quarry site. In *Aku Aku*, Heyerdahl recounts commissioning a number of the islanders to work at Rano Raraku carving a new statue. The work lasted for three days until the carvers gave up, but their efforts suggested that it would take maybe 12 to 15 months of work to carve a medium-sized statue (say four or five metres long) with two teams working constantly in shifts.

Among the many statues here a few are of special interest. One statue exhibits a roughly carved three-master ship with sails, on its chest. From the bow, a line extends downwards at the end of which is a circular figure with what might be interpreted as a head and four short legs. The figure is so roughly carved it certainly had no connection with the making of the statue itself. The carving may represent a European ship, although it's also thought it may represent a large totora reed vessel. The figure below it may represent an anchor of some sort, although it might also be a turtle or tortoise held by a fishing line. Contrary to popular belief there were a number of female statues made, some with carvings which clearly represent the vulva and others which have clearly defined breasts.

The most unique discovery at Rano Raraku made by the Norwegian expedition was that of a kneeling statue which at the time was almost totally buried. The statue now stands to one side of the outer slope of the mountain. It has a fairly natural rounded head, a goatee beard, short ears, and a full body squatting on its heels and with its forearms and hands resting on its thighs. It appears that the statue was made on the spot. The brow is low with curved eyebrows, the eyes are hollowed out and slightly oval, and the pupils are marked by small round cavities. The nose is considerably damaged; the cheeks are round and natural in appearance; and the lips are damaged but may have been quite plump and pouting. The statue is a bit less than four metres high. It may be worth remembering that just standing this little fellow upright, according to the Norwegian expedition's report, required the aid of the 'expedition jeep, tackle, poles, ropes, chains, and 20 native workers'.

Having carved your statue with toothpicks from hard basalt you lift it out of its cavity and lower it down the cliff face. (This must have been difficult because a couple of broken statues suggest that ropes broke or workmen slipped). Then you stand it up at the foot of the mountain (probably by sliding it downwards into a trench cut for the occasion) so that work on the back can be completed, and when that's done all you have to do is transport it several km to the coast where you stand it upright on a *raised* platform. Easy. Over 300 statues were either placed on ahu or are lying along the old roads in various parts of the island. Many explanations as to how this feat was performed have been suggested, but for any of them to be valid they have to be able to account for the transport and erection of the biggest statue ever placed on an ahu – the 10-metre long giant at Ahu Te Pito Te Kura.

AHU TE PITO TE KURA

On the north coast of the island overlooking La Perouse Bay, on the south-east side of a small, shallow cove called Hanga-ko-uri or Black Bay, can be found the largest moai ever moved from Rano Raraku and erected on an ahu. The name of the ahu comes from a particular stone called *te pito te kura* which means 'the navel of light'. Hotu Matua is said to have brought this stone to the island and it is believed to symbolise the island itself – the island is sometimes called *te pito o te henua* or 'the navel of the world'.

At first glance little light seems to be shed on the mystery of Easter Island here. This statue is 9.8 metres long and lies face down upon the sloping surface on the inland side of the platform. Its ears alone are each 2.2 metres long. A topknot – oval rather than round like those at Vinapu – lies nearby.

Oral history relates that the statue was erected by a widow to represent her dead husband. It is also said to have been the last statue to have been toppled, although that claim has also been made of the statue re-erected by the Norwegian expedition at Anakena. In height and bodily proportions and in general appearance the statue at Ahu Te Pito Te Kura is similar to the tall statues still buried up to their necks at Rano Raraku. If those standing at the quarry site are the last to have been made then it seems likely that the Te Pito Te Kura statue was probably the last to be erected on an ahu.

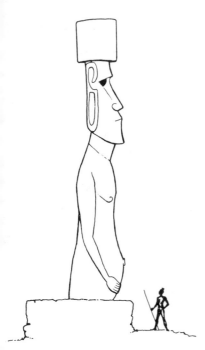

Dimensions of Ahu Te Pito Te Kura

shaped house (probably about 25 metres long originally) is said to have been the house of Hotu Matua – once again the Norwegian expedition failed to find anything of particular interest here. Of much greater interest are Ahu Nau Nau and Ahu Ature Huki.

Ahu Ature Huki

On the side of the hill above Anakena Beach stands Ahu Ature Huki and its lone statue, re-erected when the Norwegian expedition was here. In *Aku Aku* Heyerdahl describes how the statue was raised back on to its platform using wooden poles:

> ... the men got the tips of their poles in underneath it, and while three or four men hung and heaved at the farthest end of each pole, the mayor lay flat on his stomach and pushed small stones under the huge face ... When evening came the giant's head had been lifted a good three feet from the ground, while the space beneath was packed tight with stones.

The process continued for nine days, the giant on an angle supported by stones, and the logs being levered with ropes when the men could no longer reach them. After another nine days work the statue finally stood upright and unsupported on its platform. The work had required the efforts of a dozen men.

Getting the statue to the site in the first place must have been an even greater problem. It was suggested at the time that the statues could have been moved using a Y-shaped sledge made from a forked tree trunk, pulled with ropes made from tree bark. Heyerdahl eventually got together 180 islanders to pull a four-metre-long statue across the field at Anakena, and he suggests in his book that a much larger statue could have been moved given wooden runners and enough people to do the pulling.

There is a story that the statues were moved by the power of the *mana* of the

To work out how they got the thing up in the first place it is worth considering the statue that was re-erected on Ahu Ature Huki at Anakena, just up the road from La Perouse Bay.

ANAKENA

Anakena is the island's largest white-sand beach and the landing place of the legendary Hotu Matua, the founding hero of the island. There are a number of caves in the area and one of them is said to have been the dwelling place of Hotu Matua while he waited for his boat-shaped house to be built near the beach – although the Norwegian expedition found no traces of very early habitation in the cave said to have belonged to Hotu Matua. Nearby, the remains of an unusually large *hare paenga* or boat-

priests, who were able to make the statues walk a short distance every day until eventually they reached their ahu. Another explanation is that round stones were inserted under the statues and that they were pushed, pulled and rolled to their destinations like a block on marbles. If you look around the island you will find numerous round stones so it is not an unlikely idea, but it doesn't explain how the statues were moved without harming the fine detail which had already been carved on them at the quarry.

There is one plausible explanation of how it could have been done, which was developed by the American archaeologist William Mulloy, who was on the Norwegian expedition. The method he postulates would have been physically possible given the available manpower (although very difficult), and also ties in with the shape and configuration of the statues. First, a wooden sledge would have been fitted to the statue (Figures 1 & 2) – the distribution of the statue's weight would have kept the relatively light and fragile head above ground. A bipod would

then have been set up astride the statue's neck (Figures 3 & 4), on an angle off vertical (Figure 3). A cable attached to the neck of the statue would be tied to the bipod apex and pulled forward. The head of the statue would rise slightly (Figure 5), and the statue would be dragged forward. When the bipod passed vertical, the statue's own weight would carry it forward along its belly (Figure 6). By moving the legs of the bipod forward the entire process could be repeated.

It's interesting to consider that the figure is thus moved across the ground in a repetitive series of upward and forward movements, reminiscent of the islander's legend that the statues 'walked' to their ahu. It could also explain why broken statues can be seen along the old transport routes; the rope or bipod may have slipped or broken when the statue was in a raised position, sending it plummeting to the ground. There are a few problems with Mulloy's method (for a start it requires very large tree trunks to make the bipods) but it's still theoretically possible.

William Mulloy's statue-moving theory

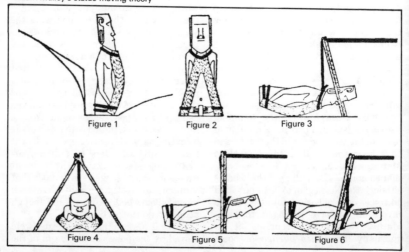

Figure 1   Figure 2   Figure 3

Figure 4   Figure 5   Figure 6

Now that you have got your statue to its ahu you have to stand it up on an *elevated* platform. Mulloy's restoration of Ahu Akivi (described in the Ahu Akivi section, following) suggests that the technique of levering and supporting the statues with rocks may have worked.

Ahu Nau Nau

Mata ki te rangi is a term in the language of Easter Island which means 'Eyes that look to the sky' and it is one of the names by which the island has long been known to Europeans. Some thought it was a reference to the craters of the extinct volcanoes which lie at the corners of the triangular-shaped island. Other more imaginative interpretations thought it referred to the islanders looking to the skies in expectation of the return of their extra-terrestrial ancestors or building patrons.

What makes the Anakena site on the north shore of the island so important was the discovery, during the excavation and restoration of the Ahu Nau Nau site in 1979, that the statues were not blind as was previously believed, but actually had inlaid coral and rock eyes – the eyes that looked to the sky – some of which were reconstructed from fragments found at the site. It's also thought the figures were painted and had inlaid earplugs.

There are seven moai at Ahu Nau Nau; four have their topknots on their heads, whilst only the torsos remain of two other moai. Fragments of bodies and heads lie in front of the ahu.

The Beach

Incidentally, Anakena Beach is a little white-sand beach which is very popular with the locals. Oddly enough, tourist brochures don't do justice to the place and if you've got the time to spare (Easter Island is a *long* way to go just to go swimming) then this is a pleasant place to spend some time.

AHU AKIVI

This restored ahu sports seven statues. Unlike most other ahu on on the island Ahu Akivi is built inland, and the moai look out towards the sea. Ahu Akivi was completely restored in 1960 by a group headed by William Mulloy and the Chilean archaeologist Gonzalo Figueroa. They used a technique for re-erecting the seven statues similar to that used to re-erect the statue at Ahu Ature Huki. Some years later Mulloy wrote:

... a surprising amount of skill was acquired with practice. The first statue at Ahu Akivi was erected in a little over a month, while the last was accomplished in less than a week ... Clearly the prehistoric islanders with their hundreds of years of repetition of the same task must have known many more tricks than modern imitators were able to learn.

Mulloy suggests that the large number of stones found in front of Ahu Akahanga on the south coast are the left-overs of stones used to erect the statues, and that one statue appears to have fallen sideways off the platform as it was being erected. He also points to the tremendous number of stones gathered near many ahu, including Ahu Te Pito Te Kura, as possible evidence that the statues may have been erected using stones to support the statue as it was gradually levered upwards.

He thought that the statue and topknot at Ahu Te Pito Te Kura could have been carved by 30 men working eight hours a day for one year; it could have been transported from the quarry to the ahu by 90 men over a previously prepared road in two months; and could have been erected by 90 men in about three months. But even if Mulloy is right there is still the problem of raising the topknots, carved from the red rock of the Puna Pau crater, to the heads of the statues.

PUNA PAU

The cylindrical, red-stone topknots which once capped a number of the statues have been variously thought to be hats, baskets, or crowns. The stone is relatively soft and easily worked. Most have a clearly marked knot on the top and a depression carved into the underside which allows them to be slotted onto the heads of the statues. The original native name for this head decoration is *pukao* which means 'topknot' and was the usual hairstyle of the Easter Island males at the time the first Europeans came to the island.

The custom of capping the statues with topknots appears to have developed later in the piece as it seems many statues did not have topknots at all. Only about 60 statues are known to have topknots, and about 25 topknots remain in or near the quarry at the small volcanic crater called Puna Pau where they were carved. The topknots were carved in much the same way as the statues, and may then have been rolled to their final location. These topknots – each about the weight of two elephants – were then somehow placed on

the statues, some of which were as much as 10 metres high. The first few European ships to visit the island do record that statues were still standing on their ahu with the topknots on their heads.

It seems that the knot on top of the stone and the depression on its underside were carved after the stone had been transported to its ahu – probably to prevent the knot breaking off in transport and to allow the head to be measured in order to carve the right-sized depression. Oral tradition suggests that a long causeway of stones was erected to the head of the statue long enough to provide a grade up which the topknots could then be rolled. Mulloy suggested that the more probable method of getting it on to the top of the statue was to tie them together and raise the statue and topknot at the same time. This would eliminate the clumsy and time-consuming method of trying to roll the topknot up an enormous ramp.

Horse and topknot, Puna Pau

THE POIKE PENINSULA

By the time the first Europeans arrived at the island construction work had ceased and the statue makers had disappeared off the face of the earth, as if they had been taken up into the heavens. It seems more likely though that they were, in fact, swallowed by the earth and consumed by fire.

The eastern end of the island is a high plateau called the Poike Peninsula. The western boundary of the peninsula is marked by a narrow island-wide depression called *Ko te Ava o Iko* or Iko's Trench, which legends record was built by the Long Ears to defend themselves against the Short Ears. One version of the story begins with the Long Ear rulers deciding to clear the Poike Peninsula of all its loose rocks so that the whole area could be cultivated. The Short Ears tired of the work and decided on war, and the Long Ears – under the command of their chief Iko – gathered on the Poike Peninsula and dug a trench which separated Poike from the rest of the island. The trench was then filled with branches and tree-trunks, ready to be set on fire should the Short Ears try to storm across.

But one of the Long Ears had a Short Ear wife who allowed the Short Ears to slip into the Poike Peninsula and surround the Long Ears. When another Short Ear army marched up towards the ditch the Long Ears lined up to face them and set fire to the pyre; the other Short Ears rushed down behind them and in a bloody fight the Long Ears were pushed into, and burned in, their own ditch. Only three of the Long Ears are said to have escaped; two of these were later killed but one was permitted to live, married a Short Ear and had children.

It was once thought that the ditch was a natural one and the story of the battle purely an invention. The Norwegian expedition, however, found thick layers of charcoal and ashes and carbonised wood, proving that there had once been a great fire here; and since much of the ash was red it must either have produced a very intense heat or else burnt for a long time. The topmost part of the trench was natural but this had been artificially enlarged further down to create a trench with a rectangular bottom, three or four metres deep, about five metres wide and running a couple of km across the hillside. It is not a continuous ditch but is actually made up of a number of separate trenches. Carbon 14 dating suggested that the great fire had burnt perhaps 300 to 350 years ago.

It's worth considering that though the Long Ears, suddenly forced to retreat to the Poike Peninsula, would perhaps have had time to fill the ditch with wood, they would certainly not have had time to undertake the heavy and time consuming work of enlarging the ditch. In fact, dating the remains of earlier fires suggested that the ditch was originally dug out around 400 AD. It may not have been a defensive ditch originally, but may have been used as such in the 17th century. Whatever, the Late Period is marked by the absence of statue carving, and the only new ahu built seem to have been used specifically for burials.

MT ORITO

Having done away – so it would seem – with their Long Ear rulers the Short Ears are said to have entered into a long period of peace until tribal rivalries and conflicts arose, resulting in a period of bloody warfare involving the toppling of the statues.

The weaponry used to fight these battles was made from the hard, black obsidian rock, some of which was quarried from Mt Orito. The *mataa* is a common artifact turned up on the island – usually a crudely shaped, blade of obsidian used as a spearhead. It's also suggested that the blades could have made highly effective weapons by fixing them in series in the edges of the flat wooden clubs which were once commonly used on the island. The quarry was also used for peaceful purposes; other artifacts found on the island include obsidian files and obsidian drill bits which would have been attached to a wooden shaft and used to drill bone, wood or rock.

From the vantage point of Rano Kau the quarry looks like an enormous grey rectangle on the southern slope of Orito, but quarrying actually took place around the whole circumference of the mountain. This is not the only obsidian quarry on the island: there is another on the island of Motu-iti off the south-west tip, and on the north-east edge of the Rano Kau crater.

THE SOUTH COAST

Apart from Ahu Vinapu, the handiwork of the 'statue overthrowing' period is best seen along the south coast where a number of enormous ruined ahu and their fallen statues can be seen.

Vaihu

One of the most impressive sights on the south coast, this ahu has eight large statues which have been toppled and now lie with their noses in the ground and several topknots scattered in front. Other topknots have rolled into the small estuary next to the site.

Akahanga

Akahanga is a large ahu with four large, fallen statues. Across the adjacent estuary stands a second ahu with several toppled statues. On the hill slopes opposite Akahanga are the remains of a village, including the foundations of several boat-shaped houses and the ruins of several round houses.

Hanga Tetenga

Also on the coast, this almost completely ruined ahu has two large statues which have toppled and broken into pieces. From Hanga Tetenga the road branches inland towards Rano Raraku. Along the track leading to the volcano you will see several fallen statues making a beeline towards the sea.

Ahu Tongariki

To the east of Rano Raraku there is a field in which several topknots and shattered statues were strewn by a tidal wave produced by an earthquake on the Chilean mainland in 1960. The ruined ahu from which these pieces were swept was called Ahu Tongariki; it was the biggest ahu ever built and supported 15 massive statues. There are several petroglyphs cut into the flat rock out-crops in front of the scattered statues. These include a turtle with a man's face, a tuna fish, a birdman motif, and one which may represent a woman with her legs spread apart.

ORONGO

Almost covered in a bog of floating totora reeds, the crater lake of Rano Kau looks like a giant witch's cauldron. Perched 400 metres up on the edge of the crater wall of Rano Kau, the ceremonial village of Orongo occupies one of the most dramatic pieces of real-estate on the island. This was once the most important ceremonial site on the island, but its significance seems to belong to a period after the construction of the great statues and ahu.

An endless winding road makes it way from Hanga Roa up the side of Rano Kau to Orongo which is perched on the rim of the crater, facing the sea. There are sweeping views of the whole island on the way up. There is an entrance fee to Orongo – about US$1 – which you pay at the ranger's office outside the entrance to the site. There is also a small booklet on Orongo available here for US$1 – it's worth getting.

The Orongo village seems to have been – at least in the 18th and 19th centuries – the centre of an island-wide bird cult linked to the gods Makemake and Haua. Makemake appears to have been the supreme deity of the island; he is said to have created the earth, sun, moon, stars and people; he rewarded the good and punished the evil, and when he was angry he made it known by thunder. During times of trouble it is said he required the sacrifice of a child. Makemake is also credited with bringing the birds – and presumably the bird cult – to Easter Island, but he is said to have been aided in this venture by another god called Haua.

There is no complete record of the ceremonies which took place here and accounts which do exist conflict with each other, particularly in regard to the time of the year when the ceremonies would begin and their duration. At the required time the people involved with the ceremonies would move up to Orongo where they would live in stone houses. During this period they made offerings and said prayers to their gods, conducted rites to propitiate the gods and held what may have been fertility dances in front of the houses.

Birdman petroglyphs, Orongo

The climax of the ceremonies was the attempt by each contestant (or his representative, called a *hopu*) to obtain the first egg of the sooty tern whose breeding grounds were on the islands of Moto-nui, Motu-iti and Motu-kaokao just off the south-west tip of the island. When the word was given for the contestants or their hopu to leave, they would descend down the cliff face from Orongo and with the aid of a small reed raft called a *pora* swim out to the islands. The contestant who found it became the 'birdman' of the year. If a hopu found the first egg he called out the name of his master across to a man stationed in a cave in the cliff face below Orongo. The fortunate master's head, eyebrows and eyelashes were then shaved, and his face was painted red and black; he became the new birdman and for the next year and went into seclusion in a special house. The advantage of becoming a birdman has never really been worked out, but it seems that whoever won the first egg also won the favour of the god Makemake. The last bird-cult ceremonies were held at Orongo about 1866 or 1867.

The Orongo ceremonial village has been partially restored and has a breath-taking setting. The Orongo houses were generally made by cutting a floor into the side of the slope. The walls were made using slabs of stone placed horizontally and overlapping each other, and the structure was roofed by laying overlapping stone slabs horizontally to produce an arch. The roofs were covered in earth and give the appearance of being partly underground. Because the walls were thick and the roof had to be supported by its own weight, the doorway is a low, narrow tunnel, only high enough for a person to crawl through. At the end of the site, where the crater suddenly drops away is a cluster of boulders carved with numerous birdman petroglyphs – figures which look something like a hybrid between a man and a bird, with a long beak and a hand clutching an egg.

Ceremonial village house, Orongo

THE MUSEUM

A few more mysteries are housed in the island's new museum which is located some distance inland from the coast and midway between Ahu Tahai and Ahu Akapu. A road from Hanga Roa leads to the museum – see the map for directions.

Odd Statues

Just outside the museum stands a peculiar statue made of red coloured rock. The statue was uncovered not far from the modern cemetery outside Hanga Roa and was re-erected by the Norwegian expedition. The intact statue stands about 2.5 metres high and appears to be crudely made. The appearance may be somewhat deceptive since the statue appears to have been badly damaged and eroded, although it appears to have a triangular-shaped head with rather large sunken eyes.

This is not the only odd statue found on the island; the seated figure dug up at Rano Raraku is another. Inside the museum there are also several oblong-shaped stone heads (the 'potato heads') which have eye-sockets and rudimentary features, including one with round ears. These are thought to be the oldest carvings on the island, pre-dating the Rano Raraku figures.

Artefacts

Other exhibits include skulls from bodies originally entombed in ahu; basalt fish-hooks and other implements; obsidian spearheads and other weapons; sketches of boat-shaped houses, circular beehive-shaped huts, and the ceremonial houses at Orongo; a statue head with reconstructed fragments of its eyes; moai kavakava statues; and replicas of rongo-rongo tablets.

The Moai Kavakava

Of all the carved wooden figures produced by the islanders the most common – and perhaps the most grotesque – are the moai kavakava or the 'statue of ribs'.

These are human figures with large, thin and markedly aquiline noses, protruding cheekbones which accentuate their hollow cheeks, long extended earlobes, and a goatee beard that curls back on the chin. The abdomen recedes, and the ribs and backbone protrude like that of a person suffering from starvation.

At least one story goes that King Tuu ko ihu discovered two sleeping ghosts (*aku aku*) at the foot of the cliff in the

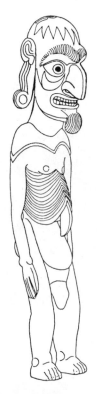

Moai kavakava – statue of ribs

topknot quarry. Both ghosts had pendulant ear-lobes reaching down to their necks, beards and long hooked noses, and were so thin that their ribs stood out. Tuu ko ihu returned home and carved their portrait in wood before he forgot what they looked like, and from then on the people of the island have always carved these statues.

The Rongo-rongo Tablets

If there is one thing on Easter Island which is likely to defy explanation for all time then it's the rongo-rongo script. The first European to become aware of the existence of a native script on the island was the missionary Eugene Eyraud who recorded in 1864 that tablets or staffs of wood covered in some form of writing or hieroglyphics could be found in all the houses on the island. The figures were carved into these tablets with sharp stones, but by the time Eyraud came across them the islanders appear to have lost or forgotten their meaning.

The old and complete name of the tablets was *ko hau motu mo rongorongo* which literally means 'lines of script for recitation'. It is said that Hotu Matua brought a number of these tablets with him, along with learned men who knew the art of writing and reciting the inscriptions. Most of the tablets are rather irregular, flat wooden boards with rounded edges, each about 30 cm to 50 cm long. They are covered in neat rows of tiny incised symbols which include birds, animals, possibly plants and celestial objects, and geometric forms. There are hundreds of different signs – too many to suggest that this writing is some form of alphabet.

Tradition says that there are three separate classes of tablets. One type records hymns in honour of the god Makemake and other divine beings. The second type recorded crimes or the other deeds of individuals. And the third type recorded those who had fallen in war or other conflicts. It is also said that tablets recording genealogies also existed. Only a few rongo-rongo tablets survive today although it's probable that at one time thousands were in existence.

The first attempt to translate the tablets was made in Tahiti by Bishop Jaussen in 1866 using an Easter Islander who lived there and who was said to be able to read the tablets. This and other similar attempts failed. It generally appeared that the natives were either reciting memorised texts, or merely describing the figures, rather than actually reading them. It seems that by this time the last truly literate Easter Islanders who could read the rongo-rongo tablets were dead, either as a result of the slave raid in 1862 or the subsequent smallpox epidemic when the survivors returned to the island.

There have been various theories concerning the nature of the script. One suggestion is that script may not actually be a readable script at all, but might simply consist of memory joggers for the recitation of memorised verse. Another is that the characters are ideographs, similar in principle to those of the Chinese script. Or to go off on another tangent one person has even suggested a connection between the rongo-rongo script and a script used by a 3000-year-old civilisation in the Indus River Valley in what is now Pakistan.

Rongo-rongo script

Index

Temperature

To convert °C to °F multipy by 1.8 and add 32

To convert °F to °C subtract 32 and multipy by 5/9

Length, Distance & Area

	multipy by
inches to centimetres	2.54
centimetres to inches	0.39
feet to metres	0.30
metres to feet	3.28
yards to metres	0.91
metres to yards	1.09
miles to kilometres	1.61
kilometres to miles	0.62
acres to hectares	0.40
hectares to acres	2.47

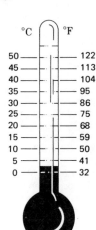

Weight

	multipy by
ounces to grams	28.35
grams to ounces	0.035
pounds to kilograms	0.45
kilograms to pounds	2.21
British tons to kilograms	1016
US tons to kilograms	907

A British ton is 2240 lbs, a US ton is 2000 lbs

Volume

	multipy by
imperial gallons to litres	4.55
litres to imperial gallons	0.22
US gallons to litres	3.79
litres to US gallons	0.26

5 imperial gallons equals 6 US gallons
a litre is slightly more than a US quart, slightly less
than a British one

Lonely Planet Newsletter

We collect an enormous amount of information here at Lonely Planet. Apart from our research there's a steady stream of letters from people out on the road. To make the most of all this info we produce a quarterly Newsletter (approx Feb, May, Aug, and Nov).

The Newsletter is packed with down-to-earth information from the pens of hundreds of travellers who write from first-hand experience. Whether you want the latest facts, travel stories, or simply to reminisce, the Newsletter will keep you in touch with what is going on.

Where else could you find out:
- about boat trips on the Yalu River?
- where to stay if you want to live in a typical Thai village?
- how long it takes to get a Nepalese trekking permit?
- that Israeli youth hostel stamps will get you deported from Syria?

One year's subscription is $10.00 (that's US$ in the USA or A$ in Australia), payable by cheque, money order, Amex, Visa, Bankcard or MasterCard.

Order Form

Please send me four issues of the Lonely Planet Newsletter. (Subscription starts with next issue. 1987 price – subject to change.)

Name and address (print) ....

....

....

Tick one

☐ Cheque enclosed (payable to Lonely Planet Publications)
☐ Money Order enclosed (payable to Lonely Planet Publications)
Charge my ☐ Amex, ☐ Visa, ☐ Bankcard, ☐ MasterCard for the amount of $.............

Card No ....   Expiry Date ....

Cardholder's Name (print) ....

Signature ....   Date ....

Return this form to:

Lonely Planet Publications	or	Lonely Planet Publications
PO Box 2001A		PO Box 88
Berkeley		South Yarra
CA 94702		Victoria 3141
USA		Australia

Guides to the Americas

South America on a shoestring
An up-dated edition of a budget travellers bible that covers Central and South America from the USA-Mexico border to Tierra del Fuego. Written by the author The New York Times called "the patron saint of travellers in the third world".

Alaska – a travel survival kit
A new edition of a definitive guide to one of the world's most spectacular regions – including detailed information on hiking and canoeing.

Canada – a travel survival kit
Canada offers a unique combination of English, French and American culture, with forests mountains and lakes that cover a vast area.

Mexico – a travel survival kit
Mexico has a unique blend of Indian and Spanish culture and a fascinating historical legacy. The hospitality of the people makes Mexico a paradise for travellers.

Ecuador & the Galapagos Islands
– a travel survival kit
Ecuador is the smallest of the Andean countries, and in many ways it is the easiest and most pleasant to travel in. The Galapagos Islands and their amazing inhabitants continue to cast a spell over every visitor.

Peru – a travel survival kit
The famed city of Machu Picchu, the Andean altiplano and the Amazon rainforests are just some of Peru's attractions. All the facts you need can be found in this comprehensive guide.

Lonely Planet travel guides

Africa on a Shoestring
Alaska – a travel survival kit
Australia – a travel survival kit
Bali & Lombok – a travel survival kit
Bangladesh – a travel survival kit
Burma – a travel survival kit
Bushwalking in Papua New Guinea
Canada – a travel survival kit
China – a travel survival kit
Chile & Easter Island – a travel survival kit
East Africa – a travel survival kit
Ecuador & the Galapagos Islands
Egypt & the Sudan – a travel survival kit
Fiji – a travel survival kit
Hong Kong, Macau & Canton – a travel survival kit
India – a travel survival kit
Indonesia – a travel survival kit
Japan – a travel survival kit
Kashmir, Ladakh & Zanskar – a travel survival kit
Kathmandu & the Kingdom of Nepal
Korea & Taiwan – a travel survival kit
Malaysia, Singapore & Brunei – a travel survival kit
Mexico – a travel survival kit
New Zealand – a travel survival kit
North-East Asia on a Shoestring
Pakistan – a travel survival kit kit
Papua New Guinea – a travel survival kit
Philippines – a travel survival kit
Raratonga & the Cook Islands – a travel survival kit
South America on a Shoestring
South-East Asia on a Shoestring
Sri Lanka – a travel survival kit
Tahiti – a travel survival kit
Thailand – a travel survival kit
Tibet – a travel survival kit
Tramping in New Zealand
Travel with Children
Travellers Tales
Trekking in the Indian Himalaya
Trekking in the Nepal Himalaya
Turkey – a travel survival kit
West Asia on a Shoestring

Lonely Planet phrasebooks

Indonesia Phrasebook
China Phrasebook
Nepal Phrasebook
Papua New Guinea Phrasebook
Sri Lanka Phrasebook
Thailand Phrasebook
Tibet Phrasebook

Lonely Planet Distribution

Lonely Planet travel guides are available round the world. If you can't find them, ask your bookshop to order them from one of the distributors listed below. For countries not listed, or if you would like a free copy of our latest booklist write to Lonely Planet in Australia.

Australia
Lonely Planet Publications, PO Box 88, South Yarra, Victoria 3141.
Canada
Raincoast Books, 112 East 3rd Avenue, Vancouver, British Columbia V5T 1C8.
Denmark, Finland & Norway
Scanvik Books aps, Store Kongensgade 59 A, DK-1264 Copenhagen K.
Hong Kong
The Book Society, GPO Box 7804.
India & Nepal
UBS Distributors, 5 Ansari Rd, New Delhi - 110002.
Israel
Geographical Tours Ltd, 8 Tverya St, Tel Aviv 63144.
Japan
Intercontinental Marketing Corp, IPO Box 5056, Tokyo 100-31.
Netherlands
Nilsson & Lamm bv, Postbus 195, Pampuslaan 212, 1380 AD Weesp.
New Zealand
Roulston Greene Publishing Associates Ltd, Private Bag, Takapuna, Auckland 9.
Papua New Guinea see Australia.
Singapore & Malaysia
MPH Distributors, 601 Sims Drive #03-21, Singapore 1438.
Spain
Altair, Balmes 69, 08007 Barcelona.
Sweden
Esselte Kartcentrum AB, Vasagatan 16, S-111 20 Stockholm.
Thailand
Chalermnit, 108 Sukhumvit 53, Bangkok, 10110.
UK
Roger Lascelles, 47 York Rd, Brentford, Middlesex, TW8 OQP.
USA
Lonely Planet Publications, PO Box 2001A, Berkeley, CA 94702.
West Germany
Buchvertrieb Gerda Schettler, Postfach 64, D3415 Hattorf a H.